To Cross the Widest Ocean

What I
Have
Learned
About
Faith

Mrs. Rick Martin

Copyright © 2005
Christian Womanhood Publications
8400 Burr Street
Crown Point, Indiana 46307
219-365-3202
www.christianwomanhood.org

ISBN: 0-9745195-5-3

Scriptures used in this book are taken from the King James Bible.

Disclaimer:

The direct quotes used in this book have been taken word for word from the cited sources. At times, a punctuation mark has been inserted to assist the reader with the clarity and understanding of certain sentences.

Printed and bound in the United States of America

With Gratitude

There are a number of people whom I would like to thank: first, I would like to thank my husband Rick and my daughter Rachel. Many times they left me alone at the computer and did laundry, meals, and countless other things so I could work. Thank you, Rick and Rachel, for your usefulness, patience, and understanding.

My husband was also my greatest encourager in this project. He did the project I hated most—endnotes, and he read and reread every page, giving helpful suggestions when needed. My husband is the best Christian I know. His great love for the Lord and burden for the lost inspires me constantly.

Next, I would like to thank two very special friends—one a missionary's daughter and the other a missionary's wife. Sandy Heidenreich Domelle is the daughter of our dear friends, Steve and Susie Heidenreich, who served the Lord here in the Philippines for 15 years. Sandy has taught missions courses at Hyles-Anderson College and has a real burden for the young ladies preparing to be missionaries as well as the missionary wives currently on the field or on deputation. Since she is a missionary kid (MK), she also has a genuine love for MKs. For eight years, Becky Sisson and her husband, Missionary Doug Sisson, have served the Lord in General Santos City, Philippines. They are doing a tremendous work in a dangerous area for the Lord Jesus Christ. Becky's deep love and compassion for the Filipino people continually makes a great impression on me. Thank you for your prayers and encouragement for this project, Sandy and Becky!

Thank you, Dr. Jim Vineyard, for allowing me to use excerpts from your missionary paper in several places in this manuscript.

Thanks to Mrs. Linda Stubblefield who patiently plowed through mounds of pages I sent to her, correcting, suggesting, editing, and encouraging. I could not have done it without your help, Linda! Linda and the staff at Christian Womanhood came up with the title of this book. Thank you so much, Linda; I appreciate you more than you will ever know.

Thank you, Rena Fish, for your careful proofreading and attention to this book.

Last and most importantly, I must thank my Lord and Saviour Jesus Christ Who placed a great burden in my heart for missionary wives. He made me realize the great potential every missionary wife has—to either help her husband reach a lost and dying world or to keep him from it. I love You, Jesus!

Table of Contents

Your Husband (continued)

4 Your Children 137

5 Your Ministry 179

6 Your Relationships 209

Above: Our first church building was built out of coconut wood. We are still in the same building; we have expanded it through the years. The old house in the background was our girls' dormitory; then was later used for boys. That building was razed in January 2005 to make way for a two-story boys' dormitory.

Inset: Rick preaching at the police headquarters

Below: Two Bible students and I visit children on our route.

Foreword

It is an honor to write the foreword of this book which was written by my wife Becky, who for more than a quarter of a century has been by my side on the mission field. How could I begin to thank her for giving her life unselfishly to the Lord, to me, to her children, and to the people whom God has called us to reach?

I met Becky Umbright on Valentine's Day, February 14, 1972. The subject she wanted to talk about the most was her relationship with Jesus Christ and her burden for lost souls. She is not only a fruitful soul winner, but she has also been used of God to train others to win souls.

As a mother, she has prayed and fasted for God to use her children. Since both of our children were born, I have heard her pray that God would send the right mate to each one. Half of this prayer was wondrously answered the day Miss Brandie Gavin married our son Ricky.

As a wife, Becky has been my help meet and encourager. I have never been able to get over the fact that she wanted to marry me! As a friend, she has brought enjoyment through her fellowship and wonderful sense of humor.

As my co-worker, she has been involved in numerous ministries. I have also been fortunate to have her as my secretary. Her tireless work in this area has been invaluable to me in my work as a missionary. My handwriting is such that often even I cannot read it and have to go to her for deciphering!

A missionary wife is under attack just like the missionary. Satan knows if he can defeat the wife, he has already defeated the husband. You will learn from one who has not only withstood those attacks, but she has also overcome evil with much good.

Becky has a servant's heart and has lifted many of my burdens. If it were not for her determination to follow the Lord's leading in our lives, I would not have been able to stay on the field for so many years. During our first four years in the Philippines, she had three surgeries, one of which nearly took her life. She has endured seeing our daughter go through open-heart surgery on two occasions. These and many other trials would have easily discouraged most any woman whose eyes were not focused on the Lord. Therein lies the secret of her usefulness: she humbly walks with God.

Next to Jesus, Becky is my best friend. I believe she exemplifies what a missionary's wife should be, and I believe you will be blessed as you read this book and gain wisdom and inspiration in serving Him.

– Dr. Rick Martin

Preface

During the summer of 2004, I began reading the manuscript *To Cross the Widest Ocean* by Becky Martin. I spent many summer hours sitting on my side porch reading this wonderful book. During this time, I often exclaimed to my husband regarding the wealth of wisdom in this book. Though it was lengthy, I hated to put it down, and I looked forward to each moment I had to continue reading it. It was the reading of this book that led me to the theme and ideas of our 2005 Christian Womanhood Spectacular (an international ladies' conference which is sponsored by the First Baptist Church of Hammond, Indiana, and of which I am the executive director.)

This book is several things all in one: it is a compilation of exciting and convicting stories of many missionaries and some of the greatest in history.

It is the true life testimony of one of the most humble, godly, successful, and fruitful missionaries in history. Becky Martin is a "just like me" type of Christian. She is personable and "copiable" both in her life and in her writing. In speaking to her, it is obvious that she is not only unimpressed with who she he is, but she does not know who she is—so allow me to tell you. She is one of the outstanding Christians of our day, and she is married to a hero among missionaries. Becky's humility and love of life is a reflection of her husband. Both are a joy to be around.

Last but not least, this book is a life-changing tool. When I read it, I was convicted of any discontent and, therefore, made more content. I was motivated to give more to my Lord, and I was thankful for the writing and the living of missionaries like Becky Martin.

– Mrs. Cindy Schaap

Top left: Ricky with pet, a small, raccoon-like animal which is now on the endangered list.

Top right: Ricky with his pet python!

Below: Ricky loved to listen to Brother Hyles' preaching!

UNIT ONE
Your Attitude

"...Be thou an example of the believers...
in spirit."
(I Timothy 4:12)

Introduction

It was July 2000. My husband had flown home to the United States to preach at some churches. He planned to be gone only for a couple of weeks because school in the Philippines starts in June. Knowing he would be gone, my husband had already planned the Bible students' first outing. He tries to have several outings throughout the school year. Since there are so many students, we usually go to the beach where they play volleyball, hold contests, and enjoy games. Truthfully, I did not want to go on the outing. July is always rainy in the Philippines, and as usual, it was a rainy, miserable day. My daughter Rachel really wanted to go, and since all of her friends were going, she talked me into accompanying the young people. I cooked some food to pack and take with us. We rode with the Arnigos, a family in our church. When we arrived at the beach, the waves were extremely rough and high. No one was swimming, so we had the whole place to ourselves.

About an hour after lunch, I asked the Arnigos if they were ready to go, and they said, "Yes." I walked down to the beach where Rachel and all the students had gathered and told her to pack up because we were leaving. I returned to the shelter and began packing the food when I heard the lifeguard make an announcement over the public-address system. He told some boys on one end of the beach to leave the water because he thought someone was in distress. I quickly ran back to the beach, but I could not see anything. I was immediately thankful that I had just told Rachel to pack. Otherwise, I would have panicked, thinking it might have been her. I was also thankful that Ricky did not go with us that day, or I would have thought it was him. As it was, I was already terrified—just knowing it was probably someone from our church or school.

Far off to my left, I could could see some boys diving, so I ran in their direction. Finally, I spotted a boy being carried toward the shore. I noticed that the rough waves made it very difficult for the rescuers to carry the boy. By the way they were carrying him, I could tell he was dead, or at the very least, unconscious. I began motioning and screaming for them to hurry. Rather than wait until they brought him to shore, I ran into the water and grabbed his head. I recognized Jessie.

Even as Jessie was being carried, I opened his mouth, cleared his airways, and immediately began blowing into his mouth. Soon he was laid on the ground, and just as I began to start CPR because Jessie had no pulse, the lifeguard knelt beside me and began pumping his heart. He yelled at me to breathe into Jessie's mouth. He vomited, and I began scraping out his mouth with my fingers. Hope arose with me. "He's still alive!" I thought. (Later I realized that it was probably just a reflex from the lifeguard's pumping his chest.) While I was trying to clear his mouth and throat, I began yelling, "Come on, Jess!" By then a large crowd of students had gathered around us, and they began yelling out his name also. Many were praying, and many were crying.

Suddenly, some boys appeared with a board. They asked me if they should load Jessie onto the board and carry him to the jeep. I nodded, and we lifted Jessie's lifeless body onto the board. The boys picked up the board, and we all ran as fast as we could to where the jeep was parked. The boys laid him on the floor of the jeep, and once again, I began performing CPR. Someone drove the jeep quickly along a rough road to a clinic about a mile from the beach.

Almost before the jeep was parked, the boys grabbed Jessie and carried him inside the clinic. I hurried with them as I continued to pump his heart. A doctor and a nurse met us and began suctioning out Jessie's mouth and administering oxygen. I have no idea how long we labored to save Jessie's life, but I am guessing at least 20 minutes. Finally, the doctor placed her hands on my arms, signifying that I should stop. She looked at me and shook her head. I started to weep.

I turned from Jessie's lifeless body and walked over to a sink and started washing my hands. I noticed they were cut and bleeding, probably from Jessie's teeth when I had tried to clear his mouth and throat. All I could think was, "How in the world am I going to tell this poor boy's parents?" I turned around and saw that some of our boys were standing beside him, trying to brush some of the sand off his body. I walked back over to where he was lying motionless and took his hand.

Some of our staff arrived. The moment was surreal; seemingly, we were all in shock. None of us could believe he was dead. Finally, we left the hospital, and I saw Rachel was waiting. I hugged her and kept thinking, "What if it had been her or Ricky? How can I tell Jessie's parents?"

We got into the jeep and drove back down to the beach. I saw the students huddled together praying. I told some of the staff to have everyone load up and to return home immediately. Aida, one of our staff ladies, and I decided that we would take a boat to the island of Negros as soon as possible to tell the parents. She had the foresight to ask the clinic not to give any information to a radio reporter who always hung around looking for a story until we were able to break the news to Jessie's parents.

Two other people decided to accompany us to Negros. Mrs. Arnigo and Mechie, a student who knew the way to Jessie's house, would also go. As we started driving back to Iloilo, I asked if we could go to my home so I could change and get some money for the boat. They said, "No," because the last boat was scheduled to leave shortly. We would have to rush directly to the pier.

"But I don't have any money for our boat fare," I explained. The Arnigos graciously offered to let me borrow money to care for my fare. I was also sopping wet, covered with sand and vomit, but I could not wash or change my clothes. As it was, we barely made it to the pier in time to catch the last boat to Negros. I kissed Rachel goodbye and said, "You or Ricky needs to try to get a hold of Daddy in the States to tell him what happened."

The ocean was still very rough, and by now, it was raining even harder. I thought the boat was going to capsize. All the way to the island of Negros, we prayed and discussed how we should break the news to Jessie's parents. We reached Bacolod City in a little over an hour. Aida decided that we should first go to her brother's house and ask him to accompany us because he was a security guard. We knew that Jessie lived in a really rough neighborhood. She questioned, "Suppose Jessie's father is drunk and becomes very angry when we tell him his son was killed?"

By then the inclement weather had worsened further. It was raining harder, and the skies were dark. We found the way to Aida's brother's home flooded. We walked through thigh-high water to get there. Thankfully, he agreed to go with us, and we waded down the street to higher ground. There we found a taxi which drove us to the general area where Jessie lived. We were stopped at the edge of another flooded street. We waded again through thigh-high water for about a block to a pitiful little shack at the end of the street. There we knocked on the door.

Jessie's mother, who was the same age as me, invited us in. I noticed that half of the shack had a dirt floor and the other half had a bamboo floor. She was cooking rice in a pot over a fire on the ground. Two small boys and a baby girl were sleeping on the bamboo floor. Jessie's father was just sitting in the shack.

We were soon relieved to learn that both parents were saved. We carefully broke the news to them about Jessie. They began weeping softly. We hugged them, cried with them, and told them how sorry we were. We asked who would return with us to Iloilo to claim the body of Jessie. I explained that we would pay for all of the funeral expenses. Jessie's mother decided to go. We had another prayer with them and said good night. Mechie decided to go visit her family and agreed to meet Jessie's mother in the morning and bring her to the pier.

Aida, her brother, Mrs. Arnigo, and I returned to Aida's brother's house. He and his family gave us something to eat and let us borrow some dry clothes. I remember watching Aida's niece iron our wet clothes, over and over, trying to get them dry. Mats were placed on the bamboo floor for Aida, Mrs. Arnigo, and me; we tried to sleep, but we tossed and turned all night. I kept playing and replaying the whole day through my mind—like a video—and thinking, "If only...."

TO CROSS THE WIDEST OCEAN
WHAT I HAVE LEARNED ABOUT FAITH

It continued to rain hard throughout the night. It was impossible for our clothes to dry in the damp air. It really didn't matter as the next morning when we got up very early, we had to wade once again through the deep water to get a taxi to the pier. When we arrived there, we found Mechie waiting with Jessie's mom and one of his aunts. We rode the boat back to Iloilo City. Thankfully, Mr. Arnigo was waiting for us in the van. He drove us immediately to the funeral home where we made the necessary arrangements. We left the funeral home to go to the church. Once Jessie's mother saw her son's body, she could not stop sobbing. Her tears flowed freely all the way to the church. My heart was broken for her.

When we arrived at the church, Ricky was waiting. He opened the van door, put his arms around me, and just held me while I cried. He told me he had finally contacted his dad and told him about Jessie. Needless to say, poor Rick was also brokenhearted and was so sorry to be so far away. He immediately started making arrangements to fly back. I woodenly walked inside our house, got several hundred pesos, took it to one of the pastors, and asked him to take it to the funeral home.

A couple of days later when my husband finally arrived, Jessie's body was in a casket inside our church. Several of the students had sat in the church all night, staying with Jessie's mother.

I walked inside the church with Rick, and we walked to where the casket had been placed. As we stood there, my husband cried and cried. I put my arms around him, and I also remember Pastor Johnnylee walking to Rick and putting his arms around him, too. When Rick finally composed himself, he went to be with Jessie's mother. In her soft voice, she told my husband how much Jessie had loved and admired him.

During the next few days, before Jessie's body was placed on a boat to be taken to Negros for burial, his body remained in the church. We held services, and several students stood before Jessie's casket and gave testimonies about this remarkable young man. At first I questioned, "Why him, God? He would have made a wonderful pastor." Later I realized that of all our students, he was probably the most ready to meet the Lord.

The next week Rick, Rachel, Ricky, and I, along with several staff, students, and church members, took the boat to Negros to attend Jessie's funeral. Jessie's casket was sitting in the poor little shack. Ricky had gathered all the testimonies written about Jessie and had placed them in a scrapbook to give to Jessie's parents. The rains had finally stopped, and the flood was gone. Rick and Pastor Johnnylee preached. Ricky wrote a poem about Jessie which was put to music and sung at the funeral. Then we all walked slowly down the long road to the cemetery.

As I write this introduction, it is April 2003. A picture of Jessie still sits on my bookcase. Two weeks ago Iloilo Baptist College had its twenty-second graduation. Had he lived, Jessie would have been in that graduation class. My husband mentioned that fact at the graduation, so Jessie has been on all of our minds. In the conclusion of this unit on attitude, I have included what my husband wrote in our prayer letter about Jessie shortly after he died. I purposely opened this unit on "Your Attitude" with this story about Jessie because he was one of the best examples I have ever met of someone with a good attitude.

Chapter One

How Important Is Your Attitude?

In September of 1977, my husband and I said goodbye to our family and friends, and we boarded a plane for the Philippines. I was 23, and Rick was 25.

We spent three days in Manila to take care of "paperwork"; then we caught a one-hour flight to Iloilo City, located on the island of Panay. To be honest, I was not at all prepared for the intense heat and humidity. My makeup melted and ran off my face. My hair and clothes became wet and clingy. I immediately decided that I would never wear hosiery again!

Although the gang of men at the airport who surrounded us yelling "Cano" (short for "Americano") were smiling, I was nervous as they grabbed our luggage. After all, everything we owned in the whole world was contained in those four suitcases. We were loaded into a very tiny rattletrap taxi and were driven to the pier. I won't go into how much the traffic scared me senseless, but fortunately I had already had a taste of that in Manila.

When we arrived at the pier, boys dressed only in shorts carted our luggage onto a bamboo outrigger boat. Holding onto a swaying rope and wearing high-heeled shoes, I navigated my way across a six-inch plank! Thankfully, I knew how to swim! By now, quite a crowd had gathered to watch us, and I didn't care to give them a show by falling in.

We rode the little bangka boat for about 30 minutes to the Island of Guimaras. There we got onto a jeepney which took us up a very steep hill to a beautiful place called the Good Shepherd's Fold Orphanage. Rick had visited the orphanage the previous year while on his survey trip, and he had already met "Mommy" and "Daddy" Irabon, the founders. We were warmly greeted and served rice cakes that had been baked in banana leaves.

Daddy Irabon had asked a little orphan girl to sing to me. I couldn't stop the tears from streaming down my face. The Irabons put us in a comfortable bamboo house for three days. They graciously fed us, provided us a private place to bathe, and covered us with mosquito nets at night. Because there was no electricity on the island, we used a lantern when the sun set. The little orphans washed our clothes by hand for us. I felt then as though I could have stayed forever in that beautiful, peaceful place.

Let me fast forward a few months. I was expecting our first baby. I was sick and vomiting all the time. I was very tired, hot, and grouchy. The honeymoon was over!

One afternoon when I came home from soul winning, someone informed me that our little dog Buster was dead. I started crying and could not stop. Although I am a dog lover, I am normally not that emotional (I'll blame it on my pregnancy). After I finally calmed down, I asked our Bible students what had happened to him. One hesitantly replied, "One of the neighbors held him down while the other ran over his head with a jeep. They are now preparing to cook and eat him."

I became so angry that I no longer wanted to stay in the Philippines forever! Truthfully, it took me a long time to get over that incident.

Let me stop right here in my narrative and ask you a question: Why are **you** going to the mission field? Is it because your husband wants to go, so you have no choice? Is it because you read a book and the mission field sounded exciting and romantic? Is it because of lost souls? After all, there are lost souls in America whom you can lead to the Lord. Were you touched during a missions conference, and in the emotion of the moment, you went forward, surrendered, and now you're having second thoughts?

I finally had to realize that I did not go to the mission field to raise a dog. I believed, and still believe, that God was and is going to use my husband to reach many lost people in the Philippines. I also knew and believed that a great deal of his success or failure would depend on me and my attitude. To be sure, the attitude of the missionary's wife or any Christian lady is extremely critical. If God has not called you or your husband to the mission field, why have **you** chosen to serve Him wherever you are? Is it because of your dreams of honor, grandeur, and heroism?

Chapter Two

An Attitude Strong Enough to Survive the Mission Field

When my friend, Sandy Domelle, *pushed* me into writing this book—okay—when the Lord *pushed* Sandy, and she *pushed* me, she was a tremendous help by sharing with me the responses she received from surveys sent out to missionary wives. She used these surveys as a teaching aid for the missions classes she taught at Hyles-Anderson College. Sandy also helped me formulate yet another survey to send. At this point, I would like to thank each wife who took time out of her busy schedule to think about these questions, to answer them, and to return them. I promised the wives that I would not use their names nor the fields in which they served, in the hopes that they would be more forthcoming with their responses.

Question How important do you think the missionary wife's attitude is?

Answers:

• Attitude is the most important issue. All it takes is one thing to go wrong, and it festers into a rotten attitude. Boom—her marriage and her testimony are shot. Keep a handle on your attitude which largely consists of controlling our tongue as well.

• The attitude of any wife is important for the atmosphere of the home—especially a missionary's wife. Your husband will either be encouraged or discouraged by your attitude. If he feels you are not content, he won't be either; and he may be tempted to leave the field and/or the ministry altogether. It isn't easy, but the wife needs to keep her attitude on topside through thick and thin. Take your worries and uneasiness to the Lord and be sweet and happy around your husband. Learn to make it on a little money and don't be a spend thrift.

Something that helps me a great deal in this area is knowing the children are watching to see my reactions to different circumstances. It is humbling to have to apologize to your children because you said or did a wrong toward their daddy. I try to remember that little eyes are watching and little ears are listening and learning. Are they learning good or bad? I have learned that they will treat their daddy like I treat him.

• I grew up in a Christian home, and I was pretty selfish. I did not want to do what the Lord wanted me to do. I went to [Bible college], and I did not really want to be there; but the Holy Spirit worked on my heart. I did not surrender to be a missionary until I was already dating [my husband]. Because of my selfishness, I did not want to leave the States; I wanted to stay here and not have to go through the hardships on the field. But the Lord spoke to my heart through a service, and I surrendered to be a missionary in 1989.

• It's my prayer that I'll always be sensitive and obedient to the Holy Spirit's leading in my life—less of me, more of Him. Attitude is the reflection of your "inner man." When self is on the throne, our attitude clearly shows it. We need to die to self daily—then our attitudes will be godly.

• Keep a happy spirit even when you are tired or sick. Nobody likes a "moper!" Stay positive. Don't sound like you know it all. When you get to the field, you will realize how ignorant you really are. Nobody likes a "know-it-all." I have watched MKs [missionary kids]. If the parents are positive, the kids will be.

• The wife should accept where God has placed her and her family. There are many things to get adjusted to; and if the wife is constantly thinking of how easy life is in the States, it could be a downfall.

• [My hardest adjustment when I arrived on the field was] the first six months. I didn't know the language, and we were working in villages. It was hard because I didn't have a church home; the only friend I had was my husband, who was gone most of the day. I depended on him to go to the market so I could buy just fruit and things. It was hard being "in the dark." I had a feeling of "Is this what I left America for?" God worked in my heart and in my life, and when I became pregnant and was able to return to the States for the birth of our son, I got "homesick" for [the mission field] and decided that no matter how awful I sounded, I would speak what I knew of the language. I decided to accept where I was and not feel sorry for myself.

• Our church presently meets in our backyard. The church uses one of our bathrooms. The nursery is in our den; one girls' Sunday school class meets in the kitchen, one on the porch, and one meets in the boys' room. Our furniture is hand-me-downs from other missionaries, so when one of the church kids writes on my couch cushion, I don't lose my Christianity. Our home is functional and comfortable.

- God has used Isaiah 50:7 to keep me set on staying and winning souls. Sometimes it seems like things are going slowly here and I get a bit weary, but God has promised me that I shall not be confounded or ashamed. Also Psalm 60:11, 12 is a comfort when it seems we need help that can only come from God.

- When we were at [Bible college], I never pictured myself as someone who could live on the mission field for 25 years—not even one year! The thought was very overwhelming to me. The Lord helped me to see myself as a missionary for just one day. That's not so overwhelming; anyone can do that, and for the last eight-and-a-half years I've tried just being a missionary one day at a time. The days add up, and I don't dread the future if I just take one day at a time.

Question

How do you face the hardships on the mission field?

Answer:

We feel very fortunate now on the field. It was quite difficult when we first went over there nine years ago. There was very little of anything available in the market. There was also very little electricity. The quality of the water was uncertain (and still is). But, things have changed so very much now. The most difficult physical thing that we face is the condition of the roads and the sanitation system (or lack thereof). Coupled with the road conditions are the driving habits of inexperienced and foolish drivers. We do not feel deprived as we are able to purchase all we need. In other words, God has blessed and provided as He always does for his children!

Question

Have you ever considered the possibility of dying on the field?

Answer:

Yes, we have considered that possibility. In 1997, there was significant political and civil unrest [in our area]. A message from the American Embassy advised us to leave. The next day we were contacted regarding evacuation, and we were airlifted out. During the 9/11 aftermath, the Muslims began to talk to some of the people who had been attending services. People were told that they should not attend and that God would kill them if they came. With God's blessing, we did continue the work. God is great!

Question

How have you faced open opposition?

Answers:

• We have no direct opposition from the government. The Devil is our biggest problem as he uses cultural traditions and other things in the lives of the people. If we did not have the full armor of God, who knows what could happen?

• You have probably heard the expression "living in a glass house." Perhaps missionaries understand that fact more clearly than anyone else. Not only do you feel exposed to the world because the people watch you so closely, but you also feel more vulnerable. It is best to dress and look as much like the natives as possible. We feel, however, that we are identified as Americans just by the way we walk. We are still advised by the embassy to keep a low profile, and we are advised by our neighbors…to stay off the street at night. We are thankful for God's provision of full armor for our physical life as well as for the spiritual warfare that is very real in [our field].

One missionary wife mentioned how she tried to make her home as comfy as possible without overextending her budget and being a burden to her husband because she decided she was there on the mission field for the "long-haul," and she might as well make the best of it. What great attitudes these women have!

Galatians 5:22, 23 says, *"But the fruit of the Spirit is love, joy, peace, longsuffering, gentleness, goodness, faith, Meekness, temperance…."* Since a person's attitude should be controlled by the Holy Spirit, let's break down these attributes and take a brief look at each one.

Chapter Three

Love

When I think of love, I think of Jesus. He was the perfect example of love. He was a great example as a missionary because He gave up His home in Heaven and lived on earth for over 30 years. Not only did He live a sacrificial life, He died a sacrificial death—on the cross for you and me—because of love. Besides the wonderful love chapter, I Corinthians 13, there are also many verses about love in the book of I John. Please allow me to share many of them.

• *"But whoso keepeth his word, in him verily is the **love** of God perfected: hereby know we that we are in him."* (I John 2:5)

• *"He that **loveth** his brother abideth in the light, and there is none occasion of stumbling in him."* (I John 2:10)

• *"**Love** not the world, neither the things that are in the world. If any man **love** the world, the **love** of the Father is not in him."* (I John 2:15)

• *"Behold, what manner of **love** the Father hath bestowed upon us, that we should be called the sons of God...."* (I John 3:1)

• *"For this is the message that ye heard from the beginning, that we should **love** one another."* (I John 3:11)

• *"We know that we have passed from death unto life, because we **love** the brethren. He that **loveth** not his brother abideth in death."* (I John 3:14)

• *"Hereby perceive we the **love** of God, because he laid down his life for us: and we ought to lay down our lives for the brethren. But whoso hath this world's good, and seeth his brother have need, and shutteth up his bowels of compassion from him, how dwelleth the **love** of God in him? My little children, let us not **love** in word, neither in tongue; but in deed and in truth."* (I John 3:16-18)

- *"Beloved, let us* **love** *one another: for* **love** *is of God; and every one that* **loveth** *is born of God, and knoweth God. He that* **loveth** *not knoweth not God; for God is* **love**. *In this was manifested the* **love** *of God toward us, because that God sent his only begotten Son into the world, that we might live through him. Herein is* **love**, *not that we* **loved** *God, but that he* **loved** *us, and sent his Son to be the propitiation for our sins. Beloved, if God so* **loved** *us, we ought also to* **love** *one another…If we* **love** *one another, God dwelleth in us, and his* **love** *is perfected in us."* (I John 4:7-12)

- *"And this is his commandment…* **love** *one another…."* (I John 3:23)

- *"And we have known and believed the* **love** *that God hath to us. God is* **love**; *and he that dwelleth in* **love** *dwelleth in God, and God in him. Herein is our* **love** *made perfect, that we may have boldness in the day of judgment…There is no fear in* **love**; *but perfect* **love** *casteth out fear…He that feareth is not made perfect in* **love**. *We* **love** *him, because he first* **loved** *us. If a man say, I* **love** *God, and hateth his brother…whom he hath seen, how can he* **love** *God whom he hath not seen? And this commandment have we from him, That he who* **loveth** *God* **love** *his brother also."* (I John 4:16-21)

- *"Whosoever believeth that Jesus is the Christ is born of God: and every one that* **loveth** *him that begat* **loveth** *him also that is begotten of him. By this we know that we* **love** *the children of God, when we* **love** *God…For this is the* **love** *of God, that we keep his commandments…."* (I John 5:1-3)

I read a wonderful example of love and of having a good attitude in the missions paper published by Dr. Jim Vineyard, the pastor of Windsor Hills Baptist Church in Oklahoma City, Oklahoma. This article happened to be written by my friend, Becky Trimble, a missionary in the Philippines. With her permission, I have reproduced her thoughts as follows:

Learning to Love Living in the Philippines

I've grown to love living here in the Philippines, although I could not always say that! I'm still a "junior missionary" as I've heard it called, being here for only three and a half years. I'm sure there are many more learning experiences and trials for me, but this is one thing that I have learned.

A wise veteran missionary wife once told me, "You will first love the Filipinos; then you will dislike them very much; then you will learn to love them for what they truly are." I could not understand the second part of that statement until about one year ago. "How could I dislike these sweet people?"

TO CROSS THE WIDEST OCEAN
WHAT I HAVE LEARNED ABOUT FAITH

I thought. Then we moved to a little country town called Tagoloan. We had just spent our first ten months in language study in a city about four hours from Tagoloan. We had learned to love our home in a quiet subdivision, the Filipino church we attended while learning the language, and the city in which we lived.

If you visit the Philippines, you will notice how Westernized the people are. You will see that you can buy a great deal of things from the States—for a price. But once you have lived here, the difference in culture pulls itself out; and that's when trusting the Lord and leaning on Him really counts.

In America, if you have a loud party going on next door all night, all you have to do is call the police; they will take care of it for you, right? Not here! Our house in Tagoloan was right across from the village basketball court. It's the center of activity. Each village has a yearly fiesta time—just like in Mexico. The people worship a chosen saint for that particular week. Many special events take place, and to defer the costs of the events, dances are scheduled every weekend for about five weeks before at the—you guessed it—basketball court. Even though the dances did not start until 10:00 p.m., the music was always turned on at around 5:00 p.m. for advertisement, so you can imagine how loud it was. The two speakers were eight feet high and directly facing the back of our house. Sometimes we got lucky, and the dance would end at 1:00 a.m., but usually it went on until 3:00 a.m.

We talked to the owner of the speaker system. One time we even called the police, only to find out that the police in the only patrol car were also attending the dance! No one could understand why the Americans were upset about how loud the music was. After all, it was the fiesta!

I was discouraged. Even when we shut all the windows and closed all the doors and turned on our air conditioner in our room, the music still vibrated in our ears. And to make matters worse, the owner of the vacant lot next door to our house decided to build a little eatery with a sing-a-long video television! Now, you must know this: in the Philippines almost every small establishment is not air-conditioned and is usually very open with lots of windows and doors to bring in air. Every day they were open, their music was on. Our church met outside our house, and we would sometimes have to go over next door and ask them to please turn down their music so we could have church. Talk about discouraging!

I begged God to allow us to find a different home in a subdivision where it was quiet. I fretted and fumed about it. I realized during that time that I actually disliked these people to whom the Lord had called us! So it WAS possible to dislike them!

But God was working on my heart. He was molding me and making me into a vessel for the finer that He could begin to use. It was not until I yielded my stubborn heart to Him and overcame my selfish desire to live in better circumstances that the Lord did indeed move our family to a quiet subdivision— just a few blocks away from some American missionary friends.

I learned many valuable lessons through it all, and I am learning that God placed me here in the Philippines for MY OWN good, as well as for the good of others.

Truly, we cannot have a good attitude without love.

Chapter Four

Joy

When I think of joy, I think of having a sense of humor. I love to laugh. In fact, one of the biggest reasons why I love being around my husband and my children is that they love to laugh. I love being with my mother-in-law, my husband's sisters, his brother, and their families. One reason is that they are so funny and fun.

My sister and brother are also extremely funny. They are very patient with their big sister, who has spent more years in the Philippines than she has in the States. Sometimes their big sister comes to the States and looks around in wonder at life in America, about which she has forgotten and therefore can't quite figure out. She doesn't know how to dress or act, and she doesn't know what to think or say. She's lost!

I remember a time when my sister and I were shopping at a Goodwill store. I saw a sign that I thought said there was a big sale on everything that was blue. I loaded my cart with every blue piece of clothing I could find. I found my sister and proudly showed her my cart. She just raised her eyebrows when she saw the cart full of blue clothing. I started pulling out items and showing them to her. "Look, Bobbie," I said excitedly, "I don't even like this; but it's BLUE, so I'm getting it." I took out another item and said, "See this, Bobbie? It doesn't even fit; but it's BLUE, so I'm buying it."

She patiently led me over to the sign which read, "Everything with a blue **TAG** is ½ off today"!

Another time we were driving from Oklahoma to Indiana. To keep awake, I was chewing on sunflower seeds as I drove. I pulled into a gas station to buy some gas, purchase a drink, and go to the restroom. I smiled and talked to several strangers and then returned to our the car. My little sister gave me one of her knowing looks as she sweetly asked, "You didn't talk to anyone in there, did you?"

"Well, of course I did," I answered. "Why?"

"Look in the mirror."

To my horror, my teeth were covered with the black shells from the sunflower seeds I had been eating!

Once several family members were meeting at a mall in Indianapolis to eat and shop. Before going to the place where we were to meet, I stopped by the restroom. While on my way to meet the others, I noticed my pretty teenage niece was already there talking with a couple of handsome guys. I walked up to them, smiled, and said, "Hello."

After my niece kindly introduced me to the boys, I walked away to see if I could find the others. I heard the boys snickering behind me. Wondering what could be wrong, I turned around, and to my horror, I saw a long trail of toilet paper following along behind me stuck to my shoe!

Needless to say, every time I go home, my brother and sister laugh over their "hayseed" sister.

I love sharing funny stories with others, and I love having them share their funny anecdotes with me. No one wants to be around someone who is glum all the time. Ecclesiastes 3:1-4 says, *"To every thing there is a season, and a time to every purpose under the heaven…A time to weep, and a time to laugh…."*

Trust me—you need a sense of humor on the mission field. However, joy is more than just laughter and happiness. It goes deeper than that. Joy comes about as a result of salvation. The Bible says in Nehemiah 8:10, *"…the joy of the LORD is your strength."*

Mrs. Rosalind Goforth writing in *Goforth of China* relates the following incident:

One of the first things we all joyously took part in on arriving at Szepingkai was the decorating of the preaching-hall, which could hold two or three hundred, and over which was the Mission Home. A large number of beautiful texts and pictures illustrating Bible stories had been secured from Shanghai…We literally covered the chapel walls with these, making the place beautiful and attractive. Mr. Reoch had had the chapel filled with fine, comfortable benches. Then, with the preacher's table, beside which was placed the literature table, and the ever-needed hymn scroll and baby organ, the preaching-hall was ready. I only wish those who pity missionaries could experience, if only for a brief spell, the pure joy we had in getting that chapel ready, and in the contemplation of what it was going to mean to multitudes in the days to come.[1]

This is just one text which illustrates how Mrs. Goforth found joy in sacrificing for the cause of Christ.

Peace

"Thou wilt keep him in perfect peace, whose mind is stayed on thee: because he trusteth in thee." (Isaiah 26:3) One dictionary defines *peace* as "quiet, order, security, calm." Certainly these words are appropriate synonyms; however, I believe true peace only comes when we surrender to God and to His will. In the book, *In the Arena*, author Isobel Kuhn, a missionary to China, writes the following account:

The difficult lessons of 1942 taught me to fear leaning heavily on human props. I had surrendered husband, child, friends, all I possessed, long ago. But this was something deeper. This was relinquishing my rights to them. This was holding them, but on the open palm of my hand. Mrs. McFarlane, principal of our language school in Yangchow and a dear warrior saint, had taught me that metaphor. She said, "Keep your treasures on the open palm of your hand. If you hold something tight clenched in your fist, God may have to hurt you in order to open your fingers and take it from you. But if it is offered on the open palm of your hand, you will hardly know when it is gone."[1]

Another missionary to China, Betty Stam, wife of John Stam, had the following to say about surrender: "It's as clear as daylight to me that the only worthwhile life is one of unconditional surrender to God's will, and living in His way, trusting His love and guidance."[2] Another time she said,

I want something really worthwhile to live for. Like most young people, I want to invest this one life of mine as wisely as possible, in the place that yields richest profits…wherever it is, I want it to be God's choice for me and not my own. There must be no self-interest at all, or I do not believe God can reveal His will clearly…I can never realize the richest, most satisfying life Christ meant for me, if I am not giving my own life unselfishly for others.[3]

The Stams were later kidnaped by the Communists and held for ransom. John wrote the following letter dated December 6, 1934, to the China Inland Mission:

Dear Brethren:

My wife, baby and myself are today in the hands of the Communists, in the city of Tsingteh. Their demand is twenty thousand dollars for our release.

All our possessions and supplies are in their hands, but we praise God for peace in our hearts and a meal tonight. God grant you wisdom in what you do, and us fortitude, courage and peace of heart. He is able—and a wonderful Friend in such a time.

Things happened so quick this AM. They were in the city just a few hours after the ever-persistent rumors really became alarming, so that we could not prepare to leave in time. We were just too late.

The Lord bless and guide you, and as for us, may God be glorified whether by life or by death.

In Him,
John C. Stam[4]

Later, some Chinese Christians found the decapitated bodies of the Stams, and miraculously, their baby daughter who was still alive. Yieldedness to the cause of Christ was immortalized in a prayer written by Betty Stam:

Lord, I give up my own purposes and plans, all my own desires and hopes and ambitions (whether they be fleshly or soulish) and accept Thy will for my life. I give myself, my life, my all utterly to Thee, to be Thine forever. I hand over to Thy keeping all my friendships; all the people whom I love are to take a second place in my heart. Fill me and seal me with Thy Holy Spirit. Work out Thy whole will in my life, at any cost, now and forever. To me to live is Christ. Amen![5]

Nine years after penning these words, Betty Scott Stam and her husband calmly and bravely laid down their lives for Christ when they were martyred by Chinese Communists on December 8, 1934. As a result of their seemingly untimely deaths, Peter Stam, John's father, said, "We are earnestly praying that it will all be for God's glory and the salvation of souls. How glad we shall be if through this dreadful experience many souls shall be won for the Lord Jesus...."[6]

Peter Stam did not have to wait long for an answer to his fervent prayers. Seven hundred students stood up in the memorial service held at the Moody Bible Institute to consecrate their lives to missionary work.

John Stam, in writing to his father some time before, had mentioned the prevailing dangers. In one of his letters, he had enclosed the following verses written by another, which he said expressed his own feelings:

Afraid?

Afraid? Of what?
    To feel the spirit's glad release?
To pass from pain to perfect peace,
    The strife and strain of life to cease?
Afraid—of that?

Afraid? Of what?
    Afraid to see the Savior's face,
To hear His welcome, and to trace
    The glory gleam from wounds of grace?
Afraid—of that?

Afraid? Of what?
    A flash—a crash—a pierced heart;
Darkness—Light—O Heaven's art!
    A wound of His a counterpart!
Afraid?—of that?

Afraid? Of what?
    To do by death what life could not—
Baptize with blood a stony plot,
    Till souls shall blossom from the spot?
Afraid?—of that?[7]

I am convinced that these missionary heroes knew that God's peace surely does not depend on circumstances.

Chapter Six

Longsuffering

The Bible word *longsuffering* means "to endure trouble or pain patiently." Not too long ago, a missionary couple I know lost their precious baby in an accident. With permission, I would like to share portions of an e-mail this young mother sent to several people:

Dear Family and Friends:

We went to the cemetery today. How beautiful his grave site was! I went yesterday and put a silk flower arrangement on his site. Yesterday was the day we buried [him] two years ago. I put some small sprays of flowers and leaves on seven other graves, including three babies. I just had to put something there that said, "You are not forgotten." What a wonderful salve it was to my soul when some friends put flowers on [my son's] grave site. My heart longed to be near his memorial stone. I felt I should return the sentiment.

Some find it hard to believe that it has already been two years since he left us. For us, it has been the longest two years we have ever known. But as I look back, I can take a deep sigh of relief, knowing not only did we make it, but [we] have come out with our hands full.

As low as we have delved into the trenches of Hell, we have to the same degree been transcended into the realms of Heaven. Most of the time spent grieving we were alone, but as the song says, "In my darkness Jesus found me...." I learned what it meant to have a song in the night, "...and in the night *his song shall be with me, and my prayer unto the God of my life.*" (Psalm 42:8) In the presence of God is fullness of joy, the Bible tells us. I didn't always feel the way I do. I recall the dread of falling asleep because of the repetitious dreams I would have of his leaving us so tragically. We comforted ourselves with the thoughts of God taking [our son] to Heaven. When certain thoughts came to terrorize me, I imagined God's huge hand catching our little white-haired angel and scooping him into His arms.

Lately I have received some astonishing letters of those whose souls surely are being lowered into the depths of Hell. I am always amazed by the heartache and sorrows that come to mankind. If you are at rock bottom, please grab my hand and let's ascend back up together. Your tragedy has great potential.

God wants to use our hardship to tear us down, so that He can build us up. In Jeremiah 1:10 God tells us how He operates: *"See, I have this day set thee over the nations and over the kingdoms, to root out, and to pull down, and to destroy, and to throw down, to build, and to plant."* That verse could translate as God saying, "Off with the old and on with the new!" Did you ever see an old dilapidated building that was not very useful? Sometimes it is listed as a "historical site" so the city will fight to keep the sad thing around though it is just taking up useful space. That stooping structure may bring some people security because it is a symbol of a nostalgic stage in their lives that was happy and safe; nonetheless, it is not productive to live in the past. That historic structure may even be violating many new safety codes, leaving the next generation a possible catastrophe with which to deal. Developers who have an eye for a bright future want to come in and erect a brand-new, modern building that will beautify the city, create new jobs, generate money, and offer an array of services to the community.

Often we get frustrated with God when He wants to take something away from us that we want, perhaps a possession, child, job, reputation, or an era. We resist God's decision to tear down our "old building." If only we could stop boo-hooing long enough to realize this is an important stage of which we must be partakers if we are to have the bigger and better! We tend to look at the present and cannot see the future.

I held on to hope and imagined a bright future after we lost [our son]; but like many of us, for a time I began to wonder if we even had a future. I wondered if the sun would ever again shine in our lives. However, we should not rush the painful phase that we are in. My dad used to tell me when we were running and I would get that pain in my side and shoulder, to lean into the pain. We should feel it, remember it, and concentrate on the anguish. We will need to refer back to that pain many times for the sake of others and our own personal growth. Pain has the ability to make us deep, sober-minded people, if we will not shun it. I was able to literally feel the arms of God around me.

I remember a night while looking out of a window that I often prayed at in the wee hours of the morning; I was telling God I still loved Him even though He took [our child]. I remember a distinct feeling of warmth near the back of my neck. I turned around, and I did not see anybody, but I knew it was the presence of God. Another time almost a year later as I prayed earnestly asking God to use us, I drifted off and was awakened five minutes later to a voice in English calling my name. Everyone was gone, and it sounded as if someone was calling me from the hallway. That was a particularly dark time in my life, and I have no doubt that it was God assuring me of His love and presence. If only we could see our hardship as a phase in one of the stages of building! God is not trying to destroy us for the sake of destruction, oh no! He is in the first stages of construction! Let's say to ourselves, "I am in the first stages of building! I will become more useful, productive, and valuable."

James 1:4 says, "But let patience have her perfect work, that ye may be perfect and entire, wanting nothing." Our sorrow may last only a few months or may be with us for a lifetime. We should allow it to work in us, to change us, to teach us, and to transform us! When stockholders invest into the market, rarely do they expect to see big returns in a week, a month, or even a year. Often the biggest money to be made is when the investment matures.

I believe the greatest temptations to make big decisions happen when we are in the midst of struggle. We should resist moving our investment elsewhere if it doesn't seem to be profiting us. We can't rush God's natural laws. Whatever happened to the idea of waiting on the Lord? What an instant generation we live in!

Psalm 37:34 orders us to wait: "Wait on the LORD, and keep his way, and he shall exalt thee to inherit the land." What if we moved a stalk of corn because it had not yet formed the ears? Most likely transplanting the young stalk would kill it [or] most likely, it would not produce. We must simply wait patiently for those ears of corn to come to fruition. We stress ourselves out trying to make a big decision in the middle of a crisis. Let's soothe ourselves with these thoughts: "I must simply rest where I am and wait for God."

In Romans 12:2 God tells us, "And be not conformed to this world: but be ye transformed by the renewing of your mind, that ye may prove what is that good, and acceptable, and perfect, will of God." You cannot stay a caterpillar if you want to fly! "And be not conformed to this world," means "be not fashioned to the age, time, or stage you are in." Instead, experience a metamorphosis! The word transformed is the Greek word, "metamorphoo." If we want to get our wings and fly, we must experience a change, and we do that by "renewing" or renovating our mind daily. We need to fill our minds with thoughts such as, "in all these things we are more than conquerors through him that loved us." When we renovate our shambled minds with victorious thoughts every morning, we will experience a metamorphosis and get our wings!

I don't think it is immodest to say that God has opened the windows of Heaven and poured out a blessing many times for me because of my renewing my own mind by taking on the traits I wish to have. God will close the windows of blessing if we get bitter.

I believe you would agree with me that this precious lady is a perfect example of longsuffering.

Chapter Seven

Gentleness

Filipinos are wonderful people who have many great attributes. One character-istic I love about the Filipino people is their gentleness. I often joke that the major export of the Philippine Islands is her nurses. One reason why Filipinas make such excellent nurses is a result of their natural gentleness. You rarely see a hospital in the United States without a Filipina nurse. I truly believe gentleness is part of their cultural makeup.

However, in this chapter I am not addressing the human attribute of gentleness. I am examining the fruits of the Spirit, and one of the fruits of the Spirit is gentleness. Are you gentle with your husband and your children? Are you gentle with your church people? Are you gentle with strangers? Maybe you're one of those drivers who could be labeled as having "road-rage."

A couple of my dresses are supposed to be washed in the "gentle" cycle in the machine because the cloth is considered delicate. On the other hand, I have a denim skirt that does not need to be handled quite so gently because it is made of rougher and more durable material. Denim is naturally able to withstand more stress on the material.

The children in Iloilo Baptist Academy, whom I love dearly, often need discipline. I can't handle some of the rough-and-tumble boys in the same way that I handle some of the soft-hearted girls. Sometimes I turn the boys over to Brother Gelladula, who is our principal, or to one of the other men on our staff. Sometimes I even ask my husband to deal with a young man. Dealing with the girls can be very different, however. Often, I can just give any of the girls one of my "looks," and her eyes will fill with tears! My look is all it takes to get the desired result.

I Thessalonians 2:7 says, *"But we were gentle among you, even as a nurse cherisheth her [own] children."* How "gentle" are we talking about in this verse? The Apostle Paul is saying that a nurse or "nanny" is very gentle with children who aren't even her own—how much more gentle she is with her own children. Paul was filled with the Holy Spirit; he could be harsh when he needed to be, and he could be very gentle as well. He allowed the Holy Spirit to guide him as the occasion demanded.

The Bible presents a beautiful picture of the gentleness of the Lord in Isaiah 40:11: *"He shall feed his flock like a shepherd: he shall gather the lambs with his arm, and carry them in his bosom, and shall gently lead those that are with young."*

We need to ask the Holy Spirit to give us gentleness and kindness when we deal with people. In order for us to help people, He alone can give us the wisdom to know how to "handle" them.

Chapter Eight

Goodness

If you look in your Bible concordance, you will see the word "good" mentioned many times. Basically, the opposite of good is evil.

The Bible mentions three men who were "good." One was Ahimaaz. During the uprising against King David caused by his own son Absalom, a watchman came to the king and said, "...*Me thinketh the running of the foremost is like the running of Ahimaaz the son of Zadok. And the king said, He is a good man, and cometh with good tidings. And Ahimaaz called, and said unto the king, All is well....*" (II Samuel 18:27, 28) Another good man was Joseph of Arimathea, who wanted to take care of the body of our Lord by giving his tomb after Jesus was crucified. The last of the three was Barnabas, who traveled with Saul (Paul) on his missionary journeys.

What did these three good men have in common? My husband, who preached a sermon on these three men, believes the good that all three possessed in common was their ability to encourage others. Ahimaaz tried to encourage King David. Joseph encouraged by trying to do a good and kind deed in providing a burial place for the body of the Lord Jesus. Matthew 27:57-61 says: "*When the even was come, there came a rich man of Arimathaea, named Joseph, who also himself was Jesus' disciple: He went to Pilate, and begged the body of Jesus. Then Pilate commanded the body to be delivered. And when Joseph had taken the body, he wrapped it in a clean linen cloth, And laid it in his own new tomb, which he had hewn out in the rock: and he rolled a great stone to the door of the sepulchre, and departed.*" Luke 23:50 adds an additional description of Joseph. "*And, behold, there was a man named Joseph, a counsellor; and he was a good man, and a just.*"

Barnabas encouraged the Apostle Paul right after he was saved. Acts 9:26-27 says, "*And when Saul was come to Jerusalem, he assayed to join himself to the disciples: but they were all afraid of him, and believed not that he was a disciple. But Barnabas took him, and brought him to the apostles, and declared unto them how he had seen the Lord in the way, and that he had spoken to him, and how he had preached boldly at Damascus in the name of Jesus.*" In fact, "son of consolation" is the meaning of Barnabas' name. A "son of consolation" is one who encourages another.

To be an encourager is wonderful. Do you try to encourage people? Or do you tear down people with your gossiping tongue? This is a tough old world in which we live, with too many heartaches. Therefore, we need to be encouraging one another all the time.

Chapter Nine

Faith

No doubt you have read Hebrews chapter 11—the "faith" chapter—many times. Many wonderful examples of people who had great faith are listed. Faith is not hope; rather, faith is substance, and it is evidence. Faith is acting. The verses in Hebrews 11 often begin, *"By faith…"* and then a name is given such as Abel, Enoch, Noah, Abraham, Isaac, Joseph, Moses, and so on. Then the verse continues on to say what each person *did.* Abel offered; Enoch was translated; Noah prepared; Abraham obeyed; Isaac blessed; Joseph gave commandment; Moses refused, chose, esteemed, forsook, endured, kept, and passed; and so on.

Recently I read the biography of Irene Webster-Smith, a single lady missionary who went to Japan in 1916. With great faith, she started an orphanage. As in the case of George Mueller, God miraculously provided for her orphans time and time again.

Years later, while she was home on furlough, Hitler invaded Poland. Irene felt God wanted her to return immediately to her orphanage in Japan. She did so in spite of great opposition. She found that securing a boat was impossible, but she could not quiet the urgency inside her. Finally after several months, she booked passage and once again sailed toward Japan. Upon arriving there however, she felt hatred in the air. Her beloved country had become so different from the country in which she had lived for so many years. Finally, the British ambassador ordered foreigners out of Japan. Irene suddenly realized why the Lord wanted her to hurry back to Japan: she must find homes for all of her orphans.

Irene prayed fervently, and the Lord answered her prayer. She found good Christian homes for nearly all of her orphans; only one 17-year-old girl remained whom it seemed that no one wanted because she was too old. In faith Irene reminded her charge that God had exactly the right home for her. The beautiful young orphan girl knew the danger Irene faced by staying. She unselfishly urged Irene to leave the country—"I will manage." However, Irene insisted that God had parents already chosen for the girl and that she would stay until the girl was placed in that home.

Irene prayed all night long. In the morning a lady knocked at the door and asked to adopt a baby. Irene told the woman she was sorry. "All the babies have been adopted."

The woman, who happened to be a Christian, shared how she had recently lost her only daughter to polio. "My daughter was only 17 when she died," she explained. The lonely mother shared how she became bitter and turned from God. Then after reading a book about Irene's orphanage, she came back to the Lord's loving arms.

Irene told the woman about her 17-year-old girl named Hana-chan, who badly needed a home. At first the woman refused and retorted that no one could take her daughter's place. Irene smiled and calmly waited. Her strong faith had told her that this woman was God's answer to her prayer!

That night the couple had supper with Irene, who had asked Hana-chan to help serve. When the couple saw Hana-chan, they exclaimed that she was the very image of their dead daughter! With tears streaming down both of their faces, they asked Irene if they could adopt Hana-chan. Irene gladly consented, thanking God for answering her prayer. Later, when the adoption papers were drawn up, it was discovered that Hana-chan was born on the very same day, month, and year as the couple's dead daughter!

With her orphans adopted, Irene was free to return to her home country. God's timing was perfect, for little did she (or the world, for that matter) realize that the attack on Pearl Harbor was just around the corner.

The Irene Webster-Smith story is only one story among many. Undeniably, Irene possessed a Hebrews chapter 11 kind of faith.

Chapter Ten

Meekness

The modern-day definition of meekness is being patient, submissive, and mild. However, my former pastor, Dr. Jack Hyles, said when Numbers 12:3 described Moses as being meek, it meant he was perfect, or well-rounded. *"(Now the man Moses was very **meek**, above all the men which were upon the face of the earth.)"* Like the man Moses, we are to be balanced in all of the many facets of our life.

Meekness also means being "even-textured" and being humble. A meek person treats everyone in the same way. The Lord does not like it when we cater to the "big shots" and ignore the "little guy." James 2:2 says, *"For if there come unto your assembly a man with a gold ring, in goodly apparel, and there come in also a poor man in vile raiment; And ye have respect to him that weareth the gay clothing, and say unto him, Sit thou here in a good place; and say to the poor, Stand thou there, or sit here under my footstool: Are ye not then partial in yourselves, and are become judges of evil thoughts?"*

Twenty-five years ago when my husband started the Iloilo Baptist Church, he put the words, "The Church with a Heart for Everyone" on a sign outside the gate. It just so happens that we have a couple of doctors and a couple of lawyers attending our church. They are treated the same way as the poorest street kid who cannot put anything in the offering plate. Everyone is welcomed, and everyone is loved.

The Bible admonishes Christians to be meek. *"But let it be the hidden man of the heart, in that which is not corruptible, even the ornament of a meek and quiet spirit, which is in the sight of God of great price."* (I Peter 3:4) The Bible says if we are meek, we will be fed (Psalm 22:26), we will be guided and taught (Psalm 25:9), and we will inherit the earth (Matthew 5:5). If we are meek, God will judge in our behalf (Isaiah 11:4), and we will have our joy increased (Isaiah 29:19). God lifts and saves the meek (Psalm 76:9, Psalm 147:6). If we are meek, we are in very good company because according to Matthew 11:29, Jesus is meek. *"Take my yoke upon you, and learn of me; for **I am meek** and lowly in heart: and ye shall find rest unto your souls."*

Are we balanced in our Christian life? Do we treat people equally? Perhaps we are not "even-textured" in our daily walk. Maybe we read our Bible, but we don't pray. Maybe we spend time in prayer, but we're not soul winners. Maybe we do all three but we don't give, or we're negligent about our church attendance. We need to be balanced and well-rounded in our Christian life.

Chapter Eleven

Temperance

M rs. Howard (Geraldine) Taylor, the daughter-in-law of Hudson Taylor, was a great example of temperance. Like her famous father-in-law, Geraldine was also a missionary in China. When I read passages like the following, I think of how well her life illustrates temperance.

I t was the medical work that was used at last to win an entrance for the Gospel into that city, and even with all the help thus afforded, conditions were far from easy. Four years of patient effort were required before we could obtain the poorest kind of little place in which to live. The house they gave us was just a small cart-inn, old and dirty, four rooms all told, with walls and floors of dried mud and a dilapidated roof of thatch leaking all over. The paper windows were heavily barred, and not made to open, and the little bit of courtyard was enclosed with high walls all round that shut out everything except the sky.

Altogether it was very like a prison, and so shabby and dirty that it would hardly have been used for a stable at home. But poor as it was, how we rejoiced to obtain it! It was privilege, opportunity, everything to us; the answer to many prayers; the chance we had so longed for to live and preach the Gospel in that proud Confucian city. I think the authorities had an idea, when they let us rent that house, that we should find it impossible to live there long, and that in that way they might soon be rid of us. But if so, they were indeed mistaken. How little it matters to us where we live, or what we have to put up with, as long as souls are saved and men and women grow up into Christ in all things![1]

The author writes the following about Geraldine Taylor:

F ew have traveled more extensively and continuously in China than Howard and Geraldine did those three years, and it is impossible to give any conception of the physical endurance that was involved. Only those who have been in those places know. They were not young; they were in their sixtieth year in 1922. They had of course taken with them what comforts it was possible to take, but nothing could save them from lying awake all night, in winter because it was so cold that no amount of bedding made them warm enough to go to sleep, or in summer because it was too hot, and the company in the inns, large and small, too lively to allow of rest. They would have to be up very early to pack and set out before daylight, and then there would be hour after hour of jolting slowly along in a cart or swinging in a sedan chair.

But those things were easy compared with the spiritual cares they carried. The burden for souls they met by the way, the pain of realizing how few could ever be told the Good News, was a constant undercurrent from which relief was found only in pouring it out before the Lord.[2]

I believe that Geraldine Taylor possessed the biblical trait of temperance, another of the fruits of the Spirit. *Temperance* means "to have self-control or self-restraint." Are you ever out of control? Do you have an uncontrollable mind, mouth, or heart? I believe one of the biggest problems missionary wives (and all wives) have is lack of self-control when it comes to spending money. Because of this problem, I will devote more time to finances in another chapter. For now, let me say that if you do not control your appetite when it comes to spending, Satan can use the unbridled weakness in that area to ruin your husband's ministry. Some missionaries have had to leave the field because of this problem.

Geraldine Taylor did not care about living in a nice house or having an easy life. She cared about seeing souls saved. I Corinthians 9:25 says: "*And every man that striveth for the mastery is temperate in all things....*" II Peter 1:5, 6 says: "*And beside this, giving all diligence, add to your faith virtue; and to virtue knowledge; and to knowledge temperance; and to temperance patience; and to patience godliness; and to godliness brotherly kindness; and to brotherly kindness charity.*" Learn to control yourself with God's help. Seek to be filled with the Holy Spirit and let Him give you His self-control.

If you are filled with the Holy Spirit, you will have these fruits of the Spirit. When people see you, they will see Jesus because you will appear Christlike.

Conclusion

Remember Jessie, the young man in the story at the beginning of this unit? Jessie was Christlike. As time passed, I found I began to think less of his death and more of his life. Maybe God had to take him to get our attention—mine anyway. Maybe God had to use his death to get those of us who knew him to look at his life.

I would like to share portions of what my husband wrote about Jessie in his prayer letter dated September-October 2000:

Have you ever known a young Christian whose testimony seemed too good to be true? When I think about Jessie Contiga, that thought comes to mind. Although only starting his second year of Bible college, he was one of the best students we have ever had at Iloilo Baptist College. Recently, the Lord took him Home. Here is his story:

Jessie Contiga was born and reared in Hamdumanan, a village outside Bacolod City, on Negros, the next island east of Iloilo. His parents were very poor but managed to feed Jessie and his five siblings by selling vegetables.

As a teenager, Jessie regularly attended a small Baptist church where he had found Christ as his Saviour. He soon began to bear a burden for others to hear the Gospel, and so he began to share it.

One day a Bible college student with whom Jessie had attended high school visited him and persuaded him to come to Iloilo. He was told that there was a Bible college that would teach him how to start a church and be a more proficient soul winner. Jessie packed his few possessions and caught a boat ride to Iloilo, where he would give his life for others.

The Bible says in I Samuel 18:5, "*David...behaved himself wisely...*" and so did Jessie. Anyone who had anything to do with Jessie at IBC couldn't have been more pleased and proud of him. He worked in the print shop doing anything his supervisor told him to do, and he was very efficient. He was a diligent student, often seen studying past midnight, and therefore, made good grades.

Jessie was known as a hard worker in his ministries. He worked in many of the ministries of IBC. He was very consistent in his soul winning and brought many people—young and old—to Christ.

Jessie was known by the staff as a servant, who without fuss would drop everything he was doing to meet another's need. One staff lady recalls asking Jessie on several occasions to take a sick student to the hospital when she was too busy. Jessie often spent the night at the hospital, watching over an ill classmate.

Jessie was known by his fellow students as an encourager who believed that wise people win people. He occasionally used short simple sayings like, "No victory without suffering," to minister to the weary. He also believed that actions spoke louder than words. He fed hungry roommates, paid another's utility bill, and slept on a church pew after giving his bed to a new student. I don't know how he did so much with practically nothing.

Jessie and the Bible college students and staff went on an outing for a day of fun. At the outing, Jessie watched two men who were painting nearby. He decided to mix business with pleasure, for soul winning was his business, and he led both painters to Christ. Jessie then went into the ocean, as some of the boys were allowed to go to a secluded place on the beach to swim with a lifeguard present…Heaven was waiting.

A lifeguard saw a hand go up, and he dove into the water. Several students also joined the search, but too much time had lapsed before Jessie was found and brought to shore. My wife gave him CPR on the beach and on the way to a local hospital, where he was pronounced dead on arrival.

That same day Becky, some other ladies in the church, and the Bible student who had brought Jessie to Bible college left for Bacolod to break the sad news to Jessie's parents. Their reaction to their beloved son's death was one of sorrow, yet acceptance.

Jessie loved the Word of God. At the end of May we gave all the second year students a Scofield Reference Bible. After the Lord took Jessie to Heaven, someone gave me his new Bible. Over 1,000 verses had been highlighted by Jessie in that short time. One verse I noticed that he highlighted was Proverbs 27:1, *"Boast not thyself of to morrow; for thou knowest not what a day may bring forth."*

Jessie had a tremendous love for soul winning. We found a list of people he had won to Christ in the 31 days before he died. There were 48 names of people he had led to Christ with the age and address of each on the list. He led 25 adults, 21 teenagers, and 2 children to Christ, plus the two painters he led to Christ the day he died. He had a strong desire to start a church someday. He had recently written a letter to his father, asking his father to build a small pulpit so Jessie could practice preaching in the dorm.

At Jessie's funeral, several people were saved, and lives were rededicated. Over a hundred testimonies were written by those who knew Jessie as a friend.

Some told how Jessie had kept a student from quitting school, and others were full of thanks to Jessie for all he had done and what he had meant to them:

"Jessie was my good friend. He had a good attitude. I didn't know anyone that was better than Jessie."

"He recruited me for Bible school. I'm thankful because he led me to Christ. I could see Jessie was serious about serving God. I want to be like Jessie and serve God."

"Jessie was my big brother at IBC. He helped me get acquainted when I first came to IBC. He helped me with my problems, advised me, and helped meet my needs. Jessie was my best friend during my eight months here. When I had a problem, I went to Jessie. I'll never forget him…he gets the credit for my being in school this long. I was his little sister, and whenever I saw him, I felt loved as a sister in Christ. I thank God for letting Jessie be my big brother here. I'll never forget his telling me that I will finish school and that he would help me. As I sit here before his body, I make a pledge that I will fulfill his dream and finish school."

"The first time Jessie went with me in our extension class, I thought he will not sustain the walk. I was surprised he can. My route in Lapaz is almost 2 kilometers from Lapaz proper. After I gave it to him, he was faithful in bringing my kids every Sunday. He was also my worker in the school ministry. When I started to open a Bible class at a high school, Jessie was there. Last Tuesday when we went there, he had eight souls won…Every time I need him, he's always there. He promised me he will go with me even though he is hungry or sick. He never refused me or complained."

Nearly all the Bible students maintain that Jessie always smiled, regardless of circumstances. Many went to him for help or advice. I believe that Jessie was as complete as a Christian could possibly be. He lived for others, and he lived to please Christ. Everything a Bible college would want a student to be—that was Jessie.

Little did I realize, during that short year he walked our campus, that I was in the presence of greatness. His outstanding attitude displayed his excellent spirit. Daniel 5:12 says, *"Forasmuch as an excellent spirit…were found in the same Daniel…."* Let's strive to have an excellent spirit.

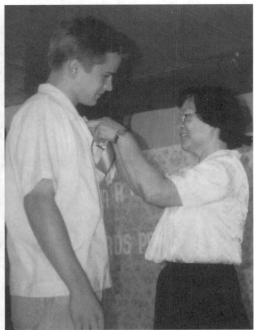

Top left: Ricky graduates from kindergarten and receives his diploma from his dad.
Top right: Ricky is pinned by his teacher, Jane Harder.

Below: Our Christian academy the first year we started it. You can see a little blond Ricky sitting in the front row on the left. I am standing in the back row, second from the right

UNIT TWO
Your Walk with God

*"And thou shalt love the Lord thy God
with all thy heart...."*
(Mark 12:30)

Introduction

Even though she was born in England, Rosalind Goforth grew up in Canada. She vividly recalled that when she was a child, her father, a famous artist, picked a flower and told her what a great artist God was. Her godly mother taught her, her seven older brothers, and three older sisters Bible verses from an early age. Rosalind was saved at the age of eleven. Although she had art lessons from the time she was quite young, Rosalind knew God wanted her to be in full-time Christian work. On her husband's deathbed, Rosalind's mother promised that she would send her talented daughter to a famous art school in England. As a result of that promise, when Rosalind decided she would be a missionary, her mother, quite uncharacteristically, resisted the idea. After a long battle, she finally told Rosalind that she could no longer fight God.

Rosalind met and married Jonathan Goforth, and in 1888, the couple left for China under the China Inland Mission. The Goforths faced terrible trials and hardships, including the loss of five of their eleven children. One of their worst experiences occurred during the Boxer Rebellion when Chinese rebels killed many foreigners, as well as many Chinese Christians.

Immediately after the death of their daughter Florence, the American consul urged all Americans to flee the country. The missionaries wanted to stay, but the Chinese Christians begged them to leave. Their warning and counsel had a two-fold purpose: not only would the lives of the missionaries be spared, but hopefully their lives would also be preserved if the foreigners left. The missionaries heeded the pleas of their converts.

In the intense heat, several missionaries, along with their children, endured an agonizing two-week journey by wagon carts. Everywhere the travelers went, people threw rocks at them. One night as they stayed in an inn, a large crowd gathered outside. The missionaries prayed together, came to the conclusion they should leave, and started to leave the walled city. The large mob attacked the defenseless missionaries. Rosalind, who was sitting in the cart holding her baby, had to fend off an attack on her baby and on herself. She was barely able to save the baby as she tried to evade an attempt to stab her. Another attacker tried to cut off Jonathan Goforth's head with a sword. The attack ultimately failed, but Goforth was terribly wounded. He passed out from the pain of his wounds; and when he came to, a man ran up to him and shouted to get the missionaries away from the carts. Goforth, who was dripping with blood, shouted for the missionaries to leave the carts. As the missionaries fled, the mob forgot them and began looting the carts. After they fought over the belongings, the people began throwing stones at the missionaries. Rosalind resolutely faced the angry crowd and pleaded with them to not kill her children. The attack suddenly stopped.

The party of missionaries straggled in to another village. As the villagers tried to keep out the missionaries, Goforth, who was literally bleeding to death, collapsed. Weeping, Rosalind and her children gathered around Jonathan. At this sight, the villagers became more sympathetic. One man put something on Goforth's neck to help stop the bleeding. The villagers then helped Rosalind and the others carry the stricken Goforth into a mud hut.

In the confusion of the mob attack, the party of missionaries became separated. One of the Goforths' children was missing. Rosalind prayed all night for her dying husband and their missing child.

Later that evening the missing party miraculously arrived with the carts at the mud hut. Rosalind later learned that a Chinese lady, with her body, shielded the Goforths' daughter from the blows of the clubs. After the attackers scattered, the missionaries climbed into the carts and started off again. Thankfully, the missionary families were reunited.

The travelers finally left the village, and as they traveled toward safety, they passed through another large crowd of people who threw stones at them. They escaped injury and finally reached the relative safety of another inn. The news of the arrival of the foreigners began bringing a crowd of people. Later that night the courtyard became packed with a mob of over a thousand. Goforth bravely went outside the inn and talked to the mob, trying in vain to calm them. The leaders demanded that each foreigner come out and face them, which they did. The mob kept screaming "Kill," yet they did nothing. For no apparent reason, the crowd finally dispersed, and the missionaries again loaded in the carts and started traveling under cover of night. The party had been warned that they would be waylaid, and they became more uneasy as they traveled.

Suddenly, one of the drivers announced that the Goforths' son and another missionary were missing. The missionaries turned around and returned to the inn. The missing individuals could not be found anywhere. A decision was made to leave a servant and a cart for the two who were missing, and the rest of the party would continue on. In retrospect, they felt this detour saved their lives from those who were planning to ambush them along the way.

All along the way, the weary travelers fought off mobs. As cruel as some people were, there were also kind Chinese along the way who tried to help them. As they came to another city, which they would gladly have bypassed for fear of the crowd, they stopped because they were starving. They also realized that if they did not take care of the mules, the animals would die. They desperately needed the mules to pull the carts carrying their children and the injured. Fortunately, the Goforths had Chinese friends in that city who convinced the mob to leave them alone. A doctor treated the wounded, and the missionaries were fed. These Chinese friends urged the missionaries to travel on and promised they would do their best to rescue the missing missionary and the Goforths' son.

Miraculously that night the missionary and the Goforths' young son were brought to the inn where the Goforth party was resting. They traveled without interruption for the next 20 hours until they reached yet another city. The next day they were able to secure passage aboard a small boat. Although God had surely intervened and seen the Goforths through this perilous time, hundreds of missionaries and Chinese Christians, including children, lost their lives. In spite of their harrowing experience during the Boxer Rebellion, after a short furlough the Goforths returned to China.

How could Rosalind Goforth, after losing her children, after seeing her husband gravely injured, and after barely surviving the Boxers' attempt to have them killed, return to the mission field? I have no doubt that Rosalind Goforth had to learn to walk with God. She was married to a man who walked with God. Jonathan Goforth was a powerful, Spirit-filled evangelist. Sometimes the crowds who came to hear him preach swelled to as large as 25,000 people!

Exactly how did Mrs. Goforth learn to walk with God?

Chapter One

The Key to Life

Matthew 13:45, 46 says, "...*the kingdom of heaven is like unto a merchant man, seeking goodly pearls: Who, when he had found one pearl of great price, went and sold all that he had, and bought it.*" In these verses Jesus beautifully portrays a merchant who is seeking precious gems. He teaches us that we should patiently seek the kingdom of Heaven just as the merchant patiently and persistently searched for the pearl of great price. After a lengthy search, the merchant finally found this priceless gem. He then traded everything he had to purchase it.

The Philippines is known as the "Pearl of the Orient" for many reasons. One reason is that the islands are a great source of pearls. I have heard that jewel markets around the world are especially attracted to the Sulu Sea, near the Southern island of Mindanao, which is abundant with pearls. The great majority of Moslems living in the Philippines live in Mindanao, and many of them are pearl divers. Author Jose Mandoriano, in his book *The Hour Before Sunset*, notes:

The life of a Philippine pearl diver of the Southern archipelago is truly exciting. As a child he grows up in a house beside the sea. As soon as he is old enough to run, his parents toss him into the water to give him lessons in swimming. As he grows into manhood the sea becomes a part of his own life. When he wakes up in the morning, one of the first things he does is to jump from the improvised balcony of his home into the sea. Then he goes to the deeper parts of the sea with pearl divers, to observe how they search for pearls. Finally, he is initiated into the vocation which provides excitement and sufficient reward.

A Moro pearl diver describes the art of pearl diving: "The pearl fishermen ride their small boats at dusk and slowly move toward the pearl beds. As soon as the Morning Star ushers in the new day, the fishermen locate themselves in strategic places. The boats usually consist of teams. Each member must be able to dive into the bottom of the sea and pick out oysters containing pearls. One of the divers ties a rope around his waist and fastens a basket to the rope. A sizeable piece of rock is often placed in the basket to aid the diver into reaching the depth of the sea. At the bottom of the water he holds the basket with one hand and looks for oysters. As soon as the basket is filled, he loosens the rope and ties it to the basket. He tugs at the cord, and the other members of the team pull the basket, and then he swims to the surface.

Some of the best pearl divers of the Mindanao area are known to remain under water for six minutes, without the aid of aqua lungs. These people of the South can dive for pearls which will provide enough money to support them for life. However, the love for the sea and the excitement which it offers to them always constrain them to return to the pearl vocation. Many of them die of old age still insisting on returning to the sea.[1]

In July of 2003, a church in the United States contacted me to ask if I would buy some pearl necklaces here in Iloilo City for them. The church was having a ladies' conference, and they wanted to present these beautiful pearls to the lady speakers. I was happy to do so because I love pearls. I suppose one reason why I am fascinated with pearls is that the pearl is my birthstone. Also, my husband's sister Ann and her husband Jerry own a jewelry store in Ardmore, Oklahoma. One day we were discussing the fact that the month of June has two birthstones, one of which is the pearl. They later gave me a beautiful gold necklace with a pearl.

The conference leaders gave me a budget, and I went downtown to look for the Moslem girls who sold them. They are easy to spot, with their long-sleeved shirts, long pants, and headdress. When I found them, they showed me all shapes, sizes, and colors of pearls. The small ones are called "rice pearls" because they look like grains of rice. Even though they are the most inexpensive, they are my personal favorites because they are so dainty. They have "egg pearls" which are shaped like eggs. "Siopao pearls" are named after a certain kind of round-shaped bread. They also have what are called "Miki-Moto pearls" and "South Sea pearls." To be sure, there is a great range in the price of these pearls. Even the inexperienced buyer can tell the pearls are real if he looks closely because flaws can be seen.

When I asked, "How much are these?" the 18-year-old girl would rub them together and then quote a price to me! I pointed to another strand of perfect pearls and asked the price.

"Ma'am! Very cheap! They are plastic!" They giggled.

In the years I have lived here, I have learned how to haggle. I went around and around with them. The girls then showed me three large pearls that had not been made into anything so the buyer could choose to have them made into a necklace, earrings, bracelet, or ring. The price of the three plain pearls was $400 (U.S.). It was fascinating talking to the girls, and they were very knowledgeable. Purchasing just the right pearls for the conference provided a pleasant outing for me.

I could not help but notice an older Moslem male, walking back and forth in the distance, who was obviously watching me. I have no doubt he was angry because once before we had given one of the girls a Gospel tract. We had offered tracts to the girls, but all of them rejected the tracts except one. I have often wondered if she was beaten for accepting the tract, and I have prayed that she at least had an opportunity to read it and get saved.

Since we are on the subject of pearls, there is another story I would like to share, so please be patient! I have a definite reason for addressing the subject of pearls! My husband told the following illustration in church one night.

One day a five-year-old girl went to the store with her mother. She saw some plastic white pearls in a box. She begged her mother for the pearls which cost all of $2.00. The wise mother told her daughter that she would have to do some extra chores to pay for the pearls. The little girl gladly agreed. After several days, the little girl finally had enough money to buy the pearl necklace. The little girl loved the necklace. She wore it everywhere—even to bed.

This little girl also had a very wise father. Every night he would read her a bedtime story and then kiss her good night. Then he would ask his little girl, "Do you love me?"

The little girl always answered, "Yes, Daddy, you know I love you."

One night the father said, "If you love me, give me your pearl necklace."

But the little girl simply could not part with her pearls. She offered her dad other things in her room instead.

He quietly replied, "That's okay, Honey. Daddy loves you. Good night."

This interchange went on for several nights. The father always asked for the necklace. The little girl, who loved her dad, simply could not give up her beloved necklace. She offered him her dolls and everything else in her possession, but her father was not interested in the other things. He was interested in the item that mattered most to her.

One night, when the father entered the room, he saw his little girl sitting on the bed crying. He asked, "What's wrong, Honey?"

The little girl silently handed her necklace to her father. The father, with tears in his eyes, took a velvet jewelry box from his pocket and handed it to the little girl. With a surprised look, she opened the box. Inside was a beautiful strand of costly, genuine pearls! He had them with him all the time—just waiting for his beloved daughter to give up her dime-store trinket so he could give her the genuine treasure.

In the same manner, our Heavenly Father is also waiting for you and me to give up and exchange the cheap "junk" in our lives for the Pearl of Great Price. That Pearl of Great Price can represent different things to different people. To me, it represents what the Bible says it represents—the Kingdom of Heaven.

What are you holding on to? Is it really worth it? Are you giving up the Pearl of Great Price because you are clinging to something worthless or artificial? Why not trade in the trash for treasure! To have a close walk with God is to have the Pearl of Great Price! Truly, it is the key to the every Christian's life.

Chapter Two

The Key to Being Successful

The Bible says in Proverbs 4:23, *"Keep thy heart with all diligence; for out of it are the issues of life."* A Christian's quiet time with God each day is an absolute necessity. We all surely know that God wants to meet with us even more than we want to meet with Him. Joy Turner Tuggy writes in her book, *The Missionary Wife and Her Work,* that the missionary wife is:

> …just an ordinary Christian, and the laws of life and spiritual health apply to her as to any other Christian. They are, however, important to her in a special sense. She has gone out as a representative of her Lord before a people who know Him not. Further, the effectiveness of her husband's ministry and the pattern for her children's lives are greatly depending upon the quality of her spiritual life and its outworking in her daily walk.
>
> Missionaries, like other people, must carefully guard their time with the Lord. We have all the familiar problems. Wandering thoughts, for example. I pick up my Bible in the morning and have an overwhelming urge to write out my marketing list…Mothers with small children have to fight for time for devotions. One missionary mother said she had been jumping up and down all through the mealtime to attend to other people's needs, and she herself got fed in small installments. Afterwards the Lord showed her, "Today you did not have an uninterrupted time to eat, but you were fed. You can get enough food in small bites. If you will allow me to, I can give you your spiritual food in that way, so don't fret about not having large portions of time." If we have an appetite, God will see to it that we have food for our souls.[1]

Question

Would you please comment on your personal devotions?

Answers:

• I have become more dependent on the Lord to get me through things—not only because I see my kids growing up before my eyes and know that they have need of a good example, but for the simple fact that my life with all its challenges seems easier when I'm close to the Lord. Another thing is that I have felt more open to attack. I have had struggles in finding the time for devotions and have had to force myself to rise earlier so as not to lack in that area. The Lord becomes more and more special just knowing that I did leave country, family, and friends for Him. I know that He knows it, and I feel like He feels my love for Him in a new way. I know I feel His.

• I am accountable to my husband and he is to me. We ask each other what we read that day or prayed for and if we prayed. That personal accountability helps tremendously.

• My prayer time has become much stronger. His Word took on a special meaning. When there is no one else, there is ALWAYS God.

• I can't make it without the Lord in the States, so I surely can't make it without Him on the mission field.

• Parts of the Bible have become more special to me and have been my lifesaver in many ways. You have to always fight to keep being faithful in your walk with the Lord. If you miss—start right up again and don't ever give up.

• My devotional time is very special. I like to wake up early in the morning when the house is still and the day is new and talk with God and listen as He speaks to me. I go into the day much calmer and more prepared for the day's responsibilities.

• I started working on keeping a journal of what I have learned in my devotions when on the field. I enjoy that.

Truly, we cannot be successful in our Christian life if we haven't learned to walk with God.

The Key to Being a Successful Mother

Sarah Boardman Judson, second wife of Missionary Adoniram Judson, learned to walk with God from an early age. The eldest of 13 children, Sarah was born in 1803 in New Hampshire. She was very much affected by the death of a missionary by the name of James Colman, who had worked with Adoniram Judson in Burma. Sarah wrote a poem about Colman which was published. This poem attracted the attention of another prospective missionary, George Boardman, who decided he wanted to meet the author.

Courtney Anderson, in *To the Golden Shore: The Life of Adoniram Judson* writes of that first meeting:

When [Boardman] discovered she was a stunningly beautiful eighteen-year-old blue-eyed girl with light brown hair, shy but gracious, who taught school, took the lead in church activities and had considered missions for herself, the outcome was inevitable. They were engaged within a few months, and were married in the First Baptist Church of Salem on Sunday, July 3, 1825, a few weeks before their departure.[2]

George and Sarah Boardman, along with baby daughter, Sarah Ann, arrived in Burma shortly after Judson's wife Ann died. Their presence helped to comfort the devastated Judson. Soon the Boardmans began ministering to the Karen, a mountain tribe in Burma. It would not be long before the parents embraced their grief of losing their daughter. The Boardmans were brokenhearted when little Sarah died.

After serving only five years in Burma, George Boardman became very ill with tuberculosis. Author Courtney Anderson immortalized the spirit of the stricken missionary.

Though he knew his days were numbered, Boardman had insisted on making the arduous expedition. He had become a great leader to the shy Karens, and had promised to visit them and help baptize them. So, carried on a cot by the Karens, and accompanied by Sarah, his two-year-old son George, and Francis Mason, a newcomer to the Tavoy mission, he had journeyed for three days into the hills to a bamboo chapel the Karens had built beside a stream at the foot of a mountain range. Here he saw thirty-four of the Karens baptized by Mason. On the way home, thundershowers had soaked the whole party; Boardman, wet and cold, was permitted to lie on the porch of a house by the river belonging to a native of Tavoy. In the morning a boat was brought up to take him the rest of the way. But it was too late. He had hardly been placed aboard when he died.

Adoniram wrote to Sarah a few days after he heard the news. His opening words may have been cheerless, but he knew he could tell her the truth:

You are now drinking the bitter cup whose dregs I am somewhat acquainted with. And though, for some time, you have been aware of its approach, I venture to say that is far bitterer than you expected. It is common for persons in your situation to refuse all consolation, to cling to the dead, and to fear that they shall too soon forget the dear object of their affections. But don't be concerned. I can assure you that months and months of heart-rending anguish are before you, whether you will or not. Yet take the bitter cup with both hands, and sit down to your repast. You will soon learn a secret, that there is sweetness at the bottom.

He added that he hoped she would stay on as a missionary to the Karens. As for her son George, she was promised that, when the boy was old enough to leave Burma, Adoniram would try to secure for him the best education she could wish. Or, should Sarah herself die unexpectedly, if she would commit George to Adoniram: "I hereby pledge my fidelity to receive and treat him as my own son, to send him home in the best time and way, to provide for his education, and to watch over him as long as I live."

For a while after Boardman's death Sarah thought she would return to America, particularly on account of her little son. Perhaps Adoniram's letter helped change her mind. At any rate, she finally decided she belonged in Burma. She knew Burmese pretty well; she knew the Karens. They liked and trusted her. She had a flourishing school which probably would not continue if she left.[3]

Once in a while, Sarah would take time off from her school and journey into the jungles and mountains to visit her nomadic Karen people. No wonder this white lady, who dressed in European fashion, became a legend herself. One of the Karen men always carried little George, whom they affectionately called "the little chieftain." These journeys were so extremely difficult, Sarah sometimes startled exploring white men!

Courtney Anderson shares a letter Sarah wrote to Adoniram, after she read his Bible translation:

My Dear Brother:

The translation of the Bible into Burmese is an event to which thousands have looked forward with joyful anticipation, and for which thousands now perishing in their sins should fall on their knees in thanksgiving to God, and through which thousands yet unborn will praise him for ever and ever.

Last Lord's-day, while reading Scripture, I was affected to tears, and could scarcely proceed, as is often the case, in reading striking passages.[4]

Adoniram greatly admired Sarah because she carried on the work of her husband instead of returning to her home country like many other widows did when their missionary husbands died.

She had even dared to carry the Word by herself through the tiger-haunted jungle. The vision of her fording streams and crossing the hills as she went from Karen village to village, her little son carried by one of the native converts who accompanied her, smiling and unafraid in the face of danger and hardship, rose irresistibly to his mind.[5]

Adoniram Judson and Sarah Boardman eventually fell in love and were married. Courtney Anderson wrote of Sarah's son George: "Little George, six years old, sobered and matured beyond his years by the harsh demands of life, spent a good deal of time by her bedside, reading the Bible to her or reciting hymns he had learned."[6]

By the end of the year, the time came for her to carry out a decision she had made about George even before her marriage. If he were to live to adulthood, he must go to America. It was a heart-rending parting. George was unusually dear to his mother: "and his nature had about it a clinging tenderness and sensitiveness which peculiarly unfitted him for contact with strangers."

But there was no help for it. "Oh! I shall never forget his looks," wrote Sarah to her sister, "as he stood by the door and gazed at me for the last time. His eyes were filling with tears, and his little face red with suppressed emotion. But he subdued his feelings, and it was not till he had turned away and was going down the steps that he burst into a flood of tears."

While Sarah, her heart breaking, hurried to her room and fell to her knees in tearful prayer, Adoniram carried the little boy in his arms to the small boat. All the way down, Adoniram comforted the boy as best he could, and reported to Sarah afterwards that "his conversation was very affectionate and intelligent." On board the *Cashmere*, Adoniram saw George's little bed properly made up in the cabin, made sure that he would be well cared for, "and he, as George expressed it, returned to 'comfort Mama.' "[7]

Little George Boardman never saw his mother again. Sarah gave birth to a total of eleven children; three by George Boardman and eight by Adoniram Judson. Only six of her children by Adoniram lived. Her only child by Boardman to live to adulthood was George. With the death of each of her four children, she learned to walk even closer with her Lord.

During Sarah's last illness before her death, Courtney Anderson quotes Adoniram who wrote to his mission board: "...She is willing to die, and I hope I am willing to see her die, if it be the divine will."[8] In the hopes of saving Sarah's life, the family made an unplanned voyage to find medical help.

In the book, *To the Golden Shore*, Sarah's son, Adoniram, Jr., reflects, "...the family gathered on deck and mother sang to the group, which included some of the sailors and officers of the ship. The hymn was 'The Star of Bethlehem.' "[9] Author Courtney Anderson describes the earthly end that was inevitable:

She knew she was dying. Adoniram spent most of his time in the cabin with her. Sometimes the children came in for a few minutes, sobered and apprehensive, but not quite able to grasp what was happening to their mother.

On one of these occasions he said: "My love, I wish to ask pardon for every unkind word or deed of which I have ever been guilty. I feel that I have, in many instances, failed of treating you with that kindness and affection which you have ever deserved."

"Oh," she said, "you will kill me if you talk so...I...should ask pardon of you...I only want to get well that I may have an opportunity of making some return for all your kindness, and of showing you how much I love you."

In spite of her tranquility, she had some regrets. She told Adoniram she wished she could see her son George, and the three children left in Moulmein. Between these wishes and her longing to leave life, she said, "I am in a strait between the two—let the will of God be done."

Her mind became liable to wander. On the evening of the 31st of August, she appeared to be drawing near to the end of her pilgrimage. The children took leave of her and retired to rest. I sat alone by the side of her bed endeavoring to administer relief and consolation to the departing soul. At two o'clock in the morning I roused her attention, and said, "Do you still love the Saviour?"

"Oh, yes," she replied, "I ever love the Lord Jesus Christ."

Life continued to recede, and she ceased to breathe. For a moment I traced her upward flight and thought of the wonders which were opening to her view. I then closed her sightless eyes, dressed her, for the last time, in the drapery of death; and being quite exhausted with many sleepless nights, I threw myself down and slept.

In the morning he was awakened by the three children. They were standing around their mother's body, weeping bitterly, and crying out for her to answer them. Abby Ann, young Adoniram, and Elnathan could not realize until this terrible September first exactly what death meant. Now they knew.[10]

By the end of the 1850s, there were over 10,000 Karen church members. Unquestionably, Sarah deserves a great deal of credit for that accomplishment. Three of Sarah's sons became preachers. Edward Judson wrote a biography of his father entitled *The Life of Adoniram Judson*.

Do you want to be a good mother? Sarah Judson was a good mother because she walked with God. When the valleys came into her life, as they will most assuredly come to yours, her walk with God was what kept her going.

The Key to Being a Successful Wife

I asked my husband who he thought was an outstanding missionary wife, and without hesitation he replied, "Charles Cowman's wife." My husband loves Charles Cowman, who was a great missionary to Japan. His wife wrote her husband's biography, *Charles E. Cowman: Missionary-Warrior,* as well as the famous devotional book, *Streams in the Desert.* The problem, though, is that it is very difficult to find information about Lettie Cowman.

I told my husband, "I read the biography she wrote about her husband, but there's nothing in there about herself."

"That's one reason why she was such a great lady," my husband replied. "She completely forgot herself."

Lettie Burd was born in Iowa. Lettie's brothers and sisters were already grown and married when she became a surprise addition to her parents' family! Author B. H. Pearson, in the book *The Vision Lives,* shares how Lettie met her husband at a very young age:

> One day Lettie's mother returned from town and said: "Today I met a dear lad down at the railway station. He seemed so clean and fine, but there was an air of loneliness about him. I invited him to the house, as I feel he just needs a little bit of mothering."[11]

Charles walked Lettie home from school each day. He was a 17-year-old train dispatcher, and Lettie was only a 15-year-old schoolgirl, but they fell in love and soon became engaged. When Charles was transferred to another city, Lettie waited for him for two years. When he returned, they were married.

Charles was not wealthy and had never attended college; but by the age of 21, he had already become the manager of the Western Union Telegraph Company office in Colorado. Charles and Lettie later transferred to Chicago, where he became even more successful.

One night while living in Chicago, Lettie went to church to hear a converted opera singer speak. Lettie was gloriously saved at the meeting; however, when she told her husband, he was very opposed to her decision. Thankfully, it was not long until Charles was saved too. Charles became a soul winner, and within six months, he led 75 of the men in his telegraph office to the Lord! Nine months after the Cowmans were saved, they attended a missionary convention in Moody Church, Chicago. B. H. Pearson relates,

> Together, she and Charles listened to the story of a young businessman who, with his wife and child, were going to Africa and depending only upon

God to supply their needs in answer to prayer. Mrs. Cowman saw her husband pull out a roll of bills that represented a month's salary and place it on the plate. As the enthusiasm mounted higher, people wanted to give their jewelry and even watches. At the announcement of this second offering, Charles disentangled his solid gold watch and chain, and looked down at the large diamond in Lettie's engagement ring. This diamond ring meant much more to her than mere beauty. She began twisting the ring from her finger. They were both ready when the offering plate reached them a second time, and into it went the gold watch and the engagement ring. Soon from the platform came a call for volunteers to go as missionaries. "If there are any young people here who will offer themselves to go out as missionaries...please stand."

Charles [whispered] to her, "That means you and me. Let's stand and show our colors."[12]

Like her husband, Lettie became a great soul winner. B. H. Pearson tells of her walk with God:

No effect can be produced without a significant cause. What was the cause of Mrs. Cowman's spiritual power revealed in her Christian life? Hers was a household name to millions and her writings were daily read by hundreds of thousands about the home altars. Mrs. Cowman's life and her unpublished diaries and letters reveal a fourfold secret.

First, it may be observed that faith is developed through testing. One of her early testings came through books. There had always been books in her life. Shortly after her conversion, she wrote in her diary: "I cannot continue to have the companionship of the blessed Trinity while reading these." Volume after volume was consigned to the fire.

No one more than she recognized the infinite variety of God's dealing with His children. She knew and admired artists, musicians, composers, writers, novelists, statesmen, and leaders in all walks of life. But she was being prepared for her special task. There can come from the mind only what enters it. Had she continued reading the yearly offerings of the secular book trade could she have written the devotional classics of her later years?

God was separating her from lesser things for His greater purposes. He was preparing her for a divine commission. **She was beginning to learn that faith is obedience.**

One morning she sat down to the piano. Here were stacks of dance music. The Spirit whispered, "Does all this glorify your Lord?" She rose and stood by the piano in deep emotion, pleading to retain her beloved music. It too was yielded.

Then there came to her a glorious hour which can be described only in her own words: "One morning, as I arose at four o'clock to pray and to do some searching (of the Word), just as I knelt, I felt an Unseen Presence so near me that I looked up to see who was there. I could not utter one word, but just felt hushed in that glorious Presence. A sweet rest filled my very being, and I knew that the Holy Spirit had come in to fill and abide with me forever. Nothing has ever been able to shake the experience of that hour alone with God. For twenty-one years He has kept through smooth ways and thorny paths, in battles and victories, in homeland and among the heathen, and this morning, as I pen this testimony, the witness still is in my heart that 'the blood of Jesus…cleanseth me from all sin.' His will is the sweetest thing on earth."

We may learn another source of the richness of her life, by looking at the Bibles she used through the years. They have been rebound. Their worn, torn leather covers, split apart at the back, are substitutes for the originals or others which gave way to constant use. The work of the best binderies has not been able to hold them together. Their backs are broken, and pages and folios lie loose where the wear has been excessive. Many of the pages are darkened by tears or the perspiration of a hand laid many times upon promises in entreaty, or through the oft-turning in search of daily inspiration and guidance.

There is scarcely a page or a chapter, from Genesis to Revelation, which has not been marked. She practiced what she wrote on the leaf of her Bible: "If we want to know God, we must give ourselves entirely up to the study of God's Word. Man was made to know and love God."

She also learned that secret of power which comes from communion with God through faithful prayer. For nearly a year she strove in vain to awaken early. Then she put the matter "definitely in God's hands." The next morning she was awake at twenty minutes after five o'clock, with the assurance that God would continue to awaken her at an early hour for this sacred tryst in His presence. She wrote at that time: "He met me and strengthened me with His Spirit."

There might not be time for other things. There was always time for God.[13]

The Cowmans went to Moody Bible Institute. One morning when Cowman told his wife that he had definitely been called to go to Japan, she answered, "Charles, six weeks ago, while alone, God spoke to me about going to Japan. I have kept it hidden within my heart, waiting for the right moment to tell you."[14] Soon they arrived in Japan and began their ministry.

In 1913, Cowman made a decision to visit every village in Japan in five years. He and 200 workers started that year, going from village to village until 1918. They had knocked on 10,800,000 doors and preached to those who would listen, leaving a Gospel tract or booklet in each home, even if no one was there.

The great Japan crusade took a heavy toll on Charles physically. He suffered several heart attacks and strokes and had to return to America where he lived out his days as an invalid. The following words are found in *The Vision Lives*:

She props Charles up in a chair. He dare not lie down now for fear of an attack. Neither of them sleeps. The days are so full.

Years later, Mrs. Cowman would say to visitors to [their home]... "I have seen the maps of all the earth upon these walls. During the nights, when Charles could not lie down because of heart pain, he would be seated in that leather rocker before the maps of the world. I would find him with tears running down his face as he pleaded; 'Lord, awaken a sleeping church. Help us to do what we could if we only cared. Help us, in this generation, to obey Thy command to preach the gospel to every creature.' "[15]

Of this time, B. H. Pearson says of Lettie, who faithfully nursed her husband until he died:

She loves Charles passionately. He has always been her "great hero." Now more than ever she loves him. God has made them for each other; they are still sweethearts. How heart-breaking it is to see Charles suffer. But instead of driving her to despair, this battle sends her to the Word and to prayer.[16]

Walking with God is the reason Lettie Cowman was such a successful wife. It is the key to making you a successful wife also.

The Key to Having a Successful Ministry

Although a chapter is devoted to "ministry," I want to add a few thoughts here. How can we have a successful ministry if we do not walk with God? It sounds crazy, yet there are people who try to do just that!

When I think of a missionary lady who had a successful ministry, again I cannot help but think of Lettie Cowman. For six years, a time she called her personal "Gethsemane," she nursed her invalid husband. Though she prayed unceasingly for his healing, her prayers for Charles' healing did not come. When he died, a huge void was left in her life.

While thumbing through her husband's Bible, she found a slip of paper with the last words he had written: "Go on with my unfinished task."[17] As she slowly worked through her grief, invitations to speak came pouring in. She also began writing, and from her pen came Christian classics: her husband's biography, *Streams in the Desert, Count It All Joy, Praise Changes Things, Thoughts for the Quiet Hour, Life Begins at Eighty,* and *Springs in the Valley.*

During and in spite of his illness, her husband started a Bible college and a mission board in the United States. Lettie continued to be actively involved with these and her husband's other ministries.

Obviously, Lettie Cowman was totally in tune with God. Her biographer B. H. Pearson tells of an incident that shows her relationship with God:

> During World War II, the son of a well-known mission executive serves on a United States destroyer, which is sunk by enemy bombs. It is almost certain that the young man has been killed. The father asks Mrs. Cowman to pray. Later he finds her radiantly happy, rejoicing in God's deliverance. "Not a bone of him is broken," she says. "God told me so. He gave me that assurance from His Word." Every report indicates that the son has been lost in action, but Mrs. Cowman's assurance is infectious. A message comes later from the son stating that he had been blown off the deck into the ocean by the force of the explosion. Though severely bruised, no bones were broken.[18]

God kept speaking to Lettie about completing her husband's "unfinished task" about which he had written.

> Charles had been called to this great ministry. Night after night during those six Gethsemane years before his death, with the maps of the world before him, tears flowing from his eyes, his voice pleading in prayer, he had cried out: "Oh, God! We could do it! The church could do it! We could get the gospel to every creature now if we only cared—if Thy church would only awaken and obey Thee."[19]

Lettie began sharing Charles' plan to reach the world with the "Every Village Campaign." She was asked to speak at the Bible college chapel, and she shared Charles' plan that he started in Japan. After chapel some people invited her to Finland where the "Every Village Campaign" was instituted. The use of the plan spread to Lapland and Estonia, as well as to Russian refugees along the border. Mrs. Cowman was then invited to Sweden where she again told of the Japan campaign. As a result, crusades were begun in Latvia, Poland, Romania, Czechoslovakia, and in the Baltic States. Doors were opened everywhere with money and Scriptures pouring in for her ministry.

Lettie Cowman was a tireless and fearless soul winner wherever she went. She gave a Bible to the prince of Egypt, who was soon to be crowned king, and witnessed to him. God opened a door for her to be able to have a private audience with His Imperial Majesty, Emperor Hailie Selassie of Abyssinia, who was in exile. She prayed and asked God to reveal what He wanted said to the emperor. The following day Mrs. Cowman shared Isaiah 54 with the emperor: *"For a small moment have I forsaken thee; but with great mercies will I gather thee. In a little wrath I hid my face from thee for a moment; but with everlasting kindness will I have mercy on thee, saith the Lord thy Redeemer. For this is as the waters of Noah unto me: for as I have sworn that the waters of Noah should no more go over the earth; so have I sworn that I would not be wroth with thee, nor rebuke thee. For the mountains shall depart, and the hills be removed; but my kindness shall not depart from thee, neither shall the covenant of my peace be removed, saith the Lord that hath mercy on thee."*

Lettie boldly told the emperor that God would restore him to his throne. Her seemingly impossible prophecy came true! She then witnessed to the emperor and his family.

Mrs. Cowman helped start crusades in 28 countries, just as her husband did in Japan. She died in 1960 at the age of 90. Author B. H. Pearson concludes:

For Mrs. Cowman, life is simple. She sees no reason why every Christian man should not be a Charles E. Cowman, a winner of souls, a leader of crusades, an evangelist to nations. "Charles E. Cowman was a humble man," she says encouragingly, "but God gave him a vision!" What God helps you to see can be. What can be should be. Therefore let it be. God sent you into the world at this time. There is no one else in all the world like you. He wants to use you. He is giving you a vision.[20]

Lettie Cowman had a successful ministry because she walked with God.

Chapter Three

The Bible

Psalm 119:1-11; 119:105: *"Blessed are the undefiled in the way, who walk in the law of the LORD. Blessed are they that keep his testimonies, and that seek him with the whole heart. They also do no iniquity: they walk in his ways. Thou hast commanded us to keep thy precepts diligently. O that my ways were directed to keep thy statutes! Then shall I not be ashamed, when I have respect unto all thy commandments. I will praise thee with uprightness of heart, when I shall have learned thy righteous judgments. I will keep thy statutes: O forsake me not utterly. Wherewithal shall a young man cleanse his way? by taking heed thereto according to thy word. With my whole heart have I sought thee: O let me not wander from thy commandments. Thy word have I hid in mine heart, that I might not sin against thee...Thy word is a lamp unto my feet, and a light unto my path."*
The secret to walking with God is to get into the Word of God. I personally like Jack Chick's Bible reading plan of reading ten chapters a day. Read one chapter from each of the following ten sections and start over as each is finished.

1. Matthew, Mark, Luke, John, Acts
2. Genesis, Exodus, Leviticus, Numbers, Deuteronomy
3. Romans, I & II Corinthians, Galatians, Ephesians, Philippians, Colossians, Hebrews
4. I & II Thessalonians; I & II Timothy: Titus; Philemon; James; I & II Peter; I, II, & III John; Jude; Revelation
5. Job, Ecclesiastes, Song of Solomon
6. Psalms
7. Proverbs
8. Joshua, Judges, Ruth, I & II Samuel, I & II Kings, I & II Chronicles, Ezra, Nehemiah, Esther
9. Isaiah, Jeremiah, Lamentations, Ezekiel, Daniel, Hosea, Joel, Amos, Obadiah, Jonah, Micah
10. Hebrews chapter 11, I Corinthians chapter 13, alternately every day.[1]

Ten chapters may not seem like much to some. In fact, one busy missionary mom with ten children shared with me that she reads twenty chapters a day! That really convicted me! Then again, I thought she probably figured she had ten good reasons to read so much a day! Others feel that if they read a lot, they are just reading for the sake of reading and not really getting a lot out of it. It may be through force of habit, or we just do it because we feel guilty if we don't, but we don't really intend to be changed by God's Word. Whether you read a lot or whether you read a little because you meditate and memorize, I am not here to judge—your Bible reading is between you and God. The important thing is to get into the Bible! For sure, Satan will fight you on this matter. I believe it is good to have a variety of plans from year to year so the Bible will not be stale but will always be fresh to us.

My husband said when he was little, his mother would have him, his brother, and his four sisters climb on her bed in the evenings so she could read the Bible to him. He also memorized countless verses as a child.

Years ago, a young school teacher was saved at our church here in Iloilo City. I heard her share her testimony, and she said that right after she got saved, she began reading her Bible and praying early in the morning before going to school. As a new babe in Christ, she prayed, "Lord, please do something to me every day that I do not have devotions. Please punish me and remind me in some way." I thought that prayer was quite impressive for a new Christian to pray.

All Christians need to have a steady Christian walk, but as a missionary I am actually afraid **not** to meet with God every day. Many look to the missionary for spiritual stability. People around us need to see us looking to God for the solution to all our problems.

1. **We must fill our life with the Bible so we can have the mind of Christ.** Philippians 2:5 says, *"Let this mind be in you, which was also in Christ Jesus."*

2. **We must read the Bible if we want to be a disciple.** John 8:31, 32 says, *"Then said Jesus to those Jews which believed on him, If ye continue in my word, then are ye my disciples indeed; And ye shall know the truth, and the truth shall make you free."*

3. **We must read the Bible so we can be strong.** Matthew 7:24, *"Therefore whosoever heareth these sayings of mine, and doeth them, I will liken him unto a wise man, which built his house upon a rock:"*

Dr. James Ray, the president of Baptist International Missions, Inc., wrote a book entitled *Incredible Journey*, in which he relates the story of a 15-year-old girl named Mary Jones from Wales. The year was 1799, and Mary Jones wanted a Bible more than anything. Her family was extremely poor, and Bibles were rare and expensive. Mary prayed for a Bible for six years! During that time, she committed many verses to memory with the help of a lady who owned a Bible. She worked hard for years doing washing, ironing, and other chores for a few coins until she finally had enough money saved for her Bible. Half the battle to owning a Bible was over when she saved enough money. The other half of the battle was walking 25 miles to buy the Bible! Mary's mother was worried about her daughter's long trip, but Mary's father said that they could not fight against God. They knelt and prayed and asked God to protect their daughter. The way was rugged and wild, and it would not be an easy trip. Mary walked barefooted out of her humble home, carrying her shoes in a bag.

That night, after walking all day, she finally arrived at a Methodist minister's house. The minister and his wife listened to Mary's story. They fed her, put her up for the night, and promised to take her to another minister's house in the morning, where she could purchase the precious Bible.

The next morning, when they went to the minister's house, that man of God began to question her. She answered,

I love the Bible. I have loved it ever since I was a little girl and heard it read at meetings when I went with my mother and father. Then the school opened, when I was ten, and I learned to read; and a Sunday school started too, and I went. But I needed a Bible more than ever then, and a kind friend, Mrs. Evans, promised that when I learned to read I could go and study her Bible at the farm. So I went, every Saturday, to study my Sunday school lesson. The farm is up in the mountains, two miles away.[2]

Mary continued to explain how she had worked and saved for the Bible.

Rev. Thomas Charles stared at Mary in awe. All of his words left him. After a few moments of silence he said to the Methodist minister, "Oh, friend Edwards! To see this young girl, so brave, so intelligent, so consistent a Christian, coming all this long twenty-five miles to me for a Bible, and I have none to spare. The Society has refused to print any more Bibles for Wales.[3]

Mary burst into tears when she heard this devastating news. The minister could not stand to send her away empty handed, so he relented and allowed her buy one of the last Bibles which had already been promised to another. Mr. Charles went to London and told the story of Mary Jones. Through the sharing of Mary's story, the British and Foreign Bible Society was born. From the birth of that Bible society came the National Bible Society of Scotland, the American Bible Society, and others.

Would you or I work that hard and that long for a Bible? Would you and I walk two miles to study it for a few hours? The answer is probably, "No." Many won't even walk into the living room to read it for five minutes. Would we walk 25 miles up and down mountains to buy one?

Our problem today is not that there is a lack of Bibles. The truth is that most people own more than one copy of the Bible. Rather, there is a lack of people who love it enough to sit down and read it.

Don't take the Bible for granted! It is not just a nice book to read now and then when we feel like it. It is life itself. Jesus said in Matthew 4:4: "*...It is written, Man shall not live by bread alone, but by every word that proceedeth out of the mouth of God.*"

Chapter Four

Prayer

One of the first Bible stories we hear as children is that of Daniel's being thrown into the den of lions. I loved the story as a child, but as an adult I have really come to appreciate Daniel even more. Because of Daniel's testimony, King Darius made Daniel one of the three presidents of his nation. The Bible says that Daniel was preferred more than the others because he always had a wonderful attitude. This excellence evidently made others jealous, so they tried to devise a way to get rid of Daniel. The only problem was that Daniel was such a good man, they couldn't find anything of which to accuse him!

Finally, a plan was formulated to bring about the demise of Daniel. The king was consulted and deceitfully advised to sign a decree stating that no one could ask any man or god for anything for a period of 30 days. Only one could be asked for anything—King Darius.

This decree probably sounded good to the king, so he signed it into law, which no one, not even the king who made the law, could change. Daniel 6:10 says, *"Now when Daniel knew that the writing was signed, he went into his house; and his windows being open in his chamber toward Jerusalem, he kneeled upon his knees three times a day, and prayed, and gave thanks before his God, as he did aforetime."* As a result, Daniel was thrown into the lion's den but was delivered.

If many of us thought that we would be executed for praying, we probably would not pray. It's hard to believe that even though we have the freedom to pray and even though we are not threatened like Daniel was, we still do not pray!

A week consists of 168 hours. How many of those 168 hours do we spend praying? On the other hand, how many of those 168 hours do we watch television?

I must admit that one of the best things that happened to my spiritual life was getting rid of my television. Rachel and I watched one together in our family room, and we finally decided it needed to go. If we cannot control something in our life, we need to remove whatever cannot be controlled. My husband (who is very strict about what is viewed) and I still have one in the bedroom. I may watch a few minutes of a news program, or my husband may watch an occasional ball game.

After I stopped watching television, I wondered how I ever got anything done before! I have also noticed that I am now shocked at the commercials. I guess before I stopped watching the television, I had become calloused to all of the obvious filth that is featured. When we read Philippians 4:8 which says, *"Finally, brethren, whatsoever things are true, whatsoever things are honest, whatsoever things are just, whatsoever things are pure, whatsoever things are lovely, whatsoever things are of good report; if there be any virtue, and if there be any praise, think on these things,"* I don't believe we can justify the viewing of television. In fact, I don't believe television falls into any of those categories, do you?

In Matthew 6:9-13 the Lord gave us an example of how to pray: *"After this manner therefore pray ye: Our Father which art in heaven, Hallowed be thy name. Thy kingdom come. Thy will be done in earth, as it is in heaven. Give us this day our daily bread. And forgive us our debts, as we forgive our debtors. And lead us not into temptation, but deliver us from evil: For thine is the kingdom, and the power, and the glory, for ever. Amen."* From these verses, we can see that prayer is to be a combination of adoration, confession, thanksgiving, and supplication.

I began writing in a journal and praying a prayer of commitment from what I read in the Bible each day. I believe that keeping a journal has really helped my prayer life. I also have a long list of people and various matters about which I pray each day. Read, study, and find ways to make your prayer life better.

I, in no way, feel that I have "arrived" in my prayer life. I want it to increase and be multiplied a hundred times over. I want my prayer life to be what God wants it to be. I have to fight the Devil on this every day.

I have had many wonderful answers to prayer in my life. I suppose the one which most stands out in my mind was when I prayed for my father's salvation. I was saved in 1971, and my mom was saved shortly after that, but I prayed for seven years before my dad was saved. My parents came to the Philippines in 1978 when their first grandchild Ricky was born. While they were visiting, my husband led my dad to Christ.

I had read Dr. John R. Rice's wonderful book *Prayer: Asking and Receiving*, and I had tried to the best of my ability to follow Dr. Rice's principles to the letter. I learned that many hindrances to prayer must be removed from our life.

Many great books on prayer are available to the one who would like to learn more about prayer. My former pastor, Dr. Jack Hyles, wrote a great book called *Exploring Prayer with Jack Hyles*. One of my favorites, that has been a blessing to a multitude of Christians, is Mrs. Jonathan Goforth's book *How I Know God Answers Prayer*. Reading books on prayer will never take the place of the best book which, of course, is the Bible!

Read about prayer but more importantly—Pray!

Chapter Five

Keeping Your Heart Right

Keeping your heart right is vital because, quite simply, you cannot be filled with the Holy Spirit if your heart is not right with God. In 1928 Isobel Kuhn went to China as a missionary. An author of several books, Isobel Kuhn wrote one of my favorite books, *In the Arena*. Isobel penned the following thoughts on the importance of keeping a right spirit:

God blessed the sinner who opened his heart to correction, and God's blessing was lost to the sinner who closed his heart to the pleadings of grace and refused to forgive.

We do not receive His blessings then because we deserve them, but only when we obey His tender injunction, *"Open thy mouth wide and I will fill it."*

In October, 1928, when I sailed for China, there were eight of us young women who sailed together. And on that ship was Miss Ruth Paxson [who] kindly consented to give us girls an hour's Bible teaching every day while the trip lasted. One sentence I never forgot. Standing in front of us, an experienced missionary, she looked into our faces searchingly and said, "Girls, when you get to China, all the scum of your nature will rise to the top."

I was shocked. Scum? Wasn't that a strong word? All of us were nice girls—weren't we? I was totally unprepared for the revolt of the flesh which was waiting for me on China's shores. The day was to come when on my knees in the Lord's presence I had to say: "Lord, scum is the only word to describe me."

I went to China eager and hopeful to be a soul winner. I was ridiculously, pathetically unprepared for the cost. It is true that I had expected poverty and had even tried to discipline myself for it. This puny "self-discipline" makes me laugh now. And makes me wonder how I could have been so unprepared for the ordinary missionary hardship.

The China Inland Mission, true to its name, reached out to the unworked interior of that great land, where by far the great majority of unevangelized Chinese were country peasants, poor people who toil and labor in mud hovels and know nothing of the luxuries of hot baths with soap, or frequent change to clean clothing. I had to learn that it costs money to be clean; I had always taken cleanliness for granted.

And so, after a happy time at language school, I found myself on a country station in a farming district, with thousands of Chinese peasants in all directions who had never been told that Christ died for their salvation. What a wonderful opportunity! In spirit I reached out eagerly toward them and then—the flesh revolted.

As in all eastern lands, and among our own poor also, these toiling people had vermin on their persons, in their homes, and in the dust of their mud floors. Fleas jumped on me from those floors and nibbled joyfully. I was likely to carry away a louse. When asked to spend a night in these homes, bedbugs walked out in regiments upon me, not to speak of flies and mosquitoes.

Their customs were different. They had no plumbing...so dogs acted as scavengers. And the lack of privacy [and] to be thronged with people hour after hour exhausted me emotionally. A woman cannot bathe without some kind of privacy. The constant traveling too was a source of irritation. So the flesh was offended on every hand, and it revolted.

My husband did not seem to mind these things.

I had been well taught in the truth of identification with Christ. I knew that these daily irritations and disagreeable things were opportunities to die to the flesh and sin. I frantically reckoned myself dead (Rom. 6:11); still I was hindered. Everywhere selfishness and self-pity would raise their ugly heads. I knew now that the scum had risen to the surface, and only the Lord could take it away.

Amy Carmichael said quite casually, "Everything personal had gone long ago"—meaning that the self-life was under her feet...I would get discouraged and put her books on the shelf saying, "You're too high for me. I cannot attain that."

I would fall on my knees and weep before the Lord asking for His help. And never did He spurn me. He was firm in correcting me but always loving. I want to testify to what God can do to change a human being, one that found she was indeed—scum.

He had to first bring me to the place where I was so exercised in spirit over producing so little fruit for Him that nothing else mattered. Physical comforts did not matter if only souls could be born into His kingdom. Moreover, He brought me to the place where I was willing that the instrument He used be someone else if necessary.

And always He will relentlessly hold you to His highest. He wants your soul not only purged and clean, but with a bloom upon it.[1]

At many different times in my life I have earnestly sought to be filled with the Holy Spirit, the most recent being this past year. There were various personal reasons for this time of supplication into which I will not go.

Suffice it to say, I needed to make a number of things right with the Lord. I read many books written by great people of faith such as Charles Finney, Jonathan and Rosalind Goforth, Jack Hyles, John R. Rice, Hudson Taylor, and R. A. Torrey on the filling of the Holy Spirit. I diligently searched my heart and asked God to show me what was not right in my life. He clearly brought things to mind, and I yielded and surrendered. I strove with all my heart to have a clean heart and life. I became consumed with the desire to be filled with the Holy Spirit. I wanted (and still do) more than anything to be filled. This is something I believe that we must all work on continually.

Keep your heart right so God can fill you with His Holy Spirit and use you for His glory.

Chapter Six

Being Filled With the Holy Spirit

Luke 11:5-13 says, "...*Which of you shall have a friend, and shall go unto him at midnight, and say unto him, Friend, lend me three loaves; For a friend of mine in his journey is come to me, and I have nothing to set before him? And he from within shall answer and say, Trouble me not: the door is now shut, and my children are with me in bed; I cannot rise and give thee. I say unto you, Though he will not rise and give him, because he is his friend, yet because of his importunity he will rise and give him as many as he needeth. And I say unto you, Ask, and it shall be given you; seek, and ye shall find; knock, and it shall be opened unto you. For every one that asketh receiveth; and he that seeketh findeth; and to him that knocketh it shall be opened. If a son shall ask bread of any of you that is a father, will he give him a stone? or if he ask a fish, will he for a fish give him a serpent? Or if he shall ask an egg, will he offer him a scorpion? If ye then, being evil, know how to give good gifts unto your children: how much more shall your heavenly Father give the Holy Spirit to them that ask him?*"

I believe every problem in our life can be solved by being filled with the Holy Spirit! I do not, however, believe that God wants us to be filled with His Spirit just so our problems can be solved. For instance, we need to be filled with the Holy Spirit so we can be soul winners. The most important thing we can do, after we ourselves receive Jesus Christ as our personal Saviour, is to help keep others out of Hell.

Dr. Jack Hyles' book *Meet the Holy Spirit* is a great book. Brother Hyles explained that the Holy Spirit doesn't necessarily come into everyone's life as He did with men like Charles Finney and D. L. Moody. However, the Holy Spirit can and will give us power to win souls and will use us to change lives. We have to keep pleading and begging for God's power. A Christian can look around and see those who have met God's conditions and claimed His power, and thus God has seen fit to give them Spirit-filled lives and ministries.

Is that what you want in your life? It's what I want! I have had seasons when I **knew** I had His power in my life. Before I was married, I was a student at Ozark Bible College in Joplin, Missouri. Although Ozark was a Bible college with a Christian church sponsorship, Rick and I already believed in faith salvation.

One weekend I went home with a girl to whom I had been talking about how I witnessed to people. That weekend she asked me to witness to her friends—basically worldly teenagers who cared nothing about God. We spent all day Saturday visiting her friends, and they were all getting saved! That Sunday they all came to church and went forward during the invitation and were baptized—numbers of them! They were all crying uncontrollably.

To say that I was amazed was an understatement. I believe that was the first time that I personally experienced the Holy Spirit's power in leading people to the Lord. I had had people saved, but not like that! The people in that little country church were looking at each other in astonishment.

I have had other seasons like that. When I was home in 1998, about a year after my mom died, two friends of my dad, who were very hard, claiming to be atheists, called me out of the clear blue sky, both on the same day and independent of each other, to ask me how to be saved. I led both of them to the Lord over the phone. I'll never forget that experience.

Once again I've been especially "thirsty" for the Holy Spirit's power on my life. Brother Hyles advised us to read the Bible verses that deal with the power of the Holy Spirit several times a day, yielding to Him. Many times a day, pray for God's power. Times come when we need to have "seasons of prayer."

Brother Hyles believed that the first time he was filled with the Holy Spirit was on his father's grave. In fact, when Brother Hyles had the body of his father moved to Memory Lane Mausoleum, he placed a bronze marker on the place where his father rested that reads: "In memory of Willis Athey Hyles, whose body now rests in Schererville, Indiana. It was at this site in May of 1950, on the grave of his father, that Dr. Jack Hyles knelt and prayed for the power of God on his life." After that he had numerous times of being filled with the Holy Spirit.

I have been asking God to show me things in my life that aren't right, and I have been trying my best to make them right. As much as Brother Hyles was filled with the Spirit, he kept on asking and begging for more until the day he died. If he needed to beg God for His power, how much more do I?

Do you want to be filled with the Holy Spirit? How can we possibly serve God without the Holy Spirit? Yet, many try to do just that.

There are some conditions that must be met:

1.   God cannot fill a dirty vessel with His Holy Spirit. In her book *Climbing,* Mrs. Jonathan Goforth tells how she believed she almost missed being filled with the Holy Spirit because she seemingly could not forgive.

The first sad details of how and why unforgiveness entered my heart cannot be given. Suffice it to say that those who knew the facts agree that humanly speaking one can scarcely imagine a case where unforgiveness was more justified; yet my dear husband, who had equal reason with myself for feeling as I did, quietly and calmly laid it all before the Lord and left it there and begged me to do the same; but I could not, or rather would not.

For more than a year, while the source of trouble remained at our station, I would not speak to or recognize that one. Four years passed. One day my husband and I were traveling by train with a number of co-workers en route to the religious fair at Hsunhsien, where the most intensive campaign of evangelism was carried on. This year I had been put in charge of the women's work there.

For months I had been deeply but secretly moved by the evident spiritual power that had come into my husband's life. I, his wife, could not but see that he was indeed filled with the Spirit of God. There had come into my soul a great yearning that I, too, might have this fullness of the Spirit.

As we sat there on the train, I asked my husband to sit with the others for I wanted to be alone. I bent my head and cried to God to fill me with His Spirit as He had filled my husband. Unmistakably clear came the Inner Voice, "Write to (the one towards whom I felt hatred) and ask forgiveness." My whole soul cried out, "Never, never can I forgive him!" Again I prayed as before, and again the Inner Voice spoke clearly as before. Again I cried out, "Never." When for the third time this was repeated, I jumped to my feet and said to myself, "I'll give it all up, for I'll never, never forgive!" I joined the others and laughed and talked to hide my agitation. Then followed the saddest part of my life. For several months I [kept] up appearances but all the while my heart was becoming harder, colder, and more hopeless.

Then one day that passage in the *Pilgrim's Progress* came to me where Christian, when going through the house of the Interpreter, came to the man in the cage who said, "I have grieved the Spirit, and He is gone: I have provoked God to anger, and He has left me." As I read this passage, a terrible conviction came upon me that the words I have quoted were true of me. During the two days and nights that followed, I was in the depths of despair, believing God's Holy Spirit had left me. My husband was away from home, and there seemed no one to whom I could turn. Then God in His mercy sent someone to me.

A young missionary whose wife had died came over to see me. It was evening, and the children were in bed. We sat on the front steps together while he sobbingly told of his wife's tragic death. Suddenly the very floodgates seemed loosed within me, and I gave way to uncontrollable weeping. When able, I told all the story as I have related it, and its sad, early details, then ended with, "I have grieved the Holy Spirit of God, and He has left me!"

"But Mrs. Goforth," he said, "are you willing to write the letter?"

I replied: "I now know what it would be to be without God and without hope, and if I could only have another chance, there is nothing I would not do."

Again he asked, "Are you willing to write that letter?"

"Yes," I replied.

"Then go at once and write it."

With a glorious ray of hope dawning in me, I ran into the house, and in a few minutes returned with the letter. It was just a few lines of humble apology. Oh, the joy that came, and the thankfulness that it was indeed not too late.[1]

Is your heart clean? Do you have something in your heart against someone? If so, get it out, or God cannot fill you.

2.   **Humbly yield.** Mrs. Howard Taylor, daughter-in-law of Hudson Taylor, said the following:

In China I came to see that there was a great lack in my life. I was often out of touch with the Lord Jesus, often weary, hungry and longing for blessing. From the very first day I landed in China, God began to show me my need by humbling me in the dust. He brought me in contact with other lives that were what I wanted to be. At last I came down to Shanghai, and there began some meetings amongst sailors on board a British man-of-war. I longed to see these men brought to Christ, but God did not use me to the conversion of one. It was the last Sunday before Christmas when a word was spoken that, under God, brought deliverance and made all things new. After the evangelistic service in the C.I.M. Hall, an entire stranger—a Christian seaman—came up to me and said earnestly: "Are you filled with the Holy Ghost?"

Filled with the Holy Ghost? I remembered no more of the conversation, but that question burned deeper and deeper into my heart. This, then, was the explanation of all the inward failure, the sorrow that seemed unavailing, the purpose that came to nothing. God had made a provision, given a Gift that I had never definitely accepted. I knew that the Holy Spirit must be in my life in a certain sense; yet, just as certainly, I knew that I was not filled with the Spirit, and was experiencing little of His power.

The Word of God was full, now I came to study the subject, of the personality and power of the Holy Spirit. Why had I never seen it? And there stood out in Galatians 3:13, 24 [that] Christ hath redeemed us from the curse of the law, having been made a curse for us...that we might receive the promise of the Spirit through faith.

I saw that I needed to give my life to the Holy Spirit of God and let Him come in all His grace and fullness, and make my life what it ought to be. The first feeling was doubt about the result. How far might I have to go? I said, "Don't mind that, He will give you strength for whatever you need."

The next morning—I shall never forget it—I gave my life to the Spirit of God. Carefully I went through some passages in the Scripture on the subject, and I saw first of all that God gives the Holy Spirit to those that obey Him, and then that we must ask and seek, "for this I will be enquired of, saith the Lord, Ye have not, because ye ask not."[2]

Have you surrendered?

3. Ask. How badly do we want the Holy Spirit? Are we willing to pay the price? Reread Luke 11:5-13 at the beginning of this chapter.

We are to keep on asking God for His Holy Spirit. Maybe He wants to see how badly we want Him. Do we ask once, and then when God does not grant Him to us, we say, "Oh well," and that is the end of it? Or do we want the Holy Spirit so badly that we keep on asking and never stop until we receive His fullness? I'm not talking about a quickie two-minute prayer.

The last line in the verses from Luke 11 says: "*…how much more shall your heavenly Father give the Holy Spirit to them that ask him?*" However badly we want the Holy Spirit, how much more does God want to give Him to us?! God is no respecter of persons. Being filled with the Holy Spirit is totally up to us. Fast and pray and show God how much you really want His Holy Spirit.

Ask and ask and ask. Never stop asking.

Conclusion

In 1905 Rosalind Goforth saw how God was greatly using her husband. He had been filled with the Holy Spirit, and Rosalind also wanted to be used like her husband was being used. In 1916 during a furlough, she said she felt spiritually numb. A friend took her to a Bible conference where she sat on the front row and listened intently to the preacher. She tells of her experience in *Climbing*:

> He drew simply a picture of an ordinary, all too common Christian life. If he had drawn the picture from my everyday life experience, he could not have given it other than he did. Sometimes on the mountain-top with visions of God and His mighty power; then the dimming of vision, coldness, discouragement, even definite disobedience. Again through some sorrow or trial, there would come a return and seeking of the Lord. In a word, an up and down life of intermingled victory and defeat.
>
> The speaker then asked all who truly sought for God's highest to hold up their hands. Being in the front seat and realizing many behind knew who I was, and that they thought of me as a "good missionary," I kept my hand down. It was too humiliating. But the Spirit of God strove with me, so up went my hand.
>
> Then the speaker drew another picture: it was the Christian life as God had not only planned it for His children, but had made abundant provision for their living it. He described it as a life of victory, not defeat, of peace and trust, not struggle and worry. All through his address, I kept thinking, "Yes, it's wonderful, but I've tried so often and failed, I doubt if it is possible." Then the speaker ended by urging us to go over the texts listed on a slip of paper. He emphasized the importance of standing on God's Word.
>
> The following morning I rose early, as soon as it was light enough to see. On my knees, I read from the list I have mentioned, all the texts given. But before I had gone half way down the list, I saw clearly God's Word taught, beyond the shadow of a doubt, that the overcoming, victorious life in Christ is the normal life God has planned for His children. In the two days that followed, clearer light came, with a dawning hope that this life might be possible for me.

The day after reaching home, I picked up the little booklet, *The Life That Wins*, the personal testimony of Charles G. Trumbull—the man who had been a great blessing to me at the conference.

As I began to read, I came to the words: "At last I realized that Jesus Christ was actually and literally within me." I stopped amazed. The sun seemed suddenly to come from under a cloud and flood my soul with light! How blind I had been! I saw as in a flash the secret of victory. It was Jesus Christ Himself!

For days I seemed as if in a dream. Fearing lest I be carried off my feet by what had come to me, I determined to seek the advice of our beloved and honored foreign missionary secretary, Rev. Dr. R. P. McKay [former missionary to Formosa]. Never can I forget a detail of that interview. Dr. McKay listened sympathetically while I told all. I ended by saying, "Do you think I am going too far in this?"

Dr. McKay smiled as he replied, "No, Mrs. Goforth."

Then he gravely added: "Mrs. Goforth, I am amazed; amazed that you have only now come to apprehend this truth of Christ's indwelling. You have been the wife of Jonathan Goforth for many years. His messages were aglow with this truth."

"Yes, Dr. McKay," I replied humbly, "I begin to realize this and wonder at my blindness. One sentence my husband so often uses has come back to me these days: All the resources of the Godhead are at our disposal!"

Dr. McKay then said: "It seems that this, the deepest truth, the union of the Divine and human, is not received by simple head knowledge but must be apprehended through the Holy Spirit's revealing."

I left Dr. McKay strengthened in the belief that what had come to me was indeed of the Holy Spirit. But I was determined to search the Scriptures and stand only on them. That summer I laid aside all secular reading and, with a concordance, dug into my Bible; and, oh, the wonderful treasures I found! The line of study was entirely on the union of the Divine and human.[1]

The Lord began to use Mrs. Goforth in a miraculous way from that point on in her life, until her death. Mrs. Jonathan Goforth had been undeniably filled with the Holy Spirit. Dear lady, walk with God!

Above: All of us at Ricky's high school graduation
Below: Rick and Ricky at Ricky's graduation from Hyles-Anderson College in Crown Point, Indiana.

UNIT THREE

Your Husband

*"The heart of her husband doth safely
trust in her...."*
(Proverbs 31:11)

Introduction

Nearly everyone has heard of the famous missionary to China, J. Hudson Taylor. Taylor went to China as a single man, but God had someone very special already picked out for him. Her name was Maria Dyer, and she worked in a school for Chinese girls run by Miss Mary Aldersey, the first woman missionary in China. Maria and her sister were the orphan daughters of missionaries. Maria was 18 when Taylor met her. In Taylor's biography, *J. Hudson Taylor; God's Man in China*, written by Dr. and Mrs. Howard Taylor, son and daughter-in-law of Hudson Taylor, Maria is described as follows:

> Maria Dyer's was a deep and tender nature. Lonely from childhood, she had grown up longing for a real heart-friend. Her father she could hardly remember, and from the mother whom she devotedly loved she was parted by death at ten years of age. [She and her sister were] brought up under the care of an uncle in London, most of their time being spent at school. Then came the call to China, through Miss Aldersey's need of a helper in the Ningpo school. In offering for this post, the sisters were influenced not so much by a desire to take up missionary work as by the knowledge that it was what their parents would have desired. Young as they were they had had some training as teachers, and as they were self-supporting and did not wish to be separated, Miss Aldersey invited both to join her.[1]

Maria was saved on the boat as she sailed to China. Now she was serving the Lord—not because that would be what her parents wanted—but because of her love for Jesus. Miss Aldersey was a very difficult person for whom to work. Thankfully, Maria had the support of her sister and missionary friends:

> ...but her heart had never found its mate in the things that mattered most. And then he came—the young missionary who impressed her from the first as having the same longings after holiness, usefulness, nearness to God. He was different from everybody else; there was a something about him that made her feel at rest and understood. He seemed to live in such a real world,

and to have such a real, great God. Though she saw little of him, it was a comfort to know that he was near, and she was startled to find how much she missed him.[2]

In order to reach the people, Taylor had adopted the Chinese dress and culture. This course of action took a lot of courage, and he was ridiculed and criticized by the other missionaries who felt Christianity had to be wrapped in Western culture. Taylor not only wore Chinese clothes, he even shaved his head except for a small patch, which he dyed black. He then had some false hair braided into his own, so he had a long pigtail hanging down his back like any other self-respecting Chinaman.

Taylor had fallen in love with his sister's music teacher before leaving for China. She, however, did not want to be a missionary and tried to talk him into forgetting about the foreign field. How sad to think that he might have given in, and a multitude of Chinese would have been lost forever as a result. May I say, if you are a young lady and you are dating a mission student with the intent of persuading him to stay in America, please do not let Satan use you. Break up with him and let him do what God has called him to do. Better yet, get your heart right with God and become what Maria Dyer became to Hudson Taylor.

When the young music teacher refused to go to China, Taylor could not get her off his mind. He longed for a wife. When he finally realized the beautiful and talented music teacher was not going to change her mind, he became interested in another young lady. He wrote to her in England and asked her to marry him. She accepted but soon changed her mind. Some believe her change of heart was because she had heard of his Chinese dress and pigtail. For a time, he even thought about leaving China, returning to England, and persuading her to marry him. Shortly after the second failed romance, Taylor met Maria Dyer.

Maria did not think Hudson Taylor was interested in her as he never made any advances. As she saw him from time to time, the interest and curiosity she had for him grew into something greater.

Although Taylor was still hoping to hear from the other young lady in England, he wrote of Maria: "...a dear sweet creature, has all the good points of Miss S. and many more too. She is a precious treasure, one of sterling worth and possessed with an untiring zeal for the good of this poor people. She is a lady too..."[3]

Maria fell in love. Taylor's son and daughter-in-law comment: "...Others did not see in him, always, just what she saw. They disliked his wearing Chinese dress, and did not approve his making himself so entirely one with the people. So she prayed much though she showed little. The love of her life had come to her, and nobody knew but God."[4]

Maria often went visiting with another missionary; although she was very busy with school, it was said that her real love was soul winning. "That [soul-winning zeal] was what drew out my interest," said Hudson Taylor. "She was spiritually minded, as her work proved. Even then she was a true missionary."[5] Dr. and Mrs. Howard Taylor note:

[Maria] proved so like-minded in all important ways that, unconsciously almost to himself, she began to fill a place in his heart never filled before. Vainly he strove against the longing to see more of her. He had loved before in a more or less boyish way; but this was different. Everything he thought, felt and did seemed permeated. He could not separate himself in thought from her. In everything she satisfied his mind and heart; not only embodying his ideal of womanliness, but being herself devoted to the work to which his life was given, he could rest in the assurance that she would help and not hinder him in his special service. Of her thoughts and feelings about him, if she had any, he knew nothing. She had always been kind and pleasant, but that she was to everyone, with a sweetness of spirit that was unfailing.[6]

In *From Jerusalem to Irian Jaya*, author Ruth Tucker relates:

In March of 1857, several months after Taylor and Maria became acquainted, Taylor made his first advance, and, typical of his style, it was a bold one—a letter containing a marriage proposal. "I then opened my letter and read of his attachment to me, and how he believed God had given him that love for me. I could hardly understand; it seemed that my prayers were indeed answered. He asked me to consent to an engagement." She sent him a hasty refusal. How could this young missionary teacher brazenly turn her back on the man of her dreams—the very husband she had prayed for? Here is where the very domineering and protective Miss Aldersey (whom Maria loved and respected) enters. She stood over her timid teenage charge and dictated the response, and with that accomplished, she wrote to Maria's uncle and legal guardian in England, pungently outlining her objections to Hudson Taylor. Her objections? He was uneducated, unordained, unconnected (with a mission society), and uncouth. And if that was not enough, he was short (Maria was tall), and he wore Chinese clothes.[7]

Some of the other missionaries suggested that Taylor should go back to England and finish his education so he could be "worthy of Maria." Maria's response was, "I would wait if he went home in order to increase his usefulness. But is he to leave his work in order to gain a name for the sake of marrying me? If he loves me more than Jesus he is not worthy of me—if he were to leave the Lord's work for world's honour, I would have nothing further to do with him."[8]

Taylor suspected Miss Aldersey was behind Maria's objection. Maria was kept from any contact with him for months until finally they secretly met in the home of missionary friends. They became engaged. When the uncle, who had done some checking up on Taylor, sent his approval, they were married on January 20, 1858. Tucker writes: "Maria was the very woman Taylor needed to polish the rough edges of his personality and to help focus his enthusiasm and ambitions, and from the start their marriage was a true partnership."[9]

I have always loved this wonderful love story of Hudson Taylor and Maria Dyer. It is a great example because Hudson Taylor became one of the greatest missionaries of all time, and his wife played a big part in his ministry. Would you like to be the kind of wife Maria was? What if God has plans to use your husband in a great way, and all that is holding him back is you?

Chapter One

Praying for Him

"Moreover as for me, God forbid that I should sin against the LORD in ceasing to pray for you...." (I Samuel 12:23)

How much time do you spend praying for your husband every day? Do you pray that he will be a good husband and father? While you are at it, pray that you will be a good wife and mother! Pray that your husband will be morally pure and that God will protect him against temptation. Pray for him to be filled with the Holy Spirit. I pray for my husband every day; I ask God to fill him with the Holy Spirit and to give him wisdom and power. After all, he is also my pastor.

As with any area of our life, if we are right with God, we are usually going to be right with others—whether it be husband, children, or church people. If you do not get anything out of this book, I hope you get this one truth: walk with God. Pray that your husband will walk with God. I sincerely doubt that very many marriages fail when both the husband and the wife are truly walking with God every day. If both of you are filled with the Holy Spirit, how can you *not* get along with each other?

The best example I have heard about a wife's praying for her husband is not the story of a missionary's wife, but a pastor's wife—Mrs. J. Frank Norris. I would like to share one instance of God's hearing the prayers of Mrs. Lillian Norris.

Norris had just been called to pastor at First Baptist Church, Fort Worth, Texas, in the early 1900s. He had just been through a battle with denominational leaders and against racing and gambling in Texas, leaving his health shattered. He was still quite young. In his autobiography, *Inside History*, Norris wrote: "I had very little faith. I wanted to quit the ministry. My unbelief changed into contempt."[1]

First Baptist was the richest church in Texas and was known as "The Home of the Cattle Kings."[2] First Baptist Church of Dallas was also "dead."

He said for two years he tried to fit in. He received a high salary, lived in a beautiful house with servants, drove a nice car, and received paid vacations that lasted the whole summer. One day he went home and told his wife he was going to quit the ministry.

She asked, "When did you ever begin?"

He answered, "I am going to quit before I begin. I didn't want to come here. I have no faith. I don't even know whether I am a Christian. I thought I was once—fact is, I don't know whether there is a God. I am going to leave it all."[3]

Norris left to preach for a friend in Kentucky. However, he couldn't eat or sleep. When he tried to preach, he failed miserably. In the biography *The J. Frank Norris I Have Known for Thirty-Four Years*, Louis Entzminger continues the story:

I got up, put on my clothes; the window was open, I didn't want to disturb the family, and I took my shoes and slipped out. I sat down for a while in the grass—and I sat there—thin, wasted away, broken, discouraged. I wondered why all these things had befallen me. My friends had turned away, everything was gone and I knew I was gone too—I am telling you I knew I would be in the asylum or in the grave in a short time. I felt myself slipping and I was terribly alarmed. I said to myself, "I am going home, get my family, and I am going to Southern California where nobody knows me. I am through with the ministry."[4]

That night before the service, he hid his bag by the railroad station. He was planning to sneak away after church that night, without telling anyone. He went to church, and as he got up to preach, the pastor leaned over and whispered:

"Do you see that man sitting back yonder?" I had already seen him. He said, "That old fellow with the red bandana handkerchief around his neck—he is the meanest man in all this country; it is the first time I have ever known him to come to church—he has a half dozen notches on his gun. If you could reach that man, you could reach this whole country." I can see him now as he sat rared back—he had on boots and spurs, and I learned afterwards bells on his spurs, and he looked at me and I looked at him; we were of mutual curiosity to each other. I stood up, tired and weak, and I looked at him, and I thought—"You poor old sinner, it's the last time I ever expect to preach, and I am going to give you the best I have."[5]

Brother Norris began to preach about the prodigal son from the Bible. Entzminger continues the story:

About that time I saw that old red-faced sinner bury his face in his hands—it was a hot night and I didn't know what it meant, but in a minute he just reached up behind and tore that old red bandana loose. I saw him bury his face in it and his frame shook like a leaf in a storm—and folks, something happened in this tired, weak frame of mine—and I stood up on my hind feet for the first time in a long time and felt strong—and I said, "If there is a man here who is a sinner, lost, and will come to the Father's house tonight, come on; come on! Come on!" And my friends, I can see that old sinner now as he got up and started down the aisle—he had that old red bandana handkerchief in one hand and his cowboy hat in the other, and you could hear his bells jingling as he came—listen folks, he didn't stop to shake hands with me, but he fell full length on his face—and when his little old Methodist wife sitting over there saw him, she let out a shout that you could have heard a quarter of a mile and came running and fell by his side, and in five minutes there were more than fifty men and women in that altar seeking Jesus Christ, and salvation came down, and that 11 o'clock train whistled and went on and they were still being saved, and twelve o'clock came and folks were still being saved, and one o'clock came and they were still shouting, and two o'clock came and we were still there.[6]

When Brother Norris finally got back to the house, it was 3:00 a.m. His wife had been calling and trying to get a hold of him.

I went to the telephone and tried to talk—I have always been able to keep control of my emotions, but sometimes they get the best of me—this was one time they did—I got Fort Worth on the line and they told me Mrs. Norris was trying to get me. When she came to the telephone and said, "Hello, is that you, Frank?" I just played the baby act, and I couldn't do anything but stand there and cry, and central kept saying, "Talk, talk, here they are." Well, I was doing my best to talk and I couldn't say a word. I turned to Sister White and I said, "You tell her." She drew back and slung it against the wall and shouted "Hallelujah! Hallelujah! Hallelujah!" and she just shouted all over the room. I said, Brother White, you tell her." He said, "Sister Norris," and that was as far as he got, and their sixteen-year-old daughter came and she tried it and she just squalled and cried. And I said, "Give me that telephone receiver"—and all the time central was saying, "Talk, talk, talk!" Finally I got my feelings under control enough and I said, "Wife, wife, we have had the biggest meeting you ever saw, more than half a hundred sinners have been saved, and they are still shouting all over this country, and the best part of it is, wife, you have a new husband—he has been saved tonight, and he is coming home, and we are going to start life over again and lick the tar out of that crowd and build the biggest church in the world."

And she said, "I knew it was happening. I have been praying for three days and nights. I haven't slept a wink, and tonight I had the answer to my prayer, and I have been praying that this thing might happen, and my joy is complete; my cup runneth over."

The next Sunday I preached, and the fire from heaven came down, and we had sixty-two converts to walk down the aisle.[7]

Norris credits his wife and her prayers for saving him and his ministry. Could your prayers for your husband ever save his ministry?

Chapter Two

Loving Him

"*That they may teach the young women to be sober, to love their husbands....*" (Titus 2:4)

In December 2002, my husband, daughter, and I flew to America to attend our son's wedding. He married Brandie Gavin, a wonderful young lady he met at Hyles-Anderson College. They are planning to go to the Philippines as missionaries. As of this writing, they are currently on deputation to raise their support. I am sure if you would ask them (or any other couple about to be married) if they loved each other, they would say "Yes." Many people do not realize that love is not just feelings, because feelings come and go. Rather, love is a decision.

On June 3, 1973, Rick and I promised to love each other from that day forward. That was a decision we made on that day. Marriage is not always easy; many times it is difficult. At times couples become angry with each other and, as a result, perhaps feel that they do not even love each other. Staying together, in spite of those times, is love.

Consider the countless little acts of kindness each day—that is love. If you are going through a time when you may feel like you do not love your husband, I recommend reading the "love" chapter—I Corinthians 13. Better yet, memorize it. The Bible says that love is patient, kind, is not envious or puffed up, does not behave itself unseemly, does not seek her own, is not easily provoked, and thinks no evil. Love bears all things, believes all things, hopes all things, and endures all things. Love never fails.

Funny, I find that I Corinthians 13 does not say anything about feelings. Suppose I do not *feel* like being patient, but I am patient anyway. What does that mean? Am I patient? Or am I not patient because I simply did not *feel* like being patient? Maybe I do not *feel* like being kind, but I decide to be kind anyway. So, am I kind or not?

Maybe you do not *feel* like you love your husband, but you decide to stay with him. You decide not to leave him, in spite of how you feel. You do acts of kindness for him, in spite of your feelings. At times your husband may be unlovable. Still, you must make a conscious daily effort and a conscious daily decision that you are going to love him—no matter what.

At the times when I have been less than kind to my husband, I have remembered how God said we will reap what we sow. I often thought that someday when my son got married, I would want him to marry a girl who loved him, was faithful and kind. I need to treat my husband in the way that I would want my future daughter-in-law to treat my son. If I want her to *"do him good and not evil"* as Proverbs 31:12 instructs, then I believe I need to do that to my husband so I will reap what I sowed.

Love is being grateful. If we are grateful, we will learn to be content as the Bible teaches. Love is forgiving. Love is sacrifice. Do you do things for your husband that you do not want to do? Are you thinking, "Well! He doesn't do things for me!"

Since feelings come and go, I believe if we do acts of love, even when we don't *feel* like it, the feelings will eventually come back. Many divorced people say, "I just don't love her/him anymore," or "I fell in love with someone else." We cannot go through life letting our feelings guide us. Christians should not live that way because that is how we end up getting into trouble. Instead, a wife needs to ask God to fill her heart with love for her husband.

I Corinthians 13:13 says, *"And now abideth faith, hope, charity, these three; but the greatest of these is charity."*

Chapter Three

Encouraging Him

A wife needs to support her husband because there will be times when she is the only one who does. If it seems that everyone else in the whole world is against him, it would be nice if he knew there would always be one person behind him. Don't be like Job's wife—she kicked her husband when he was down!

When the Sabeans stole Job's oxen and asses and slew his servants, when fire fell from Heaven and burned up Job's sheep and servants, when the Chaldeans appropriated Job's camels and killed the servants, when a great wind came and killed Job's sons and daughters, and when Job was covered with boils, did his wife encourage him? Job 2:9 says, *"Then said his wife unto him, Dost thou still retain thine integrity? curse God, and die."*

In my survey of missionary wives, I asked for frank and honest answers to the following question:

 **Question** What do you do to encourage and/or help your husband when there are trials in his ministry, such as people not responding, financial problems, etc.?

Answers:

• I try not to dwell on the negative, but to remind him of the blessings and successes. If we as wives will truly depend upon God, we won't be too overwhelmed by finances and trials. I remind myself, "It's God's work."

• One thing I do is to do something special he likes such as going on a picnic or making his favorite dinner—something to help him relax and get his mind off things.

• My husband likely would answer this question by saying I am content in whatever state I may find myself. I am not so sure that is entirely true, but I am glad he thinks so! I have learned to use as little as possible to feed the family. We purchase very little meat because we raise our own. I make anything and everything from scratch. I sew most of the girls' clothes and mine. We live very simply. As far as encouraging my husband during setbacks in the ministry, I try to point out all he's done for the ones still sticking; remind him that the Lord will bless his consistency; show up for every service myself; encourage the children to write notes of appreciation; keep a supply of "I love you" cards, knick-knacks, balloons, etc., to give to him so he knows that his wife appreciates his efforts.

•   I hope that my biggest involvement, though, has been being an encouragement to my husband in these years on the field. I have tried to help him with various projects.

Ladies, if our husband falls, we need to help him up. We should not be like Job's wife. Be an encourager!

Chapter Four

Backing His Decisions

W hen the late missionary to the Philippines, Dr. Bob Hughes, spoke at the 1976 Pastors' School at First Baptist Church, Hammond, Indiana, he was dying of cancer. Our pastor, Dr. Jack Hyles, invited him along with several others to speak at Pastors' School that year on the theme of "Don't Quit." Brother Hughes knew he did not have long to live, and he made a plea for missionaries.

Rick and I were both in the service as we were then attending Hyles-Anderson College. After hearing Dr. Hughes, my husband turned to me and said, "We're going to the Philippines."

We had been married a little over three years, and we did not have any children. We had been praying for God to lead us. I did not argue with my husband or try to talk him out of his decision. I believed if I prayed, "God, please tell us where we should go," and then God spoke to my husband through Brother Hughes and said, "I want you to go to the Philippines," it would have looked kind of funny if I replied, "Now wait a minute, Lord. I need to reword that prayer. I meant within an hour's drive of Mom and Dad."

Ephesians 5:22 says, *"Wives, submit yourselves unto your own husbands, as unto the Lord."* The Bible does not say, "Submit IF your husband loves you and acts like it all the time and you agree with him." It does not say "Submit if you want to," or "Submit if you are sure he is not just making an emotional decision because it was during the missions conference."

I was not born submissive. Allow me to let you in on a secret—**NO** woman was born submissive. Becoming a submissive wife has been a long process for me. In fact, I have still not arrived! I am still working on being a submissive wife.

 **Question**   What is your advice to a young man has who been called to the foreign field, but his wife (or fiancée) doesn't want to go?

Answers:
- For the young man who feels called to the mission field and is not yet mar-

ried, I would advise him to reconsider that maybe she isn't the one the Lord has for him, especially if she's already bucking his authority and desires before the marriage has taken place. He probably should thank God he found her true character before it was too late. As for the young man who is already married, try to be patient and more sensitive than usual to your wife. She will probably open up and tell you the fears and anxieties she's feeling if she thinks it really matters to you. She may not necessarily be totally against the idea, but she probably just has doubts. Perhaps she feels inadequate and needs encouragement.

- The wife seems selfish.
- The wife seems worldly-minded, not very dedicated, and perhaps may even need to get her heart right with God.

These replies may sound rather harsh, but perhaps there is a grain of truth there. II Corinthians 11:23-27 says: "...in stripes above measure, in prisons more frequent, in deaths oft. Of the Jews five times received I forty stripes save one. Thrice was I beaten with rods, once was I stoned, thrice I suffered shipwreck, a night and a day I have been in the deep; In journeyings often, in perils of waters, in perils of robbers, in perils by mine own countrymen, in perils by the heathen, in perils in the city, in perils in the wilderness, in perils in the sea, in perils among false brethren; In weariness and painfulness, in watchings often, in hunger and thirst, in fastings often, in cold and nakedness."

When I think of what the Apostle Paul endured so that he could take the Gospel to a lost and dying world, I am ashamed. No doubt if some of us had to face even one of those trials, we would quit. When I read of the great missionary wives of bygone years, I wonder if any American missionary today could endure such hardships.

Ann Judson went with her husband Adoniram Judson to Burma in 1812. When I think of a missionary who has made some sacrifices, I think of her. When I was a student at Hyles-Anderson College, I first heard about Ann Judson from my teacher, Mrs. Marlene Evans.

Ann suffered a stillbirth during the rough ocean voyage and had to be carried off the ship when it docked in Burma. She was still grieving for her best friend, Harriet Newell, who had died after a difficult delivery. Also desiring to be missionaries, Harriet and her husband Samuel Newell had sailed with the Judsons.

Both of the Judsons studied the difficult language for several hours a day. They labored seven years in the Buddhist country before seeing their first convert. In the meantime, their hearts were once again broken by the death of a child.

Never a country very tolerant of missionaries, the situation grew even worse for those in Burma when war broke out with England in 1824. Judson tried to explain to officials that he was an American, not British, to no avail. He and other missionaries were arrested and thrown into a death prison; they thought they would be executed at any moment. The prison was filthy, and to make matters worse, at night the guards hung the prisoners by their feet.

Ann later became known as a heroine for her perseverance in getting her husband released. She constantly sought out officials to beg them to let her visit her husband and take food to him. She daily walked two miles from her house to the prison in the oppressive heat, sometimes only to be turned away. Every day she would make her rounds to the city governor and other officials, offering money and gifts to make her husband's internment a bit more bearable. The ruthless officials ransacked her house and stole everything of value.

As she and her husband were fearful of his precious Burmese New Testament translation's being stolen or destroyed, she sewed the manuscript pages into a pillow on which he slept each night. Ann took care that the pillow was hard and that the pillow cover was dirty and ugly, so it would not be desired by the brutal guards.

Eight months after Judson's arrest, Ann gave birth to a baby girl. Three months later the prisoners were forced on a death march. Many did not make the destination. With great difficulty, Ann learned where the prisoners were taken and made the journey to the new location with her baby. As a result, Ann became very ill and was no longer able to nurse baby Maria. Oddly enough, the guards allowed Adoniram, with ankles chained together, to carry the baby around the village to beg other native mothers to nurse his child.

Finally, after enduring one and a half years of imprisonment, Judson was released. Author Gordon Langley Hall shares the account of Judson's liberation in *Golden Boats from Burma*:

Adoniram thanked the governor with all his heart, and then he half walked, half ran to the mission house.

The flickering flame from the crude-oil lamp was still casting a feeble glow through the window when he reached his own home. Inside the door, warming herself over a brazier of coals, sat a Burmese woman nursing a thin and dirty baby. He did not even recognize it as his own little Maria and hurried into the bedroom where an awful sight confronted him. Stretched over the foot of the bed lay what looked to be the lifeless body of his wife. Her fine black curls had been cut from her head which was now covered with a grubby cotton cap; the chalk-white skin of her face stretched taut over her cheekbones. She looked more like a skeleton than a human being. Shocked, he gently lifted the forlorn figure into his arms and cradled it gently to his breast as one would a child. Even then he did not know if she were still alive. When her eyelids flickered he saw that she was.[1]

A few months later, because of his knowledge of the Burmese language, the British army enlisted his aid to help with peace negotiations. While he was working with the British, Ann died. A few months later, Maria also died.

Romans 12:1 says, *"I beseech you therefore, brethren, by the mercies of God, that ye present your bodies a living sacrifice...."* I often wonder if the word "sacrifice" has become distasteful in this day and age. Ann Judson became a willing living sacrifice when she backed her husband's decision to go to the foreign mission field. Because she did not turn back, she died at the age of 36. How about you?

Chapter Five

Having a Servant's Heart

One of the saddest missionary stories I have ever read is that of William Carey and his wife Dorothy. When Carey felt God calling him to India, Mrs. Carey refused to go. Carey boarded a boat with his eight-year-old son, leaving behind his wife and two other children. The boat was delayed and Dorothy, after delivering a fourth child, "grudgingly agreed to join the mission party, providing Kitty, her younger sister, could accompany her. Obtaining funds for the additional passengers was a difficult hurdle....."[1]

Ruth Tucker writes in *From Jerusalem to Irian Jaya*: "...[it] grieved [Carey] that his wife and Kitty were continually exclaiming against him. Dorothy's health and mental stability steadily declined. In 1807, at the age of fifty-one, Dorothy Carey died."[2]

I do not want to be critical of this poor woman, who some believed suffered from mental illness possibly exacerbated by the death of her child. I have no way of knowing if she brought any of her misery upon herself because of her attitude or her relationship with God. Certainly, it is not my place to judge. I have no way of knowing whether or not she could have prevented her situation. Just because an individual has any kind of illness—mental or otherwise—does not mean it is necessarily God's judgment upon that person. However, mental or physical illness notwithstanding, the idea that I have the potential to be a Dorothy Carey frightens me. Therefore, I want to work hard to always have a servant's heart.

Are You Willing to Go?

The following is a response from a missionary wife about being willing to go to the mission field.

I believe a mature Christian should be willing to live and serve Christ anywhere. I also believe that God is wise in His calling. Whom He calls, He will enable. For the unmarried man—if he feels the call is genuine, then his choice of wife who refuses to go must be wrong. He should be willing to go—single. For the wife who doesn't want to follow her husband, I say, "Go with your husband and trust God completely." God didn't talk to Sarai when Abram was told to move from home. A husband and wife are one in Christ, and if God directs the man to serve in another country—I believe a God-fearing wife should follow. It may be unsettling and scary, but God will guide. Three years before my husband felt called to his place of service, I felt moved during a missionary slide presentation. Later that night, I asked my husband if he felt like God was going to send us to a foreign country to serve Him. We were on staff at a church, busy serving Him. He said, "No." I thought, "Okay." Surely if God wants us somewhere, He'll direct through my husband. I didn't give it much more thought.

However, three years later God did call my husband. It happened during a revival service, and I was sitting with a few bus kids far from my husband. I did not know of his week-long struggle previous to this meeting. When the preacher opened his message with "Is It Well?" my husband knew God was tapping him, not one of his students, on the shoulder for missionary service. During the invitation, I was busy with the bus kids in the baptistery. I didn't have a clue that my husband was deciding our family's future and giving in to God's leading in his life. While standing at the brim of the baptismal tank, I heard Pastor say that someone had a testimony to share, and he called my husband's name! My husband tearfully announced to the congregation that God was leading our family into missionary work. I was stunned for a brief moment, and then God reminded me of my "feeling" a while back that He'd send us overseas.

I said, "Well, I guess it's now, Lord!" I can honestly say that I felt no fear or doubt. God had "warned" me three years prior to this, so that I wouldn't be shocked by the news—and faint into the water tank! It wasn't until an hour later that I learned our destination. I wasn't happy hearing that.

This dear missionary wife continued that although she was concerned about going into a country where AIDS, malaria, and other killer diseases were rampant, she knew that she could be content and happy because they were willing to go wherever God led them. She has been there for many years now, which leads to the next point.

Are You Willing to Stay?

I have had some people say to me, "Well, you've been in the Philippines so long now, it must feel like home to you." In a way that statement is true, but sometimes

I do not feel like I belong anywhere. Although I love our people very much, I also stick out like a sore thumb since I'm an American! But then, when I am in America, I feel like a fish out of water. I suppose all Christians should not feel "at home" until they get to Heaven.

When missionaries first go to a foreign field, it is often difficult for them to adjust. However, I believe it has been even more difficult for me in the last few years than it was when we first came. It was difficult for me when my son left for America to go to Bible college. I kept telling myself, "Be glad! Be glad he wants to go to Bible college and serve the Lord!" I know it will be hard for me next year when our daughter goes away to college. I have missionary friends who have grandchildren back in America, and they find it difficult not to be able to see their children and grandchildren as often as they would like.

One of the hardest times comes when we are so far from aging parents who are ill. I was in the Philippines when I received the call that my mother had passed away. I have experienced guilty feelings as a result. I have learned to turn them over to the Lord. My father had cancer, and I felt fortunate that I was able to be with him when he died; yet, I also had guilt feelings regarding my dad too. However, I am so thankful that both were saved. I have the blessed hope of seeing them again!

At this point, allow me to share the thoughts of another missionary wife.

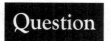

Are you willing to stay?

Answer:

Living and ministering in a foreign field is stressful. If a man also must face a discontented wife, an extra burden and stress is placed on him. A wife who cannot be satisfied in Christ alone will have trouble with adjustments and missing family and adapting to a culture. Our weak flesh will have struggles, but if we deny self and truly follow Christ, these issues should be minor ones. Ministering in a foreign culture is not for the immature Christian! If a couple is having marital problems, they are obviously not mature followers of Christ. Missionary work is not for the fainthearted!

A young wife may be excited about the big adventure of going off to a foreign country and being a missionary. Then, after she has been there for a while, she realizes it is not all that glorious after all. Sometimes it is just plain hard. Someday she may wake up and realize that those people are not thrilled that she has given up everything to bring them the Gospel. In fact, they don't even want her there.

What are you going to do when the going gets rough? Go home? That is why your relationship with the Lord and with your husband is so vital. You will not be able to stay on the field on your own power. You will need the Holy Spirit's power. You will need to give yourself to God daily. You will also need to make a commitment to Him. Did He quit on the way to Calvary? He could have, but He didn't. Why don't you promise Him that you won't be a quitter?

Let me just add here that even if you are not going to the foreign mission field, you need to learn to walk with God. You need to read your Bible, pray, go soul winning and do all those other important things, even if you stay in America. Is Jesus first in your life? Do you need to give some things up? Do you spend more time watching television than you do reading your Bible and praying? Do you love Him? Do you want to spend time with Him? The closer I get to the Lord, the more time I want to spend with Him. The more I read my Bible, the more I *want* to read my Bible. The more I pray, the more I *want* to pray. No matter how far you are in your Christian walk, you have not arrived! Once you think that, you're gone! Our daily walk needs constant care and tending, just like a garden.

If your heart is right with God, you will want to please Him. You will want to stay on the mission field, even though it is hard, because you love Him and want to please Him. Ask Him to help you stay for His sake and for the sake of a lost and dying world. John 14:13, 14 says, *"And whatsoever ye shall ask in my name, that will I do, that the Father may be glorified in the Son. If ye shall ask any thing in my name, I will do it."* Ask Him to help you to *want* to stay.

Not only do we need to be willing to go and be willing to stay, but we must have a heart for our husband's work for the Lord.

Do You Have a Heart for His Work?

I introduced this chapter with the story of William Carey, who went to India in 1793 and died there in 1834. Carey went from being a poor shoe cobbler to being known as the "Father of Modern Missions." Carey's sister said her brother was a "plodder." What she meant by that description was that no matter what happened, he would continue on doing God's work. In other words, he had perseverance and determination.

William Carey became the pastor of a small Baptist Church in Moulton, England. Although surrounded by extreme Calvinism in that day, Carey became burdened for the lost in other lands. He was convinced that God wanted people to go to these foreign lands and carry out the Great Commission. He met a lot of opposition with this "new" idea.

At a meeting with some other preachers, Carey preached a sermon entitled, "Expect Great Things from God; Attempt Great Things for God." Dr. James Ray, in his book *Incredible Journey in the Steps of Greatness*, said about this sermon:

"Little could anyone present know, including Carey himself, that he was about to change the world forever. His sermon would become famous as *William Carey's Deathless Sermon* because it initiated a movement that lives forever."[3]

The Baptist Missionary Society was started at this meeting, and Carey offered to go to India. Besides starting churches and schools and training preachers, Carey translated the Bible into Bengali, Sanskrit, and Marathi; and he translated the New Testament into other dialects as well, a total of 34 Indian languages!

It is incredible that William Carey was able to accomplish anything at all for God with his wife being such a hindrance. Author Ruth Tucker wrote the following about Carey's first wife:

> In 1807, at the age of fifty-one, Dorothy Carey died. Although Carey grieved Dorothy's death, it was probably a relief to him. She was a hindrance to the work. John Marshman wrote how Carey often worked on his translations "while an insane wife, frequently wrought up to a state of most distressing excitement, was in the next room."[4]

William Carey's second marriage was extremely happy—the exact opposite of his extremely sad first marriage:

> I am now called in Divine Providence to be a mourner again, having lately experienced the greatest domestic loss that a man can sustain. My dear wife was removed from me by death. She was eminently pious, and lived very near to God. The Bible was her daily delight, and next to God she lived only for me. Her solicitude for my happiness was incessant, and so certainly could she at all times interpret my looks, that any attempt to conceal anxiety or distress of mind would have been in vain. Nothing, however, but tenderness for each other's feelings could induce either of us for a minute to attempt a concealment of anything. It was her constant habit to compare every verse she read in the various German, French, Italian, and English versions, and never to pass by a difficulty until it was cleared up. In this respect she was of eminent use to me in the translation of the Word of God. She was full of compassion for the poor and needy. She entered most heartily into all the concerns of the mission, and into the support of schools, particularly those for female native children.[5]

It is obvious that Charlotte Carey, William's second wife, had a heart for her husband's work.

Chapter Six

Protecting Him

Many years ago a very wise pastor's wife told me, "There are two basic areas where your husband may fall—money or women. Or, if he doesn't fall, he will be accused of one of those two. That's why you should always have someone else in charge of the money. That's also why if you cannot be his secretary, find the ugliest woman you can to do it!"

My husband has always been very careful in both areas. Regarding ladies, he is never alone in our house with another girl or woman. Lots of missionaries use household help; and to be sure, they need to be very cautious. Our house is located on the same compound as our church, Christian school, Bible college, dorms, and staff houses. When my husband needs to talk to a lady staff (or any lady for that matter), he speaks to her out in the open, where everyone can see them.

Certainly I am not saying to be jealous and suspicious of him all of the time. For sure, that kind of negativity will kill any marriage. I am saying that a wife should always be careful. In I Peter 5:8, the Bible warns us that the Devil goes around like a hungry lion, seeking whom he may devour. The Bible also warns us in I Corinthians 10:12 that we are to take heed, lest we fall: *"Wherefore let him that thinketh he standeth take heed lest he fall."* If a wife becomes complacent, that is when she needs to look out the most. A wife must never get to the place that she thinks she is beyond sin. All we have to do is look at all the broken marriages—even among full-time Christian workers. But for the grace of God, there go you and I.

Here are more responses from missionary wives.

Question

Would you please share what you do to protect your husband?

Answers:

• We do live in a country where there are absolutely zero scruples. I do my best to be attractive at all times. If my husband must leave at four in the morning for one reason or another, I try to be presentable before he leaves so he remembers an attractive wife waiting for him at home. The same is true if he doesn't get home until one or two in the morning. I stay dressed and present-able like I was when we were courting. Obviously, you don't have the time to spend on yourself that you did while you were courting, and your husband ought to realize this; but he will appreciate a wife who tries to be attractive in spite of the lack of time. I enjoy leaving little notes on his pillow, by his com-puter, in his Bible, on the pulpit at church, etc. If a man feels completely loved and appreciated by his wife, he will be less likely to notice another woman. Of course, praying for him will help keep your relationship as it ought to be.

• I alone have the password to the Internet.

• My husband and I counsel women together. He never takes girls home alone from Sunday or youth activities. I dress nicely, and I am very romantic with him often.

Chapter Seven

Studying to Be a Good Wife

I Corinthians 11:9, "*Neither was the man created for the woman; but the woman for the man.*" I was not created to be a missionary. I was created to be Rick Martin's wife. If you have a husband, he is the one for whom you were created. You may play other roles. You may be a Christian schoolteacher or a church secretary, but that is not the primary reason why you were created. Is it wrong to be a Christian teacher or a church secretary? No, of course not, but we need to pray about the proper order of our priorities.

Sometimes we get so wrapped up in being a mother or fulfilling our other roles, which are usually good, that we neglect our first and most important job—the job for which God made us. I love Mrs. Beverly Hyles' book *Woman the Assembler,* and Dr. Jack Hyles' book *Woman the Completer.* I highly recommend that every wife read and study both. In fact, you should be reading all the time about being a better wife. Read books written by Mrs. Cindy Schaap, Mrs. Marlene Evans, Mrs. Judi Vest, Mrs. Frieda Cowling, Mrs. JoJo Moffitt, Mrs. JoBeth Hooker, and others. You can order these books through *Christian Womanhood,* 8400 Burr Street, Crown Point, Indiana.

Long ago I knew a lady who I thought was a wonderful missionary. She had so many talents and loved what she was doing, so I wanted to be like her. Then her marriage failed. She is now back in America, working at a secular job. That experience was a wake-up call for me.

You can be the best missionary in the world, but if your marriage fails, are you successful? I am not saying for you not to get involved in the ministry—as you'll read in the chapter, "Helping Him in His Work." I believe that is very important. But one day I looked around at all our staff, church people, and Bible students and thought, "None of these people can be Rick Martin's wife. None of these can be Ricky and Rachel's mother. I am the only one who can do that."

I came to the conclusion that if being Rick Martin's wife means that I have to give up a church activity once in a while, then I need to give it up. Pray for God to help you set the right priorities. Ask God to help you have balance. Are you doing too many church things and neglecting your family? Ask God for wisdom as you study to be a good wife. For me, I knew I needed God's help in setting my priorities in the proper order.

My first priority is God—my personal relationship with Him. That first priority does not include all of the running around we are prone to do in the name of God's Work, all the while neglecting our family in the process. On the other hand, some people avoid doing anything for God, using their family as an excuse. My personal relationship with God involves my quiet time in the morning when I read the Bible and pray.

My second priority is my husband, and following closely, my third priority—my children. I have *lots* of other jobs that I try my best to get done, but they have to fall in after these first three. I work in our Christian academy, and I spend a lot of time doing correspondence for my husband. We have soul winning, visitation, choir, and all of the other activities that other churches have, as well as a house, laundry, and meals to take care of. I just have to ask God to help me get the most important things done. I need His strength for the tasks and also His wisdom in setting priorities.

Be constantly studying and learning how to be a good wife. I am so thankful that my husband and I had excellent role models. Both of us had parents who had happy marriages.

Chapter Eight

Helping Him in His Work

As you read the title of this chapter, you possibly thought, "This is a contradiction of the previous chapter." Not at all! A wife needs to be a helpmeet to her husband. That means a wife needs to try her best to be what he wants her to be and to do what he wants her to do. I am not saying that a missionary's wife is to be his associate pastor, but I think it is especially important for a wife to help her husband when he is first starting out to build his work where the Lord has led him.

You, dear wife, may be all he has. He will need you. But even when his work is established, he will need you. He cannot very well get up in church and ask the ladies to go soul winning if you do not go soul winning. It looks funny if he asks ladies in the church to work in the nursery or in other capacities if you never help with anything.

I am not saying you have to do it all. I am not saying neglect your family and put church work first. Again, pray for wisdom. Pray for your husband to have wisdom as he asks for your help. Do not be so totally wrapped up in your family that you are neglecting what God wants you to do. Let your husband guide you in this area. I believe there is a fine line between too much or too little of either time for family or time for the Lord's work, and it is easy to cross that line. We have to see that our lives are balanced. In all honesty, this area is a continual struggle for me. When I sent out the survey forms, I received the following response from a missionary wife who wrote this personal note to me:

I have to tell you a story about your husband. I attended Hyles-Anderson College, and I attended one of Dr. Maurice Paulson's missions meetings where your husband was having a question/answer session. I asked him the question most on my mind, "What does your wife do on the mission field?"

I was prepared to hear a list of heroic deeds. I wanted to know what I would need to do—what to brace myself for. Well, your husband replied, "She's my wife." Huh? I felt kind of squashed! Later, I was annoyed. I was sure he was not giving me the whole story. But long ago I realized a missionary wife is a suc-cess if she's a good wife to a missionary—simple!

Now that I believe we have established that point, let's move on! In our situ-ation, my husband really needs me to be his secretary. It is hard on the foreign field to find someone who knows English well enough to do that job for him. That is probably the case with many missionaries. Add to that the fact that when you first arrive on the field, you don't know anyone trustworthy enough to be the secretary.

If your life is so totally involved in your children that you have no outside interests or activities, what are you going to do when they are grown and gone? You will be glad if you have developed some relationships with your people and have become involved in a ministry. If your life is so wrapped up in the children that you neglect your relationship with your husband, what will be left of your marriage when the children leave?

As I have already mentioned in an earlier chapter, when we were students at Hyles-Anderson College and attending First Baptist Church, I remember our pas-tor, Dr. Jack Hyles, preaching about Moses. Brother Hyles said that when Moses was called the meekest man on the face of the earth, it meant he was balanced and well-rounded. Numbers 12:3 says, "*(Now the man Moses was very meek, above all the men which were upon the face of the earth.)*" I have often thought on Brother Hyles' words because I want so much for my life to be balanced and well-rounded.

Jonathan Goforth was one of China's greatest missionaries. His wife Rosalind has written several books about their many experiences. In one instance, Rosalind had prayed that if God wanted her to marry, He would lead her to someone "whol-ly given up to Him and to His service."[1] She was a Christian and often played the organ for special meetings.

One night the group introduced her to Jonathan Goforth who was to preach at the meeting where she would be playing the organ. A few days later, just before Goforth was to preach, he laid his Bible on a chair and walked out. Rosalind picked up Goforth's worn Bible and glanced through it. She found it marked from cover to cover. She said to herself, "That is the man I would like to marry."[2] She said she looked beyond his shabby clothes and fell in love with a man who wanted to give his all for the Master.

In the book, *Goforth of China,* Rosalind recalls a few days after his marriage proposal, that Jonathan said, "Will you give me your promise that always you will allow me to put my Lord and His work first, even before you?"[3] Even as she said "Yes," she recalled that this was the kind of man for whom she had asked God. She continues:

A few days after my promise was given, the first test in keeping it came.

I had been (woman-like) indulging in dreams of the beautiful engagement ring that was soon to be mine. Then Jonathan came to me and said, "You will not mind, will you, if I do not get an engagement ring?" He then went on to tell with great enthusiasm of the distributing of books and pamphlets on China from his room in Knox. Every cent was needed for this important work. As I listened and watched his glowing face, the visions I had indulged in of the beautiful engagement ring vanished. This was my first lesson in real values.[4]

I am inclined to think that a lot of girls would have broken their engagement right then! But Rosalind Goforth was different. She was a woman truly dedicated to helping her husband—a man who had wholly given himself to God and to His service.

Chapter Nine

Submitting to Him

The secret to submitting is to die to self. Paul said in I Corinthians 15:31, "...I die daily." A marriage cannot have two bosses. That would be a two-headed monster! One has to be the leader, and the other has to be the follower. A wife has an important decision to make. She can decide that she is going to fight him every day for the rest of her life about this matter of submission, or she can decide that she is going to just die to self daily, and let him lead like God intended.

Let me illustrate. My daughter and I are terrified of the giant flying cockroaches we often find in our house in the Philippines. If Rick is around, we scream for him to come and kill it. If he's busy, we have to do it ourselves. One night Rachel was chasing a huge one with a broom. Unfortunately, she has a poor aim. She was knocking over lamps and kept beating everything but the poor cockroach which kept managing to escape. I am sure the neighbors thought the Martins were having a knock-down-drag-out fight! Finally, between screams, Rachel yelled at the cockroach, "JUST GET IT OVER WITH!"

What was she actually saying? She was telling him he was going to die, so he should quit ducking her broom and just lay down and die. Although I do not want to compare any wife to a cockroach, ladies, may I say the same thing Rachel said to the cockroach to you? "Just get it over with!" Just die to self. Just give in and submit. I can promise that God will bless you for your obedience.

I have had to submit to my husband regarding how I spend my time. I also had to submit to him in certain areas of child rearing. There have been times when we have disagreed about certain matters regarding our ministry. My husband is patient in hearing me out, and sometimes he will even agree with me. But when we do not, I need to give in to him and follow his wishes.

I have had to submit to my husband regarding finances. When we arrived in Iloilo City in September of 1977, we rented a small apartment. When I say "small," I mean 350-square feet. We went downtown and bought the cheapest (which happened to be the smallest) refrigerator we could find. I remember when one missionary wife first arrived and saw the appliances in the store, she laughed. She said,

"They're so tiny! They look like toys!"

We bought a two-burner stove; actually, it was more like a hot plate. We bought two plates, two spoons, two forks, two knives, two cups, and two towels. We bought a small pot in which to cook our rice and a skillet. We bought a teapot to boil our drinking water. We bought a bucket in which to take a bath and wash clothes. We bought a bed, a tiny table, and a cheap wood "couch" for the corner of our apartment we called a living room. We were then ready to set up housekeeping! I noticed every missionary we visited had large, nice homes. I did not understand why we had to be so different.

Within just a few days of arriving in Iloilo, we were out knocking on doors. I saw right away that compared to everyone we visited, we were "rich." No one we visited had a refrigerator or a stove. Most of the little bamboo shacks did not have any furniture. The occupants ate and slept on bamboo floors. Their extreme poverty was even shocking to a young couple who had been working on a bus route in a poor section of Chicago. One thought that struck me was that the people seemed content.

I remember at our first Bible study, one of the teenagers said, "Ma'am, you have a beautiful home." I was so touched by her words. I thought, "If she thinks *this* is beautiful, what would she think about our homes in America?" We lived so frugally because my husband had a plan. He was saving money to buy land and to build a church and a Bible college.

I'll be honest, submitting is not easy. That is why a wife needs to die to self—every day. My husband wrote in his book, *Missionary Relationships at Home,* "Probably the easiest way to hurt your husband's ministry, or ruin your marriage, is by not having a submissive spirit. A woman can be quiet and still not be submissive. Silent rebellion and open contention are both destructive."[1]

A wife must realize that she cannot control how her husband (or anyone for that matter) acts; a wife can only control how she reacts. Wife, stop thinking about what you think your husband should or should not be doing. Concentrate on what your part should be, and your part is to submit.

Chapter Ten

Building and Keeping a Strong Marriage

In the book, *The Missionary Wife and Her Work,* Joy Tuggy, the author, quotes Lora Parrott:

The only successful way to handle the obstacles in the road to a happy married life in the parsonage is to learn the technique of praying things through and talking things out. To harbor misunderstanding or to allow resentment to develop is a sure beginning of a breach. But to talk out the problem calmly, centering the discussion on the issue, rather than on the person, is an expression of adult emotional maturity. Real happiness in the parsonage does not come by ideal circumstances; it comes when two people, eager in God's service, have learned enough about each other to love in spite of shortcomings, in spite of unpleasant surroundings, in spite of long hard days.[1]

Dr. Russell Anderson, the co-founder of Hyles-Anderson College, is a very successful businessman. He told my husband that sometimes people become successful, and then they begin to fail. He said what they need to do is to figure out what they did to become successful and keep on doing it. A wife became "successful" when her husband fell in love with her and married her. If a wife feels that her marriage is starting to fail, she needs to look back and figure out what attracted her husband to her in the first place and start applying what attracted him in the first place.

I would like to put out my disclaimer right here and now: I am not an expert! I do love my husband though, and I believe he would agree with me when I say that we have a strong marriage. My intention is not to write a book about marriage. So many good books on the subject of marriage have already been written. My intention is to try to help missionary wives succeed on the field, and one of the chapters simply must be about marriage. It is so important to realize that if a missionary wife fails at marriage, she has failed as a missionary.

The following are just a few good ideas on marriage. In fact, you can probably think of several more to add to this list on your own:

- Focus on the positives rather than the negatives. Stop thinking about your husband's faults. Think about his good points.

- Don't be stubborn—apologize. Paul said in Ephesians 4:26: "...*let not the sun go down upon your wrath:*"

- Value and respect each other.

- Communicate—don't expect each other to be mind readers.

- Keep a good sense of humor. The Bible says in Proverbs 17:22, "A *merry heart doeth good like a medicine....*"

- Keep up your physical appearance.

- Be kind and polite. We are often polite to everyone else but not to our own spouse.

- Start and finish each day with a kiss and an "I love you."

- Remember to smile—a lot!

- Daily devotions are an absolute must. You have no doubt heard the saying, "The family that prays together, stays together."

- Go on dates. Living and working together 24/7 can make it feel like you are just roommates and co-workers. Family vacations are important, too.

- Do not let your marriage become boring and monotonous.

- Never criticize your husband.

- Don't take each other for granted. Do you appreciate him?

- Don't argue or quarrel about money, about kids, about in-laws, about "outlaws"—just don't fight about anything. Life is too short.

Chapter Eleven

Helping Him When He Is Down

Ecclesiastes 4:9, 10, *"Two are better than one; because they have a good reward for their labour. For if they fall, the one will lift up his fellow: but woe to him that is alone when he falleth; for he hath not another to help him up."*

Recently I read Dr. Jack Hyles' great book on *Meet the Holy Spirit*. I love the chapter on "Woman, the Holy Spirit of the Family,"which basically teaches about wives having the right attitude because they set the atmosphere for the home. I would like to share about a missionary wife who has had the right attitude.

Steve and Suzie Heidenreich lived about an hour from us for many years. They were (and still are) very dear friends of ours. Brother Steve bought land to build a church and a Bible college, but he also built Suzie a house so the money they were pouring into rent could be put into their work. As with most missionaries, money is always tight. For a long time, Suzie secretly saved and "squirreled away" a little money here and a little money there. She was saving to buy tiles for the rough cement floor in her house.

One day Brother Steve had a financial crisis in his ministry. When Suzie found out about it, she quietly went to her hiding place, took out several thousand pesos, and handed them to her husband. Brother Steve has testified, "She saved my ministry." Suzie was willing to sacrifice her desires to help her husband when he was down.

When my daughter Rachel and I were visiting First Baptist Church of Hammond, Indiana, in June of 2003, we stopped by to visit the Heidenreichs in their home. I asked their permission to use the above illustration in my book, and they graciously agreed. Brother Heidenreich added, "That wasn't the only time Suzie did that. She did it many times."

It may not be finances causing your husband to be down. It may be he is just discouraged about another area in his ministry. Perhaps the people are not responsive, and the work is not growing like he had hoped. It may be that your husband is carrying the burdens of several church members. He may be constantly dealing with problems. Be aware that the more your church grows, the more problems there will be.

Brother Hyles said, "You are the mood-determiner, the atmosphere-determiner, the Holy Spirit of the family."[1] Wife, comfort your husband and help him get back up.

Having Family Time

Ibelieve the common complaint of many who have husbands in the ministry is that he is too busy. He doesn't spend enough time with you and the children. Do you make it so that he *wants* to spend time with you? When he *does* spend time with you, do you gripe and complain about all the time that he does *not* spend with you? If so, then I don't blame him for staying away from you as much as possible! Why don't you just enjoy the time he spends with you, instead of wasting it arguing about the time he doesn't spend with you? Do you nag him all the time, making statements like, "Why don't you spend time with the kids?" Do you realize your kids will pick up on that discontent? They will grow up resenting their father, the ministry, and they might resent you, too!

When your husband comes home to you and the children, he should be coming home to a haven. The atmosphere should be such that he cannot wait to get home. If he walks in the door with all the cares and burdens of the day on his back, he doesn't need his wife and kids to dump more on him.

Pray about your attitude. God wants us to be joyful. People like to be around joyful people. People don't want to hang around with a grouch. Pray about his spending time with his family. Go soul winning and on visitation with him. Have the children go soul winning and on visitation with him. Doing so will build a bond between you and him, as well as between your children and him.

It is important to plan dates. If you happen to be married to a workaholic like I am, this is easier said than done! Planning is definitely the key because we just get too busy. A "Family Day" once a week, or a "Date Night" is a good idea. Save and plan for family vacations. Families need to get away from work, friends, school, television, and other outside influences, just to spend time together. My father-in-law, Dr. Russell Martin, a busy preacher with six children, always said, "Precious memories must be arranged for in advance."

Dr. Jim Vineyard publishes an excellent missionary paper called *Fundamental Baptist World Missions*. In it, Dr. Joe Finn edits a column entitled, "An Interview with a Missionary." One question he always asks is, "What special thing do you do with your family to help the stability of your home?" May I share a few of those edited responses here? (Some of these responses were written by the husband.)

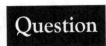 **Question** What special thing do you do with your family to help the stability of your home?

Answers:

- We have family day on Mondays; we spend the whole day together as a family. We may drive a couple of hours to see another missionary family to spend the day with them. We may drive to another city where there is a nice park and take the children, or we might just get pizza. We also feel that family devotions each night are important, reading the Word of God and praying.[1]
- We pick a day that we take off and spend together as a family. We might go and do anything—have a picnic or go to the beach, take off our shoes, and walk on the beach.[2]
- We have Mondays where we just spend time together as a family. Sometimes we just go looking around. We will go to McDonald's in the city. We have time to spend together as a family because, during the week, we are so busy with the ministry. It is important to have the time together.[3]
- My husband saves up money so we can go on vacations.[4]
- She likes to shop; so sometimes I take her shopping, or just go out and look—if it's nothing else but to go for a walk.[5]

Question How do you balance time for husband/children/ministry?

Answers:

- For me these are all intertwined. If my relationship with my husband is what it ought to be, the other things sort of fall into place.
- We have no children, but my husband only wants me doing so much for the ministry. He doesn't overload me even though we are a new church, so I have plenty of time for my husband anytime he needs me.

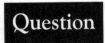 **Question** What was your hardest adjustment when you arrived on the field?

Answer:

Not being able to have a weekly date with my husband was hard. We are learning how to spend time together in other ways, like put the children to bed early and then order pizza and talk.

I have many fond memories of my childhood, and I want my children to have the same kind of memories. Don't neglect to plan your family time.

Seeking Advice

Be humble enough, and wise enough, to seek advice. Proverbs 24:6 says, *"…in multitude of counsellors there is safety."*

On the questionnaire, we also asked for advice for new missionary wives. Of course, most of this advice can be easily applied to any wife who seeks to please the Lord.

 Question Would you like to give some advice to prospective missionary wives?

Answers:

- I would tell a future missionary wife to be completely for her husband, for what he is doing, and to be totally devoted to the Lord. If those goals are in order, then any difficulty can be overcome more easily.

- Even though you are a missionary, you are first a wife and secondly a mother. Those are your priorities. You cannot fill all the roles within the ministry that might need workers. Do what you can and what the Lord leads you to do, but do not feel guilty about giving your family priority. Do not feel guilty about what you cannot do. Also, do not let your work for the Lord crowd out your personal time with the Lord.

- Keep your eyes on the Lord. Lift up your husband. Learn to pray and have a consistent time with the Lord no matter what the distractions are. I found that on the mission field I was only busier. I had to work harder on my time with the Lord. Get out to the people God has sent you to. I know many missionary wives who hold the church people at such a great distance. I have heard them say that the husband is the missionary, not the wife. If I am one with my husband, then I am also supposed to love those people. I cannot imagine loving my husband and then not loving the people that he loves.

- My advice to a future missionary wife would include, of course, to be working all the time on being a good wife—read and study about it, take all the classes you can on the subject, listen to preaching and preaching tapes. Pray a lot about your marriage and for your husband. The mission field is different. You have to not only have a strong marriage, you have to have a concrete relationship because Satan fights even harder than normal. You may not have access to all the great preaching and encouragement one day like you did at Bible college—it is very desolate and lonely. You have to have a very strong foundation. If you have marriage problems at all, you shouldn't even consider going to the foreign field. It is only harder there.

• My advice would be to expect the unexpected. Then you won't be as disappointed when you get there. That advice sounds negative, but I have met other missionary wives who almost lived in a fantasy world about what it was going to be like on the field. They were too shocked when they actually went, and they are no longer on the field. Another thing that helped me a lot when we came to the mission field was to force myself to realize that this was now my home—like it or not. I would have to find a way to like it unless I planned to be unhappy for the rest of my life. Think of it for life. Do not live for furlough. If you do, then you will only be happy for a very small portion of your life—the short times you are on furlough. You have to make the field HOME...

• Another very important thing I have learned here is how unwise it is to compare your ministry with others' ministries. That goes on so much on the mission field. Also, don't try to push your husband to start or do things; he will do what he can and in his time. I used to see other missionaries starting this and doing that, and I would suggest, "Why don't we start that too?" My husband would say that he wouldn't start something unless he knew he could continue it and do it right. Many of those other missionaries who were starting all kinds of stuff are all gone now—off the field. Some have serious family problems. Your husband knows what he is doing. Just help him out in what he needs and don't make suggestions all the time. He will start to feel like you are putting pressure on him. He needs a place of "no pressure" with you. He will get pressure and stress from every other direction on the field. Try to always provide him with a place to relax and be himself.

• Keep your relationship sweet and fun, too. Read lots of good books and articles. Do what you need to do in order to stay on the field. If you need to eat out every week, and it is possible—do it! If you need to take a day off every few months—take it! If you need to take a nap, read a good book, bake something special, call a friend, write a letter, go for a walk, whatever you feel you need to do in order to stay sane—you better do it, or you will not stay on the field. Don't try to live without any comforts and luxuries just because you are a missionary. Your supporters wouldn't want you to have to do that (if they are sane anyhow!)

• Realize no one will ever completely understand you or your life on the field. The only way that they could is for them to live it. People will make all kinds of comments and give all sorts of opinions, but take it all with a grain of salt. A man once said to me when we were back on furlough, "I don't see why missionaries waste all that money to come back to the States for furlough when they could just stay on the field and work." I wanted to retort, "Go and do it then!" I didn't—but you can understand what I am saying. They really can't understand, so don't expect them to. Just remember the Lord knows, and you are working for Him and no one else.

Do not be afraid to ask questions. If you are fortunate enough to take a survey trip (I was not), ask all the missionary wives all the questions you can. Seek their advice.

Conclusion

What happened to Maria Taylor? Besides being a wonderful wife, her children grew up to serve God. She also helped her husband found the China Inland Mission. Author Ruth Tucker credits Maria Taylor with this statement: "In [Hudson Taylor's] own lifetime the missionary force under him totaled more than eight hundred. Maria was indispensable in setting the plan in motion."[1] However, they were only married for 12 short years. After Maria gave birth to her fifth son, she became very ill. The baby died one week later. Dr. and Mrs. Howard Taylor describe the scene:

"Though excessively prostrate in body," Taylor wrote, "the deep peace of soul, the realization of the Lord's own presence, and the joy in His holy will with which she was filled, and in which I was permitted to share, I can find no words to describe." She herself chose the hymns to be sung at the little grave.

Weak as she was, however, it had not yet occurred to them that for her too the end was near. The deep mutual love that bound their hearts in one seemed to preclude the thought of separation. She was only thirty-three. There was no pain up to the very last, though she was weary, very weary. At daybreak on Saturday, July 23rd, she was sleeping quietly, and Taylor left her for a few moments. She awoke, and serious symptoms called him to her side.

"By this time it was dawn, and the sunlight revealed what the candle had hidden—the deathlike hue of her countenance. Even my love could no longer deny, not her danger, but that she was actually dying. As soon as I was sufficiently composed, I said: 'My darling, do you know that you are dying?' "

"Dying!" she replied. "Do you think so? What makes you think so?"

I said, "I can see it, darling. Your strength is giving way."

"Can it be so? I feel no pain, only weariness."

"Yes, you are going Home. You will soon be with Jesus."

My precious wife thought of my being left alone at a time of so much trial, with no companion like herself, with whom I had been wont to bring every difficulty to the Throne of Grace.

"I am so sorry," she said, and paused as if half correcting herself for the feeling.

"You are not sorry to go to be with Jesus?"

Never shall I forget the look with which she answered, "Oh, no! It is not that. You know, darling, that for ten years past there has not been a cloud between me and my Saviour. I cannot be sorry to go to Him; but it does grieve me to leave you alone at such a time. Yet, He will be with you and meet all your need."

"I never witnessed such a scene," wrote one who was present. "As dear Mrs. Taylor was breathing her last, Mr. Taylor knelt down—his heart so full— and committed her to the Lord; thanking Him for having given her, and for the twelve and a half years of happiness they had had together; thanking Him, too, for taking her to His own blessed presence, and solemnly dedicating himself anew to His service."[2]

In closing this unit on the husband, let us as wives rededicate ourselves to fulfilling God's will for our lives by being the right kind of wife. You will please God by following His plan. When you follow God's plan for your life, you will find peace and joy in the center of God's will.

Help your husband be all God wants him to be.

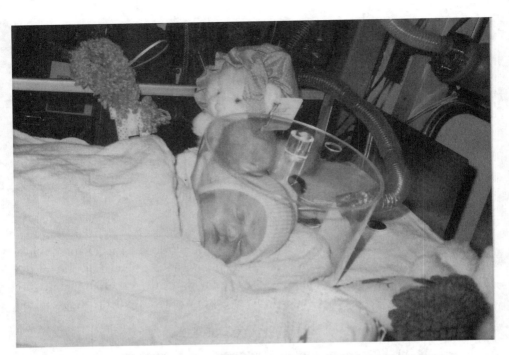

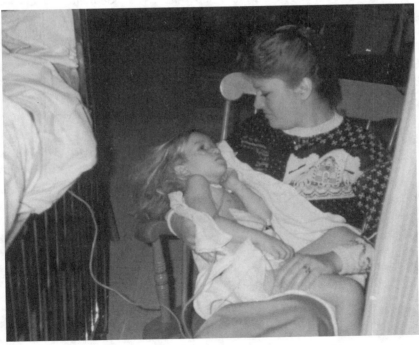

Above: Rachel is 18 days old in this photo. The story of the first 17 days of her life is given in the unit on Medical Concerns.

Below: The first time I was allowed to hold Rachel (age 3½) after her third heart surgery.

UNIT FOUR
Your Children

"Lo, children are an heritage of the LORD."
(Psalm 127:3)

Introduction

Mary Smith met Robert Moffat because her father hired him to be his gardener. When the two 19 year olds fell in love, Robert had already surrendered to be a missionary in Africa. Mary's parents, although excited about young Robert's going to Africa to be a missionary, absolutely refused to let their delicate only daughter join him, so Robert went alone in 1816. Robert faithfully waited three long years, in spite of the fact that Mary unselfishly begged him to marry another girl who would be able to go to Africa with him. Mary kept praying, and finally her parents relented. She left for Africa at the age of 24.

At that time, the colonists and the government were prejudiced against missionaries, so evangelizing was painfully slow. Robert could understand the reasons for the prejudice—many of the missionaries simply could not get along with each other. Sad to say, he even saw some immorality among the missionaries. After many delays, Moffat and some others were granted permission to enter Namaqualand, located hundreds of miles north of Capetown.

In December of 1819, Mary finally arrived from England. Three weeks later Robert and Mary were married. They enjoyed a happy marriage for 53 years.

After the wedding, Robert and Mary traveled 600 miles by oxcart to Kuruman. Needless to say, this was a very difficult journey. In the book *Dauntless Women*, author Winifred Mathews tells of Mary's thoughts regarding the journey by oxcart:

In later years, especially when she traveled with her young children, she found life in the wagon somewhat irksome. "The length of our day stages," she writes, "is about eight or twelve hours on an average, riding about three and a half miles an hour. When we span out [or unyoke] a fire is immediately made, the kettle set on and coffee or tea made. Having thus refreshed ourselves, we have worship with our people round the fire. In every place the wolf pays us a visit and the lion is on the prowl. I shall by no means attempt to prove that it is a remarkably pleasant life, for we are always heartily tired by the time the journey is done...."[1]

At first, the government would not grant permission for the Moffats to settle in Kuruman, so they went to Griqua Town. This is where Mary, the future wife of David Livingstone, was born. The Moffats also adopted abandoned African children, whom they rescued from being buried alive. When permission was finally granted to settle in Kuruman, the Moffats lived there for 47 years! In *From Jerusalem to Irian Jaya*, Tucker says:

> The Moffats' early years in Kuruman were filled with hardships. They lived in primitive conditions, their first home being a mud hut, with the kitchen separate from the house. Although Mary was not used to doing heavy domestic work, she adapted to African life remarkably well. She washed clothes by hand in the river and cooked on an open fireplace. She soon overcame her aversion to cleaning the floors with cow dung and even recommended it."[2]

The growth at Kuruman was slow. Tucker relates: "Mary, particularly, was inclined to periods of despondency: 'Could we but see the smallest fruit, we could rejoice midst the privations and toils which we bear; but as it is, our hands do often hang down."[3] After 10 years, the Moffats began to see the fruit of their labor. People started getting saved and lives were being changed! They opened a school. Mary showed the women how to bathe their babies and how to take care of them when they were sick. She taught them how to keep their children healthy and explained about the importance of discipline. Even more effective than her motherly lectures was the consistent example she displayed in rearing her own children.

In 1830 Mary took her three oldest children, Mary, Ann, and Robert, to a Wesleyan school near Grahamstown. As her children grew older, she feared the viciousness of the pagan environment. When Mary turned 14, her mother decided to take her, Ann, and Robert to the Cape to school. In 1835 Mary took her three youngest children with her by wagon to Grahamstown, to pick up the oldest three. She then set out with the six children to Port Elizabeth. She put the oldest three on the boat for a dangerous, 11-day trip to the Cape. Then she turned around, with the three youngest, and returned to Kuruman. This journey, taken without her husband, took her seven months! In fact, Mary made a total of five trips from Kuruman to the Cape, more than 6,000 miles, without her husband— via African oxcart, at the rate of 15 miles a day.

It took Moffat 29 years to translate the Bible into the language of the Bechuanas. In 1838 a large stone church was built which reportedly still stands today. This was also the year that the Moffats, with their three daughters and three sons, sailed to England for their only furlough. One reason for the trip was to have his New Testament printed. Another reason for going was their grievous health conditions. While on board the ship, Mary gave birth to another daughter. Tragically, their six-year-old son died during the voyage. The book, *The Moffats*, records the following story:

> Mrs. Moffat, who lay helpless in her berth, perceived that Jim, the six-year-old boy, was in serious plight. He had not fully recovered from measles, contracted in Cape Town, and another disease, more critical, had followed in its train. No one was able to nurse the sick boy, for seasickness had prostrated nearly everyone on board. In her extremity, Mrs. Moffat asked to have the child laid by her side, and there, while the wind howled and the ship tossed, the little fellow lay upon his mother's arm talking contentedly of the angels who should bear the souls of children to their heavenly home. "Oh, that will be joyful," babbled the childish lips, while his eyes closed dreamily, and he slipped away to join the children at play in the Father's house.[4]

Upon arriving in England, Moffat was in great demand as a speaker, but Mary stayed home with her two young daughters, born since leaving South Africa. Robert and Mary sailed again for Africa in 1843, taking Mary and Ann, the two eldest, and Jack, Elizabeth, and Jane, the three youngest, with them. The two middle children, Robert and Helen, ages 16 and 14, were left behind to attend school in England. Little did they know it would be 27 years before Helen would see her parents again!

On this journey back to Kuruman, the Moffats' daughter Mary and David Livingstone fell in love. Livingstone, one of Moffats' recruits, had gone to Africa ahead of the Moffats. Livingstone was born in Scotland, just like his father-in-law. He wanted to go to China, but God used the Opium War to send him to Africa instead. Tucker relates:

> Livingstone had been introduced to the striking, six-foot-tall veteran missionary to Africa, Robert Moffat. Moffat had a profound influence over the eager missionary candidate and tantalized him with the thrilling opportunities for evangelism beyond Kuruman in "the vast plain to the north" where he had "sometimes seen, in the morning sun, the smoke of a thousand villages, where no missionary had ever been."[5]

David Livingstone sailed to Africa in 1840 at the age of 27. Four years later, he went to Kuruman to court Mary, the Moffats' oldest daughter, who was now 23 years old. Livingstone's arm had been mauled by a lion, and no doubt he needed and enjoyed the care shown to him by the Moffats. He soon proposed to Mary. In the book *Livingstone* are the following remarks:

There never was a happier match. Livingstone and his wife were devoted to each other to an extent that the world never knew in the lifetime of either, and in remembering the heroic services of the one, the patient self-abnegation of the other should never be forgotten. They shared one another's ideals and partook of one another's confidence as fully as any happily married couple could desire.[6]

I am sure that Mary Livingstone found an excellent role model as a wife in her mother, Mary Moffat. More mothers should stop to think that their daughters will probably copy them as wives and mothers. That is a sobering thought. The Moffats also instilled other good traits in their children. *Dauntless Women* states:

Mary Moffat said of her daughter Mary that she was less openly pious than the other members of the family, but that she was a very practical Christian. "Accept me, Lord, as I am and make me such as thou wouldst have me to be," was the private prayer that her husband found among her papers after her death.[7]

A quote from the book *Livingstone* reveals how fitted Mary Moffatt and David Livingstone were for one another. "Brave, humble, quiet, sensible, unpretentious, hard-working, ever more ready with service than speech, a worthy mate for David Livingstone was Robert Moffat's eldest daughter."[8] In the book, *From Jerusalem to Irian Jaya*, the author discloses facts about the first ten years of their lives:

The wedding took place at Kuruman in January of 1845 and in March the Livingstones left for Mabosta. Later that year, after delivering his first child, Livingstone pulled up roots and moved his family to Chonwane, forty miles north. The time at Chonwane was a happy one for the Livingstones. In the summer of 1847, after their second child was born, the Livingstones moved into their third home. For seven years, the Livingstones lived a semi-nomadic life in Africa. Sometimes Mary and the children stayed home alone, while at other times she brought the children and accompanied her wandering husband. Neither situation was satisfactory. On one occasion when Livingstone was away from Chonwane for an extended period of time he wrote: "Mary feels her situation among the ruins a little dreary and no wonder, for she writes me that the lions are resuming possession and walk around our house at night."[9]

In 1846, between the birth of Robert and of the Livingstones' second child Agnes, Mrs. Moffat, along with her three youngest children, visited the Livingstones. The journey took three weeks by oxcart. Mrs. Moffat, of all people, knew from experience what loneliness and hardships her daughter must have been going through. *Dauntless Women* records:

It was plain to Mary Moffat that David and her daughter were very much in love. Indeed, with her more rigid upbringing, she sometimes wondered whether, in their joy in each other's company, they were not almost too playful and merry for missionaries. She assured herself that, except in the intimacy of family life, they were both extremely quiet and reserved.[10]

In 1850, David, Mary, and the three children, Robert, Agnes, and Thomas, set out on yet another journey, much of it through desert where they suffered from lack of water, among other necessities. *Dauntless Women* gives this insight into their deprivations:

They suffered from lack of meat; sympathetic Africans often brought the children a kind of large caterpillar, which they relished, and a very large frog, which looked like chicken when it was cooked. A dish of locusts, too, was quite a treat.[11]

When the people saw that Mary and the children traveled with Livingstone, they were no longer fearful. While the Livingstones were traveling, their fourth child, Elizabeth, was born, but she died six weeks later. Mary became very ill, suffering from paralysis. David took her to Kuruman, where her mother nursed her back to health. Later Mary Moffat wrote a strong letter of protest to her son-in-law, when she learned that David was planning to make another trip with Mary (who was again expecting) and the children. They left before the letter reached them, and their fifth child, William Oswell, was born during the expedition in 1851. The author of *Dauntless Women* writes:

His strongest advocate was Mary's love for her fearless, almost frighteningly determined husband. She longed above everything else to be with him and she shared his sense of a divine mission. He upheld her by his strong, simple faith in the overarching providence of God; and the utter confidence with which she put her life and the lives of their children in his care nerved him to fresh endeavor.[12]

When Livingstone mentioned his reluctance to Mary, of leaving her and the children while he traveled, she told him she knew why he was doing it and that her wish to spread the Gospel was no less than his; after all, she was the child of missionaries. In 1852, after many long talks and a season of prayer, Livingstone sent his wife and four children to England. They would not see each other for four and a half years. *Dauntless Women* records a letter he sent:

> How I miss you now, and the dear children. I never show all my feelings, but I can truly say, my dearest, that I loved you when I married you, and the longer I lived with you I loved you the better. Take the children round you and kiss them for me. Tell them I have left them for the love of Jesus, and they must love Him too.[13]

In *Livingstone*, the author shares the following about Mary Livingstone:

> Mrs. Livingstone's character was one of simple goodness and benevolence conjoined to a reticence in regard to her own personal feelings and beliefs unusual in evangelical circles in the middle of the nineteenth century. She was to endure much suffering and some slander during the period of necessary separation from her husband, which had to be borne while he was fighting his way across unknown Africa. Evil tongues whispered that they could not get on together.[14]

Dauntless Women paints a picture of the Livingstones. "That Christmas of 1856 was a merry one for Mary and the children. David [was] now a famous man, but he was still his wife's lover and the children thought him the best playfellow and story-teller in the world."[15] In the book *Livingstone* the author adds the following:

> One of Livingstone's profoundest regrets in later life, as we learn from a confession written by him in 1870, was that he had not devoted more time to playing with his children when he had them with him up to 1851; he never had the same opportunity again, though his delight in their society while in England in 1857 was observed and sympathetically commented upon by Sir J. Risdon Bennett and Mr. Frederick Fitch, with both of whom the Livingstone family stayed for a time. Says the former: "It was beautiful to observe how thoroughly he enjoyed domestic life and the society of children, how strong was his attachment to his own family after his long and frequent separations from them, and how entirely he had retained his simplicity of character." The latter remarks on the unity of spirit that characterized the parents. "Dr. and Mrs. Livingstone were much attached, and thoroughly understood each other. The Doctor was sportive and fond of a joke, and Mrs. Livingstone entered into his humour."[16]

In 1858, Mary went back to Africa leaving Robert, Agnes, and Thomas in England for, like her parents before her, she was afraid of the effect the heathen

African society might have on her children. Only six-year-old Oswell accompanied his parents. When they reached the Cape, Mary's father, Robert Moffat, met them. Moffat took his daughter to Kuruman, for she was pregnant and suffering from fever. Livingstone, on another expedition, did not hear of the birth of his daughter, Anna Mary, for a year.

Mary again returned to England. Unfortunately, bitter slander was being spread about their "separation." After four years in England, Mary returned to Africa again. Three short months after arriving in Africa, on April 27, 1862, Mary died. In the book, *The Moffats*, the author expresses the following:

> In the fever-stricken territory of the Zambezi, another missionary fought the hardest battle of his whole embattled life. There in the village of Shupanga, David Livingstone struggled with wild grief, for Mary, his beloved wife, lay dying. Beside her rude bed, made of boxes but covered with a soft mattress, watched "the man who had faced so many deaths and braved so many dangers, but who was now utterly broken down and weeping like a child." From the hour of Mary's death those blue-gray eyes which never showed fear carried a grief which time could not efface.[16]

David wrote in his journal, "O my Mary, how often we have longed for a quiet home since you and I were cast adrift at Kolobeng. She purposed to do more for me than ever. The loss of my dear Mary lies like a heavy weight on my heart...For the first time in my life I feel willing to die."[18]

In the book *Livingstone*, the following passage sheds light on Livingstone's feelings: "I wept over her who well deserved many tears. God pity the poor children, who were all tenderly attached to her, and I am left alone in the world by one whom I felt to be a part of myself."[19]

Dauntless Women declares, "Mary was not the victim of his selfishness," as some hotly declared, "but the partner of his enterprise, as much during the periods of separation when her part was confined to waiting and praying as when she was by his side, cheering him with her counsel, her companionship."[20]

Not only was Mary's death extremely hard on her husband and children, but her parents back in Kuruman also suffered greatly. The book, *From Jerusalem to Irian Jaya*, comments on the Moffatts' last years:

> After fifty-three years in Africa with only one furlough (1839-1843), the Moffats were ready to retire. They had suffered some severe tragedies, particularly the deaths of their two oldest children within the space of a few months in 1862, but the work was moving forward. There were several native pastors active in the work, and their son John [with his wife Emily],

who had joined them at Kuruman, was prepared to take over the mission. It was a sad departure from Kuruman and perhaps an unfortunate mistake. Kuruman was the only home they had known for half a century, and readjustments back in England proved difficult, particularly for Mary, who died only months after their return. Moffat lived on another thirteen years, during which time he became a noted missionary statesman, traveling throughout the British Isles challenging adults and youth alike with the tremendous needs of Africa.[21]

The book, *Dauntless Women*, records the loss Robert Moffat felt when his wife died: "For fifty-three years I have had her to pray for me."[22] Meanwhile, Livingstone continued on in Africa: "The more [Livingstone] encountered the inhumane slave traffic of the Portuguese and the Arabs, the more convinced he became that only the combination of 'Commerce and Christianity' could save Africa."[23]

Years passed, and Livingstone grew older and sicker as he kept up his relentless pace: "As time passed, the Africans became used to the bearded, toothless, haggard old man who often spoke to them of his Saviour."[24]

On May 1, 1873, Susi and Chuma, Livingstone's African helpers, found him dead, kneeling beside his cot. To show their respect and love for the old man, they decided to deliver his body and personal papers to other white men on the coast. After burying his heart under a tree, they dried Livingstone's body in the hot African sun until it was mummified. They then proceeded to carry their precious burden 1,500 miles. The journey took them eight months. Livingstone was given a state funeral at Westminster Abbey, attended by dignitaries. The book *From Jerusalem to Irian Jaya* states:

It was a day of mourning for his children, who came to say good-by to the father they had never really known; but it was a particularly sad hour for the seventy-eight year old Robert Moffat, who slowly walked down the aisle in front of the casket bearing the man who decades before in that same city had caught a vision of "a thousand villages, where no missionary had ever been."[25]

The Moffats had ten children, though only seven survived to adulthood. Of those, five became actively involved in African missions, and that is the reason I have chosen to write about them. My husband and I have always felt that the mission field is a great place to rear kids. Oh, I suppose I'm going to get in trouble for using the word "kids," but it is truly spoken in love! In the next few pages, we will address rearing children on the mission field. The chapters are divided by the survey questions asked and answered by missionary wives.

$\mathcal{K}ids$ and the $\mathcal{M}inistry$

Question	How do you make sure your kids are loved and not neglected in the busyness of the ministry?

Answer:

This is an area where home schooling comes in handy. We spend a good portion of the day teaching and giving one-on-one attention. In many cases, the father puts so much of himself into the ministry that he neglects his family. My husband puts a lot of himself into the ministry, but not at the neglect of the children. He involves at least one of them wherever he goes.

In the book, *The Missionary Wife and Her Work*, author Joy Tuggy shares this view from a missionary daughter:

Parents shouldn't get so involved in their work that the children get the feeling that they kind of have to take care of themselves and solve their own problems. I don't know what I would have done had I not had parents to whom I could go when I wanted to and who had not been genuinely interested in me.[1]

Our friend, Pastor S. M. Davis of the Park Meadows Baptist Church in Lincoln, Illinois, once remarked that he often sees a pastor or full-time Christian worker make a mistake with their children that lay people usually do not make. That mistake is that the "problems" of their people are put before the "problems" of their own children. We certainly want to help the people in our church when they need our help, but we must be careful not to put our children's needs on the back burner because other people always come first. I am not talking about emergencies; rather, I am referring to the day-in, day-out complications of life.

Brother Davis also said he doesn't believe we lose our kids from being overprotective; rather, we lose them from being harsh, critical, and inconsistent. If a child becomes rebellious, parents tend to become angry and draw away from them when they should be drawing closer. That doesn't mean not to discipline them, but we should never be angry. The Bible says in Ephesians 6:4, "*And, ye fathers, provoke not your children to wrath: but bring them up in the nurture and admonition of the Lord.*" Use praise instead of insults. Don't compare them with others—accept them and forgive them. That doesn't mean that we should trust them, however! Help them choose their friends very carefully, and do not let them spend too much unsupervised time with friends. The Bible says in Proverbs 13:20, "*He that walketh with wise men shall be wise: but a companion of fools shall be destroyed.*"

Can you listen to your child without jumping all over what he says? Children should always feel comfortable about talking to you about anything. If you pounce all over everything they say, they will quit talking to you and go find someone else with whom they can talk. Always correct in love.

In my husband's book, *Missionary Relationships at Home,* he included a chapter entitled, "A Missionary's Relationship with His Children." He wrote the following statement: "Missionary kids do not grow up to serve God simply because their parents are good missionaries."[2] This statement seems obvious, but sometimes we parents act as though we don't believe it by the way we rear our children! Proverbs 22:6 says, "*Train up a child in the way he should go: and when he is old, he will not depart from it.*" The key word in that verse is "train." Are we really training our children? Training involves both teaching and discipline.

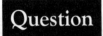 **Question**

How did you get your kids involved in the ministry?

Answers:

• Get your kids involved with the ministry and make life fun for them. Don't always be talking about America and how nice it would be to live there. You have to make a home on the field. Do all the things you would if you lived in the States—bake Christmas cookies, try to buy a turkey to cook on Thanksgiving, go to the zoo, and go on picnics. They will love the mission field if you do.

• Every time my husband goes out soul winning, he takes one of the children with him. On the first Saturday of every month, we all go to pass out tracts. At this point none of our children are old enough to lead singing, teach Sunday school, etc.

• When they were older, they started going soul winning. They always invited their friends to church.

• Our kids are involved in every aspect of our ministry. They are all soul winners, nursery workers, and ushers. They help clean the bus and the church. When our kids pray, they pray for the needs of the people. They don't pray for things they want. I think they are special people, but I must admit that I'm a little biased! When we first came to the field, we met some MKs who were what I call "proud Americans." They made little effort to mix with the nationals. My husband was quick to teach our kids that God has blessed America, but God loves all people. If we are going to minister to people on the mission field, we cannot be proud, snobbish, or condescending.

Dr. Bob Hooker, one of the staff members at Hyles-Anderson College, wrote an article for *Christian Womanhood* detailing how his six daughters were involved in the sailor ministry at the First Baptist Church of Hammond, Indiana. He stressed how important he thought it was for his children to be involved in a ministry where they could see lives being changed. I agree wholeheartedly! My son Ricky helped me on my children's route when he was small. When he left for college, Rachel became my partner. One Saturday we were walking home after visitation, and we were commenting to each other about the different families. She has seen the heartbreak of alcohol and families without Christ. She has seen lazy parents who sit around and don't work and provide for their families. At the same time, she has also seen lives changed.

Chapter Two

Teenagers

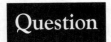 Would you please share how you handle your teenagers—boy/girl friends, and just helping them choose good friends in general?

Answer:

We told them it wasn't necessary to have a girlfriend/boyfriend until they went to college. We told them that is where they would find their future mate. We just never had a problem with that.

The younger your children are when you take them to the field, the easier adjusting will be. The older they are, the more difficult it will be. Teenagers may even be upset at their parents (or God) for taking them away from their friends. If you have basically done the "right things" in rearing your children up to their teenage years, it won't be as difficult. That thought leads me to—what are the "right things"?

Pastor S. M. Davis says, first and foremost, to have your child's heart. This is easy and natural when the child is young. As the child grows older however, he is more influenced by his peers. This is the main reason why parents need to help their child choose the right kind of friends. The wrong friends will take a child's heart away from his parents and away from God. Peer pressure is awesome. Teenagers do not want to be different. They want to blend in and to be like their friends.

I love what Mrs. Jack Schaap, the senior editor of *Christian Womanhood*, teaches. She always pointed her children to her husband. She always deferred to him and upheld him in her children's eyes. She never criticized him. Why? If you do, your children will have no desire to listen to their dad or go to him for advice when they become older.

What about dating? Some missionary parents do not wish for their children to date the nationals, for various reasons. One particular reason is that they may believe the national does not love their child for who he is—but simply because he is an American—even among Christians. Some nationals may think that dating and then marrying an American is a golden opportunity for them—a way out of poverty. Some missionaries do not mind if their child dates a national, as long as the young person is a good Christian. Their argument is that their child, especially those who have been on the field for a long time, will find it easier adjusting to life with a national than with an American.

I will not comment on this matter as I feel that it is between the parents and the Lord. I do suggest that parents spend a lot of time praying and talking about it before they wake up one morning and find their teenager in love. Guidelines must be discussed, though not too soon—let them be kids for a while, but do not wait too long either. Another consideration is that it doesn't make sense to date someone on the field and become serious, especially if your child is planning on going to Bible college in the States.

Often instances arise where MKs return to America and get into trouble because of dating. That situation can be a real snare. Part of the reason for this may be because they were not allowed to date while they were on the field or the choices were quite limited, so they when they get to the States, some of them seem to go "hog-wild." Their exposure to American kids may have been limited, and they just don't know how to date.

Keep talking to your kids. They need your wisdom. They need instruction about boy-girl relationships. They need to hear you tell them to be careful about whom they date and to ask for advice about whom they are dating. They need to hear you talk about staying pure. Daughters need to be taught how to say "No" to a young man. Sons need to be taught not to ruin a young lady's reputation. I know some missionary daughters who, when they go to the States and are asked for a date, request the young man to first call their father and ask for permission to date. I like that policy very much.

In the book, *The Missionary Wife and Her Work*, Joy Tuggy explains how difficult it is for MKs to adjust to the opposite gender when they go to America:

Missionaries should strive to be informed about the adjustment problems their children must face and be prepared to help them. Help should be given the student not to feel so different. The facts as presented in this study were worthy of careful note, for of all problems, those of social adjustment were the greatest. Concerning this type of problem the findings were as follows:

Out of 34 studies, 6 claimed to have no particular problems, but the remaining 28 mentioned this type of problem 132 times. The most common were adjusting to heterosexual friendships. "I had to learn how to act in front of girls. I'm still learning how to act in front of them."[1]

When it's time for your child to go to America for school or whatever, it can be a wonderful time in his life, but it is also a scary time. They are making decisions that will stay with them for the rest of their life during this period. We need to help them so they won't become "shipwrecked." When I look at my beautiful daughter-in-law (beautiful on the outside and on the inside), I thank God for leading my son and Brandie together.

Question	Would you like to tell about when your children went off to college (or left home)? How did you handle it? How did you help your children with this?

Answers:

- It was very hard on me when my first child left. I really missed her a lot. But over the years being away from the States and seeing three more leave for college, God has helped me not to miss them so much. I still have times when I think about them and cry, because I want to see them. They handled looking forward to going to college well. They still call a lot, and they want me to come to the States to see them.

- When my first son left for college, I thought my heart would break. Waving goodbye at the airport as he happily boarded his 747 to cross the ocean, I realized it was the hardest thing I'd ever done. He was only 17 years old! He was excited about college and training for the ministry. Many a night I'd look up at the moon as I prayed for him, and I realized the same moon would be shining down on him eight hours later. God was watching out for him, I knew. His first semester at college he was in a minor accident—without me there! But God is faithful, and He comforted us both. The summers were difficult for our sons with no home to go to. They were shuffled around between friends and relatives. Those were the toughest times for them.

In the book *In the Arena*, Isobel Kuhn cites the pain she went through when she sent her young daughter off to boarding school. She offers helpful advice:

The Lord spoke to me. He said something like this: "Well, dear, you have indulged your grief. You have gone over your loss minutely and by detail. The last time you would give her a bath, the last night to tuck her into bed, the last energetic bear hug from the impetuous little arms, the last sight of lovely childhood. And now I would counsel you. What good did it do you? Emotionally you are as worn and limp as a rag. It did not profit you physically. It did not help little Kathryn at all. It was a drag on your poor husband. Of what use was it to indulge your grief?

Next time—for this is only the first parting of many times to come—let

Me counsel you to gird up your loins and try to be a soldier. There are many small helps you can use, especially in the area of the mind. Refuse to let your mind dwell on your loss. It will not make you love her less. Deliberately think of something more helpful, or anything, rather than your loss. I have given you a thing called common sense—summon that to your aid. Common sense will tell you to avoid all scenes which harrow the feelings. Singing or music, for instance. Deliberately plan your good-by so that emotion will be strained as little as possible. When you return home after the loved one has left, change the furniture of her room around so as not to stir up memories, which cause useless grief.

"But Lord," I argued, "wouldn't that make me hard? I do not want to lose the ability to feel."

"You will not," He promised. "In fact, it will go all the deeper when it is not allowed to evaporate in bursts of emotion. Sublimate your feelings: rechannel your attention toward helping someone else.

And so He taught me—bless His precious name! Never again did I allow myself to be so broken up over a grief. And I found that common sense was a good aid. Also my love and my concern for my children certainly have never become less.[2]

When I first went to the mission field, I talked with some older missionaries who had been here quite a while and who had reared their children here. They said they really made an effort for the missionary children to get together at times. Two or three times a year, all the kids would fly (or take a boat) to one of the missionary's homes to spend several days. A few of those children grew up, went to Bible college, married their childhood sweethearts (other MKs from the Philippines), and came back as missionaries. Our mission board, Baptist International Missions, Inc., has a field conference once a year. The MKs love to have fellowship with each other. I think it is important for them to "rub elbows" with other American children now and then. Maybe when they go back to the States, Americans won't seem so strange to them. Perhaps things won't seem so foreign, and it will be easier for them to make friends when they return stateside.

As I have already mentioned earlier, this is a very important time in your children's life as the decisions they make in the next few years—where they go to school, who they will marry, what they will do for the rest of their life—could be totally disastrous. People talk about "cutting the apron strings"; yet, on the other hand, we need to stay involved in our children's lives to a certain extent. There's a difference between "cutting apron strings" and letting your kids grow up—especially letting a boy learn to make his own decisions and become a man—and staying in close contact with your children. Let them know they can (and should)

ALWAYS come to you for advice—no matter what their age is. If a church member comes to some pastors/missionaries for advice, some give it—no matter what the age of that church member. Yet, if their own child will come to them, they will say, "You're old enough to make your own decisions." What a contradiction! I don't believe there's anyone who has reached an age where he no longer needs advice.

I'm sure you have seen broken lives as I have; and it's frightening. Just because your child is safely tucked away at Bible school doesn't mean they are out of the Devil's reach. Let me take that thought a step further—just because your child is safely married to a Christian does not mean the Devil can't touch them anymore. Not only that, just because your child is in full-time Christian work does not mean they cannot fall. When I look at those who have made "shipwreck" of their lives, I say, "But for the grace of God—there am I—or my children." Throughout our lives, we need to stay on our knees and urge our children to stay on their knees.

Chapter Three

Your Kids' Spiritual Life

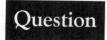 Would you please share what you do to help your kids spiritually?

Answers:

- I tell them they need to have their own private devotions every day. They cannot rely on their parents' spirituality.
- We involve them in every activity of the church. We home school our children, using Christian curriculum. When they enter the seventh grade, they are required to read assigned Bible passages over which they are quizzed daily to make sure they've read the assignment. We do our best to protect them from worldly influences—no television, radio, etc.
- Everyone agrees that family devotions are important. Be sure you make having devotions a top priority every day. You could easily make or break your child's spiritual life, depending on how you handle this important subject. Not only that, we need to teach our children how to have their own private walk with God. Mom and Dad will not always be there to hold their children's hands and lead them in this walk. By the time your child leaves home, be sure he knows how to walk with God, especially when Mom and Dad are far away. This is vital. They need to learn to "gird up their loins" so they'll be ready when temptations come.
- Be the right kind of example. Mom, if you are not submissive to your husband, how can you expect your children to be submissive?

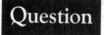 Can you please share something about your family devotions?

Answers:
- At this point in our children's ages, my husband conducts family devotions like a children's church. We each choose a song, and we all sing it. Then

he brings a short Bible story and/or principle and applies it to a child. Then two or three of them pray, and we ask a couple of them what they learned to see whether or not they followed his thought.

Deuteronomy 6:6-9, *"And these words, which I command thee this day, shall be in thine heart: And thou shalt teach them diligently unto thy children, and shalt talk of them when thou sittest in thine house, and when thou walkest by the way, and when thou liest down, and when thou risest up…And thou shalt write them upon the posts of thy house, and on thy gates."*

The chapter on "Walk with God" goes into more detail about devotions, but let me make this point in particular: children should grow up with memories of serving the Lord together with their parents and of having their parents reading the Bible to them. They should remember Mom and Dad praying for them. Those memories and prayers will follow them for the rest of their lives. My husband and I both have fond memories like that.

Chapter Four

Helping Kids Adjust

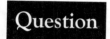 **Question**
What tips have worked well for you with helping your children or family make the needed adjustments to the mission field?

Answers:

• We did not have the usual adjustments. My husband and I had both lived overseas, so it was not as scary. This prior knowledge of the field is probably what helped our daughter the most. We learned to laugh at ourselves a lot. One time my daughter needed to try on something at a store in our city. The dressing room was just a closet in the middle of the floor. The lady kindly unlocked the door for us. My daughter and I walked in, and the lady shut the door behind us. When we were ready to go, we discovered that the young lady had inadvertently locked us in! I forgot any [language] I had learned, and my daughter was trying to stick her head out underneath the door and yell in English. Finally another customer noticed and sent someone over. However, the person didn't have the key. Another worker came over, and that individual didn't have a key either! After all was said and done, it took five people before someone could let us out. As we exited, the onlookers applauded! We laughed so hard, and so did the people.

I don't compare the people with whom we work to Americans. Every culture has its own quirks, even in the United States!

• One thing that helped the kids to adjust and learn the language was attending Sunday school and junior church with the people. The kids had an opportunity to attend an English class, but we said "No." They didn't get much from the lesson for a while, but soon they came home and said, "I think he talked about Jonah today." Soon they were singing the songs and helping me with the language. Children are very flexible and adapt very quickly. Their conflicts arise when they see Mom has a bad attitude and isn't happy.

• Keep a regular schedule for everything. We had a family breakfast each morning at 7:00. This was also devotion time, where we read the Bible together and shared prayer requests. Our noon meal was at 11:00, and supper was always 5:00 because it gets dark by 6:00 every day. Also, we never knew from day to day what we would be doing for electricity that night. We always had "Family Day" each week. Sometimes this activity had to be broken up into sections [as when children are sick]. Another tip that worked for us is, we allowed our children to collect and take care of the pets they chose. Our additional family members have included monkeys, macaws, cats, dogs, ducks, iguanas, parrots, chickens, and various other wildlife.

• Despite having new American friends on the field, our oldest children still missed "home" very much. Their dad took them to Pastors' School one year, and they learned to write letters.

Don't let well-meaning Christian people, whether your friends and family back home or other missionaries or your church people on the field, pressure you about the way you rear your kids. I think it is fine to ask for advice, but ultimately it's between you, your husband, and God. Don't try to fit your children into a mold to please other people. Sometimes we're more concerned with what people think of our kids than we are for the kids themselves. This is where consistency really matters. If we have different standards when people are around to see us than at other times when no one is looking, our kids will see right through that pretense.

Adjusting to America

Children have to adjust when they go to the mission field, and children who have been on the field for a while have to adjust when they go back to America, be it for college or another reason. For some it means "leaving *home* to go to America." Any young person has a big adjustment when he goes to college—how much more so for those reared on the mission field! Stay actively involved in their lives. My husband spent a small fortune calling our son often when he went to college. I'm sure as our daughter leaves for college in 2004, our phone bills will skyrocket again. Those calls to stay connected are worth every penny. Your children need your continued guidance. They need to know that just because you are halfway around the world and/or that you are busy with your ministry, that does not mean you no longer care about them. I know money is tight, but try to fly your child home at Christmas or during the summer months. Try to fly to the States and see them occasionally throughout the years they are in school. They need you. Don't wait until they have gone off into sin to pay for an airline ticket. (Remember, our Father owns the cattle on a thousand hills!)

I believe it's really beneficial for kids to get a part-time job to help with their school bill, but I also see nothing wrong with parents' helping them out financially from time to time while they are in school. Some may disagree with me on this matter. I am not saying pay for everything and hand them their education on a silver platter. I know if they work for their education, they will appreciate it more and also develop character. This method of character development may be especially needful for children who have not learned good work habits and may tend to be a little lazy. Still, I see nothing wrong with helping your children a little though. Teach teens how to handle money when they go off to college. Hopefully, they have been taught to tithe since they were young. Letting them work and help pay the bills will give them a proper perspective, but don't let them become so overburdened that they quit school.

It has been my observation that children who are reared on the foreign field aren't as independent as American children. Some MKs seem more attached to parents simply because of the circumstances of missionary life. For example, in the Philippines, kidnaping for ransom is big business, so my husband and I did not let our children go off our compound (our house, Christian school, church, and Bible college are all together on one compound) without one of us.

MKs have unique struggles when they go to the States. Because many may have led a more sheltered life, they may seem more immature compared to their American counterparts. In fact, that is one reason why my husband and I were happy to have the privilege of rearing our children on the field. To give you an example, when I turned 16, I got my driver's license and immediately went out and got a job. My son Ricky didn't experience that privilege until he was 18.

It seems that every time we go back to the States, we are shocked at some of the changes—mostly bad. Kids in the States grow up too fast. Some readers will think I'm a little old-fashioned, but I will go ahead and state it: I'm shocked when I go to the States and see little girls (and sometimes even young boys!) wearing makeup, bleaching their hair, wearing worldly clothing and anything and everything that the world is doing in the name of fashion—even in Christian homes. As for tattoos and excessive body piercing—I won't even go there!

My daughter, like most little girls, loved jewelry (*lots* of it!) and nail polish, and all those things when she was growing up. I am not saying those are wrong, but we parents are often pressured when our children say, "But so-and-so's mom lets her!" We cave in and let our kids have their way so they can be like their friends. They have to do it because everyone else is doing it. If they don't, they are labeled. I am not saying to look dowdy; that is almost as bad a testimony as looking worldly. Rather, we must use a little common sense. Sometimes I think parents are actually afraid of their children. We're afraid of our kids' being different or of their being laughed at. We are afraid to say "No." We should be teaching our children to stand up for what is right instead of blending in with the crowd. I am not saying to rear your kid to be a weirdo, but weren't Daniel and Joseph and Moses different? Wasn't Jesus different? What's so bad about being different?

Kids in elementary schools talk flippantly about "boyfriends" and "girlfriends." In the Philippines, children hardly ever talk about that subject—sometimes not even into their late teens. We should not encourage that kind of thinking by teasing them or by letting siblings tease each other. There is plenty of time for that stage of life at the appropriate time. Let children be children for a few years. The boyfriend-girlfriend stage will come soon enough.

MKs may even have an odd sense of humor—different than Americans. They take on the traits of the culture where they were reared. They need to be prepared for Americans to be intolerant of this fact. Missionary parents need to help their children in these areas.

Some MKs, mainly boys, are teased and harassed because they are different. When this happens, I believe some kids are tempted to do foolish or even sinful things just so they will be accepted or admired. MKs think much like the people with whom they grew up—in whatever country to which their family has been called. Americans may more easily accept someone who looks foreign rather than an American kid who looks like they do, but talks, thinks, and acts differently. It is sad that sometimes even Christians can be so intolerant of someone who is just a little different. Without trying to sound negative at this point, I feel that missionary parents are sometimes naïve in thinking that when they send their kids to Bible college, their children will be welcomed, loved, and accepted. Boys, especially, need to be prepared.

Have you taught your son to be strong? I have had MKs express their hurt feelings to me about the times they have attended a Christian school and have been labeled as "strange." Many MKs cannot stand life in America and can't wait to return to their foreign home. Probably home on the mission field seems more secure to them because it is more familiar to them. Others who may have been unhappy on the mission field look forward to life in the States. Then when they finally return stateside, it turns out to be a huge disappointment. As a result of this unrealistic expectation, the MK can become very vulnerable and easily backslide.

Teenagers greatly fear being different. That fear may be one reason why it is good for your kids to visit America occasionally through short furloughs and visits while they are growing up. Maybe then the adjustments won't be so overwhelming when they return to the States.

We need to teach children courage so they won't be afraid of being ridiculed because, I believe, that is when they are tempted to do something wrong—especially boys—as if they have to prove themselves. It takes more courage not to buckle under the laughter and temptation. In James 4:7, the Bible says *"Submit yourselves therefore to God. Resist the devil, and he will flee from you."*

The book, *The Missionary Wife and Her Work*, shares the following report:

A missionary daughter, now grown and married, wrote…

MKs have quite a reputation. Some are misfits and come back to the U.S. not knowing how to dress, wearing sloppy mismatching "missionary barrel" clothes. Some have a very noticeable holier-than-thou attitude, partly because they've had a good Christian background and because people have led them to think that their parents are the most wonderful people in the earth to deprive themselves and go to the backside of the desert. Some kids have never had other kids their age to play with, have been taught completely by their parents and so have only adjusted to a grown-up world. Some have been stuck away in boarding school and have been moved from place to place until they feel very insecure. This can cause them to be shy introverts, or it can make them rebel and want to show the world that they really are worth something. Most of the missionary kids I've known are well-adjusted and above average in intelligence and ability, and for this we praise the Lord. They have had the advantage of travel and of having many people praying.[1]

An MK can feel like "a fish out of water." Remember that these children can feel adrift, lonely, and homeless. They do not ever entirely "fit in," whether on the foreign field or in America. How fortunate for the MK who has learned to adapt—wherever he is! Don't make them feel like they have missed out on a lot of things by being an MK. The advantages far outweigh the disadvantages. MKs do not need pity; rather, they need love, understanding, compassion, guidance, acceptance, and prayer.

Chapter Five

Rearing Kids on the Field

 **Question** What are your basic thoughts and needs for rearing children on the field?

Answers:

• Expect them to fit in. They will adjust to the culture and language more quickly than you will. I take my kids through a lesson in American history on the Fourth of July, and we celebrate Thanksgiving, Valentine's Day, and so forth. I try to make these times "big" and special to them, so that when they, most likely, choose to return to the States as young adults for college or whatever, they will fit in there just as easily.

• We are trying to rear our children like my folks reared my sisters, my brother, and me. Expressing pity for your kids because of "having" to rear them on the mission field without the "luxuries of America" is a grave mistake that many missionaries make. I believe children should be reared to be thankful for what they have rather than wishing for what they do not have.

• Your children really watch your attitudes. DO NOT criticize the nationals. Your children get a negative and superior attitude toward them if you criticize them. We make sure that our daughter's education is taken care of. I think our children have the same basic need on the field that they have in the States—security. Schedule and routine are important. I have noticed missionary moms tend to feel bad that their children have little or no social interaction with other children their age. I wish my daughter had more friends, but at the same time, we do not want to sacrifice her spiritual life in order for her to have a social life. We have seen missionaries ruin their children by allowing them to spend unsupervised time with unsaved and ungodly children.

• One must keep a schedule. In keeping a schedule, it helps the children feel secure. Make sure you talk about the good things that God has given you. If there is some kind of problem, my husband and I do not discuss it in front of the children. Sometimes the children need to know about these things, but we must not constantly complain about what is going on. Attitude is important. Your attitude will carry over to your children. They watch us even when we are not aware of it. They know firsthand what it is like to be on the mission field. Wouldn't it be great for them to want to return to the field if it is God's will? Or have we turned away our children because of our attitudes?

• Children are adaptable; if you are happy, they are happy as well. If you hate your life on the field; they will also hate life on the mission field. They need love and attention. They need your time. They need to come before the ministry and church people's needs. They are your children; the Lord wants you to put them before others—that is why they are given to you.

• Concerning the rearing of children on the field: I think that in many ways it is the same as in the States: following God's guidelines, being the right example before our children, being consistent, etc. I would like to suggest a book which deals with rearing children in another culture. It is not a Christian book, nor was it written for only missionaries, but it gives good, practical advice on many pitfalls parents make as they rear their child in a different culture. It also tells of the tendencies and attitudes the children develop and carry with them into adulthood: *The Third Culture Kid Experience,* by David Pollock and Ruth Van Reken, Intercultural Press, Inc., Box 700, Yarmouth, Maine.

• We try to spend time with our children and not let the missionary work occupy all our time. We speak English at home so that the children know it well. Don't let the children run with the children in the streets. Be careful what influences you allow in their lives, whether it be other children to play with or something else. Don't have a television. When I went to the field, our [language] teacher gave us a television, telling us it would help us with our [language]. I believe that it hurt me spiritually and has also done damage to the rest of my family. I am so thankful my husband and I decided not to have a television in our home. We spend time with our children playing games, reading books, and going to the park.

• My husband and I believe God gives a special grace for rearing children on the mission field. After all, He called us to our place of service; and we have to trust Him to protect our children here. It is sometimes difficult, but we need to try to let them lead as normal lives as possible on the field. Our children have been involved in sports, as voluntary firemen, in music school, and in other activities. Of course, some fields could not offer such a wide range as we have in a European country.

Once again, allow me to quote my friend, Mrs. Sandy Domelle:

Missionaries on deputation want to wait until all their kids are done with high school so they don't have to worry about them on the field. I went [to the field] with two years of high school left. I wouldn't trade those two years for anything. I think things that happened, whether good or tough, have helped me in life now. I think I have more of a heart for missions because I lived there and experienced it and, as a result, may be able to help those preparing to go to the field. I also hope I can help kids who have come home from the field. I wouldn't trade that for anything. I experienced things living in a foreign country that I wouldn't have if I hadn't gone. I think these parents are robbing their children of a blessing.

To be sure, there are some differences when rearing children in a foreign country, but there are also similarities. Children must be taught to obey so that when the time comes that they realize they are a sinner and need to get saved, their response will be obedience—not rebellion. I don't need to tell you that being a parent is an awesome responsibility. God has given you a living soul, and it is your responsibility, first and foremost, to see that they are saved as soon as possible. Do you want to know how to make this job more difficult? Rear a spoiled brat!

Children must be taught to be truthful, which can be particularly difficult as in many foreign cultures lying is thought to be clever—not sinful. They must be taught to love and forgive. Teach them to work hard. Teaching is not saying to them, "Work hard!" Teaching is showing them how to do something and then working with them to see that they learn to the do the job correctly. That requires patience. I have found that children are more likely to enjoy doing some particular chore if they know how to do it well.

Children must be taught self-control. Spanking seems to have become a "lost art"—even in Christian homes. Parents are not doing their children any favors when they rear them in such a way that no one can stand to be around them. Too many erroneously think that if their darling child doesn't want to do something, he should not be made to do it.

I thank God I had parents who made my siblings and me do what we were supposed to do—whether or not we wanted to do so. I thank God that my husband had parents who made him do what he was supposed to do, whether or not he wanted to do so. This training is vital. When God asks a spoiled child to go to the mission field (or to serve Him in other ways), he does not do it because he has learned that he does not have to do anything he does not want to do. If we were reared correctly, we do what is right to do—whether or not we want to.

Rear your child so he will be an asset—not a liability—to God and to His work. Dr. Jack Hyles always taught from the pulpit and in his books, "Do not rear your child to be a quitter." If you quit the mission field, what are you teaching your kids by your example?

$\mathcal{K}ids\ and\ \mathcal{F}amily\ \mathcal{L}ife$

 Would you please share what special things you do with your family to help your home life?

Answer:

Every Monday is "Family Day." We celebrate all birthdays on Monday, whether or not the actual date falls on Monday. All our church members know that Monday is "Family Day," and they respect our tradition and do a good job of staying out of sight and sound. We mainly do whatever the children want. We play games of all descriptions, watch a special video, take walks, or have a picnic. We do our best to make each child feel loved and appreciated and a welcome member of the family. We'll cook a favorite meal, bake cookies together, do a puzzle with the older ones, etc.

In Dr. Jim Vineyard's missionary paper, Dr. Joe Finn asks the following question in his article entitled "Interview with a Missionary": "What special things do you do with your family that have helped the stability of your home?" The following are two answers he received.

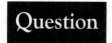 What special things do you do with your family that have helped the stability of your home?

Answers:

• We try at least once a week to have fellowship with other American families. We do seasonal activities together. In the winter, we go skiing, sledding, and ice-skating. In the summer, we enjoy swimming, camping, etc. I try to involve my kids as much as possible in the ministry here. My older boys have been helping me with the remodeling of the church building.

• We go for walks, go to the park, go to the zoo, get some ice cream, and talk about changes and the differences in their lives here.

John and Betty Stam were missionaries to China who were martyred. Betty was the daughter of missionaries. The book *The Triumph of John and Betty Stam* depicts Betty's family life:

> They were a close-knit family. They derived maximum pleasure from outings to the beach and to the lovely wooded countryside surrounding them. In spite of their main duties, the Scotts devoted as much time as possible to their children's upbringing. But it wasn't "all work and no play." Time was set aside for outdoor games and athletics, as well as for family prayers and reading children's books together.[1]

Do you know why family life is so important? Because Satan hates us, and he hates what we are doing. He will try everything he can to stop us, and one key way is by attacking our homes. We need to make our family our priority. We aren't going to be able to accomplish anything for God on the mission field if Satan has destroyed our home and we have to leave the ministry.

Educating Your Kids

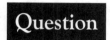 **Question**
What tips and thoughts would you give about home schooling during deputation and on the field?

Answers:

• While on deputation, formal schooling seems impossible. Child and parent alike must give grace to each other. An outsider looking in will see areas to criticize. All that can be done is our best in each particular situation. Be very thankful if you have bright, eager learners, as I did. Take the "school" out of schoolwork. Try to make learning as fun as it really is. Both learning and teaching are fun. Never say, "Go do your schoolwork." Instead say, "Let's learn something together today!" The biggest obstacle we all face in the home school is: "I can't." *"I can do all things through Christ which strengtheneth me"* is the grace we need to succeed.

• I would advise all parents to home school their children rather than send them to the native schools to learn the native customs. Many couples would never dream of sending their children to the American public school; yet, they don't seem to think it bad to send their children to a public school in another country. As a result, they lose their children. A public school is a public school in any country and is operated by worldly humanists. The children can learn the language of the country from church or neighborhood kids with parental supervision. The "good" customs can be taught to them, and the "bad" customs can be explained as soon as the parents think the child is old enough to handle them.

• I home schooled our kids. After the boys left for college, our daughter felt extra lonely. We were blessed to be able to put her in a new ACE school in our town not long after that. She loves the social interaction there. All that to say that we need to be sensitive to our kids' needs. In home schooling, even with the best curriculum, you need to have a library of your own. Our town has a mockery of a library—not a single reference book there! Take books with you. They're very hard to find in third-world countries anyway. A computer encyclopedia is a great tool too. Also, you need to use the curriculum with which you feel comfortable. Try them out before arriving on the field.

• Examine various curriculums and see which you feel the most comfortable using. A Beka, for example, has a good phonics, learning-to-read program but later could be very exacting and difficult for some students, and very trying for some mothers who do not really feel cut out as a teacher to teach various levels at the same time. ACE or Alpha Omega are more geared for self-study and perhaps less strenuous on the teacher. Many other choices are available, and each has advantages and disadvantages. Choose that with which you feel most comfortable.

• If you must home school, try to get started before arriving on the field. Having a semester or two of experience will help you to know what materials you must take along, whether or not your chosen curriculum will work for you, and it'll give you confidence.

• The most important thing is to get the basics down. After that, I do not feel the exact facts they learn in any course are as important as simply the discipline involved. Keep on a schedule; have a regular time to study. Some situations might allow a certain flexibility, but do not allow yourself to cancel or change school hours every time someone comes by the house or when something that is not an emergency arises. Look for places you can visit, factories you could tour, etc., to use as field trips.

• Home schooling is a difficult task in and of itself. On the field, you need to be flexible, but you MUST also keep a schedule! Your children need to learn school is important—even if Mom is the teacher. You must carry on like a "real school." We try to maintain that rapport when working with our children. They will try you when they would not try their teacher in school. Mom also needs to learn the time when to be teacher and when to be Mom. Don't carry over your frustrations from school to other areas. That is hard for us Moms not to do. I have gone to my husband and asked for his help and insight on certain matters. Don't be afraid to ask for help and suggestions. We make sure that we keep up with the schedule set out just like our home church does. Do not get so behind in school that the children do not have a break for summer, etc. They need some time off. They can do extra work during the summer to keep their mind fresh, but give them a break. That is important for them as they are still children, and every child needs to be able to be a child.

• I used Landmark Freedom Baptist Curriculum because of its organization, and it came with weekly quizzes. While we were on deputation, we usually went out for six to eight weeks at a time, so I would pack six to eight weeks of quizzes for each subject (per child). We never covered all the material. Generally, one week of work will take a kid on deputation two weeks to complete. I would rather go slowly than do nothing at all. When we travel, each school-age child had his own personal backpack for his school books. I also kept a separate backpack for quizzes, answer guides, grade records, etc.

Once on the field I found we needed to build a library so the kids could do research papers. Whenever someone asked, "What do you need?" I answered, "Encyclopedias and biographies." I picked up a few books while on deputation, but most were sent by churches after we reached the field. I have also kept a "vertical file" of newspaper articles, magazine articles, and maps. This might not be necessary if we had Internet service.

• The best tips on home schooling which I can give you come from an organized missionary lady who has successfully home schooled eight children who are now grown and serving the Lord:

1. Don't take it too seriously.
2. Don't be too hard on yourself.
3. Remember each child is different; don't try to force him into a mold. (Each child has different needs, abilities, limits, and so forth.)
4. Schedules are important, just so it doesn't come before the needs of the family. For instance, the schedule says we need to do "this and this," but one child is sick and the teacher is exhausted. It might be better to take off a day instead of staying by the schedule.

Many wonderful books on home schooling helps are available.

• I think home schooling is a real problem with new missionaries. So many missionaries are now sending their kids to local schools or boarding schools. I am totally and completely against this practice. I believe missionary wives are not being educated as to the benefits of home schooling (not to mention their God-given responsibility); therefore, they do not know that it is really their best option. I am shocked at the number of missionary wives with whom I speak who know so little about home schooling. They are frightened by the prospect of home schooling their kids and say things like, "Oh, it's just not my personality to home school" (Personality has nothing to do with whether or not you can successfully teach your kids!) or "I just wouldn't know how to do it." There is a great need for future missionary wives to get a good overview of home school—what it is and how to do it. Kids are being sacrificed on the altar of "missions" left and right because missionary wives don't have a clue about home schooling. How to home school should be one of the top five things a missionary wife learns before going to the field.

• For deputation I home schooled the children so we could be flexible and go with my husband when necessary. [In our country] it is not allowed to home school your children. We have had our children in the schools right from the start. But I have taught the younger children to read English. Of course, we have run into some problems having our children in their schools, but our children have often expressed how glad they were that they weren't shut off from the children and culture around them. This has been a super opportunity to reach their friends with the Gospel.

• I am still learning. One missionary mentioned having lots of books for your children to read. Our children can't run to the local library and check out books for fun. They really enjoy the library while we are home on furlough.

I would like to share Sandy Heidenreich Domelle's experience regarding education on the mission field which was sent to me via email:

When we were in Manila, I wanted to go to [a Christian academy] because the other MKs went there. My parents allowed me to visit the school one day with [a friend]. I went to the Bible class, and the teacher walked in with his shirt unbuttoned showing his hairy chest, and a huge cross dangled from a necklace—not very impressive! He couldn't decide what he believed and kept probing the students on what they thought about certain verses of the Bible. I gave my opinion on one verse, and he asked where I was from. When I said "Hammond, Indiana," he said that he had heard of the "Hyles crowd" and that I would need to change my thinking now that I was out in the real world. I went to Economics class, and the teacher was teaching on a budget. He stressed that you should always pay your bills before you paid your tithes. Then in P.E. class those in charge said I had to wear shorts. Of course, that was out of the question. By the end of the day I thought, "This is going to be something I will talk about for weeks."

When I walked in, my parents asked me how it went; and when I told them about everything, my dad asked me, "Is that the type of school you'd want to attend?" I knew full well before they ever let me go visit that I would never go. I told them at the ripe age of 16 that I guess I was destined to be the strange bird with the other MKs. Thankfully, we moved to Panay just a few months later. I didn't spend as much time with [my friend] after that because I knew who she hung with and that what she was taught was not what I needed because I knew it would change my thinking. All that to say, I know why I don't think MKs should go off to boarding schools. Those in places of authority won't uphold and teach all that the parents have instilled in their children. I am amazed at how many [missionary wives] are willing to send their kids off and how many send their kids to the public schools.

As with every other aspect of rearing our children, when it comes to educating them, we must seek God's will, ask His help, and do our best.

Chapter Eight

Missionary Kids Becoming Missionaries

 **Question**

Some MKs have a desire to become a missionary themselves. If yours did, and realizing that God gets the glory, what do you believe you and your husband did, humanly speaking, to help this to come about?

Answers:

• We have one son who has surrendered to go to [the mission field]. He will be 13 years old next month. First of all, we did not discourage him. If he feels the Lord leading him that direction, we want to encourage. We are doing our best to get good cassette tapes, computer programs, etc. so he can learn the language. We are looking into good Bible colleges that would enable him to become involved in a Spanish ministry to help him get a head start. We are also encouraging him to become acquainted with some of the missionaries already serving in order to ask questions and get advice.

• Our son is planning to do missionary work. His involvement in the ministry here on the mission field was extensive, and allowing his participation may truly be all that we may have contributed to his future plans. He saw the many needs of our foreign field, and the great opportunities there are world-wide.

• We are proud of our children and excited that all are in full-time service; three are planning to go back to the mission field. Of course, we realize that God does not call everyone into full-time service, and another missionary whose children may be in secular service might be as "successful" as us if his children are in God's will and serving through their local churches. But I do believe there is a secret that allowed our children to be open to God's call back to the field. I believe if we had been critical of the country, the culture, and our people, that could have "turned our children off." We did not criticize things we did not like, nor did we compare everything to the U.S. Not being critical and not complaining are very important. Then, we emphasized the positive. There are things they got to do and places they were able to see as MKs that average kids in the States did not. We tried to make everything an adventure. Being [on the mission field] was not drudgery, but exciting.

Regarding this same subject, the book, *The Missionary Wife and Her Work,* elaborates:

Most mission fields can testify to the heartbreak of missionary children who have been sacrificed to "the Lord's work" and who will never enter into the heritage of glad, fruitful service which could have been theirs.

Some have become embittered. For these, there is no excuse. Whether their parents were right or wrong, the Lord Himself did not fail them. It is to Him that they are personally responsible. He has ways of blessing and triumph in which He will lead any missionary child, regardless of his parents' mistakes.

Still, missionary parents do need to evaluate very seriously their responsibility before God for their children.

There is plenty of evidence to support the fact that the children of missionaries are not only the best source of future missionary recruits, but also that they make the best missionaries.

The children of missionaries were characterized by Edward Judson as "the involuntary inheritors of their parents' sufferings and reward" in the dedication of his "Life of Adoniram Judson." Since Edward Judson was "one of them," he spoke from experience.[1]

The book, *From Jerusalem to Irian Jaya* gives an example of MKs who became missionaries:

One of the most distinguished medical missionary families in all history was the Scudder family, beginning with John Scudder, a young medical doctor in New York City who, after reading a booklet appealing for missionaries, left his growing practice and in 1819 sailed for Ceylon with his wife and child. The Scudders served for thirty-six years in Ceylon and India, and during that time thirteen more children were born to them, nine of whom survived to adulthood. Of those nine, seven became missionaries, most of them specializing in medicine like their father. In four generations, forty-two members of the Scudder family became missionaries, contributing well over one thousand combined years of missionary service.[2]

Betty Stam was reared in China along with sisters Beatrice and Helen and brothers Francis and Kenneth. All returned to serve on the mission field. The book *The Triumph of John and Betty Stam* testifies,

It certainly wasn't an automatic decision that each of the children eventually took up missionary work. The reason why they followed their parents' example was that when they grew old enough to make up their own minds, they looked back with affection on their happy childhood and the firm but kindly discipline administered to them. It worked for them. They admired their parents' ideals and dedication to their Christian calling. Obviously they felt in no way deprived if they were prepared to bring their own families up similarly.[3]

In my husband's book, *Missionary Relationships at Home,* in his chapter entitled "A Missionary's Relationship with His Children," he tells about a survey trip he took to Haiti. This survey trip resulted in the surrendering to go there by the first foreign missionary out of our church in Iloilo City. To say that Rick did not like Haiti is putting it mildly. In fact, he stated quite adamantly that the happiest day of his life was the day he left Haiti! He wondered how any American could stand to live in that God-forsaken place. Haiti is the poorest country in all the Americas. We ourselves live in a third-world country; yet, he said living in the Philippines was nothing compared to the poverty and ugliness of Haiti. I could go on and on, but I think you get the picture.

He visited Missionary Don Dryden and his family and was greatly impressed with the Dryden children. He said they had good attitudes and loved Haiti. He wondered how in the world the children could possibly love the ugliness he had seen. Then he realized that they loved the land because their parents loved it! My husband states,

Did they have problems? In my estimation, more than the vast majority of missionaries I've known.

Somehow Brother Dryden and his wife made living in Haiti fun. Their house is located near the edge of Port-au-Paix. They had a big yard and lots of animals. God has used [Brother Dryden] for many years to see many souls saved in Haiti. He was also a pretty good dad![4]

My husband wrote to Brother Dryden and commented on his children, asking how he reared his children to want to serve the Lord in full-time Christian work. The following is a portion of Brother Dryden's answer:

Thank you for your remarks concerning our children. They are our main ministry. Our calling/vocation is the Gospel ministry as missionaries. We always called Haiti "home." We always looked forward to getting back. We bought land and built "our house" where our children could grow up. The Lord let us rear them all here. It has been a privilege. They were allowed to mingle with the Haitian children. We opened our yard for them to come in and play with our children. Their friends were allowed to come in our house and they to theirs under controlled supervision. When Haitians were visiting, we spoke Creole with them and among ourselves in their presence.

I remember our first furlough. We were at a church on a Saturday night showing our slides to a youth gathering. When we all got settled in the motor home for the night, we heard Lydia crying. She revealed how the slide presentation had made her homesick and said, "When are we going home?"

Another thing I feel which contributed to our children's doing so well in Haiti was that I included them in the ministry. When I would go off into the country on my motorcycle for a conference or a Bible School class, I took one of the children (alternating) with me. As they got older, they had a motorcycle to ride on. When I was collecting Bible school materials or building something for the churches, the kids helped me. They were very much a part of the work.[5]

Brother Dryden's son and his wife are now back in Haiti as missionaries. My husband also added,

Children need to see their mom and dad enjoy life. My observation is that children [who] desire to return to the mission field, even though they realize there are many difficulties are a product of their parents trying to make serving God fun and exciting. A lot of humor will help your children see that a Christian truly has overcome the world.

My dad was very strict, but he was so fun to be around. He was the preacher of a large church and carried a heavy load. I knew the ministry was not easy but grew up wanting to be in it.[6]

My husband and I have had many "highlights" in the years we've spent in the Philippines. Surely one of the greatest was August 2004, when our son and his wife came to the Philippines to work with us. To God be the glory!

Conclusion

The reason I chose to write about Mary Moffat at the beginning of this unit was that five of her children returned to Africa as missionaries. I would like to conclude this unit by writing about Mary's grandson Robert, son of David and Mary Livingstone. Unfortunately, not all stories have happy endings. My prayer is that YOUR story, your life on the mission field with your husband and your children, will have a happy ending.

David and Mary Livingstone's son, Robert Moffat Livingstone, was named after his missionary grandfather. In 1852, when Livingstone sent his wife and children to England, they lived in poverty. At the time, Robert, who was very strong-willed and independent, was seven years old. The family moved from place to place. When his father finally came to England, Robert, age 12, was sent to boarding school in Scotland. His father wrote stern letters to him, as he was always getting into trouble in school. The letters did not seem to help.

In 1858, Robert's mother went to Africa to join his father. Three months later, she was dead. Livingstone wrote each of his children a letter. *Incredible Journey in the Steps of Greatness* shares lines penned by Livingstone: "With many tears running down my cheeks I have to tell you that Mama died last night at seven o'clock. She loved you dearly and often talked about you. You must all love each other more than ever now."[1]

If Robert had difficulties before, they were increased now with his mother dead and his father far away. He quit school, which angered his father. Livingstone accused his son of being lazy. "Livingstone, in a letter to his son Thomas, expressed the possibility that Robert was only interested in making capital out of having a famous father."[2]

Robert decided to go to Africa and discuss his future with his father. Author, Dr. James Ray, comments, "This request was really a son's craving to be with a father he had never known. The trustees of the mission made provision for Robert's journey to Africa but thought nothing of the funds he needed to go inland to his father. His father had told a friend that if he saw Robert, to tell him that he would have to work his way out."[3]

Mary Moffat was very worried about her grandson. After traveling all the way to Africa, Robert was never able to locate his father. He got a job on an American ship and went to America in 1863. Robert decided to enlist and fight to help free the slaves.

His father was fighting the slave traffic in Africa. This would be his chance to do the same. This act reflected a deep respect for his father and a longing to be like him. Perhaps this would be his chance to prove worthy of acceptance of a father he little knew.[4]

Livingstone soon received a letter from his son.

The letter revealed a young man who was growing up. Robert expressed regret that he had thrown away his chances of education. The letter from a field hospital in Virginia continued, "I have changed my name for I am convinced that to bear your name here would lead to further dishonor it." These words must surely have pierced David's heart. Robert went on to describe two skirmishes: "I never hurt anyone knowingly in battle, have always fired high. In that furious madness which always accompanies a bayonet charge which seems to possess every soldier, I controlled my passion and took the man who surrendered prisoner." He then signed the letter with the name of Rupert Vincent.[5]

Not long after this, Livingstone requested the American ambassador to England to try to find out about his son. Livingstone learned that Robert had been captured by the Confederates and sent to Salisbury Prison in North Carolina. There the starving men caught and roasted rats for sustenance. The prison, built to accommodate less than 2000, was packed with 9000 captured soldiers.

One day the men who were desperate for food rioted. Guards fired on the men, and Robert, who was not even involved in the riot, was hit. In December 1864, Robert died in that prison camp. He lies buried in an unmarked grave with thousands of other soldiers.

Incredible Journey in the Steps of Greatness concludes,

What David Livingstone had accomplished for Christ was immeasurable. The cost had been staggering. His family could not have survived had they been with him Africa. Had he stayed with them in Britain, the work of Christ would have suffered. The slave trade would have continued to damn millions of people to untold suffering. When Henry Stanley found David Livingstone in Africa, he told him of the death of his son. Livingstone was fighting the hated slave trade in Africa, and his son had only tried in his own way to "be like his dad," who fought to set slaves free.

As recorded in his diary, Livingstone uttered words long over due, words of praise and esteem, words for Robert. "If I had been there, I would have gone to fight also. I am proud of you son."[6]

I'm sure you can walk into any Christian bookstore in America and find countless books on rearing children. The following thoughts may be greatly oversimplified, but rearing children basically boils down to three things:

1. Love God and teach your children to do so.
2. Love your kids and show them you love them by spending time with them and giving them lots of affection.
3. Discipline properly. If a child doesn't learn to obey his parents, how can he learn to obey God?

I highly recommend Dr. Jack Hyles' various books on rearing children, as well as Dr. Tom Vogel's book, "*May I Suggest....*" Dr. Jeff Owens has a two very good books on the subject of character. It is vital that we teach our children character. Many great books on rearing children are available through Christian Womanhood, 8400 Burr Street, Crown Point, Indiana 46307. This chapter is by no means a comprehensive study; rather, I have tried to address specifically the rearing of *missionary* children. I strongly urge you to read as many books as you can on this important subject. Of course, every Christian's most important guidebook is the Bible.

God gave us a precious gift when He gave us our children. May we, with His help, be the right kind of parents.

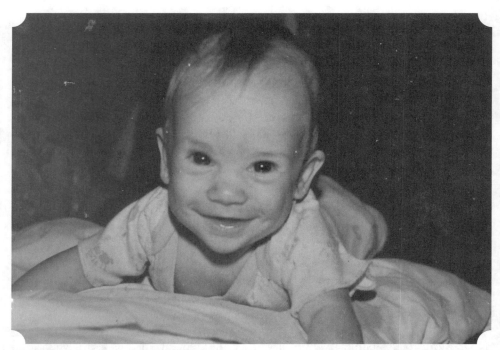

Above: Rachel loved to lay on a pillow on her dad's desk and watch him work for the longest time.

Below left: Rachel and her monkey MoyMoy

Below right: Our family at Rachel's kindergarten graduation (Rachel was 5, and Ricky was 12.)

UNIT FIVE

Your Ministry

"Therefore seeing we have this ministry...."
(II Corinthians 4:1)

Introduction

Maude Cary was reared on a Kansas farm. Her godly Christian parents often invited traveling preachers and missionaries to their humble home. Maude's mother graduated from college and the Boston Conservatory of Music, and she was an outstanding Bible teacher. She led each of her children to the Lord.

When Maude heard of the murder of Dr. and Mrs. C. S. Leach, medical missionaries in Tunisia, she surrendered to be a missionary. Maude enrolled in Bible college. She had to drop out a few times due to her mother's bad health, yet she was still determined to go to the mission field. Her mother also shared that joy and did not try to hold her daughter back from going to the foreign field.

Maude and some other missionaries boarded a ship for Morocco in November 1901. The sea was rough, but they finally arrived safely in Tangier. On Maude's twenty-third birthday, she mounted a mule, along with the others, and took a 200-mile trip to the interior. Each night they slept in tents.

After arriving in the city of Fez, the missionaries began their language study. In the book *Miss Terri*, author Evelyn Stenbock commented: "The honeymoon was over; the excitement and romance of the long-anticipated missionary ministry had already begun to fade."[1] Maude quickly learned that being a missionary was hard work, and sometimes she found the work was even boring.

There was great opposition to the Gospel in this Moslem land. In fact, the missionaries wore Moroccan clothing so they wouldn't attract so much attention. The foreigners were called "Nazarenes."

There was much fighting among the Berber tribes inland, and travel in their territory was dangerous. To put down the tribes, the cruel king used barbaric methods and it was not unusual to see the gory heads of conquered tribesmen hanging in the city square.

Slavery was still practiced, especially the selling of captured women and children. Conversions from Islam to Christianity were virtually unknown.

Muslims were assured that they could guarantee themselves entrance into heaven by killing a Christian. In the wild interior, tribesmen were quick to use this privilege.[2]

Maude and the other missionaries took camping excursions out to the villages to witness to the people. They were often stoned and attacked by dogs. When Maude would sleep with a family in their tent, the fleas and lice would keep her awake all night. After Maude had only been in the country for a year, a bloody revolution broke out. One of the missionaries was shot and killed. The missionaries prayed for wisdom. Should they quit and go home?

During this time of indecision, a beggar woman came to the door of the single lady missionaries who were living together. She was starving and asked for bread. The girls fed her and then began to witness to her.

"Does He love even me?" she asked. She began to weep. She was unwanted, cast out and forlorn, and the message of John 3:16 was music to her ears. The missionaries decided to stay.[3]

Miss Cary set out to be a witness to people with perhaps the hardest of hearts on earth—the Moslems and the Jews. Did Miss Cary have a ministry in Tangier? Just as God had a ministry for Miss Cary, He has a ministry for you and me too.

This unit is divided into six categories: the what, where, when, who, how, and why of our ministry.

What Missionary Wives Said About Their Ministry

I would like to share what missionary wives shared about their involvement in the ministry.

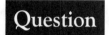 **Question**   Can you tell about your personal ministry?

Answers:

• I help my husband with office work mostly, but it is getting so that I am busy with our four little ones and am not able to help him as much. I feel that as they get older, I will be able to do more. My mother-in-law reminds me that they are my ministry right now.

• I teach the children's Sunday school class. I must also realize my limits, and because of home schooling, I may not have as much time as someone without children.

• My involvement in the ministry includes helping with the children's Sunday school class (training the teachers, teaching children's songs, etc.) and teaching a monthly ladies' meeting. I also disciple new lady converts. There is more I would like to be involved in once the children are grown.

• I am very involved with our ministry. I am a teacher by trade, so it is only natural that I would do a lot of teaching here in our ministry. I teach phonics to a group of illiterate adults six days a week. I co-teach with my husband a huge group of children on Sunday mornings. I teach music five afternoons a week. I work with special music and act as a music coordinator for our church. On the bus routes, I run the program while my husband drives. I am the registrar and secretary for our 600-student Bible correspondence course. Mostly, I enjoy staying beside my husband as he ministers.

• I am involved in the ministry by going soul winning; teaching Sunday school, the children's clubs, and teen activities; helping with music; cleaning and decorating our church and Sunday school; working with the nursery; and teaching a Sunday school teachers and children's church workers training class. Oh, yes, and I am kind of like the secretary too, I guess.

• I do whatever is necessary so that the people can easily hear the Gospel. Right now it is nursery, Sunday school, teacher, coffee maker, potluck meal preparer, singer, etc. I am also the church secretary. I love this job.

• I am the Sunday school teacher for the four-year-olds to twelve-year-olds, the nursery worker for ages three and younger during church nights, the director of the kids' club on Wednesday nights, the soul-winning babysitter, and a visiting partner with my husband.

Also in our survey, we asked the wives if there was anything they wish they had learned before going to the field. Here are the "Wish Lists!"

What do you wish you had done differently?

Answers:
• Before we left for the field, one of us should have taken a computer class. We had no idea that a computer would help us keep in touch and even help with home schooling the kids.

• [I wish I] knew how to disciple people and get them in church.

• In our work, my music skills have been absolutely mandatory. Until coming here, there was always someone who could play the piano much better than me. I took lessons as a child, but I wish I had gained much more training.

• I wish I had learned to play piano, even basic. Our daughter is learning. Our language study is important, and my husband would rather I put my effort into the language rather than piano right now.

• I wish I had learned more about follow-up and getting people in church after they are saved. Also how to encourage our people to do right.

• Some things I wish to have learned before coming are piano playing or some other instrument to help my husband with the song service, and secretarial and computer skills.

• I wish I had majored in education so I could do a better job home schooling my children.

• I wish that I could play the piano; that would be a great help in our ministry here. I am taking lessons again after 20 years, so maybe one day I will be able to play for church! I wish that I could sew better. I wish that I knew sign language for the deaf (I am also trying to learn that now!), anything that would help us to reach more people. I also wish I knew more about the computer so I could use it to help more in the ministry. So many things you can learn that would help you on the field.

I would also like to include the following good advice from two missionary wives:

• Be flexible, but realize you're not omnipresent. At times, I call myself a "floater" at church. I may not be on the schedule for "nursery duty" or whatever, but I'm often stepping in to fill in gaps left by others. I stay behind the scenes and try to handle the little "surprises" that come up that may be a distraction to the service. Also, I've gradually shifted along with the Sunday school program as our church has grown. Don't get too attached to a particular class, as they will multiply, and you'll end up saying "goodbye" and moving on with another group. Can't tell you how many times in five years that's happened! It used to be "solo mio" with up to 20 kids from babies to teens! Be prepared to be "used."
• Don't be too disappointed if the multitudes don't get saved right away or change right away. It won't be like the States. Change might come slowly, but it will come so take the small blessings as they come. Recognize them and cherish them.

Rosalind Goforth, missionary to China, wrote the following in her book, *Climbing*.

My husband had sent word ahead to the evangelist for coolies to meet us at the railway station, which was out in the open country, the mission compound being some two miles distant.

When about a quarter of an hour from Tzuchou, the sky became suddenly darkened by dense clouds from the north. Just as the train reached the station, the storm, in all its fury, broke upon us with blinding clouds of dust and sand. We could scarcely see inches away and with great difficulty reached the shelter of the station, which would soon be closed. No evangelist or coolies were in sight. Our letter had evidently miscarried. There was nothing for us to do but to face the long walk over rough, plowed fields leaving our "boy" (servant) to watch the baggage. Dr. Goforth led the way, carrying the heavier child, while the amah and I followed as best we could with the younger one. Darkness had set in. The wind, with rain, seemed unabated. Stumbling, sometimes falling over the hard clods of earth, trying to keep my husband in sight, shivering with cold, the amah and I, while sharing the burden of the child, groaned and wept all the way. Again and again I vowed nothing would make me go out with the children again!

At last we reached the mission. No time was lost in getting coolies off for our baggage. In the meantime, Chinese bread and a tin of sweetened, condensed milk were secured. With some boiling water, soon all were warming up with bowls of hot bread and milk. On the arrival of our baggage, bedding was spread on the brick, platform beds, and the children were soon asleep. But still I kept vowing to myself that this touring life must cease.

The following morning women began to pour in. One fine Christian woman with a bright, shining face came in saying, "Mrs. Goforth, you don't know what a help it is to us all, your coming out as you do with your children. Everyone knows what a home and comforts you give up just for the sake of bringing the good news to us women."

Oh, how my heart thrilled as she spoke! Little did she know what her words meant to me. The vowing of the night before vanished. Joy filled my heart, and I knew that the Lord understood. He had borne wonderfully with my faintheartedness.

It was a wonderful life! Sometimes when letters would reach us from the Homeland expressing pity for us, how my husband would laugh as I read them to him! "Pity," he would say, "why this is the most glorious life possible!" Yes, it was indeed![1]

What about the ministry? Serving God can bring you joy!

Chapter Two

Where Does Your Husband Need You Most?

This need will vary widely because no two missionaries (or wives) are alike, and no two mission fields are alike. The important issue is to pray about it and ultimately let God tell you, through your husband, or at least with his approval, where to serve.

When Rick and I arrived in Iloilo, although we started language study, we began soul winning immediately as English is widely spoken here. We had eight at our first Bible study which was held in our tiny apartment one week after we moved in.

After the Bible study was finished, my husband walked across the street and led some teenagers to the Lord. One of those teenagers is now a faithful pastor's wife. These teenagers went with me to gather children for the Bible study every Friday and Sunday night. We brought them to the apartment where they sat on the floor. I tried, in my broken Ilonggo, to teach them a Bible story with some visual aids. It wasn't long before the teenagers could teach the stories as well as I could. The children went home when their Bible study was over, and then the adults would file in.

Before long, a couple of Bible college graduates from Dr. Armie Jesalva's school in Cebu came to work with us. (That work in Cebu City had been started by the late missionary Bob Hughes.) These graduates rose early in the morning to go soul winning. They would return for lunch and a siesta, and then go out again in the afternoon. Sometimes I would accompany them. Sometimes Rick and I would go out visiting together. At times Rick and I had other things we had to do, such as prayer letters. If you asked my husband, he would probably tell you that my doing his correspondence is most important to him because communication with those in the States is vital to the missionary.

A missionary wife with children will, of course, find her time more limited.

Rick and I thought it was very important for me to stay involved even when I was pregnant. I remember being out on visitation one day while I was pregnant with Ricky and fainting in the middle of the street! That incident surely drew a crowd! Even while the children were small, I stayed very involved. One reason I wanted to stay involved was to keep my own heart right with the Lord. I also wanted to be an example to the women in our church. We did not want the ladies to get the idea that they could be "out of commission" for several months (or even years), using the child as an excuse to keep from serving God. The children take priority, but we have to be careful about not putting God and His work on the back burner all the time.

Also, I believe it has been good for our children to be involved in the ministry since they were very young. As babies, I took them with me when I went soul winning. A mother is tempted to make excuses in her mind like, "It is dirty, and my baby may catch a disease. I'll just stay home with him."

One ministry in which I am currently involved is our Christian academy, which we started when our son Ricky was ready to start kindergarten. This ministry is probably my favorite, and I have greatly enjoyed the time I have spent there. Look for a ministry in which you can work. Pray about it and seek your husband's advice.

I want to be involved in our Christian school because I want to be where our children are. They grow up so quickly, and they are gone before you know it! I enjoyed the years that Ricky and Rachel worked on a route with me, helping me bring children to church.

When you and your husband go to the field, of necessity the work will be his life. Wife, what will you do all day, every day? Yes, you have your house and your children, but someday your children will be gone. I knew I could not sit around my house all day thinking about how homesick I was. I realized I had to keep busy. I knew I needed to let God use me in some area.

Please do not misunderstand me. I am not saying that "just" being a wife and mother is not important or not good enough. I am saying that for your own state of mind, find something in which you can easily "lose" yourself. Finding this niche will also be a great help to the children—to see their mom actively involved in the ministry instead of sitting around and complaining that Dad is always gone. Including the children in the work is also wise.

Just as surely as I have special loves in our ministry, there are also those areas that I do not necessarily like or enjoy! I believe it is very important for every missionary lady to find her "niche," or **where** God needs you to serve.

Chapter Three

When God Can Use You the Most

Obviously, the answer as to when God can most use you is when your heart is right. Since this concept has been addressed elsewhere in this book, I would like to examine two additional areas that are perhaps overlooked.

A. First, I believe God can use you most when He has allowed you to go through a trial. Why does God allow His children to go through trials? I believe that God approves trials for the purpose of testing us and for the purpose of making us stronger. It may be that He wants to teach us something so He can use us in a greater way in His ministry. Charles Hadden Spurgeon said, "Most of the grand truths of God have to be learned by trouble; they must be burned into us by the hot iron of affliction; otherwise, we shall not truly receive them."

Nobody likes or enjoys trials. We would much rather stay in our comfort zone. However, the Bible says in Isaiah 55:8 that God's ways are not our ways.

Job 23:10 says, *"But he knoweth the way that I take: when he hath tried me, I shall come forth as gold."* One of the greatest examples of people triumphing through trials is Job. Two other great Biblical examples of people who endured trials, only to have God use them in a mighty way, were Joseph and Esther. Their trials were of particular importance because in both cases the whole nation of Israel depended on how each handled his adversity. What if a whole nation depended on how you or I handled our unique trial? Would a nation be lost because we did not pass God's test?

When trials come to others, too often we are quick to patronizingly quote a Scripture like Romans 8:28, *"And we know that all things work together for good to them that love God, to them who are the called according to his purpose."* However, when trials hit us smack in the face, we begin to wonder a bit about the validity of that verse! We declare, "Lord, surely *'all things work together for good'* does not apply to ME in this CASE!"

I love II Thessalonians 1:4, 5, 11, and 12: "...*for your patience and faith in all your persecutions and tribulations that ye endure: Which is a manifest token of the righteous judgment of God, that ye may be counted worthy of the kingdom of God, for which ye also suffer...Wherefore also we pray always for you, that our God would count you worthy of this calling...That the name of our Lord Jesus Christ may be glorified in you, and ye in him....*" When persecutions and tribulations come, I have to realize that God believes that I have the patience and faith to endure it. What an awesome thought to think that God trusts me! I surely do not humanly feel like I can handle what He has allowed.

I want to say, "Wait a minute, Lord! You need to take another look at me. I'm not strong at all—I don't think I can handle this!" Yet God, Who is ALWAYS right, thinks I am worthy of the HONOR of suffering for His sake. He allows the challenge to come so I can be glorified in Him and He in me.

I have been praying earnestly for the past year for God to fill me with His Holy Spirit. One reason has been the writing of this book. I feel so unworthy and so inadequate to write a book about missions and the missionary wife. I really need His power and wisdom to undertake such a task. I have not just been praying about this matter during this year of writing. I have prayed for many years for God's Holy Spirit to fill me, and as I said previously, He has answered me many times. This year, however, I have been especially earnest about praying for the filling of the Holy Spirit, even to the point of getting some things straightened out in my life that needed my attention. I told the Lord, "I want the filling of Your Spirit more than anything. Do whatever You need to do to me for that to happen."

Truthfully, that prayer was frightening for me. Before this time I would say, "Do anything to me—but please don't touch my family." As I think about that selfish prayer now, I think how sad it was that I could not trust my family to God! After all, God does choose to take some people Home to be with Him. Our loved ones belong to Him, so why am I trying to hang onto them? Rick, Ricky, and Rachel are not mine to hold close, to keep, and to protect. I need to give them to Him to do as He pleases, as well as myself. It has been a long struggle, but I believe with His help that I am slowly coming around. I am thankful God is so patient with His children!

In 2003 we were going through a terrible trial, but Rick had been praying for God to purge our church because he wanted to see a real revival. It was an extremely difficult time, but I can now see the beginnings of Romans 8:28 in that trial. The ordeal was good for us, it was good for the church, and it was good for those involved.

When my son Ricky was two years old and we had been in the Philippines about three years, I had a ruptured tubal pregnancy, and I almost died. Along with my physical body's suffering such a severe trauma, I also experienced tremendous grief over losing our baby that I wanted so very much. I also think I was "tired" spiritually at that time.

About that same time, an elderly aunt, who was my father's last surviving relative, passed away. I had led her to the Lord by phone before I left for the Philippines. Because my aunt was childless, she left $2,500 to each of her nieces and nephews. After tithing on my inheritance, I used the remainder to fly home for a month. I do not think then that I realized how badly I needed the trip of returning to my roots. I stayed in the home of my childhood and slept in my former room. I was spoiled by my mom, my dad, my brother, and my sister. I had a wonderful childhood growing up in the huge, two-story house overlooking a lake out in the country. I spent my summers swimming and fishing and my winters ice skating. We owned four horses, and rarely a day passed that I did not go riding.

Do you know what I did every night when I lay in my bed? I cried and begged God to let me stay there. I did not want to go back to the Philippines. No, I was not having any marital problems, and I still loved my husband very much. Truthfully, I just did not want to be a missionary any longer. The feelings and emotions I experienced were not what I expected to feel. In all honesty, I felt being a missionary was too hard, and there were too many trials to face. Yes, God had blessed our ministry, but the question I asked over and over was, "Why did He let me lose my baby?"

Ricky had just turned two, and he was always sick. I agonized, "What if Ricky died too?" I was so homesick for the simple, carefree life I had enjoyed in my youth. I thought after three years I would be over that feeling; however, if anything, it was worse. Oh, how I argued with God those long nights!

My guess is that 99% of all missionary wives have experienced these conflicting emotions at one time or another. What can I advise? I can only advise the simple answers I discovered. Just ask God to give you the strength of character and courage to go back anyway—even though you don't want to return. By the time that month was over, was I spiritually back to where I should have been? No! But I hugged and kissed my family members goodbye, got on that plane anyway, crossed the widest ocean again, and returned to Rick and our ministry. My husband never even knew about that time of testing in my life until many years later.

At some time a test or trial may come to your life. Will you have the faith to pass God's test? Will you do what He wants you to do—even if you don't feel like it? You must. A whole nation may depend on your obedience.

B. Secondly, I believe God can use you most when you have found your niche. Of the many missionary stories that I read while doing research for this book, one that graphically stands out in my mind is the story of Hiram and Sybil Bingham, a couple who went to the Sandwich Islands, better known today as the Hawaiian Islands.

In 1806, a young boy named Henry Obookiah saw his entire family killed during a bloody civil war in Hawaii. Shortly afterward, a ship from New York stopped at the islands. The captain agreed to let the brokenhearted boy work aboard ship to pay his passage to the United States.

Henry decided to go to Yale because he had a great desire for an education. Penniless, the 17 year old sat on the steps and wept. A theological student found him there, and upon hearing his story, offered to give him daily lessons. The student not only tutored Henry, he also led him to Christ! In 1816, Henry and some other boys from the Sandwich Islands entered a foreign mission school.

At that time, the natives of Hawaii were known for their incredible acts of barbarism. Sons often buried aging parents alive so they would not have to take care of them. Human sacrifices were common. Hiram Bingham estimated that more than half of the babies were murdered by strangulation, or they were buried alive.

In 1819, Hiram Bingham met the Hawaiian boys, and as a result, Henry surrendered to go to the Sandwich Islands with his wife Sybil, 12 other missionaries, and the Hawaiians, who were extremely burdened to see their people saved. Sadly, Henry Obookiah died a few months before the missionaries sailed.

As soon as they arrived, the missionaries set to work and began to see people saved. Churches and schools were started. Sybil started teaching the female chiefs who had a great desire to learn how to read. It wasn't long before they were being saved, including the king's mother. In the book, *From Jerusalem to Irian Jaya*, the author, Ruth Tucker, writes:

> Perhaps the most dramatic conversion was that of Kapiolani, a chieftainess who like many Hawaiians had lived in dread fear of the goddess Pele who, according to tradition, resided in the fuming volcanic crater of Kilauea. After turning to Christ, Kapiolani, in front of hundreds of horrified onlookers, taunted Pele by climbing up the volcanic mountain and descending into the crater to demonstrate the impotence of this false god. In bold defiance Kapiolani cast rocks and "sacred" berries into the lake of lava as she ridiculed the superstition of the people. Then, returning to the bystanders, she testified to the power of Jehovah. This dramatic incident did more to pave the way for Christianity in Hawaii than all the missionary diatribes against Pele put together.[1]

Sybil Bingham had found her niche! Before long, some 3,000 people were attending church services in Honolulu alone! The Binghams were strong believers in the power of the Gospel to change lives. Only eight years after the Binghams started their missionary work, 12,000 were attending church and 26,000 were in the mission schools! In the book, *Blazing the Missionary Trail*, testimony of the many salvations was recorded.

At one service 200 persons were brought under deep conviction and followed the missionary to his house saying, "We have lived long in sin. What shall we do to be saved?" Kapiolani and others wept for joy as they helped to direct these inquirers to the Saviour. Mr. Clark at Hilo wrote that his house was frequently thronged with people seeking to know the way of salvation.

On Wednesday, January 6, 1830, in Honolulu, 300 children assembled for their weekly service. On Friday, more than 1,000 women gathered for prayer. On Sunday, more than 3,000 assembled for worship. Concerning Monday, January 11, 1830, Bingham says: "Our houses were thronged from before breakfast until the darkness of a rainy night set in. They pressed upon us so incessantly, with their questions and wants, that we could hardly find time to eat the most simple and frugal meals." And he adds, "This was a specimen for many a day for many of the laborers in that field."[2]

The Hawaiian missionaries truly believed in the importance and necessity of prayer which they passed on to the new converts. Records showed 15,000 being in attendance at weekly prayer meetings. *Blazing the Missionary Trail* disclosed the power of their prayers.

In 1838 there began in the Islands and continued unabated for six years, one of the most remarkable revivals in the history of the missionary enterprise...the missionaries preached from seven to twenty times a week to congregations frequently numbering from 4,000 to 6,000 through earnest prayer and fervent efforts to reach the lost.[3]

On July 1, 1838, 1,705 converts were baptized in Hilo! The Binghams had only been married for two weeks when they sailed for Hawaii, and this was only four weeks after they had first met! I have to say that I don't recommend this! However, God greatly used Mrs. Bingham in her husband's remarkable ministry.

God can greatly use you as well. Mrs. Bingham's "niche" was the school for female chiefs. The conversion and Christian growth of these women led the way for great revival in Hawaii. Find your niche—something you do well—something in the ministry that you love doing. Then face your trials courageously and keep your heart right. You will see that is **when** God can use you.

Chapter Four

Who Can Be Used?

In this chapter I would like to observe the lives of a few ladies who have served the Lord and briefly discuss the way in which they were used in their various ministries.

John and Mary Williams, missionaries to Polynesia, endured their share of grief and heartache as seven of their children died. Still, they maintained an indomitable spirit. In the book *Dauntless Women*, author Winifred Mathews writes that Williams said:

In every other respect we enjoy a greater share of happiness than usually falls to the lot of man. We are happy in each other, happy in our work, and, with trifling exceptions, happy in the people among whom we labor.

Mary's tender heart was sad for the old women whom she saw huddled in their huts, dirty and uncared-for and unwanted. Before Christianity came to Raiatea, she knew that they would have been killed by their children or friends as soon as they became a burden, but although, as Christians, the islanders spared their lives, they did nothing to make them happy. So she asked a few of the younger women in the church to help her to gather these poor old people into classes, which were held twice a week.

Her first care was to make them decent clothes. She cut out dresses, which her native helpers put together. She fashioned bonnets for them out of native bark cloth and coconut fiber and trimmed them with grasses and shells. As soon as the clothes were ready, she invited the old people to a feast. The blind, the lame, the deaf, the decrepit—all were there, some seventy or eighty of them. "We were despised and neglected," said one; "now we are sought out by our elder sister."[1]

On Mondays Mary met with the older women, as well as the younger women who were helpers, for Bible study and prayer. These happened to be women who, in the not too distant past, had been cannibals and had practiced infanticide.

She scorned her ill-health, was even resigned to the loss of her babies, as she looked round the circle of brown faces, alight with intelligence, awed by the wonder of the love of God, and heard the new disciples read in their own language a chapter from one of the Gospels, which her husband had translated. How richly worthwhile it was! In her heart she thanked God for the great privilege of being a missionary. In after years, many of the women in that class became missionaries in their turn, accompanying their husbands as teachers to other islands.[2]

As her husband started branching out to other islands, Mary often accompanied him, along with some of the saved nationals, teaching the Bible to the women and children. These women were hungry for the Word of God. As a result of the Williamses' work, the family lives of the natives showed great improvement.

John Williams made many evangelistic excursions to the surrounding islands, and he was greatly used of God until he met a martyr's death. God also greatly used his wife Mary to minister to the women of Polynesia.

Another missionary couple, Agnes and William Watt, went to the island of Tanna. *Dauntless Women* shares Agnes Watt's feelings toward the island people:

Agnes was filled with pity for the Tannese women. Many girl babies were left in the bush to die immediately after birth, while those who were allowed to live were sent away at an early age to their future homes to become the slaves of their husbands. The women sensed Agnes' sympathy.

Agnes held sewing classes regularly for the women, who helped her to make hundreds of women's dresses. Some people at home, she felt, thought that the missionaries put too much importance on clothing, but among the natives it was the badge of Christianity. When a new tribe "took the worship," as they expressed it, then the cry was for clothing. If a man became disaffected toward the church, one of his first acts was to lay aside the cloth or girdle that he had begun to wear. Agnes generally had blisters on her fingers from cutting out so many garments.[3]

The Watts had no children of their own, so they adopted and reared several Tannese children. Tanna was a difficult mission field, and it seemed to some that the Watts had little to show for the 25 years spent there; however, Agnes genuinely loved those seemingly unlovable people. Agnes also helped her husband translate the Bible into Tannese. Perhaps Agnes' greatest gift to the Lord's ministry was her unquenchable faith.

For 28 years Horace and Lillias Underwood served as missionaries to Korea. When they returned to the States in very poor health, Mr. Underwood soon died. In 1918 Lillias wrote a book about her husband's work. From *Dauntless Women*, I would like to share some of Lillias' inspiring words:

Writing of the many dangers that they faced together, when death at times seemed very near, she quotes Kipling's line, "*A reckless seraphim hanging on the rein of a red-maned star,*" with the comment, "It has occurred to me that my experiences have been nearly as strenuous as that angel's and my husband was much like that red-maned star." Words to be found in her earlier book about missionary life in Korea are an epitome of her own life: "If in these pages you have seen much that leads you to think the land is a difficult one in which to live, if you have read of political unrest, bad government, riots, robbers and plagues; if you have learned that missionaries have died of typhus fever, small-pox, dysentery and other violent forms of disease, this will only serve to remind you that the more valuable the prize to be won, the greater the difficulty and cost. If you desire to share in the joy of this great harvest, and are worthy, you will fear no danger, shrink from no obstacles, either for yourselves or for your loved ones, whom you are asked to give to the work. There is no more place on the mission field for the fearful and unbelieving than in heaven itself. Let the applicants [for missionary work] be reduced until only the resolute, the consecrated, those who believe in God, the people and themselves, are accept-ed for this mighty privilege, this high calling."[4]

The list is endless of the ministries in which God has used missionary ladies. Truly, you do not have to fit yourself into someone else's mold. Maybe you are not a great Bible teacher like Mary Williams. Perhaps you are not a great linguist like Agnes Watt. Maybe you have not specialized in music. Possibly you feel inadequate in every area. Maybe you are thinking, "There are so many other ladies who could do this ministry so much better than me!" God isn't looking at our ability; rather, He looks at our availability. The Bible says in I Samuel 16:7b, "*...for the LORD seeth not as man seeth; for man looketh on the outward appearance, but the LORD looketh on the heart.*" Do you want a full and rewarding life? Find out what God wants you to do and do it!

Who? How about **you**? Are you ready to volunteer for the Lord's ministry? Just surrender your heart, and I promise that God will use you.

Chapter Five

How Can We Be Used?

How do missionary ladies serve the Lord? First and foremost, if you are married, you serve by being the right kind of wife for your husband. It is very difficult for your husband to do what God has called him to do if you are not the right kind of wife. This subject was addressed in the chapter on "Husband." If you have children, your children must have priority. We don't want to go out and save the world, only to lose our own kids. This was discussed in the chapter on children. Therefore, we are going to take a little time and space here to mention what else missionary ladies do to serve the Lord.

Although this book is primarily for missionary wives, I have mentioned a few single ladies who have done a wonderful work for God. One of my favorites is Amy Carmichael, who had an orphanage for children in India. My friend, Sandy Domelle, gave me a fabulous book written about her entitled *Amy Carmichael of Dohnavur* by Frank L. Houghton.

Years ago I wrote a letter to one of my heroines, Mrs. Elizabeth Elliot, the widow of Missionary Jim Elliot, who was killed by the Auca Indians in Ecuador. We were discussing reading great books as opposed to wasting our time on frivolous reading (because I LOVE to read!), and she advised me to read everything I could written by *her* heroine, Amy Carmichael.

Amy was a prolific author who wrote a total of 35 books! Miss Carmichael spent a short time in Japan before going to India where she spent 55 years of her life without taking a furlough. On the fly leaf of *Amy Carmichael of Dohnavur*, Elizabeth Elliott penned the following words taken from her book, *Introduction to Mountain Breezes: the Collected Poems of Amy Carmichael*:

Amy was aghast when she learned of the hideous underground traffic in little children who were given or sold to Hindu temples for the purpose of prostitution, from which there was never the possibility of escape.

One day a little girl appeared as Amy was having her "chota" (early morning tea) on the veranda. The child had been led, it seems, by an angel. There was no other explanation. The child had told the terrible truth about servitude, and Amy began what became known as the Dohnavur Fellowship of South India.[1]

Another great missionary, who was also single, was Gladys Aylward of China. Gladys had an orphanage just as Miss Carmichael did. Since Gladys was turned down by the China Inland Mission, she worked as a parlor maid, saved every penny she earned, and paid her own fare on a train that traveled through Europe, Russia, Siberia, and into China. That journey, in and of itself, is an incredibly interesting story, but even more arresting is the dangerous journey she took with over 100 of her children, over the mountains and rivers, during the war to get them to a safe place.

From Jerusalem to Irian Jaya shares some insight about the willingness of God's servant, Gladys Aylward, to make a difference.

I wasn't God's first choice for what I've done for China. There was somebody else...I don't know who it was—God's first choice. It must have been a man—a wonderful man. A well-educated man. I don't know what happened. Perhaps he died. Perhaps he wasn't willing. And God looked down and saw Gladys Aylward.[2]

Another of my favorites is Mary Slessor of Calabar, a single missionary to the region which is now known as Nigeria. The job God had tailor-made for Mary was very unique. She was a pioneer missionary, going into the worst parts of Africa where no one else would go. Mary lived in a mud hut and worked by herself. She became a jack-of-all-trades: nursing the sick; teaching; adopting children whom she rescued from being buried alive; and perhaps strangest of all, mediating disputes between warring tribes. The people of Calabar were steeped in witchcraft, and Mary often risked her life trying to right a wrong. She earned quite a reputation as a peacemaker; and she felt that as a woman, she would not pose the supposed threat a man would to the unreached tribes. Much influenced by David Livingstone, she also set up trade routes in preparation for missionaries who she hoped and prayed would follow. She died in her little mud hut at the age of 66, after spending 40 years selflessly blazing the trail in Africa.

How will you serve the Lord? Maybe you won't have an orphanage or settle disputes between two tribes at war! More than likely, you will teach a Sunday school class, and yes, I have done that. Maybe you will work with the deaf, and I did that for a season when our deaf ministry was just getting off the ground.

Perhaps you will work in a Christian academy or Bible college, and again, I have done both. Maybe you will have a route that you visit, and you will bring people to church. I have done both for many years. Maybe you will work with the music in your church, and I especially loved working in this area of the ministry.

Maybe God will use you in the area of counseling. I have a beautiful, wood napkin holder that was made by my friend Suzie Heidenreich which sits on my kitchen table. The paper napkins held by the holder are probably used as much to wipe the tears of the women and girls who sit at my table and tell me their heartaches as they are for their intended use.

Maybe you will have to play the part of hostess often. We have many visitors from America—pastors, groups of teenagers, groups of Bible students, friends, and the list goes on. A missionary can wear many hats. My job description is: "Whatever Rick tells me to do—I do it!" My jobs have changed many times through the years.

Most importantly, I trust you will be a soul winner. One Saturday when we were out visiting the route, I invited a mother whom I had invited many times before. This time she said "Yes!" to my invitation because we were having "Baby Day," and we were taking and giving each mother a 5 x 7 picture of her with her baby. Because she wanted a picture of her baby, this dear lady came and got saved the next day!

Several months later while we were visiting the route, I stopped in front of this lady's house and noticed blood covering the ground. I thought perhaps a dog had been killed. The neighbor children came out and told me this lady had died just a few hours earlier inside the house. This news was incomprehensible to me because I had just seen her the previous Sunday, and she seemed well. I learned that she had started vomiting blood that week from an advanced case of tuberculosis. She went to the free government hospital, but she had waited too late. She was only 39. How sad I was, but how grateful I was that she had gotten saved! As I left her house, I kept thinking, "What if I had decided to stay home that day because of a headache or some other minor excuse?" We need always to be faithful soul winners.

Find out **how** God wants you to serve Him on the mission field, but make sure you include soul winning as a part of your service.

Chapter Six

Why Serve?

Why do you serve the Lord? What are your underlying motives? Why are you going to the mission field? I have already addressed this subject in the chapter on "Attitude," but I would like to share a story regarding our motives about serving God.

One day a Chinese man named Mr. Su was riding down the street in a rickshaw when he heard an unfamiliar sound emanating from Jonathan Goforth's church in China. Mr. Su had been drinking, and his curiosity got the better of him, so he staggered into the building. A meeting was in progress, and he saw Mrs. Goforth playing the organ with her son accompanying her on the violin. Mr. Su found a seat on the front row. After the special music concluded, Mr. Goforth began preaching from the Word of God. The visitor became angry when Goforth started explaining the meaning of sinner to the crowd. The book *Goforth of China* elaborates further about the incident:

> Mr. Su later told how angry he became that this foreign devil would dare tell all the people about him, and, literally, show up all his sins and faults. Then, gradually, as he became sober, the truth went home and when the invitation was given for any who believed what had been said, to indicate it by raising the hand, he looked around, expecting that every hand would be up, for it seemed so wonderful to him. But there were none, and saying to himself, "The cowards," he himself put up his hand. Later others followed. Then as several men passed the inquiry room, Mr. Su followed.
>
> The following day he came to Mr. Goforth, saying, "Pastor, take me with you everywhere you go. I want to learn the secret of how it could be possible when last night as I stood in the inquiry room, my whole past life seemed to drop from me as a garment. I have no desire for those things which bound me with chains. I want to learn this secret that I may help others."[1]

Mr. Su never turned back from his life-changing decision! How can you read a story like that and NOT want to go to the mission field?! Does this happen all the time? Of course not. In fact, just a few pages before this wonderful story, Mrs. Goforth wrote that it was not uncommon during the early visits to that city to be spat on when they were on the streets. I cannot help but think that perhaps God had special blessings for them, such as the conversion of Mr. Su, because these missionaries endured so much for His Name's sake.

You say, "But I can be a soul winner at home." Yes, you can, and if that's what God wants you to do, by all means, do it. But have you ever asked Him if He wants you to go? Have you ever surrendered? Have you ever volunteered?

When the late missionary to the Philippines, Bob Hughes, preached at First Baptist Church of Hammond and Hyles-Anderson College in 1976, he asked, "Why do we need a call when we have a command to take the Gospel to the whole world?" He continued, "You want a call? Give me your phone number! I'll give you a call! 'There's a call comes ringing o'er the restless waves; send the Light! Send the Light!' " His clarion call for missions touched our hearts.

In Matthew chapter 19, Jesus has a discussion with the rich young ruler. The Lord told him to sell everything, give it all to the poor, and follow Him. The young man just couldn't give it up. Jesus then told His disciples that "...*a rich man shall hardly enter into the kingdom of heaven.*" (Matthew 19:23)

What was their response? The Bible says they were amazed; in fact, they were "exceedingly" amazed! Jesus then says, "...*with God all things are possible.*" (Matthew 19:26) In the very next verse we see that Peter had a bad attitude and a wrong motive. He informed the Lord Jesus that he and the other disciples had left everything to follow Him, so what were they going to get in return? I love Jesus' answer in Matthew 19:29, which I call the missionary's promise: "*And every one that hath forsaken houses, or brethren, or sisters, or father, or mother, or wife, or children, or lands, for my name's sake, shall receive an hundredfold, and shall inherit everlasting life.*"

Sometimes full-time Christian workers, including missionaries, have a bad attitude like Peter's. "What do I get, God?" Peter asked. "What's in it for me?" Don't make bargains with God for your service. Your service should be out of a heart of love. Think about the fact that Jesus died for you. Don't you love Him for that? Don't you want to serve Him for that? And if God is using someone and blessing someone's work for Him, don't envy, compare, or attack that person. Avoid jealousy; just praise God that people are being saved! We are supposed to keep our eyes on Jesus. If we watch another, that means that person has come between us and Christ. Don't take your eyes off Him.

Why serve? Because Jesus loves you and because hopefully, you love Him. Why serve? Because a lost and dying world needs to get saved. Don't hold your husband back if he is brave enough to go! Be glad that you are married to a man of God! Why serve? Go because Jesus went to the cross for you.

John 21:15 says, "*So when they had dined, Jesus saith to Simon Peter, Simon, son of Jonas, lovest thou me more than these? He saith unto him, Yea, Lord; thou knowest that I love thee. He saith unto him, Feed my lambs."* Jesus asked Peter this same question twice more. Then in verse 19 Jesus said, *"...Follow me."*

Through the years on the mission field, I have found myself following Christ, but often I find I am trying to follow Him with the wrong motives. You may "follow Jesus" to the mission field, but if you have the wrong motive, you won't stay long. I believe there is only one thing that can keep you on the field, and that is love. Only love enables you to take everything Satan can throw at you and stand fast. Pray for the right motives, and pray for love. Love has no substitute. Love is **why** we serve.

Conclusion

I admire Maude Cary so much because of the people she tried to reach for Christ—the Moslems and the Jews. They are not merely indifferent; they are antagonistic. In the book *Miss Terri* the author shares some more insight about this remarkable woman named Maude Cary:

"Maude witnessed for Christ to rich and poor, whether they listened eagerly or not."[1] In return, young men insulted her. Children would hit her and throw rocks at her. "She held her head high and trotted home gracefully, but in her heart she acknowledged that she was not really willing to be a fool for Christ's sake.[2]

Maude had other trials to bear including frequent illness, criticism from fellow missionaries, and worst of all, a terminated engagement that left her brokenhearted.

After 16 years of labor, the little group of missionaries finally had one convert whose name was Hoosein. Though others showed interest, severe persecution by their people easily caused them to reject Christ.

In November, 1924, a Bible conference was held in a hut owned by a Moroccan Christian. Five baptized believers were present, the fruit of a quarter century of labor among the tribes. The change in their lives was remarkable, especially in relation to their families. Formerly they considered that the only way to maintain authority was to keep their wives in constant terror of being beaten. The average Berber was haughty—so haughty that he hardly ever spoke a kind word to his wife, nor did she dare to sit down beside him. The believers no longer beat or even threatened their wives. They showed kindness to the children and concern for the welfare of the whole family.

Ten men, all professing to be Christians, were imprisoned for their faith one winter. The five baptized believers were the objects of hatred and scorn in their village, but they stood firm in their faith in Christ.

Miss Cary had for years delighted in teaching the little boys of Sefrou. Her first classes were sort of a junior church. It was not among the Muslims that signs of "fruit" first began to appear. Some Jewish boys listened and believed.

In time, three young men stood out as converts of the frail American woman: Judah, Simeon, and Simon. Other Jews, too, professed to believe in Christ. Saturdays were full days because dozens of Jews, sometimes up to two hundred of them, came to listen to the preaching of the Word of God.[3]

After 23 years on the mission field, Maude took her first furlough. She was now 46 years old. When she returned to the field rested and rejuvenated, she picked up where she left off. She conducted two classes a week for Moslem boys and one for Moslem girls. She also had two a week for Jewish boys and one for Jewish girls. The following is the story of one little Moslem boy named Mehdi whose life was touched by Maude Cary:

A light appeared in the form of an unassuming little woman of another race. Miss Cary was one of the hated Christians. Women liked her, but most of the men considered her a meddler. Mehdi eyed her contemptuously at first, since his opinions were those of his elders.

Some of the boys accepted invitations to go to her home. When they gathered in groups outside, they talked about her, and Mehdi tried to shame them for listening to such blasphemy. But when he was told that the American woman spoke both French and Arabic, he became curious. There could be no harm in looking in to see what the strange woman did. Or would there be? Some said the Christians worshiped idols, which was certainly blasphemous. Others said they killed Moslem children. But his playmates came out alive, so in the end Mehdi determined to go to the missionary's home.

The room was pleasant. There were interesting pictures on the wall which caught the attention of the new boy in class. As he wondered about them, the foreign lady began to read, and his attention turned to her. She spoke Arabic well and read smoothly from a book that was printed in Arabic. It was not the Koran. He soon recognized it as a book about the hated Christian leader. He felt guilty listening to the forbidden doctrine.

That evening the lad told his father about the strange woman and her teachings. Wisely, the Moslem priest explained that some of the Christian teachings were true but that what she said about Jesus Christ could not be believed.

"Jesus was one of the saints," his father pointed out, "but He was not God, or God's representative. Our prophet, the great Mohammed, is the only true representative of God, as you know."

Perhaps because the boy sincerely agreed with him, his faith in Islam unshaken, his father allowed him to continue going to Miss Cary's classes.

A respect for Maude Cary began to take root in the mind of the young

Arab. He liked to be in the clean, peaceful classroom. He listened intently to what the missionary had to say, but when she spoke of Jesus, Mehdi closed his mind. By degrees even Christ became less repulsive to the young man, for he realized that Miss Cary's chief desire in their midst was to share the message which meant so much to her. Her method of teaching the rowdy boys impressed him too. She never used a stick to rap their heads if they disobeyed; rather, she used impressive words, gentleness and unmistakable goodness.

The boys and girls in Miss Cary's classes did not go home empty-handed. They were often given pictures of Bible scenes. Every picture meant much to young Mehdi. From the first time he entered the classroom he studied the pictures on the wall intently, contemplating the stories they told.

The collection was a treasure that filled many free moments. Mehdi sat alone and studied them, recalling the stories that Miss Cary told. They also served to impress on his young mind and heart the lessons from God's Word that Miss Cary taught—lessons well watered with tears and prayers.

When Maude took her first furlough and the Bible classes stopped, Mehdi felt that a void had come into his life. He applied himself vigorously to his schoolwork, and with his friend, Mohammed Bouabid, he was chosen to take special training. They were both in their late teens when Miss Cary returned to Sefrou. In the spring of 1929, Mehdi and Mohammed both received Christ as Saviour.

It was not long before Mehdi, the older of the two converts, lost his job. This was not surprising, because both boys made a clean break with Islam, which brought shame to their families and relatives. They were outspoken in their witness for Christ. Mehdi received temporary relief from the extreme persecution when he was sent to Meknes to work in the Bible shop. There, as he studied God's Word and fearlessly shared his testimony with others, he grew by giant steps in the things of the Lord.

"If a person is unwilling to share his knowledge of the way of salvation with others," he reasoned, "it is doubtful that he has ever been born again!"
One day Miss Cary showed the young convert from Islam a picture of a large church congregation in America. He was stunned.

"How can thousands sit at home and enjoy one another's fellowship," he commented, "and leave so many here without the gospel?"

With his whole heart he entered into missionary work side by side with the foreign "infidels."[4]

One day a soldier named Lejb Feldman knocked on the lady missionaries' door. He was a Polish Jew in the French Foreign Legion. He had attended a few Bible studies with a friend, who had also given him a Hebrew New Testament. He hated the Army, tried to escape from it, and ended up in prison. There he started praying and reading the New Testament.

Out of prison, the aesthetic young Jew became more aware of God's hand upon him than ever before. He sought peace more earnestly, never going to bed at night until he felt a measure of peace with God. One night as he prayed, he seemed to see the Lord pointing to the cross and saying, "I suffered for thee." It was an unforgettable experience. The next morning he awoke, a new creature in Christ Jesus. Immediately he shared his experience with his buddies and their wives.

Lejb's greatest desire now was to see another Christian.[5]

His greatest desire took him to the home of Maude Cary. She began teaching him about the Lord, and her willingness to teach Lejb led to meetings with other Legionnaires. Like the Moslem, Mehdi Kksara, Lejb's Jewish family wanted nothing to do with him after he became a Christian. Mehdi and Lejb joined some of the missionary men when they went street preaching in the market place.

Perhaps of even greater curiosity to the milling crowds was the presence of Lejb Feldman and Mehdi Kara on the side of the "Infidels" in market debates. A Jew, a Muslim and a Christian, all saved by grace, were sharing the truths of God's Word with unbelievers. Both men were exceptionally capable and convincing speakers. But it was not only their words that drove home the message. The very presence of the unlikely trio of co-workers was an unbeatable argument for the cause of Jesus Christ.[6]

Though the missionaries endured objects thrown at them and being spit on, they kept on for the Gospel's sake. Maude Cary spent 54 years on the mission field, braving wars, illness, and persecution. She died at the age of 88. Only a handful of people attended her funeral. Shortly after Miss Cary's death, the missionaries were expelled from Morocco.

In the book, *Operation World*, author Patrick Johnstone says that today, although Islam is the state religion of Morocco, the government tolerates other religious groups as long as they confine their ministry to expatriate communities. The breakdown is 99.8% Moslem, .05% Jews, and .16% Christian. Of those listed as "Christian," .01% is considered "Protestant."[7]

Under "Missionaries," Mr. Johnstone reports that there are approximately 150 Christian expatriates in Moroccan ministries inside and outside the country.

The Church in Morocco has become a reality, but at great cost. There are possibly 400 indigenous believers who have confessed Christ, as well as other secret believers. There are eight cities in which Christians gather in little groups. Persecution of believers and intimidation of seekers has steadily increased since 1968. Individuals who become followers of Christ are open to charges of treachery and illegal contacts with foreign organizations and are subject to prison sentences. Missionary work, as such, is no longer permitted, and all former mission centers were closed. Christian workers remain on in various secular roles as nurses, teachers, etc., and quietly contrive to share their faith and encourage believers.[8]

God has a ministry for you, too. It isn't always easy; in fact, it's often difficult. But, I believe the happiest people on earth are saved people who have found what God wants them to do, **why** He wants them to do His work, and are doing exactly that!

Above: Rachel poses with her classmates at kindergarten graduation exercises. Rachel is in the front row on the left.
Below: Rick baptizes Rachel.

UNIT SIX

Your Relationships

"…Love one another."
(I John 4:11)

Introduction

Marcus and Narcissa Whitman were married February 1836. The newlyweds had a rather unusual honeymoon—traveling by wagon all the way to Oregon!

Born in the early 1800s in New England, both were saved at young ages. Narcissa, the daughter of a judge, was beautiful, well-educated, and a talented singer. She ran a kindergarten; however, she had a great burden to reach the American Indians out West. One Sunday in church, she was touched by the story of the Nez Perce Indians begging for the "Book of Life." Feeling the call of God on her life, Narcissa volunteered for the mission field; but the American Board of Commissioners for Foreign Missions, which was involved in Indian evangelism, did not accept single lady missionaries.

Marcus also heard one of the speakers who was traveling to churches recruiting missionaries and raising money for the project. Likewise, Marcus also felt called to take the Gospel to the Indians. Consequently, Marcus heard of Narcissa's wanting to go and of her subsequent rejection by the mission board. Marcus decided he needed to meet this interesting young lady who wanted to be a missionary to the native Americans. The couple fell in love. Marcus was 32 years old when they were married. The morning after the wedding they started West.

They would not make the trip alone. Another missionary couple, Henry and Eliza Spaulding, journeyed with them as they too felt called to reach the American Indians.

Several years earlier, Henry Spaulding had been in love with Narcissa, and he had asked for her hand in marriage. She had refused his proposal. This rejection made the situation rather awkward and strained for the two couples. One author suggested that Spaulding was a difficult man to tolerate. Another writer suggests that Whitman was the one who was perplexing and hard to handle.

Although the trip was extremely grueling, Narcissa enjoyed the beautiful scenery as the party slowly traveled Westward. She kept a journal, and it was obvious from entries that she was happily married. No doubt the fact that she was expecting her first child had something to do with her joy.

When the wagon train finally reached Oregon, the Spauldings and the Whitmans decided to split up because quite simply, they could not get along. Spaulding decided to work with the Nez Perce Indians, a tribe who was truly hungry for God. The Whitmans chose to minister to the Cayuse, who hated the white man and were well-known for their treachery.

Upon reaching their respective destinations, Spaulding and Whitman both had to work quickly to build shelters before winter came. Each built a rough, temporary lean-to which was barely adequate, but they knew it had to see them sufficiently through the cold months.

The day before Narcissa turned 29 on March 14, 1837, she gave birth to Alice. The first summer both Spaulding and Whitman planted crops and worked on a rudimentary form of farming. Both would diligently work on learning the language of their tribe. Whitman was a medical doctor, so he also made use of those skills.

In the autumn of 1838, more discord would come to the fledgling ministry. In the book, *From Jerusalem to Irian Jaya*, Ruth Tucker shares this account of the cause:

> The fall of 1838 brought three new missionary couples, whose presence brought further conflict. In the words of one biographer, "It seemed that the reinforcements had brought not help, but dissension only." These were often bitter. One of the wives described a typical flare-up: "It came on so sharp that I was compelled to leave. It is enough to make one sick to see what is the state of things in the mission."[1]

One Sunday afternoon in June, when Marcus and Narcissa were reading, they suddenly noticed that Alice was missing. Panic-stricken, the couple searched everywhere for their precious little girl. Tragically, the two-year-old had walked to a nearby stream and drowned. The death of the Whitmans' daughter ultimately helped to heal the division among the missionaries. Even the Spauldings traveled the long distance from the work with the Nez Perce to be with the Whitmans during their grief.

Narcissa never had any more children, but she and Marcus adopted several orphans. They took in a family of seven children whose parents had both died on the wagon train West. In the book *Doctor in Buckskin*, author T. D. Allen elaborates,

> Winter had caught the wagon train on the other side of the Blues. Because of delays, food rations had given out. Game could not be had. Measles had gone through the wagons like a prairie wind.
>
> Little bands of hungry, desperate travelers began to straggle into Waiilatpu

and camp in the Whitman meadow east of the house. Marcus doctored...day and night. Narcissa cooked and nursed and mended, her face drawn with worry, her tears near the surface.

With some of the first half-starved, half-frozen families came word of the Sagers. Marcus and Narcissa listened with aching hearts to the captain of that band. Their wagon had dropped out of line, one day late in May, long enough for Mrs. Sager to give birth to their seventh child—a baby girl. Mrs. Sager had made a slow recovery but they must move on with the wagon train or be left among warring Indians.

Near the Continental Divide, Mr. Sager took sick. Just before he died, he said, "Captain, I want my family to stop at the station of Doc Whitman."

In less than a month the mother, too, was dead. Now a German doctor was driving through with the six older children in an ox cart. Women of the caravan were caring for the baby.

"I hope you can take them in when they get here," the captain said. "That's what their father wanted."

"Seven children added to those we have already?"

Only a few days later, the captain of the first band came to the kitchen door and called, "Doc Whitman, come outside and meet your new family."

Before the pathetic little outfit, the captain introduced the children. On the far side of the cart a black-haired boy, his arms on the wheel and his head on his arms, sobbed aloud.

"That's Francis," the captain explained. "He's ten."

In the cart at the front, sat a brown-haired boy, taller, more reserved but with tears flowing down his cheeks and dropping off his chin onto his ragged jeans. "That's John in front. He's fourteen."

On the near side of the cart, the frightened girls huddled together, bare heads bleached by the sun, bare feet caked with dirt, hunger the one fact bare on their faces. "Can't keep the girls straight," the captain said. "Catherine's the one that broke her leg, jumping on the wheel. Then there's Matilda Jane and Elizabeth and Hannah Louise. An old woman's got the baby."

When they reached the house, an old woman waited by the kitchen door. Saying nothing, she got rid of the Sager baby by dumping it into Narcissa's arms. Marcus pulled down the soiled rags in which the baby was wrapped. Figuring back to May, the child must be five months old and yet she looked about three weeks and too poor to live through the day. Tears ran down Narcissa's cheeks.[2]

The orphans found a home with Marcus and Narcissa.

As more and more settlers continued to travel to Oregon, bringing diseases with them, the Cayuse became even angrier with the settlers. Ruth Tucker, in *From Jerusalem to Irian Jaya* explains what happened:

> Their villages were ravaged by a plague, and within the space of eight weeks nearly half of the four-hundred-member tribe had suffered painful deaths. Though Whitman had tried to help, the situation only grew worse, and suspicion mounted among the Indians that he was purposely poisoning them with his "medicine."
>
> The end came suddenly. It was a dreary late November afternoon in 1847. Two Indians appeared at the mission house door. Others were stationed outside. Without warning, the massacre began. There were seventy-two people living at the mission, including more than a dozen men, and the murderers were Indians whom the Whitmans knew well. Pulling tomahawks out from under the blankets they were carrying, the small party began the slaughter, starting with Dr. Whitman. When it was over, fourteen were dead. With the exception of Narcissa, the women and children had been spared, only to be held in terrifying captivity until their release some five weeks later.
>
> News of the Whitman massacre spread rapidly. American troops were sent in, and the missionaries in the interior were ordered out. In the spring of 1850 the five Cayuse Indians responsible for the murders were brought to trial, convicted, and sentenced to die; and on June 3 all of Oregon, it seemed, came out to watch the hangings.[3]

I wanted to use the story of the Whitmans because, in spite of their great sacrifice and courage, they seemingly had a problem with their relationships—those with other missionaries, as well as their relationship with the people to whom God called them. Without trying to be negative, I believe these very important relationships need to be addressed in order for the Lord's work to progress.

Chapter One

Relationships With People in Your Ministry

Your most important relationship, of course, is your relationship with the Lord. Secondarily would be your relationship with your husband and your children. Since I have included separate units about "Walking With God," "Your Husband," and "Your Children," this chapter will be limited to your other relationships.

Following are some opinions of missionary wives regarding this subject of relationships. Some have had to adjust greatly to different cultures from various fields. (As with other chapters, I have not mentioned names or countries in order to keep their remarks confidential.)

 Can you please share some insight about relationships on the field?

Answers:

• [Interaction with nationals] was much easier [than expected]. They were much friendlier and forgiving. I also did not listen to the negative talk from other missionaries as negativity can build a barrier between you and the people. You will discover their little quirks soon enough.

• People are people no matter where they are. Sin is the same, and we deal with the same problems as are dealt with anywhere. I've heard people say that methods in America won't work on the field, but we've found that they do. You may have to use illustrations and examples they will understand, but the same basic Bible principles work. Any information they have of America is from movies, so they think we are all rich with houses and cars. When we say, "There is no money," you can tell they don't really believe us. Other than this, they are normal people, just with different customs and foods.

• In many ways, they think and do things differently than we are used to. One must respect their ways, as long as they are not against the Bible. And of course, if they are, then we need to be patient when showing them what the Bible says. Also, we need to realize that we will not have a close friend and not be able to share everything with the nationals. Unfortunately, they will sometimes use you to get what they want. Don't be bothered or take it personally when these times happen. We just need to do right and be the right kind of example. We cannot change people; only God can. We are here to teach what God can do for them.

• I have never been treated with anything but respect and admiration. Everyone's dream here is to leave and go to America, so they are baffled that we chose to be here just for them. So, it's different in that you see what America means to the world. It certainly makes me appreciate my country even more!

• Our field is different in that the people are more difficult to get to know. They are polite (most of the time) but are very stand-offish and lead very private lives. They stay in their circles of family and friends.

• The people God called us to [a former Communist country] are a little hard to interact with because of their fear of strangers.

• Nationals do not think exactly the same way I think. That was very difficult for me to realize. In many ways I still get frustrated. But, when it all comes down to it, we are all just the same—sinners. People are people with all the same basic needs—no matter where they live.

We need to pray about these relationships all the time because Satan will try to destroy them. Rick and I have found Filipinos to be very warm, friendly, and easy to love. Some missionaries are in "colder" countries such as Europe and former Communist-ruled countries. People in those countries often tend to be more closed and less receptive to the Gospel. Buddhist and Moslem countries come to mind also. It may be more difficult to work among people who are seemingly hardhearted, so extra love and patience is needed.

Chapter Two

Counseling People

Hardly a day passes without someone asking me for advice. Some questions are minor, and some are not. You will not have all the answers, but you can point them to the One Who does. Sometimes people just need to talk, and it will mean a lot to them that you care enough to sit and listen.

I have young ladies come to ask about boyfriends. Many times I will say, "Let me ask Pastor, and I will talk to you later about what he said." Then we talk about all the pros and all the cons, and about being careful. We talk about listening to God, about listening to what Pastor says, about being obedient, and about the great cost of disobedience. Then we have prayer together, and I talk to my husband about the young man.

Sometimes my husband will say, "No! He's not good for her!" Sometimes he will respond with: "No! *She's* not good for *him*!" Sometimes he will answer, "It's fine for them to 'court,' " which is the word widely used here in the Philippines.

An outstanding Christian girl in our church started dating one of the young men who was also in our church. When she starting dating the young man, who was a new convert, I had my doubts. However, the young man really started growing in the Lord in a great way. They were both very involved in the church. Recently he surrendered to go to Bible college and become a preacher. This "outstanding Christian girl" was very upset! She did not want her boyfriend to be a preacher! She wanted them just to be lay people in the church.

Consequently, I had an appointment with this girl, and we talked for a long time. I told her she should be encouraging him, not holding him back. "After all," I reminded her, "you are the one who helped him to grow in Christ!" We prayed, and she cried. She is slowly coming around to the idea of becoming a pastor's wife. I believe she will make a great one because she really loves the ministry.

Another young lady came to me worried about the prospect of turning 30 with no prospects of marriage. She had decided that she must get married right away. It did not matter who, what, how, where, when—as long as she was married. Becoming a mail-order bride is a big business in the Philippines. My husband and

I have spent many hours counseling with young ladies about this matter. Sometimes you wonder how someone can be so naïve and gullible. It is sometimes hard for Americans to understand. Americans have never lived in such abject poverty. Americans do not have parents who from early childhood put the heavy responsibility on older siblings of taking care of their many younger brothers and sisters and of making sure they are educated. Some feel if they can marry a foreigner—any foreigner—then they can go abroad, get a job, and support their brothers and sisters. In some cases, this man is a total stranger, or he is very old.

In a few cases we have had ladies who have graduated from our Bible college leave to work in a church and marry a new convert in the church. Many a wife becomes extremely unhappy because, after a while, her husband who has not been grounded in church will not even let her attend church. We encourage our lady graduates to marry our men graduates, who are mature Christians and want to serve God.

Not long ago a girl on our staff asked advice about her boyfriend, who had graduated from Bible college and was getting ready to leave and work in a church. They have been in love with each other for many years and want to get married. The problem is, his parents do not like her and do not want them to marry. They want him to marry another girl who is also serving the Lord in full-time Christian work. The girl they have chosen for their son to marry does not like him, and she is in love with another. To further complicate matters, the son does not like his parents' choice. The bottom-line motivator in the Philippines is that children are usually very obedient to their parents—even when they are grown adults. Therefore, this son is patiently waiting for his parents to change their mind. As you counsel people, to be sure, you will find some very strange situations.

A few times I have had a lady come for advice because her husband beats her. Often the beatings have something to do with the wife's attending a Baptist church. However, most of these battered wives were already being beaten before they ever came to our church. In two cases, the husbands were saved (my husband led one to the Lord) and have since died. One brave lady continues to come and continues to be beaten. I often wonder, "If I were in her place, would I endure the beatings, just to be able to go to church?" Their plight makes me think twice about staying home from church just because of a little headache.

Sometimes a lady seeks counsel about going abroad to work because of the poverty. It is not uncommon for a wife to work abroad for years as a maid or in some other type of menial labor. She leaves her husband and children and sends back the money she earns to her family. We *always* recommend that they a wife not do this. We have seen so much heartbreak when this happens. Many times the husband, who has been left behind, will take all of his wife's hard-earned money and run off with another woman! In most cases the children who have grown up without a mother's influence do not turn out very well—especially if their father becomes a womanizer.

One time a young lady came to me, told me that she had been raped and was expecting a child. I was heartbroken for the girl, who was engaged to be married to a pastor. My husband and I talked to the pastor and the girl's family together. We suggested they go ahead and get married, stay in a private place with family until the baby was born, and then give up the baby up for adoption. We told them to pray diligently about the will of God in this matter and to let us know their decision. We assured them that we would back them on their choice. When the couple decided to give up the baby for adoption, I was able to find a young couple, also in the ministry, who had no children and were thrilled to have this beautiful baby. The mother and her husband have gone on to start a church and now have other children.

Many have come to ask for financial advice and for medical advice. Recently, in the space of two weeks, five people—three people in our church and two friends attending other area churches—have all learned they are in advanced stages of cancer. This discovery has been such a shock to our whole church. The medical bills for these people have been astronomical. We have given to them personally, and we have urged our people to give. We have asked people to give blood, and most importantly, we have asked them to pray. It is so hard to watch people you love suffer.

Unfaithful husbands have caused many ladies to come for counseling. Parents have come to ask about problems with children. One lady had a daughter who was being "courted" by a lesbian and wanted to know how to keep her young teenage daughter from falling into that trap. My advice was to keep her daughter with her at *all* times—never to let her out of her sight—day or night—at home, church, or wherever she went. I told her to not let her talk on the phone because this young girl is attracted to this older girl and doesn't believe she is a lesbian. I advised the mother to talk to the other children in the family and make sure no notes or messages were passed. I told her to love and pray for and with this daughter constantly and to win back her daughter's heart.

When children are very young, their parents have their hearts. Later, they will give their hearts to someone else. This "someone" could be a good choice, or unfortunately, a poor choice, and that is what we must constantly watch for in their friendships. We must always keep our children's hearts, and we must always make sure that God has our children's hearts.

Teenagers often come to ask advice about unsaved parents who have persecuted them. Widowed ladies come. I have had ladies whose husbands have become backslidden come just to talk to someone who will listen to their heartaches. In many cases, there is no answer.

As a missionary wife, you will have them come to you for advice also. Sometimes you are tired or busy. Maybe you will have your own heartaches with which you are trying to deal; however, it is better they ask your advice, than to go to someone who will not steer them in the right direction.

Counseling and caring for others is an awesome responsibility that is humbling. I am constantly praying and asking God to give me wisdom to help these people who come for consultation. I am frightened by the idea of giving someone the wrong advice. How very vital it is to always walk with God and to be filled with the Holy Spirit so God can use you to help your people.

The Bible says in Psalm 139 that no one knows us better than our Heavenly Father. *"O LORD, thou hast searched me, and known me. Thou knowest my downsitting and mine uprising, thou understandest my thought afar off. Thou...art acquainted with all my ways. For there is not a word in my tongue, but, lo, O LORD, thou knowest it altogether. Thou has beset me behind and before, and laid thine hand upon me...Whither shall I go from thy spirit? or whither shall I flee from thy presence?...My substance was not hid from thee...Thine eyes did see my substance, yet being unperfect; and in thy book all my members were written...Search me, O God, and know my heart: try me, and know my thoughts:"* (verses 1-5, 7, 15, 16, & 23)

When you counsel, tell people that God knows them so well because He made them. God loves them. Teach them that they can always go to God. He is always there, any time, any place, ready, waiting, and willing to listen.

Chapter Three

Helping People

The following are a few simple ideas that I have learned about how to help people:

1.   Disciple them. When people get saved, we need to teach them to read the Bible and pray so they will grow in Christ. They need to be taught Joshua 1:8, *"This book of the law shall not depart out of thy mouth; but thou shalt meditate therein day and night, that thou mayest observe to do according to all that is written therein: for then thou shalt make thy way prosperous, and then thou shalt have good success."* When I disciple a convert, sometimes I compare reading the Bible with reading a love letter. I explain about the excitement a girl feels when she gets a love letter from her boyfriend. She is so excited to read it that she drops everything she is doing just to open that letter. Likewise, the Bible is a love letter from God, and a Christian should be just as excited to read it as to read a love letter from someone special. Explain that God talks to the Christian as he reads his Bible, and a Christian talks to God when he prays.

Mark 1:35, *"And in the morning, rising up a great while before day, he went out, and departed into a solitary place, and there prayed."* If Jesus, Who was the Son of God, needed to pray, how much more do you and I need to pray? I explain that the Christian life is like riding a bike uphill—you have to constantly work at it or you'll start going down backward.

Teach them I John 1:9, *"If we confess our sins, he is faithful and just to forgive us our sins, and to cleanse us from all unrighteousness,"* so they will always keep their heart right with God. Teach them Hebrews 10:25, *"Not forsaking the assembling of ourselves together, as the manner of some is; but exhorting one another: and so much the more, as ye see the day approaching,"* so they will learn that it is important to go to church and hear how to live for God.

Encourage them to read I Corinthians 13 to learn about love. Have them read Hebrews 11 to learn about faith. Teach them about the Holy Spirit.

2.   Help their children. Titus 2:4 says: *"That they may teach the young women to be sober, to love their husbands, to love their children."* Help them to understand that not only should they love their children, but they should also discipline them because if they do not discipline their children, then they don't really love them. The Bible says in Proverbs 13:24, *"He that spareth his rod hateth his son: but he that loveth him chasteneth him betimes."*

My husband and I have a burden for the children of our staff members. We already have a Christian school for them, and we have decided to buy musical instruments for them. When I go to the United States, I look in pawnshops for used musical instruments to bring back for the children. We find teachers to teach them how to play these instruments. We have found that learning to play an instrument has helped with their character building. Instead of watching television so much, they practice. They also love playing in our church orchestra.

3. **Help them serve the Lord.** Don't just say, "You need to go soul winning." Instead, say, "Would you go with me tomorrow to visit someone?" Don't just tell them to do something without trying to teach them how. There are so many ways they can serve the Lord, but remember that the most important is to bring others to Christ.

4. **Respect them.** Just because their culture is different than ours does not mean ours is better. Unless there is something sinful, it simply means it is different. We cannot look down on them and their ways just because things are not done the same way we do them. Criticizing them and making fun of them—especially in front of our children—is so demeaning.

5. **Show gratitude.** Our sweet people at our church and the graduates who have left to start churches are always bringing us gifts—usually food. I am so touched by this display of love because they are very poor, and I know what a sacrifice it is for them to give. Therefore, we must always show our gratitude. Showing gratitude to people encourages them.

6. **Help them through trials.** Our people in our church are our family. When they hurt, we hurt. When a loved one dies, we need to be there for them. When they are in the hospital, we need to visit them. Matthew 25:35-40 reads, *"For I was an hungred, and ye gave me meat: I was thirsty, and ye gave me drink: I was a stranger, and ye took me in: Naked, and ye clothed me: I was sick, and ye visited me: I was in prison, and ye came unto me. Then shall the righteous answer him, saying, Lord, when saw we thee an hungred, and fed thee? Or thirsty, and gave thee drink? When saw we thee a stranger, and took thee in? or naked, and clothed thee? Or when saw we thee sick, or in prison, and came unto thee? And the King shall answer and say unto them, Verily I say unto you, Inasmuch as ye have done it unto one of the least of these my brethren, ye have done it unto me."*

7. **Be patient with them.** Sometimes when someone knocks on the door seeking some advice or help in another way, it is not convenient. Still, we need to be unselfish and focus on their needs—not on what is inconvenient for us.

Americans are often very blunt and frank and come right to the point in a conversation. Many other cultures are very different, and you have to be patient and wait for them to finally broach the subject. They may be shy and embarrassed with Americans. It may be very difficult for them to bare their soul to you and humble themselves to ask for your advice.

8. Mentor them. I recently received a sweet letter from Mrs. Cheryl Caalem. Cheryl is the first person my husband led to the Lord when we arrived in Iloilo in September of 1977. She was just a teenager. Now she is one of the most outstanding Christian ladies I have ever known. She is the wife of Pastor Billy Caalem, one of our graduates. He was our youth pastor for many years and did a tremendous job. Then the Lord led him back to the mountains of Leon to start a church where he grew up—the same place where the New People's Army (Communist Rebels) murdered his father. Brother Billy and Cheryl have also started a Bible college and Christian academy. As of this writing, August 2003, Brother Billy and his graduates have started 36 churches. Several of his graduates have also started Bible institutes and Bible colleges.

Brother Billy gives his wife a great deal of credit; therefore, it is very humbling for me to receive credit from her. My husband and I love her and her family very much, and we are extremely proud of her. Cheryl faced an incredible amount of opposition from her family, and it was not easy for her to become a Christian and grow in Christ, but she persevered.

Cheryl began her letter as follows: "Dearest Ma'am Becky (My Friend and Mentor)…" A mentor is a wise and trusted advisor. I honestly do not know how wise I am, and I hope I can always be trusted. When I think back through the years, I truthfully cannot think of what I actually did for her. She went with me every Saturday to visit our children's routes. We came back to my house, hot, tired, and thirsty, and I fixed us a large Coke. Often I "dragged" my husband away from his studies and "made" him play Monopoly or some other board game with us. We always laughed and had fun and just talked. All that I really did was love her, and honestly, Cheryl was and still is a very easy person to love.

This past July 27, 2003, I took some visitors from the United States to Brother Billy's church. They knew the visitors were coming, but they did not know Rachel and I would be there as ours was a last-minute decision to accompany the visitors. It was rainy season, so the bad roads were even worse than usual, and we had to walk over muddy, slippery dikes in the rice field to get there. Cheryl wrote me the following letter after we left, and she gave me her permission to share portions of that unedited letter:

Dearest Ma'am Becky (My Friend and My Mentor):
   Greetings to you and Pastor and Rachel; a great day in Jesus' name! Please

allow me to write to express my thanksgiving again for all your goodness to me ever since. I know you may be tired of my repeated thoughts, but I'm sorry I just can't help it. Pardon, Please. I just can't contain not to express myself, it just bothers me if I don't say what's in my mind to people closest to my heart.

I would like to thank you so much for your surprise visit to our church last Sunday. We never thought you would be coming. We did not prepare more than usual. But it was one of the blessed services we ever had in the church here in town, and we are so grateful for your presence. The preaching, [speaking of the American visitors] the music given by one of the best violinists [speaking of our daughter Rachel] were great. Your visit reminded us of the Lord's coming one day, when we really get caught on our usual work day. My husband has a belief that the Lord will come on a Sunday. Thank you for enduring a bumpy road just to be with us.

I would like to thank you also for the gifts [Cheryl's birthday is July 18—the same as my husband's]. They were the best gifts I received this year for reason that from whom it is from. They are treasures to me. Thank you so much from the bottom of my heart.

Thank you for the friendship of many years. I'm so thankful to the Lord for the privilege. Thank you for the blessed life you help me to find. Truly, a wonderful life in the Lord that I never regretted I trod. Thanks for all your guidance to the many choices I have to make since I was just a new Christian, I'm so glad I heed your counsel.

Thank you more for welcoming my daughter now to your school, a great school for the training of disciplined servants of God.

I will always have a great love and respect for you. For all you have done for me, my family, the ministry, and my country as a whole. For serving here unreservedly, thanks for loving us Filipinos. I love you and will always. Thank you! You are always in my prayers.

Much love always,
Cheryl

Truthfully, I think Cheryl is the one who has mentored me!

9. Love them. I John 3:14 a says, *"We know that we have passed from death unto life, because we love the brethren...."* Cheryl Caalem wrote the following story about one of her and Brother Billy's Bible college graduates:

Mrs. Marvelita Cabaya Capilitan was one of our best Bible college graduates. She is one with such a good attitude, no matter what. You can never detect she is having problems for she is good at concealing them with her positive, joyful attitude. Whenever I need help, I love to call on her first, because

I know she'll do it the closest to what I expect. Marvelita came to my house one afternoon, as she often does when she is in the town. We talked a while, and laughed some, as she sat on the steps of the church while I was washing clothes that Thursday afternoon. I remembered my son had a school project. He was supposed to make a centerpiece out of soft drink straws. I remembered that some of our girls from Culabao knew how to weave mats. I asked Marvelita if she knew how to weave, and she said "Yes." I asked her if she could help me with my son's project, and she said "Yes." That was her attitude—she was always willing to help. I watched her walk out of the church, carrying the plastic straws. I never thought that in a few days, she would be dead.

That night she became very ill, and they brought her to the hospital. She was expecting a baby but was only in her third month. I never visited her. Every time someone would come from the hospital I would ask about her. They would say she was better and coming home soon. I thought everything was all right. The following Thursday one of our workers, who was staying at the hospital with Marvelita, her husband, and her mother, came to us late at night. They said they needed to take Marvelita to the hospital in Iloilo City. We quickly followed them. When we reached the hospital, we saw many doctors rushing around, trying to take care of her. We did not know she was so serious.

We stood beside her bed and told her to be strong. We told her to keep fighting. When she heard our voice, she would look up and smile at us. I was overwhelmed with pity. I blamed myself for not visiting her at the hospital all week. It was so selfish of me, considering the many services she rendered to my family. One of the doctors asked me what was my relation to the patient. I said, "She is our Bible college graduate." The doctor asked why we did not bring her to the hospital sooner. I told the doctor, "Marvelita stayed in the Aleosan Hospital this whole week." Then the doctor told me it would be a miracle if she survived. I told my husband and we prayed. He called Pastor Martin to request prayer. While my husband was talking to Pastor Martin on the phone, we could see the doctors doing CPR on Marvelita. Then they came out and said, "She is gone. We are sorry."

That broke my heart. We tried to comfort the mother and the husband. A few minutes later, Pastor Martin arrived. It was a comfort to have him there. We knew, as the body was being sent to the morgue, the real Marvelita was being taken by angels to the presence of the Saviour she so faithfully loved and served.

Marvelita had only been married six months to her pastor-husband. She was dedicated and showed a willingness to sacrifice. Brother Billy's Bible college is located in the mountains. Since it is in a small village, most of the students go out to work in other village churches that Brother Billy and his workers have started. Most of the students do not have money to pay for transportation, so they walk. The farthest church was located near the town of Alimodian, a distance of over 40 kilometers, or 26 miles. Cheryl said Marvelita had volunteered to go there. Every weekend she had walked over 50 miles, round trip, to that village church. Why did she do that? The answer is—*love.*

Learn to love people.

Chapter Four

Relationships With the Unsaved

1. Learn to adapt to the country and culture. Dealing with unsaved people can be very frustrating in America, let alone in a foreign country where you also have language and cultural barriers. Always remember that you are the only "Jesus" some people may ever see. I am ashamed to say that at times I have lost my temper—especially with taxi drivers. For a long time, I told people that I didn't think Manila taxi drivers had a soul! They can be *so* aggravating! Still, they are our means of transportation, so when I pay the fare, my practice is to always give the driver a Gospel tract.

When my daughter Rachel and I were in Manila in June 2003, we were riding in a taxi. Imagine my surprise when this particular driver quickly handed me a Gospel tract before I could give him one! That was a blessing! Always keep your temper, be polite, and be a good testimony, even when people try to cheat you.

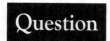 Can you please give some advice about dealing with the unsaved in your country?

Answers:

• Unfortunately, in the culture in our country, there is much lying. Sometimes the people lie because they want to please, so they say anything they think you want to hear even if it is not true. This is in the business realm also, so it is difficult to deal with people telling you something will be ready at a certain time, and it is not. But [they] are very friendly and warm, and it is great working with them.

• I try to be a little guarded. Our cultures and upbringing separate us dramatically in the areas of morals, ideals, and goals.

• We don't try to Americanize them and criticize the areas of their culture that aren't unbiblical. We still preach against [sin].

• It is best to not go into the country with pre-conceived ideas regarding your interaction with the nationals. Their mannerisms and ways will be different from ours. For example, here, when someone hears of a great tragedy, they may laugh instead of cry. This is how they express their emotion. They are also blunt. They don't mean to be unkind, but they will tell you like it is. They may say, "You are getting fat," when actually they are trying to say, "You are getting healthier and more content with the ways and food in our country." They may say, "Give me your dress," and actually mean "I like your dress and wish I had one like it." They may laugh when they see your child crying, but it may be because they don't know what else to do. They may laugh when they hear you try to speak their language, but it's probably because your accent sounds strange to them. They may not open up to you or talk to you much at first, but it could be because they want to watch you. Remember, you are strange and different to them. When you first reach the field, watch, listen, and learn. Take note of how they greet each other. Observe how they show respect to the older people. Notice how the women respond to the men. Do they sit on separate sides of the church? Is it improper to look a member of the opposite gender in the eye? Do not have the idea that "the American way is the only way." They may have a reason why they do things differently. Keep in mind that they've been there longer than you have!

2. Love and pray for the unsaved. Sometimes people are difficult to love. An ultimate example of this point is Imogene Carlson, who was interned, along with her husband and children, in a Japanese prisoner-of-war camp in the Philippines during World War II. I will not go into all the details of all the horrific things this family suffered. In her book, *American Family Interned, Philippines WWII*, she shares the following:

The many lessons learned during internment prepared us for the years ahead. The Lord taught that we should love our enemies and do good to those that persecute us. He was so right, as always. When we started praying for our guards and pitying them because they didn't know the Saviour, our hatred melted away. How we longed to tell them of Jesus.[1]

3. Ask God to give you a burden for the unsaved. *"Ask of me, and I shall give thee the heathen for thine inheritance...."* (Psalm 2:8) If you do not have a burden, ask God for one. Ask Him to love people through you. Beg Him to break your heart for people.

When I see an older woman or man, I try to think, "What if that were my mom or dad?" How would I want people to treat them? If I see a middle-aged man or woman, I think, "What if that was my brother Eric? What if that was my sister Bobbie?" If I see a younger man or young lady, I try to think, "What if that was my son Ricky? What if that was my daughter Rachel? How would I want people to treat each of my loved ones?"

4. **Ask God to keep bitterness out of your heart.** Another way to word this point is to hate the sin and love the sinner. Geraldine Taylor was the daughter-in-law of Hudson Taylor. She and her husband Howard were also missionaries to China. One time some Chinese people who hated the foreigners spread a rumor that if they were to go to the missionaries' house, they would receive lots of money. The gullible people believed this lie and went to the missionaries' house. Mrs. Taylor relates this story in the book *Mrs. Howard Taylor, Her Web of Time*:

Carts began to gather at the gate. Every hour brought a steady stream of people from far and near. They received them politely and explained over and over again that it was all a mistake—they had no money to give away. But they had come for money; their disappointment was bitter, and it gave way to suspicion until gradually evil suggestions were whispered among them. They would have their revenge. The unmarried ladies were in the upstairs room, Howard was out in the front courtyard with the men, and Geraldine in the women's guest-hall. At last the rough elements of the city pressed in among the country people; they poured over the walls, and invaded the whole place, smashing everything they could lay hands on, and carrying off whatever they fancied. They forced their way upstairs to the room where Ruth Brook and Mary Hodgson were, and the ladies had to come down and leave them to despoil that room too. Mary slipped over to a friendly Chinese neighbour and escaped all harm, but the crowd mishandled Miss Brook, knocking her about, bruising her and stripping her clothes off with violence. While trying to help her into the guest-hall, Geraldine was attacked by the crowd and treated in the same way. A woman from the country who was carrying a hoe hacked at them and cut Geraldine's head open so that the blood streamed down her neck. She succeeded in holding her torn garments about her, and was standing waiting to be struck down, wondering at her own calm, when she saw a Chinese gentleman pushing through the tumult towards the doorway in which she stood facing the mob. She did not know him but "I could see at a glance that he was friendly," she wrote afterwards, "and looked at him in surprise as he took his stand at my side." I asked his name. "My name is Wang," he answered. "I intend to stay here. I will not leave you."

His presence saved our lives, for he stayed beside us and in some measure restrained the violence of the mob until the Mandarin came, and everyone fled before him. Then Mr. Wang disappeared.

The Mandarin was newly appointed to the city and very zealous in the exercise of his business. He had been out on an official errand when news of the riot reached him, and he was in full Mandarin attire when he leapt in among the people, seized four men by their queues, two in each hand, and shook them soundly, raging all the time in a manner that struck terror into the hearts of the offenders. He came just in time to prevent the men in the front courtyard from stoning Howard, who, though badly cut and bruised, was not seriously injured. The Mandarin's escort of soldiers filled the court and tied twenty-four of the men they had seized by their queues, making them kneel down to receive their sentence.

Mary Hodgson remembers a small incident which shows Geraldine's thoughtful care of others even in the hour of her own need. "On the day of the riot, Mrs. Taylor sent some medicine to one of the rioters who had been seized by the Mandarin's men and tied up at the front door of the mission premises. This act seemed to have quite a good effect on the people, who said, 'These foreigners can't be so bad after all, if they treat these men like that.' "[2]

Geraldine Taylor kept bitterness out of her heart, even when she almost lost her life.

5. Help others like Jesus did. One of the ladies in our church asked me to go with her to visit a certain family. She said, "Ma'am Bec, I received a letter from a girl in a Bible college in Cebu City. She is burdened for her parents and asked us to visit them and lead them to the Lord."

We went to a place outside of Iloilo City. Many times finding a certain location is not like it is in the United States where streets and houses are numbered. There was just a clearing and a dirt path with several nepa huts, so we walked around asking where the family lived until we found it.

The father was outside sawing a piece of wood. We introduced ourselves, and he told us to go inside and talk to his wife, so we went in. I will never forget what I saw when I walked inside that little broken-down house. The body of a little three-year-old girl was lying on the table. A candle stuck in an empty beer bottle had been lit beside her. The grief-stricken mother explained that her little girl had just died during the previous night, and her husband was building a casket. They were extremely poor. My heart was broken for that family. We sat down with them and led them to Christ. We could hardly talk because we were so sad for them. We told them how their precious little girl was in Heaven with Jesus, and that they would surely see her again someday. I did not have any money, except for our fare, so we went home, got some money, and returned with it.

We thought of the sister of the dead girl, far away on another island. I knew she would be happy when we wrote her to tell her that her parents were now saved, but she would be devastated to hear about her little sister.

Still, God's timing never ceases to amaze me! The Bible college student had written a week ago. We arrived at the home just hours after the little girl died. Perhaps if we had gone there before the little girl died, the parents would have been hardhearted and not listened to the Gospel. Maybe God had to let the little girl die in order for the parents' hearts to be softened so they could be saved.

The Philippines is such a poor country. People all around us are always hurting and are always in need. Of course, their greatest need is spiritual, but we cannot ignore their physical needs. We need to try our best to help them like Jesus would have helped them.

6. Win them. We have had countless soul-winning experiences through the years. Let me share one.

One day I was visiting the children on my route when two young ladies who were sisters walked up to me and introduced themselves. They said they would like to come to our church as they were "Protestants." I was delighted and told them the time of the church service. They were saved, as were two other sisters, and this family became so faithful to our church. However, the father was a staunch Catholic and did not want his daughters attending a Baptist church, but they were adult women so he did not forbid them. He just grumbled about it all the time, and since he could not stop his daughters, he forbade his wife from attending. These girls always asked everyone to pray for their dad to get saved.

One day I was visiting one of them at their house when the father walked in. They introduced me to him. Everyone was staring at me as if to say, "Now's your chance! Lead Dad to the Lord!" I began to talk to him about the Bible when he suddenly got up and walked out of the house. The daughters were so horrified and so embarrassed. Filipinos are usually so polite, and his response was very out of character. I told the girls I understood his reaction and told them to just keep praying for him.

I became so burdened for that man. I guess for one thing he reminded me of my dad. I had become burdened for some other professional people with whom we did business occasionally. It was awkward to witness to them because they were so busy. For instance, a doctor might not listen when he had a room full of waiting patients. I thought I would write a form letter about how to get saved to give to these people. We made several copies and gave the letter to several people. One lady called me from Manila and could barely talk because she was weeping so hard. She thanked me for the letter and told me that she had received Jesus as her Saviour!

One day after church I gave the girls the letter and asked them to give it to their dad. I did not tell them what it was, and that night the girls came back to church very upset. They said their dad opened and read the letter, and he became very angry. He tore up the letter and marched back and forth ranting and raving about "that Rick Martin and that Baptist church!" He told his girls, "Tonight when you go to that church, you tell that Rick Martin that I'll be there first thing tomorrow morning to talk to him!" They were very frightened—for very good reason.

We were all pretty worried! We decided to ask everyone to pray. The next morning the man came to our house. My poor husband, who had no idea I had given the man one of my letters, was very polite to him and asked him to come in and sit down. Meanwhile, I was "hiding" in the other room, praying, biting my fingernails, and waiting for the man to punch my husband in the face!

My husband asked, "What can I do for you?"

The man answered, "I need you to tell me how I can get saved." I was shocked! His reply certainly was not what I had been expecting!

His salvation was so precious, and the girls were so happy. That dear man and his wife became very faithful. A couple of years after that, he became ill and died. When Rick and I went to the funeral, one of the daughters threw her arms around my neck, sobbing and thanking me for giving her dad that letter.

We must win them to Jesus.

Chapter Five

Relationships With Other Missionaries

The phone rang. It was my mom. "You won't believe what that crazy dog has done!" she said. My mom and dad had just moved back to Indiana from Texas, and Greta, their German shepherd, had ridden with them in their new white van. Greta probably would have been okay in her new surroundings if my parents had not soon thereafter driven to Oklahoma to visit my sister and had left the dog behind in the strange new yard. Greta was scared and lonely. Suddenly, a white van pulled into the driveway next door. I'm sure Greta thought, "Great! Verne and Mary [my folks] are back!" She jumped over the fence and ran to the van. The driver had left the door open, so Greta jumped in and sat in the middle of the front seat, waiting for my mom and dad to get in the van and drive her back to Texas.

Mom continued, "Well, while we were in Oklahoma, our next-door neighbor had a heart attack, so they called the ambulance. They wheeled the guy out to the ambulance in the stretcher when, lo and behold, a German shepherd was sitting in the front seat! They tried to shoo her out, but she just sat there and growled at them. The wife of the heart attack victim told the EMTs that the dog belonged to their new neighbors who were in Oklahoma. The EMT quickly radioed the police. The police officer who responded loved dogs and had no problem coaxing Greta into his police car; but he had to take her to the dog pound. Thankfully, our neighbor is back home now and is doing great. Your dad rescued Greta from the dog pound. Guess who the policeman was, Becky?"

When my mother told me his name, I realized he was a friend of the family whom we had not seen in many years. As a result of this "wild" incident with Greta, this police officer and his wife became friends with my parents while they lived in the same small town.

One time when I was home visiting my parents from the Philippines, this couple came to visit. The wife was obviously upset; and when I asked her what was wrong, she said that her husband's unwed sister was expecting again. "She cannot possibly keep the baby as she can barely care for the two children she already has." Suddenly God laid a missionary couple on my heart who were unable to have children. I told this police officer's wife about them, and she responded, "Let me talk to my sister-in-law."

She returned that night and said, "My sister-in-law is willing to let the baby be adopted. Why don't you call that couple?"

I had prayed about the matter throughout that day. With a trembling heart, I called the missionary couple and told them the story. Needless to say, they were thrilled. I warned them, "What if you spend all that money to fly to the States, and when she has the baby, she decides to keep it?"

They expressed that they were willing to take the risk. When the delivery time came, I asked the couple if the mother had changed her mind about giving up the baby for adoption, and they said, "No." I called the missionaries and told them to come for the baby, warning them again that there was still a chance the mother could change her mind. The baby stayed with my parents. The missionary couple flew in to the local airport, and Dad picked them up at the airport. My husband and I were traveling to churches at the time. I prayed and fasted for three days, hoping all would turn out well. It did!

If God opens a door (literally—the door of a white van!) and gives you an opportunity to help another missionary, take a risk and try to help however you can. God will bless you for it. A very special bond remains between that missionary family and us.

After sending out the questionnaire, we received a variety of responses from the ladies regarding relationships with other missionaries. I also found several observations in Dr. Jim Vineyard's missionary paper that I thought would be helpful.

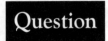 **Question** Can you please give advice about dealing with other missionaries?

Answers:

• We spent our first four years working with [the missionary's name]. His family and the other American missionaries there were a big help to us. We spent holidays together, went soul winning together, and babysat each other's kids.

• Pray for God to give you an older lady on your field who is godly and helpful. You may be shocked at how well God can answer that need.

• We were fully prepared to be opposed by the atheists, the Charismatics, the cults, and the local ministerial association. I suppose we were taken by surprise by the confrontations from other missionaries. Especially difficult were the assurances that nothing that we had done in the States would work here, and that [our mission field] was "such a hard country." Thankfully, this only happened a couple of times, and we simply ignored this sort of advice.[1]

• We spend very little time with other missionaries. This is on purpose. The nearest American missionaries that we know are about four hours away. Our best friends are [our people]. We want to avoid giving the impression that we have to "get away from it all" and spend some time with some Americans. After two and a half years, we would rather spend time with [our people] than with Americans.[2]

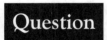 What was your hardest adjustment(s) when you arrived on the field?

Answer:

"Other missionaries. It is normal to want to talk to people who speak English, but it limits the amount of contact you have with the people you are trying to reach."

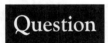 What do you wish you could have learned before going to the field?

Answers:

• Better interpersonal relationships with other women on the field (missionary wives). I thought all missionary wives were submissive and that they believed the husband was the pastor and the leader of the church. I was so wrong and naive.

• I would have liked to have known that the biggest problem is missionary relationships, to be more alert for and able to handle correctly situations involving relationships with other missionaries.

Question What advice would you like to give to a new missionary wife?

Answers:

• With other missionaries, keep your distance but stay friendly. Don't be too close as well. Bad things can happen to marriages and ministries if a too-familiar relationship is formed.

• I try to remember how far short I fall of what God wants me to be to other people. I try to remember the beam I have in my own eye before I try to remove the mote from someone else's eye. Some bitterness comes from things that we imagine people have done to us or thought about us. So I try not to judge someone else when I feel hurt over something. Actually, if I am busy enough in the Lord's work, I don't have a problem with bitterness because I don't have time for it.

• As to other missionaries who are teaching the same Gospel but don't necessarily have our standards in other areas, we pray for them to see many souls saved. The missionaries who teach another Gospel, we try to warn folks about them.

• Another thing that was hard to bear was the disillusionment that came when I found out all Christians are not honest. Probably that comes to all in the ministry, but with the isolation of the field I think it is worse. We encountered numerous corrupt Christian leaders. But harder yet, we experienced harsh misunderstandings from other American missionaries, some who cheated and lied to us and even tried to get us kicked out of the country. On the other hand, as years passed we've made dear friends with other independent Baptist missionaries and have added wonderful (occasional) fellowship to our lives. Someone here told us that missionaries are like manure! I didn't like the sound of that! Then he explained that they do a lot of good when spread around but stink when they pile up! I came to understand and accept that the field is a fertile place for the Devil to stir up people problems.

Specific Challenges of Missionary Relationships

1. **Working with another missionary.** My husband and I do not work with other missionaries, so I cannot give any firsthand experience on this particular area, but I would like to relate a story from the book *Reluctant Missionary*, written by Edith Buxton, the daughter of C. T. Studd. The title tells it all, doesn't it? Studd, his daughter, and son-in-law Alfred Buxton were missionaries in Africa:

Long before we reached Nala, I knew I did not fit. I did not like my fellow missionaries, and I am quite sure they did not like me. I became critical, often speaking ill of my neighbours. I was bored. Had I not been happily married, I could not have stood the isolation. There is no place like Africa for finding you out.

My change—whatever you like to call it—came about two years after my arrival, in answer, I suppose, to my first honest prayer to God…

I said to God, "Here am I, a missionary; I have left home and friends to come out here and You let me be ill and You don't heal me."

An inner voice began to speak. It seemed to say, "What are you doing? You have been given a pair of hands and feet and you don't use them except for yourself all the time."

I saw myself for the first time as I was before God: first and foremost an egoist, selfish, self-centered, dishonest in small mean ways. If God's command was to *"love thy neighbour as thyself,"* then surely I was wanting here. I did not like my missionary neighbours, nor the Africans. In fact, I was trying to do God's work with the tool of an unloving heart.

I began to put things right as far as I could see and, with my obedience to what I believed God was trying to say to me, there came a change—a sense of God's presence. I felt a new peace in the battle of life.

And in the evening by the glow of the log fire, with the night watchmen outside murmuring, I would sit, the door shut, with my Bible on my knee. I would read by the flickering light of an old Nestlés milk tin filled with palm oil and a rag dip. What peaceful hours they were; the fever of my heart seemed stilled. I was slowly finding what I believe are the only true ways to live this life and work. That inner voice would persist, "It is no use your preaching about the love and gentleness of Christ on Sunday, while pushing your houseboys about during the week."

I could anyhow make a beginning in sharing my storeroom. I kept this room locked because of the boys, but in the back of my mind I think I had Alfred as well. He had a way of lingering in the doorway and saying, "The runner is just leaving for Poko; 'So-and-So' has a fever. Let's send him a box of biscuits." I would let him have them, but with bad grace and say, "Well, anyhow, don't take the Petit Beurre, take something else."

I mentally gave God the key, but when I was in there one day I shoved underneath the shelf with my foot the case of butter, most precious of all our commodities. I did hope no one would be needing butter. All of a sudden Nala seemed to run out of butter, so I gave away the butter, remembering something in the Bible which said, *"Give and it shall be given unto you."*[3]

Edith continues with her narrative to say that her mother shipped her several cases of butter right after this happened. She notes:

There was one missionary in particular who made me furious. She was the daughter of a doctor. No day seemed to pass but she would ignore me, or show aversion with some marked slight. I naturally reacted to her as she did to me, with an equal dislike. God showed His way to be indifference to other people's animosity to us and we must not take to heart the hurts and frustrations that we met in our path. We must love friends and enemies alike because He sent the rain on all, the just and the unjust alike. And that equality of love, God's love, not human love, was what I must seek between me and my fellow men.

"What shall I do about her?" I asked. That morning I had read from the Bible in Mark 3, "...there came a woman having an alabaster box of ointment of spikenard very precious; and she brake the box, and poured it on his head." The idea came to me, "Send her something of value now." I can't remember what it was, perhaps just a tin of butter! Anyway, I wrote that verse on a piece of paper and sent it off. In no time at all she arrived with some fresh baked cakes piled on a plate. When we met, all the barriers that had separated us seemed gone before we spoke a word. Actually we said little, but we smiled and thanked each other, and there was gentleness and freedom between us. This understanding which came about, like the crack of an eggshell, remained for the rest of the time we were together. The barriers never returned.

One evening when Alfred was away, there came a knock at my door, and there stood another missionary, Mary. She had come out from England with her sister. She sat down and said, "We have all noticed a change in you; I have come to ask what has happened." I said I had for the first time in my life seen myself, as I was before God, selfish, dishonest, unloving. I had bared my heart to God's estimate of me and had, in so far as I could, accepted His criticism and tried to put things right in the light which I had received. I shared with her such experiences as I had had—no matter how humiliating it was to myself. With a cry of real anguish she got up, opened the door and fled. I found her after quite a search.

"Mary, whatever made you do that?" She came back and said how some word had pierced her heart; she must make it right with another missionary at once. I had hardly known her and her sister, but again this led to an open understanding between us and a happy working in our daily life.

Some of the elders came next. "Tell us," they said, "what has made you new?"

Again I shared with them some of my adventures with God. With open eyes and mouths they said, "But, Mama, we can understand this! Much of what is preached to us in the pulpit is like a cloud of words. We cannot see through it."

And so, with a softer tread, I started to walk the path of service with a new and contrite heart. There was much yet to be done in me, a work that would go on to my life's end. But I had made a beginning.[4]

2. Choosing your friends. God has been so good to give me some wonderful friends here on the mission field. Some have been Americans and some Filipinos. We must be very careful about choosing friends because of their great influence on us and our thinking. The Bible says in Proverbs 14:7, *"Go from the presence of a foolish man, when thou perceivest not in him the lips of knowledge."* The Bible tells us to stay away from foolish people. Proverbs 14:16a says, *"A wise man feareth, and departeth from evil."* If we're smart, we'll stay away from people who drag us down spiritually.

3. Staying away from negative/critical people. I always told my kids, "You are who you hang with," and that is true of us adults too. If we hang around negative people, we will be negative. If we hang around critical people, we will be critical. On the other hand, if we make friends of people who are godly, that will naturally have a positive influence on us. Once I heard my husband jokingly say to a friend that he (referring to himself) "had the gift of criticism!"

4. Having fellowship with those with a similar doctrine and philosophy. This may be hard to do on the mission field. Maybe the only other fundamental Baptist (American) is miles from you. You may become so hungry for fellowship with another American that you'll just grab the first one you see! There can be a great danger in this, and we need to be careful. My best friends are the people in our church. I do not spend that much time with other missionaries except for conferences three or four times a year.

5. Helping other missionaries. At times other missionaries will need your help, and you will need the help of other missionaries.

I will never forget the friendship of Jim and Judy Joines when they were here in the Philippines. One time our son Ricky was sick and in the hospital for about two weeks. Judy, who lived over an hour away, rode the jeepney every day to come and visit us in the hospital. With three small children, it was very difficult for her to arrange her schedule to do that for us. I will always remember her personal sacrifice.

One time I was very sick with hepatitis, and I was worried about Ricky getting it. Again, the Joines family came to our rescue. Ricky stayed with them during my convalescence. Actually, I believe that sometimes he would rather have stayed with them anyway because their son Jamey was his best friend. I will never forget their great love and sympathy during the time I had a ruptured tubal pregnancy and almost died. I will never forget their prayers and encouragement when our daughter Rachel was born with a life-threatening heart condition and had to be taken on a Medi-Vac plane to the United States for emergency heart surgery. I will always remember how they bent over backward to make my mom and dad feel welcome when they came for a visit. Jim and Judy Joines left the Philippines to start a work in Mexico in 1988. Brother Jim passed away in May 2003 as a result of an explosion that had occurred three months earlier.

When you help out another missionary, or they give you a helping hand, especially during a crisis, your hearts are knit together.

6. Learning from other missionaries. When Rick and I first came to the Philippines in 1977, many missionaries offered advice. Sometimes the advice conflicted! Sometimes we agreed and followed the advice; sometimes we chose not to follow a certain piece of advice. Sometimes we were sorry! Keep in mind that when you step off that plane for the first time, you are green! It is good to learn from other missionaries, especially from those who you can see have the hand of God upon their ministry. They have learned a thing or two in the years they have been on the field. Learn from them and pray for wisdom when you receive conflicting advice.

7. The importance of developing a good relationship with other missionaries. Even if there are missionaries for whom you may not personally care and with whom you may not want to spend time in particular, you should try to develop a good relationship with them. The reason is that we are all in this together. I am not talking about ecumenicalism. I am talking about the fact that fundamental Baptist missionaries need to be friends, not enemies, with others of like faith. We should not be fighting each other, nor should we be jealous of each other. Rather, we should be helping each other.

8. Helping the children of other missionaries. My husband has always loved children and has a very sympathetic heart for them. He has always seen their great potential. Though he is extremely busy, he takes time from his hectic schedule to write letters to children of pastors in the United States whom he has met, as well as to children of missionaries.

When the lady missionaries get together at conferences and so forth, we are always asking and giving advice to each other regarding our children and other matters. The older ones can talk about the pros and cons of educating the kids on the foreign field, medical advice, and other subjects. At these conferences, my heart is really touched when I see the love these missionaries have for one another's children.

9. Settling misunderstandings. You may notice that often the worst wounds are from the people who are closest to us. We must always realize that no matter how deep the hurts are, God can heal them. Not only that, He can turn them around and use them for good. Romans 8:28 says, *"And we know that all things work together for good to them that love God, to them who are the called according to his purpose."*

Without a doubt, the best way to solve a misunderstanding is to do it the Bible way—go to that person and talk it out. Do not talk to other people about the problem.

10.   Encouraging other missionaries (especially during a crisis). Mel and Carol Brown were missionaries in Manila for several years. They were a real blessing to our family when Rachel was born and needed emergency heart surgery. When we flew her to the Heart Center in Manila, Brother Mel and Carol met us at the hospital. They took us to their home and took care of us for a week—driving us wherever we needed to go, feeding us, doing our laundry and anything else we needed.

Another missionary couple who were a real blessing to my husband and me were Mr. and Mrs. Howard Quinlan, who started a work in Angeles City, about an hour's drive west of Manila, where Clark Air Force Base was located for so many years. When Ricky was a little boy, he was bitten by a dog that later died, so he needed rabies shots. We did not know the Quinlans, and they did not know us. Needing help, I just called them impulsively and asked if Ricky and I could come and stay with them for ten days so he could get his rabies shots from Clark Air Force Base. Not only did they agree, they drove all the way to Manila to pick us up at the airport. They also contacted an Air Force serviceman who attended their church and asked him to help get me access to the base. Since I had been told by another missionary, who was formerly in the Air Force, to get on the base "by hook or by crook" and to go from there, I was unsure as to how Ricky and I would be handled. Perhaps some Air Force personnel do not seem to want to help those in the non-military community; however, I found the doctors and nurses in the base hospital to be extremely kind and helpful.

Rick and I owe a huge debt of gratitude to various missionaries who have helped us through the years, especially when we were having a crisis. The least we can do to repay the kindness that others have shown us is to try to help someone else. To be sure, you reap what you sow. "*…For whatsoever a man soweth, that shall he also reap. And let us not be weary in well doing: for in due season we shall reap, if we faint not.*" (Galatians 6:7b, 9)

Chapter Six

Relationships With People Back Home

Our daughter Rachel was born with a heart problem. When she was one week old, we flew to Manila to take her to the Heart Center. After a few days and several tests, the cardiologist there told us he had previously performed the operation she needed, but all the babies on whom he had conducted the surgery had died. He therefore suggested that somehow we transport her to the United States, but even that was risky since the flight would take over 30 hours. The medical team did not think she could survive the trip.

Rick's sister Connie and her husband Bill, who was a member of the Oklahoma State legislature, contacted Congressman Mickey Edwards to ask if something could be done to help. Congressman Edwards called the Clark Air Force Base in Angeles City and asked if they could help us. We were contacted at the Heart Center, and the medical personnel at Clark Air Force Base offered their services. An ambulance was dispatched to pick up our baby to take her to the base. After a round of several more tests, the doctors determined they could not do the needed surgery there; rather, they decided to Medi-Vac her to America—if we would pay for it. Of course, we did not know how we could pay for the expenses, but we said "Yes" anyway.

Rachel arrived in Oklahoma City in the middle of the night. My sister Bobbie drove over 100 miles to Children's Hospital of Oklahoma and waited several hours for Rachel's arrival. The next morning Children's Hospital was teeming with all of our family members. Rick's four sisters and his brother drove from all over Oklahoma to be there. His folks drove from Kansas City. My folks and my brother drove from Indianapolis. Rick, Ricky, and I had to take a commercial flight, so we did not even arrive in Oklahoma City until after Rachel's surgery.

We will never forget how our family was there for us during Rachel's crisis. They surrounded us and supported us, doing countless acts of kindness for us.

Every need was supplied. The nurses commented several times about what a wonderful, supportive family we had.

We will never forget how the dear people of the Windsor Hills Baptist Church in Oklahoma City, pastored by Dr. Jim Vineyard, visited us in the hospital, prayed, and brought what seemed like tons of food for our huge family. Other churches and friends across the country called or sent gifts of money, beautiful flowers, and darling stuffed animals for Rachel. Most importantly, they prayed.

I will share more about Rachel's ordeal in the unit on "Medical." For now I would just like to say how much of a vital role the people back home will continue to play in your life.

Relatives

Canadian Walter Gowans was deeply burdened for the people of the Sudan area of northern Africa. An estimated 60 million people lived in this region south of the Sahara Desert— without a single missionary.

Gowans' wonderful mother is described in *From Jerusalem to Irian Jaya* as follows:

> Gowans' staunchest supporter—his mother—sought additional recruits to join in the venture with her son. The fact that she had already sent a daughter to China did not dampen her eagerness to send off her son. She was an ardent missionary enthusiast, as Bingham [another missionary] readily observed while talking with her in the parlor of her home. She had invited him to her home after hearing him speak at a meeting. Convinced that he would make an ideal partner for her son, she passionately presented to him the needs of the Sudan. She was a persuasive woman, and "the next morning," wrote Bingham, "when I went to call on Mrs. Gowans, it was to announce that I expected to sail in two weeks to join her son in a common enterprise. Was she glad? She was the whole board and I was accepted on the spot."[1]

Walter Gowans, Rowland Bingham, and another missionary recruit, Thomas Kent, were told by missionaries upon reaching Africa: "Young men, you will never see the Soudan [Sudan]; your children will never see the Soudan; your grandchildren may."[2] Even though they were warned that they would not survive, they went ahead. Gowans and Kent died a few months later. Bingham, after two failed attempts because of illness, finally returned to Africa for the third time in 1901.

Thankfully by then, quinine had been discovered and was successfully being used to cure malaria. Ruth Tucker stated:

But another factor that affected the staying power of the [missionaries] was prayer. Mrs. Gowans, according to Bingham, was "one of the greatest prayer helpers that ever blessed and strengthened" the Sudan Interior Mission. "With her prayer and faith she carried us from the first seven barren years into the years of harvest."[3]

Even after her son died on the field, Mrs. Gowans continued to support the missionary endeavor he had started. Unfortunately, not all mothers are so enthusiastically behind their children when God calls them to the mission field.

When Relatives Oppose Your Decisions

Isobel Kuhn and Rosalind Goforth were both missionaries to China. Both had saved mothers who were adamant about not wanting their daughters to go to the mission field. Mrs. Goforth records her experience in her book *Climbing:*

Then came a letter from my sister pleading with me to return, as Mother was sobbing day and night and seemed failing fast.

On reaching home, I was shocked at the change in Mother. She would not speak to me and seemed broken-hearted. My distress was now very great. Could it be God's will for me to break my Mother's heart? At last, one day, as I listened to her pacing her bedroom floor, weeping, I could stand the strain no longer and determined to find out God's will so plainly I could make no mistake. Going down to the parlor, where the large family Bible rested on a small desk, I stood for a moment crying to the Lord for some word of light. Then I opened the Bible at random, and the first words my eyes lit on were: "Ye have not chosen me, but I have chosen you, and ordained you, that ye should go and bring forth fruit." I knew at once God was speaking His will to me through these words, and in an instant the crushing burden was gone. Running to Mother's room, I begged her to hear what I had to say. Unwillingly, she unlocked the door and stood while I told her of my prayer and answer. For a moment only she hesitated; then with a cry I could never forget, she threw her arms about me, saying, "O my child, I can fight against you, but I dare not fight against God." From that moment till her death eighteen months later, Mother's heart was entirely with me in the life I had chosen.[4]

In the book *In the Arena,* Isobel Kuhn tells about her mother:

"If you go to China it will be over my dead body. I will never consent," was my mother's bitter remark.

I sat with my mouth open, staring at her in aghast silence. My dear mother, who had first taught me to love the Lord Jesus, who had been president of the Women's Missionary Society for as long as I could remember, who had opened her home to the China Inland Mission for prayer meetings? My dear mother, who was all that, to be so bitter because her daughter felt called of God to be a missionary?

"If you want to do Christian work, that is fine. You could be a YWCA secretary here in Canada. That is quite a respectable position. But a foreign missionary! Only those who cannot find work to do at home or who are disappointed in love go to the foreign field," Mother continued, bitter in her opposition.

Again my mouth fell open in utter amazement. Such an appraisal of a foreign missionary call had never entered my head before. Could it be true?

"No, Mother." I had weighed the evidence, and I spoke with conviction. "That is not true in all cases, whatever it might have been in some."

"Well," wailed Mother desperately, "but you would be an object of charity! Just think of people passing the hat around for my daughter! I could never take the disgrace of it."

For the third time I was utterly astonished. What an interpretation to put on people's giving to the Lord's work on His far-flung battle line! And this from the president of the Women's Missionary Society! I myself had newly found the Lord, and giving to His service that others could have what I now enjoyed was a sweet joy to me. That filled me with resentment. I fear there are too many church members who have that view of giving to missions.

My mother was adamant and became hysterical if the conversation along this line continued. I was set to obey the Bible, and it said, "Honor thy father and thy mother." How could I prepare to be a missionary when my mother said it would kill her? And she would never consent.

I went to my father, who had always been an earnest lay preacher and who had offered me to God for China when I was born. Here surely I would find encouragement! But, no.

"I'm willing for you to be a missionary, but I won't help you financially," he said. "You'll have to take up Bible study somewhere. You might just as well learn to trust God for your finances now. Better learn such difficult lessons in America than in China. If God wants you to go, He will provide the funds apart from me. I'm not giving you one cent."[5]

About a year later, Isobel's mother died. Before her death, she became reconciled to her daughter's being a missionary. Both Mrs. Goforth and Mrs. Kuhn could have let their relationships keep them from God's perfect will for their lives. Thankfully, they did not.

We need to pray for our parents, friends, and relatives, especially when they are opposed to our going to the foreign field. Love them, try to put yourself in their place, and seek to understand how they feel. That however, does not mean that you should give in to them.

Communicating With Relatives

When Rick and I went to the Philippines in 1977, there was no e-mail service. We were not able to have a phone for many years. Once in a while, we used another missionary's phone, but those times were rare as the overseas fees were very expensive. We wrote letters every week though, and our parents were faithful to write to us weekly. Needless to say, the highlight of the week was going to the post office and finding a letter.

Iloilo Baptist Church has been privileged to send out four foreign missionaries. Two are in Haiti and two are in Africa, and they are doing a great job for the Lord. When Juanito and Rose Eden Genada, and their children, Kennedy and Christine, were back for their first furlough in 2001, we had many long chats. They live in the very difficult city of Gonaives, Haiti. They shared how that once a month, they would make the extremely dangerous (because of bandits) trek on horrible roads to Port-au-Prince to pick up their mail. Many times Juanito said his wife would cry because even though a whole month had passed, there was not even one letter from home. They made the long journey back to their desolate little town, empty-handed. The picture of Rose weeping over no mail broke my heart, and I resolved to be more diligent to write to our missionaries. The Bible says in Proverbs 25:25, *"As cold waters to a thirsty soul, so is good news from a far country."* The following are some thoughts from various missionary wives on the subject of communicating with people back home.

 **Question**   Would you please share how you keep in touch with family and friends?

Answers:

• Stay in touch as much as you can with those at home. We lived without a phone or computer or even a vehicle for the first four years on the mission field. It is very lonely, and I felt completely isolated from my family in the

U.S. It was hard. It is so much better this term with a phone and e-mail.

•   Keep in touch as much as possible, and tell them the good things and exciting things. Don't complain about being there and how different it is.

•   Make an effort to write to your immediate family, even if they don't write to you. Get the Internet if you can. I buy a calling plan for 2¢ a minute and can talk to my parents from the computer to their telephone. The connection is not always great, but at least they hear their grandkids. Also, get a scanner; I think ours was $75. It doesn't cost anything but Internet service to scan your pictures and send them via e-mail. My family feels like they watch my kids grow up. I thank God for technology and certainly take advantage of it!

•   With people back home, maintain a healthy relationship, but don't gripe over bad things that happen because they will only see the bad not the good and will think negative of the field.

•   Let the grandparents know what those grandkids are doing! Send pictures! Our parents are unsaved and don't understand our being here, but we do what we can to keep in touch.

•   We try to send birthday and Christmas presents to them from here. They have enjoyed small things from the country here like carvings or baskets or whatever the national people make.

•   I e-mail at least twice a week. Don't be afraid to send them little goodies from the field, if possible. Pictures are very important! We bought a video camera, and we video our birthdays and Christmas celebrations for them. We try to keep everything positive as they worry about us enough already.

•   It is good to have pictures of relatives and frequently show them to the kids, especially when they are smaller, so they will know who their grandparents and aunts and uncles are when they go on furlough.

•   We now have a satellite phone that we can use in the jungle. God has really blessed us with this new addition to close our communication gap. Family members can go to a website and text message us on our satellite phone free of charge. It's free for us, too. We receive the text messages instantly. Other than that, I write a letter every day to our children at college—sort of like a daily journal. I mail these letters every three or four days.

•   It is very important to keep up family ties with loved ones in the States. When we first came here, we didn't have e-mail. Just be sure to make the time for it. My parents recorded themselves reading some children's books and sent the cassette along with the books to our girls. The girls love to play the cassette and listen to Papa and Nana "read" to them.

•   You have to make the effort. Sending prayer letters to family members [isn't enough]. Write personal letters or call on special days and don't quit if you don't get a response.

Winning Relatives

Before Rick and I left for the Philippines, I called my unsaved uncle who was in the hospital and led him to the Lord. He had been diagnosed with cancer, and I was quite sure he was going to die. He did a few months later, and I was so glad he had gotten saved.

I also had an elderly great-aunt whom I called. She was also saved by means of the telephone. I did not want to go to the field knowing that I probably would not see her again and that I did not know whether she was saved.

In the spring of 2001, my dad called to tell me that another uncle had cancer and was not expected to live long. I called him from the Philippines and led him to the Lord over the phone. He was really a rough character, and he was the last person on earth that I ever expected to get saved! He died a month later.

I don't know why we find it so hard to call our relatives and lead them to Christ. Many of us (myself included) think it is easier to talk to a perfect stranger about the Lord. The worst that can happen is that your relative will get angry and hang up on you. That is a small price to pay when you consider they just may say "Yes" and receive Jesus as their Saviour.

Supporting Pastors and Churches

Have you ever attended a missions conference and heard the term "rope holders"? Have you ever wondered where that term originated? The word came from William Carey, missionary to India. Dr. James Ray, in his book entitled *Incredible Journey in the Steps of Greatness* writes:

On March 20, 1793, the mission board met and set apart Carey and another missionary for service abroad. Andrew Fuller said on that occasion, "There is a gold mine in India, but it seems as deep as the center of the earth." Carey replied, "I will venture down into that mine to dig, but remember you must hold the ropes."[6]

That's why pastors and churches back home have become "rope holders"—a symbol to missionaries. The missionary's relationship with them is very important; after all, they are the ones who support him financially and in prayer. We are their ambassadors as Christians to a foreign country. They cannot go, but they can send us. We need each other.

How can we develop our relationship with them? By communicating! That is why a regular prayer letter is so important. If they pray for us and support us, the least we can do is keep in touch with them!

If a supporting church asks for a picture or some memento such as flag or a native recipe, send it! They know we are busy, but they are also busy. They are not asking for items so they can be a bother. They are trying to keep missions before their people, and they are trying to make their people burdened for you and your ministry. Help them all you can with whatever they ask for.

Lastly, we can pray for them. We can let them know how much we appreciate them and that we could not do the Lord's work without their prayers and financial backing.

Visitors

The Lord obviously thinks hospitality is very important. If you don't believe it, read these verses:

- *"…given to hospitality."* (Romans 12:13)
- *"A bishop then must be…given to hospitality…."* (I Timothy 3:2)
- *"For a bishop must be…a lover of hospitality…."* (Titus 1:7, 8)
- *"Use hospitality one to another without grudging."* (I Peter 4:9)

Please do not think that I am criticizing my husband in any way when I share this, but he generally does not enjoy having visitors. I am simply stating a fact that he would be the first to acknowledge. My workaholic husband only feels this way because visitors tend to take him away from his work. When Americans come to visit, they need you more than when you would visit a church in United States. They cannot easily find their way around. They do not have access to a car, and they do not know the language.

On the other hand, I cannot work 24 hours a day, seven days a week like my husband does! I need a little variety. I need a little fellowship, so I don't mind visitors. Though I may get a little behind in my work, I can usually catch up after they leave.

In this day and age, lots of people, especially pastors, are visiting the mission field. Their visit gives them a burden for missions. We find in Lamentations 3:51: *"Mine eye affecteth mine heart…."*

Even though my husband feels the disruption in his schedule, he really goes out of his way to see that visitors enjoy their stay. We invite them to eat in our home, and besides having them in our own church services, we often send them to one of our graduate's churches so they can experience what it is like to go to a service in the province. My husband often puts guests in a hotel and asks me to prepare a basket of goodies to place in their room. Sometimes he buys books for them or some other gift like a wood carving or a "Philippines" t-shirt. He asks me to do laundry for the guests. If a lady comes, he often asks me to take her shopping. (Shopping—it's a dirty job! But somebody's got to do it!!)

Let's ask the Lord to help us to be hospitable to visitors—another important relationship.

Conclusion

In closing this chapter about relationships, would you like to know what happened to the Spauldings who went West with the Whitmans to work with the Indians? Before the Whitmans were martyred, Henry established a church, and Eliza conducted a school for children. She made hand-painted books and translated hymns into the Indians' dialect. The Indians loved the artistic Eliza's beautiful Bible charts she made for teaching purposes.

Twenty-four years after the massacre of the Whitmans and the subsequent ousting of the Spauldings by the military, Henry returned to his beloved Nez Perce tribe. This time he traveled alone because Eliza had already died. He baptized more than a thousand of the Nez Perce and Spokane Indians. He worked with them for three years, until he died. The work was then continued by Kate and Sue McBeth, who set up a training school for Indian preachers. The Nez Perce were known for evangelizing other tribes.

Although Henry and Eliza Spaulding got off to a rocky beginning on the mission field because of their incompatible relationship with the Whitmans, they were able to put that rudimentary start behind them and go on to do a great work for God.

Bad relationships with other people are not God-honoring. Ask God to love other missionaries and the people of your chosen country through you. Don't be a stumbling block. Learn to get along with people so God can use you to be a channel of blessing.

Above: Rachel and her friends enjoying the water at camp.
Below: Seven-year-old Rachel goes out soul winning.

UNIT SEVEN
Language
and Culture Shock

*"When thou passest through the waters,
I will be with thee."* (Isaiah 43:2)

Introduction

Malla Moe, a strange lady with a strange name, was born in Norway in 1863. She always considered herself an "uneducated farm girl." At the age of 15, most children were finished with school. They were then confirmed and admitted as members of the state church, so it would be a long, drawn-out process before Malla finally understood the Gospel and was saved. A dying aunt once asked Malla to meet her in Heaven. Malla, deeply moved, began to weep and promised her aunt that she would.

A few years after her aunt's death, Malla heard a rare salvation message and gave her heart to Jesus. It was difficult for her to grow as a Christian in what was described as a cold, religious atmosphere. Her father's death had a great impact on her as he wept and pleaded to his children from his deathbed to be ready to die by giving their hearts to God. Malla sought comfort from God and received the assurance of her salvation.

When Malla was 19, her mother died; so she and her younger sister immigrated to the United States where they joined another sister. At the time Malla arrived in Chicago, R.A. Torrey was pastoring the great Moody Church where Malla began attending. One night the founder, D. L. Moody, preached. After the service, Malla was sitting in the almost empty auditorium when Moody walked up to her. Moody asked Malla if she was saved, and she replied that she was. Moody then placed his hand on Malla's shoulder, gave her a gentle shove, and told her to get to work for the Master!

This encounter had a great effect on Malla. She began attending meetings conducted by Swedish evangelist, Frederik Franson, who had also been greatly influenced by D. L. Moody. Franson became the first commissioned missionary out of Moody Church. Franson met Hudson Taylor, missionary to China, and George Mueller, who had an orphanage. Meeting these great men motivated Franson to begin training missionaries.

Malla did not want to be a foreign missionary. After all, she had just immigrated to the United States! She was happy. Besides, couldn't she just do missionary work in her newly adopted land of America?

Franson approached Malla about going to Africa. She told Franson she was uneducated, and besides, she had a young sister for whom she had to care. Franson told her he would pray for her that night. In the book, *Malla Moe*, the following is recorded:

> The promise to pray coming from many a person was simply a piously polite way of dropping a matter. But from Franson, one had to feel that this would be the subject of an all-night vigil on his knees. That night following the meeting Malla made arrangements to visit a friend. Franson had gone to his host's house. When Malla arrived at the friend's apartment, she found that the girl had not yet returned. While she was waiting in the front hallway, something happened. She felt the Hand upon her again. This time it was crushing and insistent, so heavy that she fell to the floor. In a flash, she remembered Franson's promise. She knew without a doubt he was right then praying for her and she knew that God was once again pushing her out beyond the shores of self-dependence, out where she could no longer rest in any human ability. "O power of God! What can I say now? I have already given myself to You, body and soul. If you want me to go to Africa, my answer is yes."
>
> When the friend arrived, she found her there on the floor of the hallway, crying. But the crisis had passed, and peace had come.[1]

Malla enrolled in Franson's two-week long missionary course. He did not care how much education his missionaries had; all he cared about was were they filled with the Spirit of God, and did they know how to trust God.

Before the little band of missionaries left for Africa, Franson advised them: "Fast and pray. If you are sick, fast and pray; if the language is hard to learn, fast and pray; if the people will not hear you, fast and pray; and if you have nothing to eat, fast and pray."[2]

The missionaries arrived in Africa and began to try to adjust to the climate and the food. They were revolted when they saw the Africans eating a mixture of corn and soured milk and insects!

> The Africans were much less attractive to Malla than her preconceived notions of them. She told the Lord that if she were ever to work among them, He would have to give her a divine love; her own would never reach them.[3]

European settlers living there tried to lead the missionaries into believing that the Africans were happy. They said the Africans had no:

> ...inhibitions about the hereafter, [and] no bothersome moral codes.

According to reports, you could hear their happy songs as they tramped in rhythm mile after mile along deep-worn trails, as they hoed and weeded their gardens, as they danced to the beat of sticks. Their language was the beautifully rich and versatile Zulu. The men had words to describe to the finest detail the wealth in their cattle kraals or to discuss the day's news as they lazed their hours away in front of their huts. By the outdoor cooking area you could hear the language flow from the loose tongues of the wives, accented more noticeably than the men's with the clicks borrowed from the speech of ancient bushmen.

Work around the huts was well organized—laid out for the women, girls, and boys, by the men, who did practically none of it. While the males cultivated their conversation and drank beer, wives and girls cultivated the fields, brewed beer, cooked and cared for the kraal (group of huts), the family home. Boys herded the cattle, which meant for the most part playing or lying in the sun. The men may have found time now and then to build part of the huts, cure leather, plow, or help with the harvest, and create fancy carvings on wooden pillows, know sticks, or wooden milk pails.

Theirs was a gay and hospitable life, so the saying went, so free from strife and sadness…Crops were good, cattle were fat, there was plenty of beer to drink. Why should any missionary want to inject into this scene his doctrines of the hereafter and disrupt this peaceful life?[4]

Despite this glowing description, Malla was slowly finding out that the minds and hearts of the Africans were very dark indeed. They had a great fear of evil spirits, and their culture was degraded by witch doctors and black magic.

As few as eight, or as many as 200 people, might live in a kraal. They often have some sort of fence, if you could call it that, made of reeds, around the edge. Men prized their cattle above wives (usually several) or children, so they were in the center of the kraal. The beehive-shaped huts were 10 to 20 feet wide, made of woven branches, and covered with grass. The floors were polished with cow dung. A hole in the middle of the hut held a fire and cooking pot. There were often grass floor mats, all shapes and sizes of pots and utensils, blankets, spears, and other possessions hanging from the roof.

When the lady missionaries visited the kraals, they were disgusted to find dogs, chickens, and pigs with their noses inside the unwashed cooking pots. Huge crowds gathered to watch the white women.

The missionaries became very discouraged when a chief forbade them to settle in his territory. Another matter also troubled and discouraged Malla:

Malla's early days with the cattle on the mountains had prepared her for some of the trials she met, but language study was not one of them. Her school foundation was meager, and she lacked the systematic and disciplined mind necessary to learn from books in the usual way.

When Mr. Wettergren left them for Durban, the new missionaries found themselves without a language teacher. Malla, apparently the slowest of all to catch on to the strange word forms and clicks, started rising at four in the morning to study. This produced some improvement, though Malla's progress was liberally sprinkled with periods of deep discouragement. Her bouts with the language became bouts with Satan. She began seriously to question why she had come to Africa in the first place. Her enemy said to her that Franson was a blundering idealist, and she had better return home.[5]

One time when Malla was visiting a kraal, she was called to the hut of a dying woman who had been in labor for several days, but her baby could not be delivered. With very limited medical training, Malla could do nothing for the laboring mother except to remember Franson's advice. She fasted and prayed. Later, the mother safely delivered a healthy child!

A few days later when Malla went to visit the mother, she told her how she had wept when she saw the laboring mother's suffering and how she had prayed earnestly for her.

Tears started to stream down the woman's face. At that moment something melted in Malla's heart. "Why, she can cry just like us." This was the first African she had seen cry. For the first time Malla felt something of a kinship with the people's suffering and heartache.[6]

The little group of missionaries finally received word from Haugerud, their fellow missionary, that they were to go to start a work in Swaziland. The missionaries were excited and prepared to go. Little did they realize that shortly after he wrote his letter, Haugerud died of a fever.

This was a trying time for Malla's faith. It was now almost a year since they had sailed from New York, and the future looked blacker than ever. Paulson, she felt, had betrayed then by breaking with the group in the first month. Gullander, the only remaining man, did not care for the place of administrator.

Besides, Malla had lost more than a leader in Haugerud. Before leaving on the survey trip, he had proposed marriage to her. Her mind was saying that she had answered definitely enough, "I did not come to Africa to get married, but to serve the Lord." But her heart now was saying that when she answered him she did not anticipate this loneliness, and had he returned, she might have changed her answer.[7]

Shortly after Haugerud's death, three wagons of supplies and one wagon of missionaries, pulled by 16 oxen, left for Swaziland. Five weeks passed before the missionaries reached their destination. Malla suffered yet another loss. Soon after the party left for Swaziland, Malla's dear friend Augusta died shortly after giving birth to twins.

This was the signal for further discouragement for Malla. This would make four lost so far from their original eight. She could not understand how God worked. Her enemy came again and assured her that it was Franson and not God who had sent her to Africa. She might have dropped it all right then and returned home, but as she thought on it all, she saw Jesus suffering on the cross for her. She knew she came to Africa to obey God, and she would serve Him to the end.[8]

Malla Moe was almost defeated by language, discouragement, and culture shock. Satan can definitely use these tools to get missionaries to quit the mission field, as Miss Moe, one of the greatest soul winners about whom I have ever read, almost did.

Chapter One

Language

A s a missionary, I feel there are many areas where I should have tried harder. Language is one of those areas. My son and daughter, who both were born in the Philippines, speak the language fluently like a lot of MKs do. Oh, how I envy them!

Allow me to share what some missionaries and their wives said in the survey about learning a language. As already mentioned, some responses are from Dr. Jim Vineyard's missionary publication.

Question   Would you please share about learning a foreign language?

Answers:

• Our children learned the language much quicker than either my husband or me. Of course we had many more things to think about. But let your children help you. That makes it fun for both of you. Even while working around the house, I would think and try to speak to them in the language. Practice helps, and it's fun to practice with family.

• Learning a language is difficult—probably the most difficult thing I have done. Yet, it is so important in being able to communicate with and to help the people.

As my husband says, "When you learn the language of the people, you learn the heart of the people" (the way they think). As a mother, language study can be very difficult and often interrupted (caring for sick children, trying to continue with home schooling, caring for a newborn, etc.). Just do the best you can and learn all you can. You may not know the language as fluently as your husband who must preach in it, but don't become discouraged. Your priority is your home.

The language study can be picked up and continued on later or little by little as your schedule will allow, but your little ones will be little only once. Don't neglect the home front. Summer months, when you aren't home schooling, may give you an opportunity to devote more attention to language study. Continue to make it your goal to know the language, and strive to constantly improve (even if it's only a few new words each week.) Take the opportunity to practice your language on children and women at church. The best way to learn it is to use it. Possibly try to teach a children's Sunday school class. You may have to write out your lesson word-for-word to begin with, but it will give you the opportunity to practice speaking in front of others.

• Learning the language has been my greatest adjustment.

• Get as much language training as you can. Be patient with yourself as you are learning the language and do not be afraid to make mistakes. You will! The more we have learned the grammar of the language, the more we realize that though we know the formation of the signs, the syntax of the language is almost equally as important.

• I think that it is extremely important that the wife go to language school or get some kind of intensive schooling in the language. It was hard for me because I was 36 when I started language school. Using what you know helps more than anything.

• Even if your field of service uses English as a national language, it will make an impact if you learn some of the local dialect anyway. You identify better with the people. When our son preached his first sermon in the local language—the people went wild with delight. I was shocked by their response. I still haven't mastered the language, but I am trying. English is the national language here, but the folks love to hear us try in their language.

• We spent our first year in language school. If possible, it is best to go to a regular school, not just have a tutor, although I suppose in some countries that is not possible. The less formal the situation, the easier it is to allow things to interfere with the learning experience. It is also important to try to use what you learn. Force yourself to speak to others, although you know you will make mistakes. I know that is easier said than done! I still make plenty of mistakes after 28 years, and I am still very frustrated that after making one sentence, people will say, "Where are you from?" Use the language!

• I guess our biggest shock was the language barrier. Even after language school which we took from a secular place, we still felt sorely inadequate. We could give directions to the next town but couldn't tell folks about getting to Heaven because we hadn't leaned those words yet. The Lord did send a seasoned missionary our way, and he helped my husband immensely with the religious words and practices.

• I would say start learning on deputation. Don't wait until you get to the field. You will have that much head start. You can learn from books, tapes, etc., while driving in the car and during rest times.

- I am hard on myself due to the fact that I am a teacher. I want my grammar to be correct, when my neighbors could care less—they just want to talk to me. We do not have a [language school]. While this has slowed down our language, it has actually helped with the people in our city. They love to help and to correct me! We are still learning. Don't spend too much time with people who speak English. When we went to the States, I prayed the whole year that we would not lose the language. When we returned, I was told my [language] was much better! I was even able to have phone conversations, which were very hard for me.

Irene Webster-Smith sailed to Japan in 1916. During the journey, she talked to Japanese sailors and memorized 5,000 words in those three months. In the book *Sensi*, author Russell Hitt relates:

On Sunday, she went with the others to the huge Mission Hall in downtown Kobe, where she listened to a three-hour sermon in Japanese. The 5,000 words she had learned from the sailors did not help her understand it, and she found later that a good many of those words would not be used in church or anywhere else! That evening she squatted on the Mission Hall floor, sitting on her feet Japanese style, for a three-hour Christmas program. She had really been initiated!

After Christmas she traveled to Tokyo, where she had been assigned to stay...while studying the language. To her deep disappointment, she learned that she could not enroll in the language school in the middle of the year. She had to engage a tutor, who came an hour a day, four days a week—quite a contrast to the five hours daily her fellow missionaries were receiving!

Irene studied diligently during the weeks that followed. She kept her nose buried in a pocket Japanese-English dictionary. She memorized Scripture verses in Japanese. At church gatherings, at services in Akasaka Hospital where she played the organ, and at prayer meetings, she kept her ears tuned to the peculiar idioms of the difficult Japanese language.

In the spring, Mrs. Braithwaite took ill and had to be hospitalized. Irene was left in full charge of the household, and this very circumstance forced her to speak Japanese constantly. When she went to the meat market, if she did not know the names of the meats hanging in the open shop, she would ask the butcher, "What's that?" He would answer in Japanese, and she would try to memorize the name.

She followed the same formula when she visited the vegetable and fruit stalls, bought stamps at the post office, visited the pharmacy, or shopped for household items. Soon, most of the shopkeepers in the Akasaka district knew the friendly missionary who was learning to speak Japanese with an Irish accent![1]

Japanese is surely one of the hardest languages to learn; yet, Irene had a great determination to master it. In the book *On Being a Missionary,* by Thomas Hale, the author suggests the following about learning and mastering a language:

Learning a language is one-third natural ability, one-third exposure, and one-third motivation. If we have two out of the three, we'll succeed. We all ought to have the motivation, and we can all get the exposure. The natural ability is nice, but not necessary.

There are no shortcuts to learning a language. It takes discipline and persistence. Don't be discouraged. You may apply yourself for six months and see no progress. Then, all of a sudden, you will notice you are speaking and understanding more easily.

A major hindrance is our self-consciousness—or, more accurately, our pride.

Just mix up two little endings, and you'll soon be saying things like: "The ball picked up the boy and threw him through the window." Or, if you are into more complex sentences, you might say: "After eating the cow, the cabbage hit the stick on the head with the shopkeeper."

Don't think to yourself: "Almost all the nationals I deal with speak English, so I don't really need to learn this language." Yes, they may speak English, but they will rarely speak it well enough to understand spiritual matters. If you want to communicate with them on a spiritual level, you will need to do that in their language, not yours...the best way to really learn a language is to immerse yourself in it. Observe; listen; and speak, speak, speak. It won't come naturally to introverts and perfectionists, but there is no other way to become fluent.[2]

Philippians 4:13 says, *"I can do all things through Christ which strengtheneth me."* Learn the language! I cannot stress too much the importance of learning the language.

Chapter Two

Adjusting to the Culture

Culture shock happens when that which is familiar in our lives is gone and we are suddenly bombarded with new things, many of them unpleasant, which are a shock to our system! In our survey, we asked missionary wives what were their biggest adjustments when they went to the mission field.

 **Question** Would you please share how you adjusted to the culture?

Answers:

• I had not gone on the survey trip with my husband, so all was new to me upon our arrival. The filthy, dilapidated buildings and the rampant poverty were appalling. Beggars were all around, and so were thieves. I was so glad though, to see brilliant flowering shrubs and trees here and there. God had some beauty in the midst of it all for me. With all the extra work of boiling all our water; dust, dirt, and roaches everywhere; home schooling; language study; and the ministry—I finally gave in and hired a part-time worker to clean the floors and do my ironing. It was a real sanity saver for me.

• Getting used to all the paperwork and realizing that the biggest difficulty is relationships with other missionaries (they are as human as me!).

• [I miss] Christmas in winter and American holidays though we celebrate as much as we can. I also miss some of the American food.

• The greatest adjustment was driving on the other side of the road. It can be quite dangerous when you don't remember what side to drive on or which way to look crossing the road.

• Probably the thing we miss most is that our families are so far away. We have children who wouldn't know their grandparents if they met them on the street.

• We don't think alike, our humor is different, our way of consoling is different, and our way of celebrating is different. So, we need to accept them as such. Think: "We are the strange ones in their country, and we are not always right." [The nationals] think of us Americans as loud, impatient, bossy, rich, and arrogant with lots of rules.

• When the sellers see our white skin, the price goes up. We jokingly call this "skin tax." Also, we are the only foreigners in our area, so when I go to the market, I get swarmed with curious people; it ends up being an emotionally draining experience.

• I certainly miss my family. I miss the food. I miss the orderliness of having things done just like that. For instance, when I went to get my phone, all I did was call the 1-800 number, and I had my phone in 30 minutes. I didn't have to do anything [whereas on the mission field] you have to wait and wait.

• Probably the greatest adjustment when you go to a foreign country is you don't have Americans close by. We were stripped of our cultural identity. It's more of a cultural adjustment to the ways they do things, and the way of their thinking is not the same as Americans.

• Well, of course, you miss the people. That's what we miss most—the family and friends. As far as material things, I can't really say that we miss a whole lot.

• No electricity, no running water, far away from loved ones, far away from our home church, lack of communication, lack of proper medical care, isolation.

• Having grown up where the people were so friendly and warm even to strangers, it was difficult to be in a culture of people who were not friendly, who were very cold and suspicious of strangers, and who did not smile. I did not know that there was such a difficulty in finding good food. This is a constant struggle. Also, having grown up in a safe culture going to a place where crime and criminals were constantly around has been a difficult adjustment.

• There are a lot of what I consider hardships on the field. The worst I deal with is visas, which can be difficult sometimes to get due to the government.

• The Catholic church attacks us by writing newspaper articles against us, and local priests warn their people against us. The constitution guarantees religious liberty, but Catholicism is always a threat. We have experienced many Satanic attacks and have learned that God is able to give us victory through His Word and prayer.

• I suppose the first adjustment when we arrived on the field was getting over jet lag and getting used to the new climate, elevation, people, language, land, etc. It seemed like a different world. Yet, we were so happy to finally be where God had called us that we didn't mind the adjustment. I think that flexibility is so vital. Deputation helps you to be more flexible, but every missionary needs to learn to be flexible; to be able to bend and not break when the "winds" of adjustment, culture shock, fatigue, discouragement, etc. come your way. Remember: "This too shall pass."

• I shop in regular stores. We go to several different stores to get everything, and it takes most of one day each week. I used to go in the market but that is so unsafe now and very hot and tiring as well that I would rather pay a few cents extra on each thing to go in a nice, clean, air-conditioned store to buy it.

• To be honest, there were several big adjustments that had to be made. The greatest physical adjustment we had to make was getting used to the unchanging weather, which is always hot. There are no distinct seasons. The greatest mental adjustment was the culture shock. Though fairly modernized and English-speaking, it is in no way America. Their humor is different. Their music is different. Their government is different. Their driving is different. Their business dealings are different. They bank differently, have different store hours, and most frustrating of all, they socialize in a different manner. It's real easy to get resentful when being confronted with all of these differences at once. To help overcome this, we had a saying that we repeated for months in our home: "Different isn't always bad; it's just different." We had to focus on what we were here for and that was to tell these people about Jesus. Our greatest spiritual adjustment was getting used to having such a great distance between us and our dear friends and family in the States. Adapting to the lack of fellowship with other American believers was not easy. There are no other American fundamental missionaries here. In fact, we rarely see Americans. Most of the tourists we happen to meet are from England or Canada and are not Christians. We do not have others around to "pump us up." It is a rare treat when we get to hear another preacher. One must stay close to the Lord and spend plenty of time in His Word to remain strong. Our fellowship with God has been strengthened as a result. Also, as our little flock continues to grow in the grace and knowledge of the Lord Jesus Christ, we are finding that we continue to have richer and greater fellowship with them. It all takes time and patience. It doesn't happen all at once.

• Being able to just run down to Wal-Mart or to the auto parts store and find what I need quickly, easily, and cheaply. Having the same product sent to us takes a lot of time and results in a duty to pay on top of the shipping. I miss the price of gas there! We also miss the interstate! You can only go so far and so fast on an island. We miss the mountains, pine trees, rivers, and lakes. We miss several different traditional things during the holidays. There are no fireworks on the Fourth of July. Instead of going sledding, I mow my lawn Christmas Eve. A Thanksgiving turkey would cost us about $40.00 (US). We all miss America—the rich history of the United States, the national anthem, baseball, hot dogs, apple pie, grandparents and friends, Wal-Mart, McDonalds, snow in winter, leaves in the fall, guns and hunting, air shows, parades, voting, ladies' meetings and fellowship dinners, and revivals.

- We were told by this language school that we were to go to Hong Kong first and get our visa. We got to Hong Kong, and they said it would take about a week. We were there for a week, and we still didn't have our visas. So they said, "Maybe tomorrow." And so, we went and they said, "Maybe tomorrow." They kept telling us, "Maybe tomorrow." That went on for over six weeks, waiting in Hong Kong for our visa. Hong Kong is a very expensive place, and we were trying to find places to stay; it was very difficult. Finally, after six weeks, we received our visa. We got into [our field], and the water was shut off; there were no curtains on the windows; there were no pillows or blankets on the beds, no food, nothing in our apartment. We had nothing to eat. The next day we had to go and get things to eat, and I think the biggest adjustment for my wife was when we had to get on the bus. She had never before been to a third-world country. She got on this bus, and it was cram-packed with people. There were holes in the floor, cracks in the windows, and people were spitting on the floor; she about lost it. So that was quite an adjustment for us— just getting used to the culture.

- Probably our biggest adjustment would be to learn how to deal with the Communist government. We were so used to freedoms here in America, just to say what we wanted to say, do what we wanted to do, and not think anything about it. We have to be cautious.

- I am still working on adjusting to the traffic. Also I am missing the "Southern" courtesy and am trying to get used to the fact that things are done differently and not always efficiently. [My wife] had a hard time with the heat.

- Getting used to the inefficiency of the government and most businesses. Things move a lot slower here. One missionary put it this way, "It takes a lot of time just to live here." One example of this is that it took six months to get my telephone hooked up.

- Isolation—being away from contact with people back home—we were completely cut off from the outside world. We lived in a little village that was out in the middle of nowhere, so we didn't have a telephone, and we weren't able to get the mail every day. Also, there was no electricity or running water. We had the opportunity of going on a survey trip, and that was good for us. That helped out more than anything else; we pretty much knew how it would be.

- Getting used to living around the filth and lack of sanitary conditions and the general rudeness of many of the people. The sanitary customs of many of the people are third-world, and the government moves extremely slow. I have traveled all over the world, and there is no place like the United States of America! God truly has blessed our country. It was also an adjustment to realize the need for constant vigilance and security of your person and possessions.

• We had about 600 pre-labeled envelopes to use for our prayer letters that immediately sealed themselves because of the high humidity. The termites also ate some of our clothes and mementos that were still packed in some boxes.

• Have you ever stopped to wonder what it must be like for a missionary wife to not have the convenience of 24-hour grocery stores and restaurants after being accustomed to it here in the States? Have you considered the stress that she is under when the power or water gets cut several times every day for long periods of time? What about the culture shock that she must continually go through? One missionary said that culture shock can be compared to the torture of being tied down with your forehead under a continuous drip of water. One drop is no big deal, but after a while, they all start to get to you.

These responses vary widely, partly because the mission fields vary widely, and partly because the missionaries themselves vary widely. What might be irritating to one may not be so bothersome to someone else.

My friend, Suzie Heidenreich, wrote the following story:

When we first arrived in the Philippines, it was the very first time any of us had ever been on an airplane. Actually, it was the first time for a lot of things. When you go to a different country, there are so many adjustments that you wouldn't think of. We arrived in the Philippines at midnight, and a veteran missionary picked us up at the airport. We had never before met him. There had been a revolutionary outbreak to try to overthrow the president just a few weeks before we arrived. There was Steve, me, and our three youngest children, ages 16, 14, and 11. The missionary took us to a guesthouse so we could rest. By the time we waited for all of our luggage and got to the guesthouse, it was already 3:00 a.m. The guesthouse was set up like an apartment. It had two bedrooms, a living room, a bath, a kitchen, and a little room off the end with just a sink, so you could wash your clothes. Right smack in the middle of that room was a tree! It went all the way up through the roof.

We learned later that the Filipino family who owned the house did not want to cut down the tree because it was a coconut tree, so they just built the roof around the tree.

We were all getting ready to settle in for the night. We all took a shower and were refreshed. There were three sets of bunk beds, so we all just got in a bunk and got ready to sleep. Since we were all somewhat excited because we were about to start our new life and because of the difference in time [the Philippines is 12 hours ahead of the United States], we all had a difficult time trying to fall asleep. A storm was brewing when we first landed, and as the night went along, the winds became stronger and stronger. We couldn't help but chitter-chatter all about the events going on with the revolutionary attempt.

Shortly after we had just fallen asleep, we heard this terrible "BANG!" My husband yelled, "Hit the deck!" and all of us dove for the floor. It was a terrible racket. We were all shook up! We were sure we were in the middle of another revolutionary war! We were scared to death, but eventually, we all fell asleep on the floor.

When we woke up the next morning, we didn't know what to expect or what to do. My husband slowly walked over to the windows to see if he could see anything and then slipped out the door to see if he could see anything outside. When he came back in, all the kids and I were practically huddled in a corner, scared to find out what had happened. He told us to get up, and he took us to the back of the apartment. He showed us where the tree trunk was in the middle of the room. He pointed up and told us that the tree was a coconut tree, so naturally it had coconuts growing on it. Through the night as the winds blew harder and harder, those coconuts were falling off the tree and hitting the tin roof of the apartment! That was our big war! We had a good time sharing our "event" with the veteran missionaries!

You will also have stories to share as the time goes on. The famous missionary to China, Hudson Taylor, had a daughter-in-law named Geraldine Taylor, who was also a missionary to China. Geraldine Guinness went to China as a single lady missionary in 1888. She later married Howard Taylor, the son of Hudson Taylor.

When Geraldine would go out on the street to visit people, crowds of Chinese would throng her. Sometimes there were so many people pressing around her that her feet would actually be lifted from the ground by the surging mob. There was several inches of dust on the ground which, when stirred by the crowd, would choke and blind her. She could not go out of the house without "a hundred eyes following every movement."[1] For her, an unchaperoned woman, to go out soul winning "constituted the greatest breach of Chinese etiquette,"[2] so the people said cruel things about her, thinking she was a loose woman.

Upon arriving home, Geraldine would be covered with dust from head to foot. Dust was in her throat, eyes, nostrils, and even the pores of her skin. Just from being out a few hours she said, "Our garments look as though we had wandered for years in the wilderness."[3]

When Geraldine married Howard Taylor, their honeymoon consisted of traveling with her father-in-law to Chinese villages to preach the Gospel. At night they had to stay in filthy inns and sleep on hard brick beds. The amazing thing is, when you read her book, you get the impression that she loved every minute of it!

I Timothy 1:12, *"And I thank Christ Jesus our Lord, who hath enabled me...."* Ask Jesus to enable you to adjust to the culture.

Chapter Three

Loneliness

When I left for the mission field in 1977, I was sure I would probably be home-sick; however, I had the mistaken idea that only single missionaries could be lonely. In our survey, we asked missionaries how they dealt with loneliness.

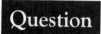 **Question**

What should a missionary do when lonely?

Answers:

• Go to the Bible! I have found so many things that I did not see before, maybe because I was not in that particular situation. Also, it helps to have a hobby (sewing). I also enjoy reading. Also, music and preaching tapes are very important to listen to on the field. We need to hear the music from home and the preaching also. It will refresh us!

• I still struggle with it. I would love more ideas. What helps me the most is to be close to my husband and children. I am trying to have a closer relationship with the Lord to help with that more also. Sometimes I find just staying busy helps too. Finding something I enjoy doing or trying to surprise my husband with something is lots of fun for me. I am glad that my husband and I can talk, and we spend lots of time doing just that. I am able to express my feelings to him. I want to learn to lean more on the Lord. Little by little, I feel the Lord is helping me. My husband mentioned getting your home pastor to send you sermon tapes. Our preacher does, and we enjoy them. It caused my oldest son to love him. Christian magazine subscriptions, newspapers, or other good Christian literature to read. I really enjoy lots of good Christian music. I can't seem to get enough of it.

• I've never really felt lonely. [My husband] and I [talk] a lot and bounce ideas between us. We seem to always have a project, whether at home or at church, to work on together. I also enjoy our church ladies a lot.

• I haven't been lonely, to tell you the truth, so I haven't had to deal with it. But some things I would say to do are keep American traditions and holidays, decorate your home or at least one room "American." Fellowship, if at all possible, with any Americans around you who would empathize with you but also help you make any transitions needed. But at the same time I would make a close national friend to help you understand and learn the national ways. Also I am an animal lover, and they have always been great companions for me.

- I dealt with loneliness in two ways: first I realized that I was probably going to be lonely for the rest of my life. I grieved over it in a way. Then I tried not to dwell on it. I try to stay busy (no need to try really—it's always busy!) and focus my "world" around my family and our church family. I talk a lot to my husband. He is a good listener and understanding of my need to talk out all that's on my mind and heart. **I pray about my loneliness. If anyone can understand being lonely in a foreign country—Jesus can.**

- I don't know of any way to avoid loneliness on the mission field, especially if there aren't any other missionaries in your city. Only the Lord can reach you at the depths of loneliness that can come.

- I really haven't had much of a problem with loneliness—yet! I stay too busy to get lonely. There are days, especially around Christmas, when I really miss my family. I allow myself a few minutes to think of past good memories with them, maybe look at a photo album, etc., but then I don't allow myself to dwell on our separation, loneliness, and other negative thoughts. Also, we schedule time to get together with other missionary families. It is so nice to talk with another American and for your children to have other MKs to play with. We as missionaries can get so busy that we don't take time to fellowship with others. It doesn't mean you are more spiritual if you stay secluded from other Americans or don't take a furlough or say you don't need fellowship with others. This practice might hurt your family more than it helps your ministry in the long run.

- Loneliness is basically a communication problem. My days are full, but I still find the time—usually at 5:30 in the morning after I have already had my walk with God and my walk with my husband (we walk together every morning, rain or shine)—to communicate with our family back in the U.S.A. My husband and I work together on projects for our children. At the moment we are making Christmas presents for them.

- Prayer and Bible time! Make times with my husband and children special. E-mail, if possible. My best friend is a missionary, and we talk over the Internet for free once a week. Not long, just a quick hello and hearing a familiar voice helps. I have a set time to be on the Internet, or else it can get out of hand!

- This can be a difficulty. It may sound trite, but we really have to make

Jesus our best Friend. We can go to Him at any time for comfort and help. On the human side, we do have to be careful, just as a Stateside pastor and wife, about making people in the church our best friends, but we can have various activities together, and we can make the ladies feel our home is always open to them. This can be one advantage of working together with another missionary couple…If this is not the situation, then we have to depend on times together with our husband as our friend, although that is different than having a female friend. Sometimes we can try to fill a "void" with reading, crafts, or other activities that can fill leisure time.

• There's no way around it, sometimes I get very lonely and miss the States or my family. Now in the recent years it has sometimes been extremely tough with the older ones leaving home for college, marriage, or the military. You can't avoid it, but it does help to stay busy with church, home, garden, outside activities, and of course, the best remedy is crying to the Lord. He understands.

• My wonderful husband has not neglected to keep our date night. That keeps me sane, I must say. I do have friends now with whom I can converse and enjoy fellowship. I just pray when I feel lonely and try not to complain. I told my husband about my first six months' difficulties after we had been here more than two years. God gets you through more than you think you're able to handle. I just try to be positive, and it helps me tremendously. I also write to my friends and family through e-mail and feel like I'm not so far away. I get the *Christian Womanhood* magazine that I love, too. I feel like these things keep my life "normal" and make me feel like I don't live on the other side of the world.

• Plan to stay no matter what anybody tells you. God called you there, and He's not likely to change His mind because you feel tired and lonely.

• There is no avoiding being lonely; you just accept it. What helps me is thinking thoughts about why we are here, and wasn't Jesus lonely? Wasn't Paul lonely?

• My hardest adjustment on the field was the loneliness. I am social, so it was very hard for me to come somewhere so isolated. You have to make your family your social group and later your church family after you have a church.

About four months after my husband held his first Bible study in Iloilo City, we ran out of room, so we began looking for another place to rent. We found a large, old, rundown house and moved in. There were two bedrooms and a bathroom upstairs, which we made our living quarters. We started a Bible college in June, with 13 students and three staff members. They lived in the larger downstairs portion. They were a great group of kids, although I realize time has a way of softening our memories! I quickly found out that living with people, especially when you're pregnant and grouchy, is not easy. I'm sure our students and staff would also say it is not easy living with two spoiled Americans!

My two-burner "stove" and refrigerator were downstairs in the kitchen, so the students and staff could use it. They put raw fish in the refrigerator so all my food smelled like raw fish. They used my pots and pans, which were often burnt to a crisp. They used my electric iron but forgot to use the adapter so it burnt to a crisp too. The students had their own budget for their food, which they cooked together as a group. I would make spaghetti for Rick and me for supper. The next day at noon, I'd go downstairs to heat the spaghetti for lunch, only to find it gone. Filipinos are very hospitable, so if anyone would drop by, anything on hand was served. That is their custom. We paid a couple of the students to wash our clothes by hand, as we didn't have a washing machine. You would think I'd be grateful, wouldn't you? I wasn't. The clothes were clean enough—too clean in fact. They were scrubbed and bleached to death. They were threadbare and discolored. I became grouchier and grouchier! You would think, being surrounded by all those people all the time, I could never get lonely—right? Wrong!

There were times when I thought I would die of loneliness. I was slowly making friends with our people, but still they were so foreign to me. I'd much rather spend time with our people now, but back then they were so strange to me—everything was, and I was shy. I didn't have any children yet, and my husband was so tied up in his new ministry. God really helped me through this adjustment period by giving me a good friend—Mrs. Steffy. She and her husband had been missionaries in the Philippines for years. She would invite Rick and me over for supper. She could take the goods from the market and make it into something wonderful! Her beautiful home was a haven for me. On days when I was overcome with homesickness and loneliness, I would hop on a jeepney and go to her house—uninvited. No matter what she was doing, she always welcomed me with open arms. She would drop everything and act like my intrusion was the most wonderful thing that had happened to her all week! Thanksgiving and Christmas would have been unbearable without her. She counseled this green missionary on the culture, housekeeping, and homesickness. She loaned me missionary biographies. When I read about what those great ladies of the past went through, I realized how trivial my little trials were. She was just a little taste of home. I will be forever grateful to her. I pray that God will give a Mrs. Steffy to every lonely missionary lady.

Romans 12:21, "*Be not overcome of evil, but overcome evil with good.*" Our God is a great God; He can help us overcome loneliness! If we will let Him, He can also help us forget about ourselves and help others.

Chapter Four

Advice

Proverbs 8:33 says, *"Hear instruction, and be wise, and refuse it not."* The following points contain some pertinent, helpful advice.

 What advice would you give new missionaries regarding adjustment?

Answers:

- Don't stay cooped up in the house. Take walks if it's safe and explore on your own. Be yourself. Just don't be loud and rude as we can so often be. Adjust your wardrobe accordingly without going the worldly way.

- Getting into a schedule as soon as possible is very helpful. Children (as well as us adults) feel security from having a schedule. Also, give each child his own responsibilities.

- We took a survey trip about a year before we actually left for the field. I got to see firsthand what I was getting into. That gave me some time to adjust and try to get necessary items before actually living there. I was so glad that I was able to go on the survey trip with my husband. Our children haven't had to make big adjustments since they have grown up all their lives there. I would think that a survey trip would be helpful for older children just as it was for me. Ask the missionaries there lots of questions. Find out how much things cost, how you will probably be living, how you will shop, cook, etc. It would be best if you could stay with another missionary instead of in a hotel. That way you can see firsthand how a missionary lives in that country.

- Prepare yourself mentally and emotionally before going. Make sure you realize you are not there to make it another America and don't try doing it. You will be disappointed. If you are prone to homesickness, take as much of "home" with you as possible—decorations, food, holiday stuff, etc. Be prepared spiritually. Know your country before you leave; it will help you adjust more quickly.

• It is helpful if she can contact any missionary who is currently on the field to which she is going. Ask that missionary wife what are the top 10 things that she recommends that she bring from America or ship from America. Talk to that missionary wife as much as possible to get a "feel" of the living standards. This information will be very helpful. I did this and learned of many items that I should take.

• Be content; keep on your knees. Remember it is a rough time on your kids too.

• Don't be afraid of feeling awkward. Everything is different, and at first, you will feel out of place. Just be yourself, and the people will see right through you. They will see that you are there to help them and because you care about them. Do things "your way" like bake cookies with your kids and deliver them to your neighbors with a smile.

• I wish I had learned not to be so demanding of myself. If I had learned to relax a little at the first when culture shock was settling in, I could have accomplished the same or maybe more. For example: Even though we lived under extremely isolated and primitive conditions, I fretted a lot about the domestic issues—cooking, cleaning, and laundry. I was very unwise and refused to accept the fact that housekeeping in the jungle cannot be the same as it was in the United States. It seems silly now, but at the time I broke down and cried out of frustration.

• This is what older missionaries have told me: "Just expect anything that first year." That's when you're the most vulnerable, and Satan knows that, and he just throws everything at you. That first year was the hardest year we ever had. After that we were able to understand a little bit why the [nationals] did what they did and the different facets of the culture. They would try to cheat us all the time just because we had a white face. I guess the advice to the missionaries would be to just be patient, stay close to the Lord, and expect it to be rough.

• We try to make everything an adventure and special. We try to point out the blessings in whatever we are doing. Sometimes it may be hard, especially when your child asks you, "Why would God let someone break into our home and take all of our things?" That was a hard one to answer. I realized real quick that my children were watching my reaction to this crisis. I honestly just wanted to fall apart, but I had to straighten up and take care of my children at the time. I told them God knew about this and could have prevented it, but He protected us as we were not home when all of this happened. I told them that we must pray for the [thieves] and we did. One cannot pray for others and hate them. We really placed them in God's hands.

In the book *On Being a Missionary*, by Thomas Hale, the author addresses the basic differences between the West and most third-world cultures:

First, the West is time-oriented. The Third World is event-oriented. This means that church in Nepal begins half an hour late and runs for three hours. Church is an "event." People who have to walk two hours to church don't want a one-hour service!

A second difference is that the West is "crisis-oriented" and the Third World is not. Westerners place high value on avoiding crises, on planning, on preventing problems. Third World people are decidedly non-crisis oriented; they prefer to deal with problems as they arise. Why prepare for problems that might never arise?

A third difference between the West and the Third World is that the former is task-oriented and the latter is person-oriented. In the Third World, relationships are more important than performance. It's very hard to fire someone on the mission field—think of the loss of face. Speed, efficiency, high standards are all of secondary importance.

In the West we promote individualism and distrust authority. But in the East, community is most important, and elders are respected. In the West romantic love is supreme; in the East courtships are most likely controlled by parents. In the West we minimize class division, but in the East one is expected to keep his place. The West is eager for progress; the East is more fatalistic.

We, as they do, tend to think our own culture is the norm by which to judge behavior. We Westerners like to tease and kid each other; it's a sign of friendship. But to the Asian, such teasing would result in "loss of face." Think the best of others. Give people a second chance. Err on the side of trusting a person, even knowing you may get stung. That's not gullibility; better to get stung ten times than mistrust an honest person once.

In short, be a decent, positive person. Remember the prayer of the little girl, who said: "Dear God, please make bad people Christians, and Christian people nice."

Culture shock often begins to take hold in earnest six to eight months after one's arrival. The initial romance and excitement of the new country has mostly worn off and the new missionary is trying to set up house and get into the work. The language is coming slowly; he has already had seven bouts with dysentery. He doesn't like the food. There are inconveniences and problems at every turn. He thinks: "Thirty more years of this!"[1]

The author Thomas Hale, who is also a medical doctor, continues on to say that culture shock can produce fatigue, discouragement, depression, a critical spirit, guilt, pessimism, and self-pity. He gives advice on how to overcome culture shock:

> The best way to overcome culture shock is to expose oneself to the culture and the people. Reach out, make friends, and adapt. The need to expose oneself cannot be emphasized too strongly. Entering into another culture means enjoying and respecting that culture and participating in it. Let's look at some of the practical ways to stay on top of this bugaboo called culture shock.
>
> First, recognize it. It's normal. You will survive it. You will simply get used to the things that shocked you at first.
>
> Experiencing culture shock doesn't mean you weren't cut out to be a missionary; it happens to anyone who crosses culture boundaries. The only people who can escape culture shock are missionary children and very short-termers. It's hard to have real culture shock when you've got an air ticket out of the country in six weeks.
>
> Second, pray earnestly for God's grace and enabling. The struggles you are facing are not only cultural; they are also spiritual.
>
> Third, determine that in all but ethical and religious matters you are going to adapt to the nationals; you adapt to them, not they to you. Cultivate a positive attitude; don't adapt grudgingly. Look for the good things in their culture; there will be many.
>
> Fourth, go out of your way to make a circle of friends.
>
> Fifth, put yourself in the nationals' shoes.
>
> Sixth, cultivate an attitude of exploration, of adventure. Be willing to try new things, new foods.
>
> Seventh—and this I include with caution—maintain close links with your fellow missionaries. It is not a cure, but periodically we need the refreshment, encouragement, and counsel that can best come from those of our own culture.
>
> Retreating back into our own cultural milieu, however, can become habitual; this is its danger. We come to rely on the people and things of our own culture, and thus become isolated from the people we've come to serve. Retreating in this way may shield us from culture shock for a time, but in the end it will prolong our adaptation.
>
> Eighth and last, don't take yourself too seriously. Learn to laugh at yourself.[2]

Paul said, *"I am made all things to all men, that I might by all means save some."* (I Corinthians 9:22) Try to learn as much as you can from experienced missionaries. There is a great incentive to your adjusting to your new land—the salvation of lost souls.

Chapter Five

Weather, Housekeeping, and Food

In this chapter as the title indicates, we will discuss several aspects of weather, housekeeping, and food! In her book, *Sometimes I Prefer to Fuss*, Verda Peet writes the following:

Officially in Thailand there are three seasons—dry, hot and rainy. "It is so hot in Bangkok that you want to take off your skin and sit round in your bones," said one friend. In April I always went round with my face an unbecoming shade of beet, without any exertion whatsoever. But it was only Westerners who looked hot. I used to marvel at how calm and cool our Thai neighbors appeared. The weather seems to have little effect on the beautiful dark skin of the Thai. They themselves prefer fair skin and don't understand the American obsession for laying in the sun to achieve the tan they naturally possess. Then foreigners go in for prickly heat. Our small Peets often looked measly, and I once asked [the] Stateside doctor what to do about prickly heat.

"Keep them cool and dry" was his infuriating advice.

One of the tourists said to a friend: "When we were coming down the steps of the plane, I thought I was feeling the heat of the engines. I guess it's the climate here!"

Your arm sticks to your desk or your papers stick to your arm. It is impossible to study without a fan, and if you use one your papers fly all over the room. I know I complained a lot about the heat, especially when darkness brought little reduction in temperature so that I wakened in the morning feeling as hot and tired as when I went to bed. I consulted one of our mission doctors. She gave me a long and impressive list of things that can happen to you in the heat; circulatory instability, heat edema and salt depletion, ending with chronic tropical fatigue.

Then she spoiled it by adding, "Heat reduces the willingness to work rather than the capacity for work."

It is extremely easy to be lazy and cantankerous in the heat. I looked forward to the rainy season because sometimes, for a few hours, the rain would bring some cooling relief, [but] the constant dampness, the mold on walls and books and the unpleasant odor of washing that had taken three days to dry, was strangely depressing.[1]

Joy Tuggy, in her book *The Missionary Wife and Her Work*, wrote that missionary ladies need to learn to adjust their housework to their physical strength and missionary duties. Too many mothers try to do all they did in America, even though learning a new language and culture, home schooling her children, and helping her husband with the mission work. Add a baby to this list, and see what happens! Missionary housekeeping is time-consuming and can also take much of a woman's strength—especially in primitive conditions. She needs to be aware of her limitations and ask the Lord to help her get her situation in perspective. Many hire helpers. As with anything, there are pros and cons. If you have a teenage son or daughter, you must be careful about young girls or boys working in your home. Unfortunately, I have also heard of more than one missionary running off with the house girl.

Take note of these comments which we received from our survey regarding housekeeping.

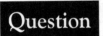

Can you tell about housekeeping on your field?

Answers:

• No hot water or dishwasher or clothes dryer! You just slowly adjust to a tiny refrigerator and an oven without a thermostat. At first everything is irritating.

• When we arrived, it was my first time ever on foreign soil. We did not know that the houses did not have closets or heaters! We planned to rent and thought those things would come with the house. The first house had water and electricity and a phone, so I didn't complain much. Little by little the Lord supplied our water heater, stove, washer, and refrigerator. Until then we just had to grin and bear it.

• We have the basics: washer, refrigerator, stove. The things we don't have, one just adjusts to being without. Of course, there have been many a day where I would have liked a dryer, especially on days and days of rain. When the laundry is hanging out under the house and won't get dry, I realized I must stop wanting and figure out a way to get them dry. One would be surprised at what can be done when you decide to figure a way to do it.

• We have the basic appliances, but we are not dependent on electricity because the electricity here is very unreliable; for instance, our oven and refrigerator are gas. We have battery packs which we keep charged up when the electricity is on, and these help to run our computer and other small appliances when we don't have electricity for a long time. We have kerosene lamps in every room.

In I Peter 5:7 we find a precious promise: *"Casting all your care upon him; for he careth for you."* Perhaps you are thinking, "I don't want to bother God with little things like the weather and housekeeping," when, in fact, God cares about every facet of our lives. Take it all to Him in prayer.

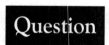

Food

Matthew 6:25 and 26 say, *"Therefore I say unto you, Take no thought for your life, what ye shall eat, or what ye shall drink; nor yet for your body, what ye shall put on. Is not the life more than meat, and the body than raiment? Behold the fowls of the air: for they sow not, neither do they reap, nor gather into barns; yet your heavenly Father feedeth them. Are ye not much better than they?"* No doubt, every missionary has a funny food story. Food is more important to some people than others. A wife and mother, of course, has to plan and prepare so she can cook for her husband and children, as opposed to single lady missionaries. My children and I love Filipino food. My husband can take it or leave it. He doesn't think it's very funny when we tell him: "Where He leads me I will follow, what He feeds me I will swallow!"

The following are some responses from our survey regarding food.

Question

Can you share about the food in your country?

Answers:

• Things have changed through the years. I don't have to cook the gelatin or make mayonnaise anymore, but most food is still made from scratch and is very time consuming.

• I do have basic appliances now. I used a kerosene burner for quite a while. You just learn to make one-pot meals. The open markets are everywhere and are where we would get most fresh things. Where we are, we do have some small grocery stores about the size of a garage. Everything is cooked or baked from scratch. There are no easy mixes.

• Here they eat rice and beans every day. I fix that some, but also fix

American food. Food preparations take longer because there are less convenience and prepared foods, but it is healthier.

- We do have open markets, and we buy the fruits and vegetables that we can get. It's much cheaper and also helps the nationals. Other foods we buy in the store, but we do not have much variety. Make sure you know how to make things from scratch—cakes, biscuits, spaghetti sauce, and many other items.

- Food preparation is dramatically different. I feel lazy in the U.S.A. because most of the food prep is already done for you. The worst part of food prep is fighting the lines at Meijer [the grocery store]!

- [My hardest adjustment] was cooking with very limited supplies. Most everything you cook or bake will be from scratch. Know what is available in the country where you are going. I thought I was prepared, and in many ways I was, but it may be a challenge to be creative with meals when you only have a very limited variety of ingredients. (And that's not because of limited funds. The stores here just do not carry many things.)

Chapter Six

Another Word for Culture Shock

M y husband does not like the words "culture shock"! He feels it has a "nega-tive" connotation, and he likes for things to stay "positive!" He suggested I use the word "adjusting" or learning to be "flexible," which is exactly what we need to do when we go to the foreign mission field.

Studies seem to indicate that the top two reasons why missionaries quit are poor health and not having good relationships with the people. However, others say loneliness is the greatest cause of missionaries' leaving the field. We tend to criticize that which we do not understand. Poverty can be a shock. I thought the people on my bus route in Chicago were living in poverty, but it is nothing com-pared to here. Culture shock affects different people in different ways. It affects men differently than women. It affects teenagers differently than it does younger children.

Needless to say, so many changes all at once can cause a lot of stress. You must learn a new language, a new culture, and on top of that, you have to try to help your kids adjust. You're terribly homesick, and it's humiliating to work on a new language—only to have people laugh at your efforts.

After the "honeymoon" period when you first arrive, frustrations begin to mount up. Learning to cope with things that we take for granted back home—like plumbing, electricity, transportation, and even meals, can cause a great deal of stress—not to mention getting accustomed to an extreme climate change. Here are a few tips for effectively combating culture shock. Oops! I mean "adjusting!":

C — Commit yourself to be joyful; learn to be content. If you are filled with the Holy Spirit, you will be joyful.

U — [You!] should be thankful. If you're in a third-world country, you should surely realize you have a lot for which you should be thankful.

L — Learn to be flexible. If life hands you lemons—make lemonade!

T — Taking yourself too seriously? A sense of humor is vital!

U — [You!] should be an encourager; don't tear down people.

R — Reduce stress. I know—easier said than done! Stop and smell the roses now and then!

E — Emotional health: be patient with people and look for their good points. Be kind!

S — Set reasonable goals. Don't be lazy, and do be responsible.

H — Human limitations can be divided into emotional, intellectual, spiritual, and physical. Emotionally, we need companionship! Don't neglect family. Intellectually, our minds need refreshment! Read! Spiritually and most importantly, don't neglect Bible reading and prayer! Lastly, take care of your physical health!

O — Overcome with courage. Quit the pity-party! Jesus knows what you're going through. After all, He left His home too!

C — Cultural changes. Look for the good in your new home instead of dwelling on the bad. Forget about your old life in America—that's in the past!

K — Know how to forgive. Forgive others and keep bitterness out of your life. While you are at it, forgive yourself too! Don't be so hard on yourself!

One of the best things my husband ever did for me was to take me to visit the Bible Baptist Church in Cebu City, just two months after we arrived in the Philippines. This church which was started by the late missionary Bob Hughes is currently pastored by our friend, Dr. Armie Jesalva. The church was having a missions conference when we visited. When I looked around and saw that church full of happy faces, I felt as if God was saying to me, "This is why you are here!"

I was amazed by that wonderful church and kept thinking, "Someday, we'll have a church like this!" It made me want to hurry back to Iloilo and get to work! Visiting Bible Baptist Church in Cebu City gave me a vision at a time when I really needed to see what the future could hold.

I remember when our first missionaries, Leny and Marjorie Funtecha, graduates of our Bible college, came home from Haiti for their first furlough. When it was time to go back, Marjorie had tears in her eyes and mentioned how much they missed Iloilo Baptist Church.

I said, "Marge—go back to Haiti and build your own IBC." I am so happy to say that they have done just that!

"...*but this one thing I do, forgetting those things which are behind, and reaching forth unto those things which are before, I press toward the mark for the prize of the high calling of God in Christ Jesus."* (Philippians 3:13, 14) Of course you are going to miss your home church! Do you know what the remedy to that is? Build a great church! Make it your home church!

Conclusion

What happened to Malla Moe? Did she get so discouraged with language and culture shock that she quit the mission field and went home? Not on your life!

When Malla reached Swaziland, she told God she wasn't satisfied with the progress she was making, so He gave her an idea. She decided she would actually go live with the people in their kraal. God had answered her prayer and had given her a great love for the people. She always said, in her charming accent: "Nothing as powerful as love!"

One day a young man named Johane came to Malla, wanting to learn to read. He had an extremely difficult time grasping how to read, but she patiently taught him. She also led him to Christ, but his life showed no great change.

Malla constantly prayed and fasted and begged God to send her a preacher for her ministry. One day God clearly told her that Johane was the one, but she had her doubts.

Johane came to Malla one day, very discouraged because he still could not read. She told him to pray, to which he answered, "I have prayed, but it doesn't help." Malla was afraid Johane would leave and go back to work in the gold mines.

That night, as Malla slept with the native women, she suddenly woke up. The book *Malla Moe*, tells the story:

When she looked up she saw Johane sitting at the low door of the hut, trembling with fear.

"What is the matter with you?" Malla inquired.

"I cannot stay in that hut. I will die."

"What is it?"

"There is danger! I heard a voice saying, 'How many are your days?' " He could hardly speak from the fright. "I said, 'I don't know.' I tried to see who was talking to me. The face was like a mist, but He wore a white gown with a brass girdle. He answered me, 'I know how many days you have, and you shall receive your reward from Me.' Then He threw a shining sword at my side. Oh! I'm going to die."

By this time Malla was sitting up. She remembered the lad Samuel.

"Oh! It's God talking to you. There's no need to run away or be afraid. Let us pray."

She prayed in her bed, and the boy prayed down there by the door.

"Go back to your hut now. God is everywhere." He seemed comforted and she saw him head back.[1]

The next day Malla looked everywhere for Johane, but he was nowhere to be found. The author continues the story of Johane's calling.

Just before sunset he came running, carrying his spelling book, his large white teeth showing through his handsome black face...

"What are you laughing at? I've been so frightened. I didn't know what had happened to you."

He came resolutely over to her. "Nkosazana [Mother], now I can read."[2]

Malla listened in amazement as Johane read to her. The day before, he could not read anything! Johane said, "God has taught me to read! I went up to the mountain and prayed to Him. He said He would teach me, and when I opened the book I could read."[3]

From that moment forward, Johane read the Bible constantly! He boldly preached the Gospel with great power! He taught Malla much about the culture, how to approach the Africans, and how to win their confidence. He taught her about the African mind and how to get past their mental barriers.

There must always be food on hand, and all must be made to feel welcome to stop and share some of it. News travels fast in Swaziland. Malla learned the lesson of hospitality so well that her house later became famous for miles as the place you could get food to refresh your body and a breath of Heaven to renew your soul. She was getting along well in the language. Her experiences, her joys, her sorrows, her thoughts, her prayers had to be in Zulu.[4]

The people declared, "She sits with us in the huts, she eats our food, she knows our names, she never forgets us."[5] Author Maria Nilsen describes Malla's overwhelming passion for souls:

"Are you saved?" she would ask anybody and everybody she met. "You must get saved."

To her, any instruction which omitted this issue was worthless. And why should not Malla be so firm on this issue? The bitter years of the fruitless religious atmosphere of her youth were sufficient. Hers was a message that even the Swazi could understand and that would meet their need. This message was reaching their hearts and changing their lives. Why were they coming? What drew them?

They wanted to know the God who could take someone so human and make him so divine. There was a spirit of joy among them. Even down to the newest believers, they were anxious to win their own people, and they gave themselves incessantly to evangelizing.[6]

After the Boer War ended in 1902, Malla took her first furlough. She only took two throughout her entire life, and she left for Africa in 1892. She would die on the field in 1953. The book *Malla Moe* adds, "She stirred her audiences to evangelism. She asked them, 'What are we here for, to have a good time with the Christians or to save sinners?' "[7] The writer elaborates on the results of Malla's personal evangelizing:

We must not be misled by the quantity of her results into thinking that the quality was any less. She talked to an African boy one day and led him to confess Christ. Later the boy remembered a chicken he had stolen from a white man and sent him money for it. The man returned the money with the comment, "I believe in that kind of religion."

A witch doctor heeded her counsel one day. Not only did he voluntarily give up his lucrative profession and influential standing, but he gave up polygamy, which to him meant a fortune in wives.[8]

The author again addresses soul winning in the life of Malla:

Soul winning to Miss Moe was not a habit; it was a drive. She did not speak to people because she was naturally an extrovert. All she knew was that men needed the message. She was afraid not to obey God. "When I see with what little effort souls can be won, I tremble to think of the many opportunities I am missing, We must do what we can. God will save them."

One day upon her arrival at a neighboring mission station, she was asked, "Did you walk these twelve miles?"

"No," she replied, "I have been running part of the way, and I've had the joy of leading sixteen souls to Christ."[9]

She would witness to anyone—including the famous, the important, or the rich. One missionary told her he wished he was as courageous about witnessing as Malla was. Malla retorted that she was also afraid, but that she was more afraid of God than man. She openly wept for people who would not get saved. Another incident that happened during Malla's second (and final) furlough shows her soul-winning zeal:

Malla had learned never to accept any situation as closed to personal witnessing. The crew of the ship was made up almost entirely of sailors from India who spoke little or no English. In spite of this she went out of her way to show them little kindnesses and developed a friendship with the captain.[10]

When Malla arrived in New York, she called two pastors of the two biggest churches and asked them to meet her downtown in an hour. The pastors couldn't miss spotting her, passing out Gospel tracts in the same old costume she had worn on her last furlough. The following story is another excerpt from the book *Malla Moe*:

What a picture. The timeless little woman with two dignified pastors in tow! She led them at an African pace from store to store, looking for New Testaments in that certain Indian dialect. She ordered one hundred. Handing two parcels to each pastor, off she started again, this time for the subway. It was high noon when they came up from the subway into one of New York's typical sultry August days. The packages were not at all light. The pastors looked at one another. Nothing to do now, but go through with it. Malla led the way. She was the only one who knew where they were going. Ever so many blocks down the street…Ties were no longer straight, perspiration was rolling down the faces of the once immaculately attired [pastors].

Triumphantly onward [she] led them till at last they came to a long pier and the ship on which Malla had come from. The party had no sooner reached the deck when scores of small dark men gathered around from every direction. They tried to help one another understand what she was saying. Malla had [the pastors] open the packages and start giving out the Testaments. The men kissed the books, while tears streamed down their cheeks. Some slipped them into their shirts, while others ran off to their cabins to hide them. They came close to touch the woman and pat her Africa-tanned face. By this time the captain had arrived.[11]

Malla handed the captain a book entitled *The Life of Moody* and said, "I want to meet you in Heaven."[12] Author Maria Nilsen tells of the captain's response:

The officer looked at her, quietly reaching for his handkerchief as he spoke. "Miss Moe, you are the most remarkable woman I have ever met." Turning to the pastors while he wiped away a tear, he said, "She has been sunshine on the whole trip. She is one of the most unique persons I have ever met."[13]

The following is yet another soul-winning experience from *Malla Moe:*

Once in the Midwest, Malla was trying to convince a strapping young Swede that he ought to accept Christ. The boy had been deeply moved by a recent narrow escape from death, but was resisting her urging. Malla always felt that if she could once get a person on his knees, he would yield to her pleas to pray and be saved. While the young man stood there, the arms of his Christian sister around him, Miss Moe got down and pulled his feet out from underneath him. Before he could get up, she had him praying, and he was soundly converted.[14]

Soul winning permeated the life of Malla Moe:

The urge to evangelize was on her soul, and nothing could stop her. Every activity was viewed in terms of how it helped in bringing men to faith in Christ.

Her letters, her prayers, her conversations were filled with longing that men would come to Him. Many were the times she could not eat or sleep because she was crying over certain ones she wanted to see yield to the Lord's claim on their lives. She got particular joy out of person-to-person evangelism. She made occasions for it. To her, wherever there were people, there were openings for witnessing. She saw opportunities where others didn't. Once news came that there had been a terrible gang fight. Many men were wounded and lying in the hospital. Malla gave the other missionaries no rest until someone took her to the hospital. She found one lying there wounded. He himself had committed murder. She spoke to him about Christ, and he believed. When he recovered, he was put in jail. Malla bought a Bible and sent it to him. Later she received letters from him about how he was reading and having prayer with the other prisoners.

Another time she went to a prison and asked for permission to read the Bible and pray for the prisoners.

"I'm sorry," the guard said, "there are no prisoners at the moment."

"Aren't you a prisoner?" she asked. "If you are not saved, you're a prisoner."

He admitted this was true and later attended a meeting where Malla had the privilege of leading him into the faith.[15]

Malla's witnessing efforts are summed up as follows:

One might make the error of supposing that because she approached everyone to speak about his soul, her batting average of persons actually persuaded was low. Not so. Her times at bat were phenomenal, true, but her hitting average was also high. Which, altogether, means that the sum total of persons introduced to the love of God as she knew it through faith in Christ, though she kept no count, amounts to a multitude.[16]

Malla's third term lasted 31 years until she died at the age of 90! She refused to take another furlough because she was afraid she wouldn't be able to return to Africa, and she wanted to die with the people she loved so much. Malla did not let difficulties with language and culture shock keep her from serving the Lord!

Romans 8:37 aptly describes the life of Malla Moe, "...*we are more than conquerors through him that loved us.*" Let's conquer language and culture shock so we can bring the lost to Christ!

Above: Rachel with her singing group

Below left: Rachel with two friends—the little girl and the parrot share the same name, Joy!

Below right: Rick with Rachel and some kids at camp

UNIT EIGHT

Finances, Deputation, and Furlough

"...I have learned, in whatsoever state I am, therewith to be content." (Philippians 4:11)

Introduction

When I think of a missionary who lived beyond reproach in the area of finances, I think of J. Hudson Taylor, one of the most famous missionaries of all time. Taylor was the best example I could think of when it comes to a great pattern for us to follow in our dealings with money.

When Taylor felt God wanted him to go to China as a missionary, he decided to attend medical school. He worked part time at a hospital to pay for his room and board. Before leaving home, Taylor carefully studied what the Bible had to say about giving. He decided he should give at least one tenth of his income to the Lord. Part of his salary included the cost of room and board.

He came to believe that he really should tithe on that portion of his income as well. However, doing so meant he would not have enough for his other living expenses. He moved to a cheaper place so he could tithe on his entire income. Moving to a more economical place was farther for him to walk to work, but he was able to save money on his rent. Besides that, he was able to economize on his eating expenses as well. He soon discovered that he could live on much less money than he had previously thought possible. What money he was able to save on food and rent, he gave generously to the poor where he carried out his evangelistic work.

In the book *Hudson Taylor, Founder, China Inland Mission*, by Vance Christie, Taylor is quoted: "My experience was that the less I spent on myself and the more I gave to others, the fuller of happiness and blessing did my soul become."[1]

In order to live as frugally as possible, Taylor adopted practices such as sewing sheets of paper into a notebook, rather than to buy a bound one which cost more money. For breakfast he ate a half a loaf of brown bread and would take a handful of apples for his lunch at work. That night he would eat another half loaf of brown bread for supper. He drank nothing but water. He shared his cheap room and walked four miles one way to work each day. He believed his Spartan lifestyle would prepare him for any deprivation he might face on the mission field. He wanted to develop a strong faith in God.

Taylor knew he would be far from home and unable to ask for help from anyone when he went to China. He would need to depend on God alone. He wondered if his faith would be strong enough. He decided he needed to exercise his faith so it would become strong. He needed to learn to move man, through God, by prayer alone.

Dr. Hardley, his busy employer, had asked Taylor to remind him when his salary was due. Taylor decided that instead of speaking to Dr. Hardley about the matter of being paid, he would just pray. Several days after his salary was due, Hudson was praying, but he had still received no paycheck. Finally, his only resource was a half crown piece.

Late that night, a poor man knocked on his door, begging him to come and pray for his dying wife. On the way to the home, Taylor learned that the man was a Roman Catholic. When he asked him why he didn't call a priest, the man replied that the priest refused to go to the house without first being paid. The poor man confessed that he did not even have money to buy food for his family.

Taylor felt guilty about the coin in his pocket, but he reasoned that he only had a little porridge remaining for supper that night and for breakfast in the morning. He began to feel irritated with the man. The two men climbed a flight of stairs into a run-down building. When he entered the apartment, he was appalled by their abject poverty. Five children were crying over their dying mother, the affects of malnutrition written on their faces. Heartbroken for the family, Taylor felt God's prompting to surrender his last coin to the needy family. Still, he resisted. He tried to comfort the pitiful mother but felt himself to be a terrible hypocrite. How could he tell lost people of a loving Heavenly Father when he himself did not trust Him? He became so convicted he could hardly talk. He finally surrendered the coin to the man and immediately felt great joy.

The next morning as he ate his final bowl of porridge, the mailman brought a letter in which he found four times the amount he had given to the poor family the previous night. The author records: "Right then and there he determined that all his future earnings and savings would be invested in the Lord's bank, a bank which he knew could never break."[2]

He continued to pray for his employer to pay him as his money again ran out. Not only did he need food, he also needed to pay his rent. He reasoned that perhaps he should speak to Dr. Hardley since his landlady was poor and quite dependent upon his rent money. He decided again that he would be unfit to be a missionary if he did not completely trust in God and depend only on Him.

Finally Dr. Hardley mentioned Taylor's salary, and Taylor was immediately relieved. However, his relief was short-lived when he learned that the doctor had already deposited the day's revenue in the bank. With that said, the doctor walked out the door and headed for home. Taylor immediately knelt and prayed and asked God to take care of him. Later, his work done, Taylor started for home when the doctor suddenly returned. He told Taylor he had just seen one of his patients on the way home, who finally paid his overdue bill. The patient remarked that he felt strangely compelled to pay the doctor immediately. The doctor handed over that money to a grateful Hudson Taylor.

Another time, when Taylor was furthering his medical training at a different school in preparation for China, his father offered to help him financially, as did the Chinese Evangelization Society. He thanked both for their generous offers, but after much prayer, he decided not to accept either. He was so determined to learn to depend only on God, and as a result, he learned many valuable lessons from God.

In 1853, Taylor set sail for China. The book *Hudson Taylor, Founder, China Inland Mission,* says:

Hudson was to receive a salary of eighty pounds [about $400 American at that time] from the CES for his first year of service in China. It quickly became apparent that such compensation was woefully inadequate. By comparison, single missionaries serving with other societies in Shanghai at the time received more than three times that amount in salary in addition to having their expenses paid for rent, medical treatment, procuring a Chinese teacher, and books. Though Hudson cared nothing about being equally compensated, he did at times suffer embarrassment over the fact that his clothes were noticeably shabby compared to those of his missionary acquaintances.[3]

The CES had a very bad reputation in China because of its many debts. Taylor finally resigned. Author Vance Christi writes:

He later explained his personal convictions on this matter: "To me it seemed that the teaching of God's Word was unmistakably clear: 'Owe no man anything.' To borrow money implied, to my mind, a contradiction of Scripture—a confession that God had withheld some good thing, and a determination to get for ourselves what He had not given. Could that which was wrong for one Christian to do be right for an association of Christians? Or could any amount of precedents make a wrong course justifiable? If the Word taught me anything, it taught me to have no connection with debt. I could not think that God was poor, that He was short of resources, or unwilling to supply any want of whatever work was really His. It seemed to me that if there were lack of funds to carry on work, then to that degree, in that special development, or at that time, it could not be the work of God."[4]

Thus Taylor became an independent missionary and trusted God alone to supply his needs. Taylor's beloved wife Maria totally agreed with her husband's beliefs regarding finances. Maria's parents had also been missionaries in China. They died, leaving her an orphan at the age of 10. The author reveals Maria's feeling on the important matter of finances:

> Exactly two weeks before they were married, a situation arose which allowed Maria to affirm her willingness to share Hudson's life, even with the full awareness that doing so would sometimes involve financial sacrifice and trials of faith. Weeks earlier Hudson and the Joneses had invited Maria and Mrs. Bausum to come to their home for dinner. When that morning came, they found themselves with virtually no food or money. Their ministry to the poor had exhausted their resources, and mail after mail had come without any new supply of funds.[5]

Finally a letter arrived just in time with the needed funds.

> That evening Hudson gave Maria full account of the day's circumstances and events and then stated soberly: "I cannot hold you to your promise if you would rather draw back. You see how difficult our life may be at times."
>
> "Have you forgotten?" she responded. "I was left an orphan in a far-off land. God has been my Father all these years. And do you think I shall be afraid to trust Him now?"[6]

Shortly after they were married, Taylor had to assume the responsibility of directing a hospital for a short while. Author Vance Christi shares another example of Taylor and finances:

> The expenses to keep the hospital and dispensary operating were enormous and, as before, Hudson needed to look in faith to God to provide. One morning, after he had been overseeing the medical work for a few weeks, the hospital's cook anxiously informed him, "The very last bag of rice has been opened and is disappearing rapidly."
>
> "Then the Lord's time for helping us must be close at hand," the missionary responded reassuringly.[7]

A check arrived before the bag of rice was empty!

When Hudson Taylor started the China Inland Mission, no appeals were made for funds. CIM missionaries were not guaranteed set salaries, and their appeals for support went only to God in prayer. They were not allowed to borrow or go into debt. They were to look to God to supply all their needs.

Taylor said, "God's work done in God's way will never lack God's supply."[8] When the CIM was challenged by a lack of funds, Taylor's faith never wavered.

One time he said to another missionary, "We have twenty-five cents and all the promises of God!"[9]

Once Taylor preached at a conference. During the closing meeting, despite the fact that CIM was never mentioned and no offering was taken, some people surrendered to be missionaries while others took off gold watches, rings, and other jewelry to give for missions.

By the time Hudson Taylor died, the China Inland Mission had sent over 800 missionaries to China, and over 2,000 Chinese had been trained for full-time Christian service. In his lifetime, about eight million dollars had been given to the mission—a lot of money now, how much more back then! Hudson Taylor definitely had the right attitude regarding finances!

Chapter One

The Right Attitude Regarding Finances

The right attitude regarding finances was extremely important in the life of Hudson Taylor because he would be used of God to start the great China Inland Mission, whose financial stand came from Taylor's personal convictions that God had taught him through the years. The Bible says in Luke 12:34, *"For where your treasure is, there will your heart be also."*

Charles Cowman, the great missionary to Japan, said, "I wish to transact the business of the mission society in such a careful manner that the angels may look over my ledger at the close of the day."[1]

To be honest, I did not want to address the area of finances, but my husband strongly urged me to do so, stressing how important it is. My husband says that a good missionary never has too much money. Many in the States erroneously believe that a missionary with a thriving work does not need additional support. On the contrary, a good missionary can never be given too much money.

While preparing to write this book, I wrote to my dear friend, Mrs. Sandy (Heidenreich) Domelle about this matter of finances. I am also greatly burdened how a missionary wife can be such a great hindrance to her husband and to the Lord's work if she has not learned to be content. Sandy wrote the following, printed with her permission:

Contentment is such an important part of any area of service in the ministry. If a wife isn't content, all kinds of problems will arise. Philippians 4:11 says, *"Not that I speak in respect of want: for I have learned, in whatsoever state I am, therewith to be content."* I told the ladies in my class [at Hyles-Anderson College] that it doesn't matter where you live, what hardships you have to endure, how much money you have or don't have, or how much time you have with your husband (preachers' wives' biggest complaint is usually that their husband is **always** gone, and they never have time with him) if you are content—everything around you will feel and seem normal, and you won't worry about all the things you do [not have]. Most problems I hear right now from wives are because they aren't content with either where they are (they lack the comforts of home), or they aren't content with what the Lord has called their husband to do.

Concerning the area of finances, let me share some illustrations. A missionary just came home from the field. Every time they come back to the States, the wife insists that they need all kinds of things to take back. They spend hundreds of dollars on their purchases (actually thousands because of the bigger items such as appliances) to make their home Americanized. Then it costs them about $5,000 to $7,000 to ship the sea container. The entire time this family is on furlough, it is a stress on the husband to raise not just monthly support and the necessary monies for return tickets, but also money for the supplies and sea container. This couple literally argues about these things in front of people, and the wife always says that he just doesn't understand how important it is for her to make her home on the mission field Americanized. She says it is the only way she feels she can survive and feel safe. Talk about giving him the guilt trip!

Finances are such a big issue with another couple who are overseas that the wife told her husband either he goes to the U.S. embassy to ask about jobs such as teaching that pay while they are on the field, or she will pack up her kids and fly home. She says she's tired of living off of nothing. She said she did not choose to marry him, be carted halfway around the world, starve her and her family, and put up with living like the natives.

Then there are couples with whom my dad talks, and he advises them that when they start deputation to live off only their love offerings. He tells them to deposit any support money that begins to come into a savings account. He strongly advises them not to touch this money until they get to the field. This money is to help the missionaries start their work. So many young married couples think this plan is ridiculous, and they say they cannot survive with just the love offerings. Yet, we have married couples with four or more children who can do this, who have done it, and who have had success when they got to the field because of following my father's advice.

Women automatically want to take everything they possibly can with them. That involves money because they have to ship their belongings. When we went to the Philippines, my dad only allowed each of us to take the two suitcases the airline limit allowed and one carry-on bag. That was the sum total of each one of my family members' belongings! We bought some things in Manila from a missionary family before they left. A few odds and ends were given to us by another family. The furniture my mom accumulated at her house in the Philippines has now been passed on to my brother and his wife, who are still serving God in the Philippines. Other than that, we purchased the things we needed on the field.

One family we knew believed that when you went to the field, you did not need to live poor like the people. They always used to say that my parents were true missionaries because they wanted to look like the people, eat like the people, dress like the people, and smell like the people. They made comments like, "There are different classes of people to reach. We chose ours, and you chose yours." They would only buy American products. They would buy several boxes of imported cereal at $6.00 a box. I am not against their practices; at times, we would pay extra for a box of cereal too. My point is that they did this weekly.

Sad to say, in most cases it is the wife and her desire to spend that puts the stress on the marriage and moves them off the field.

Mrs. Domelle knows about this problem firsthand because she not only went to the mission field as a teenager with her parents, but she also taught on missions at Hyles-Anderson College and counsels with many missionary wives.

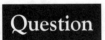 **Question** How important do you feel that self-denial and self-control are in the area of finances, for example?

Answers:
• Self-denial is very important because, in most cases, you are going to a poor country and you don't want to flaunt money before the people. Possibly your money won't be worth much where you are going, and you need to learn to live frugally.
• I think the era of faith missions is dying. So many folks wanting to go to the mission field get discouraged and depressed before they even arrive because of…the monthly support that is required of them to raise. As a result, they miss out on a lot of blessings.

We happen to be serving [on an expensive field] where the cost of living is greater than most places in America, but we do not make half of the money that a mission board will require a [small family] to raise for coming to the field; yet, we have always paid our bills. My husband learned early in life to do without, growing up in a pastor's home where the salary wasn't always available to give after the church had paid its bills. I was reared in a family that was financially secure, but my parents did an excellent job teaching me to be humble and to wear hand-me-downs and to not expect the best of everything. We could learn a lot by reading the books written by missionaries of old who did actually live by faith. Everyone wants the blessings and wonderful stories of God's goodness, but they do not want to live the way you must live to receive those blessings. If you never lack, how can God bless? If we can learn to put our trust and faith totally in God, the self-denial, the self-control, etc. will follow.

| **Question** | Would you please share ways of spending and/or saving by which you have helped your husband and/or his ministry in the area of finances? |

Answers:

- We raise our own meat; I sew my clothes and the girls' clothes. I bake from scratch. I never tell my husband we "need" something unless it is an absolute essential—like we are on the last diaper and surely could use more! When we've decorated the church for special meetings, I've made most of the decorations. Decorating was very challenging for me at first, but my husband did an excellent job of encouraging my first feeble efforts so that I plunged ahead without getting discouraged.

- Think small—deputation trains you to get by with the basics. Then, don't add on anything until you are on the field. Our housing is "small" because of overcrowding and cost. Anything bigger is just considered a bonus. The first reaction of all U.S. visitors is "small." I've gotten used to it, so we're still in the same "small" house almost five years and three kids later.

- I use coupons, go to thrift stores, and buy everything on sale.

- I realized that God would supply—and that He'd supply according to His timetable. We continued our faith promise giving at our church during deputation, and we continue to do so to this day. God says if we'll give, He'll bless. We have found Him faithful.

- Ensure that you have enough support to live and function on your field. You cannot anticipate every circumstance that will arise. Some circumstances will arise that no amount of prudent planning can foresee. However, you can plan wisely for the things you can see. Remember, missionaries must live by faith. Raise what is reasonable and prudent. Then by faith, trust God to bring it in. God has never failed to supply our needs. Never has anyone been able to adequately define the line between faith and foolishness. Frankly, I believe whatever is not of faith IS foolishness.

Another outstanding example of a missionary who had the right attitude regarding finances was C.T. Studd, missionary to China, India, and Africa. Studd, a famous sports figure in England in the late 1800s, was particularly known for his humor and for his great zeal for the lost. Studd sacrificed everything for the mission field and expected other missionaries to do the same—even his two daughters who, along with their husbands, labored with their famous father in Africa. He was the son of a very wealthy man, and before he left for China, he received his inheritance at the age of 25. It was a great fortune, and he gave nearly all of it away to the Lord's work and decided to live entirely by faith! He saved a small portion of his inheritance for his wife-to-be, Priscilla Stewart. Studd's son-in-law, Norman Grubb, tells what happened in the book *After C.T. Studd.*

Before his marriage, on receipt of his inheritance from his father's estate, he had heard God's call to follow literally the command of Christ to the rich young ruler, "Sell all that thou hast, and give to the poor, and thou shalt have treasure in heaven: and come, take up thy cross and follow Me." He had obeyed up to the point of distributing all his property between various Gospel agencies, with the exception of £2,000, which he withheld as a dowry for his bride. When Priscilla Stewart heard of this, she said, "Charlie, what command did the Lord give you concerning your money?"

"To sell all."

"Have you done so?"

"Well, yes, with the exception of this £2,000 that I am giving you."

"Charlie," she said, "I am not going to marry a disobedient man. Either you obey completely or you don't have me."[2]

The soon-to-be Priscilla Studd certainly had the right attitude when it came to finances! As a result of her statement, C. T. Studd gave his entire inheritance to the work of the Lord.

Let me ask you a question. If you are having financial problems, does that mean that God has made a mistake? God is incapable of error. Does it mean that He does not love you? Does it mean He forgot about you or overlooked you? No! He can be trusted in all areas of our lives, including finances. Maybe we cannot understand, but we can trust. There are no accidents in the life of a Christian. God's ways are always right. Just because we don't like them does not mean they are wrong. God knows what is right for us as well as what we need. We just need to learn to trust, no matter what.

Chapter Two

Deputation

As I write this chapter in January 2004, my son Ricky and his wife Brandie are on deputation for the Philippines. They started deputation in March of 2003, and Lord willing, they plan to fly to the Philippines in August 2004, after 18 months of deputation.

As they tell me of their many experiences, I am remembering back some 27 years ago when my husband and I were on deputation. When we started, my husband determined that we would work very hard and do deputation for only 12 months. Then, we would leave for the field, by faith, no matter what amount we had raised. God blessed Rick's hard work and his faith.

When Ricky and Brandie first started out on deputation, for the first few months they kept their apartment in Hammond. They loaded up their trunk with everything they thought they would need for a meeting: a display table, slides, prayer cards, and so on. They had one small problem with their car. They couldn't lock it because they couldn't unlock it. Their car had a trunk release button.

One morning they got up early to leave for a meeting and were packing their car when they noticed their black bag was missing out of the trunk. This bag held everything that went on the display table, including a picture album with pictures from our work in the Philippines. This loss was just devastating, but what could they do except leave for their meeting?

That same day, 8,000 miles away in the Philippines, I received an unusual e-mail which turned out to be from a neighbor of theirs. This man said that he and his wife found a black bag in their backyard, and it was filled with Filipino souvenirs. No name or address could be found in the bag except my husband's e-mail address in the Philippines. The nice man said he had no idea how the bag got in his yard. I called Ricky when he got home from the meeting and told him about the e-mail. He immediately went over to his neighbor's to retrieve his bag. He figured out the thief who stole it was pretty disgusted when he saw what was inside and just tossed it into the neighbor's yard as he was running away.

Ricky used the opportunity to witness to his neighbor, who was already saved and attending another church. He also took him and his wife some ice cream, along with his deepest gratitude!

From that day on, Ricky and Brandie decided they could no longer leave anything in the trunk of their car; so after every meeting, everything—display board, slide projector, black bag, and so on—was carried upstairs to the apartment. When it was time for a meeting, everything that needed to be packed in the car was placed by the front door so they could be on their way quickly and efficiently.

Soon after this incident, Ricky and Brandie were driving to a meeting several hours away. As they neared their destination, driving down the interstate, a man and woman on a motorcycle passed them. Ricky said to Brandie, "Look! That's how we should travel." They began to joke about how they would carry their suitcases, display board, and so on. "And we could put the slide projector in that little trunk on the back of the motorcycle…slide projector…uh…Brandie! Did we bring the slide projector?!"

Oh, no! They had indeed forgotten it. They turned around, drove all the way back to Hammond for the projector, turned around again, and drove all the way back to the church. Needless to say, a very tired young missionary couple presented their work to the church the following morning.

We all have deputation stories to tell. We have funny stories, horror stories, and very warm stories of wonderful people and how kind they were and how they sacrificed for the cause of Christ and the cause of foreign missions.

One very good idea my incredibly organized daughter-in-law implemented was to keep a photo album with a picture of every church, every pastor and his family where they have visited. In some cases, the pastor wasn't there or they weren't able to get a picture, so she would use the Sunday morning bulletin. Then she had typed all the information about the church on a piece of paper which she placed beside every picture. My husband and I have been on the field 26 years. We have been back to visit many of the churches we visited on deputation; and in many cases, the pastors have come to the Philippines to visit us. How I wish I had thought to keep a photo album like Brandie's!

The following comments are what missionaries say about deputation. Please keep in mind that many of these thoughts also apply to furlough, which is discussed in chapter four of this unit.

 What thoughts would you like to share about deputation?

Answers:

• Enjoy deputation—[don't always be] longing and looking forward to the end of it. You will only be unhappy living for the future. It will come to an end soon enough and then you will be on the field. Once you get to the field, you will actually long for some of that fellowship with other Christians (on deputation you can almost feel "peopled out" at times!) Meet other missionaries. Learn from them. Have fun and see the country as you travel. We still lie awake once in a while and just remember some of the fun times we had on deputation—lots of memories.

- Deputation was one of the most thrilling times of our ministry. We had the privilege of visiting some of America's greatest churches and hearing some of her greatest preachers. We only had a few uncomfortable experiences and were for the most part treated like kings and queens wherever we stayed.

- I should have taken a map-reading course. Our biggest arguments began ten miles outside of every big city. My husband would ask me to find our exit on the map while he drove. I usually found it just as we whizzed by in the wrong lane. Talk about strain!

- [Deputation] doesn't last forever—I promise! Some wives shun it like the plague; others look on it as an exciting challenge. Do what you have to do to make it as pleasant, fun, and rewarding as possible. Even if you cannot make up your mind to enjoy it, I would advise you not to complain about it—you will sour everyone around you! The wisest thing I did was to keep my mouth shut. Pride keeps humans from learning the lessons of life that God is trying to teach. Deputation is one of those classrooms of life for the missionary and his wife.

- [My advice regarding deputation is] to make it short and simple. Give yourself a date to be on the mission field with or without the 100% support. Many churches doubt folks will even make it to their field after three years of deputation. Once you are actually on the field, you are likely to pick up new support.

- Learn as you go. Go to **give** and not to **get**. Collect ideas in a notebook. Realize you'll soon be called on to use them. Be teachable—not proud! Trust God to care for your needs and don't talk about them too much. Don't get too spoiled with the extra attention from hubby along the deputation trail. Get ready to say "goodbye" every day for long hours. Just when you think you've had enough of each other's company, you'll find yourself wishing he were with you more. Do order needed ministry items while on deputation and plan to ship them with you. Specialty items like flannel graph (Betty Lukens is great), the Lord's Supper supplies, offering "bags," and even some used songbooks from a church we collected along the way. We also went to an office supply and stocked up on basic office needs.

- Learn to live on little. Be consistent with your children's discipline and schooling. **Talk** to your husband when a problem arises (but not in front of the pastor!) Be friendly. I am naturally outgoing, but I have a close friend who is a missionary wife, and she is more to herself. While I would walk around and shake hands, she stood by their display and smiled and talked to people as they would come by. She did an excellent job on deputation of being outgoing in her own way. I met many people at churches who fell in love with her. Be yourself. That was advice given to me by another missionary wife the day we left for our first meeting. She did not mean not to have discretion, but that God created each of us to be something special and unique. What one lady is like is not the same as her friend. I believe that God created me for my husband and our field. I see it more and more every day. Deputation was a time to grow up and gradually get our families used to not having access to us as quickly or as easily as they would like. Do not compare your support or your husband's preaching with anyone else's. I know many missionary wives who get discouraged and, in turn, discourage their husbands because they are too busy worrying about the missionaries that started deputation when they did. Don't be too serious all the time. Be able to laugh when it is called for. Sometimes it is good to laugh or else you will cry. Plan things that make deputation fun for your husband and children.

• Take mini-breaks and do fun things or have the husband leave the wife and or children for a little while as he does local traveling. Be helpful, kind, and courteous as much as possible.

• Be flexible, be a servant, and see how God uses many different types of people and their different styles. Be teachable. Get ideas.

• Learn to keep quiet. [Sometimes] when you spend more time with your husband, there will be more opportunities for arguments, so the more you learn to hold your tongue when frustrated at something your husband does (like his driving), the less hassles. Have things to do in the car—cross stitch, letter writing, doing things with the kids, anything to pass the time more quickly. Also, be determined beforehand to have a good time. Make it a learning time with your kids or even just yourself. We traveled in states I had never been to before, and I learned many things about them. Have a testimony, devotional, or a Sunday school lesson for ladies and a Sunday school lesson for children prepared ahead of time.

• [Deputation] is not a contest to see who can get to the field quicker. The Lord will keep you on deputation as long as it is necessary. He knows when you are ready to go to the field. Also, be as much a help as you can be when you stay in someone's home. Sometimes I just found that the pastor's wife just wanted someone with whom she could talk.

• Think of deputation as a ministry, rather than being overly concerned about how much support you have raised. It seems to take longer now, and it can become drudgery if you only think of how far you are from your goal.

Realize your ministry at that time is to the churches you visit. Center on being a blessing and a soul winner where you are.

- Remember that deputation is a ministry too. Enjoy this time and realize that in God's time you will get to the field.

- Be careful not to overdress (too fancy for the church you're in) or under-dress (too casual). Try to fit in with the people and church where you visit as far as too much or too little makeup, jewelry, hairdos that are extremely different, clothes that are so much nicer than what the people in the church are wearing, etc. Without going overboard, you should try, as much as possible, to respect the pastor's wishes in the matter of a lady's dress.

- Don't get in a hurry to leave for the field before you have all the support you need. Realize that deputation is a training time. Getting to the mission field doesn't automatically make you a better Christian. Rather, it is a good time to work on making the Lord and your husband your best friend. Something I wish we had done was to keep notes of all the blessings the Lord gave us and all the answers to prayer.

- There desperately needs to be training in these areas of dealing with pastors and their church members. When we traveled on deputation and followed behind some missionaries, it was pathetic. I could share many situations with a pastor's being upset over the missionary before us. They stirred up folks and really caused irritated feelings because of how they handled themselves and situations they created without stopping to think and do things right. Pastors appreciate tact, common sense, wisdom, and respect. We [tried to] do what was right and to treat people right [by] going to all the functions provided and planned for us. Mistakes are often made when talking with church members, saying wrong things, or by giving advice to people in another man's church.

Also, in missions class we were taught to have dates and meetings set up a year ahead. Have a first-class presentation.

 **Question** Would you please address the matter of taking children on deputation?

Answers:

- Try to allow enough traveling time for frequent stops to stretch and for the kids to run off energy. Find interesting places to visit as you travel to give the kids something to look forward to.

- Do not expect your children to be perfect angels all the time. It is not fair to put undue stress and pressure on them. Make sure you think of their needs: nap time, snacks, breaks, etc. If you plan your traveling with them in mind, it will be more enjoyable for everyone. Make stops at playgrounds or rest areas where the children can exercise. Your rewards in Heaven are not determined by how many meetings you can cram into your schedule. Plan "off days" during your travels when the family goes to a park or does something fun together. Help your children create positive memories of deputation. Give your children a way to be a part: singing in the churches or passing out prayer cards, helping set up/take down the display board, etc.

• We traveled in a motor home, and it was such a blessing and answer to prayer. It worked for our children as they knew where their bed was. For the most part, they knew where they were sleeping every night. We were also able to have a place to go to be by ourselves, either for quiet time, discipline, or whatever. I would make sure that my children kept their nap times, etc. Even on deputation, we need to keep a schedule for both us and also our children. Still, there is also the need to be flexible. Our children still talk about the special times in the motor home.

• Traveling with kids on deputation is a challenge. They have to spend endless hours in a car or van. They have to sleep in hundreds of different places. They have no or almost no schedule. They go through a lot. Sometimes we adults have to be reminded that they are kids. They have to have the life of a child—it isn't fair to make them be little adults. My idea is to make it as fun and enjoyable as possible. We read dozens of books in the car because it helps kill time. We used lots of tapes—Patch the Pirate tapes, other story tapes, and music tapes. We tried to stop for little breaks during a trip. When we stayed in people's homes, the kids stayed in our room in their sleeping bags—no matter how much the hostess insisted they stay in their own room. They were still very young, and they were afraid. Is it fair to make them stay alone in a strange place? If they were afraid to go in their own Sunday school class, I would ask permission for them to go together to one class. If they were in the same class in their own church every Sunday—fine. But, is it fair to them to have to go to a strange class every week and sometimes two or three times a week in a different church? The same is true with nurseries. I guess not everyone would agree with me on this, but I wonder too what makes some kids grow up to hate the Christian life and others grow up to love it. I have seen missionary kids put through the roughest of times by their parents, and I wonder how they are going to feel about it all when they are older. You will only be in that church for a service, maybe a few—you have your kids to rear for a lifetime. Sometimes we really want to impress others at the expense of our kids. They need to be allowed to be kids—happy and carefree. They have their whole lives to be adults later. One more thing about that. I have learned when we are traveling with the kids, to be sure they aren't hungry. If you are staying somewhere that no food is being provided (and that happens), you can excuse yourself and go get the kids something to eat. You can wait a long time for food (and many times we did when it was just us), but it isn't right to make your kids wait long times to eat when they are hungry. Sometimes I have asked the hostess where we were staying if I could make a peanut butter and jelly sandwich for the kids, and they were more than happy for me to do so.

• The people you visit on deputation do not expect your children to be perfect, but they do want to see that they are making an effort. Teach your children to eat whatever they are given (that means that Mom and Dad can't be picky either!) and to appreciate everything that is done for them. Children who can say, "Please," "Thank you," and "It's nice to meet you," are always given high marks even if they spill their milk at supper. Teach your children not to interrupt when you are talking to adults. A friend of mine said she taught her children to squeeze her hand if they needed her and she was talking. Keeping children occupied in the car decreases whining, complaining, and fights between siblings. We did school work, practiced special music (to sing in the churches), prayed, memorized verses, played "I Spy" and the alphabet game.

• If your attitude isn't what it should be, then your children will balk at traveling. Our children were ages 9, 10, 12, and 13 when we began deputation. My husband and I both tried to make it fun for them. Our children understood that we were doing a lot of driving—over 100,000 miles in two years. We made sure that they had snacks at regular intervals. Most children are content if their tummies are full. They use up their energy stores a lot faster than adults do, and if your kid is de-energized, he will make it known in various unacceptable ways. Besides the groceries, we stocked up on loads of children's books. Our children love to read. We brought along crossword puzzles. These were things we gave them so they could control themselves and be content. We stopped at national parks and monuments where we made picnics with our sandwiches and drinks.

• Control [your children]. We were in many churches that before us had been a couple with little "terrors," and everyone was prepared to receive us with our "monsters" as well. Don't be afraid to take care of them. My children are little. Traveling with little kids means coughs, colds, flu—you name it. Take your concerns to your husband and have him deal with the pastor. You'll find that most pastors are very thoughtful and understanding.

• Make frequent stops. I find it works nicely if we go about three hours traveling and then stop at a rest stop and play ball or Frisbee, or visit a McDonald's play area. My husband sometimes has races with the children. We usually stop for about an hour. Traveling during nap time sometimes works well. I also have things for them to do in the car—coloring, drawing, blocks, books with stickers, etc.

• We did deputation with teenagers. At times they "checked out" and stayed with family instead of traveling. We know of a missionary whose wife was really having a horrible time on deputation with three small children. He decided to rent an apartment for her for 30 days just to rest. We know of another missionary who had a very well behaved three-year-old. On deputation he became absolutely horrible. The couple was in despair when someone suggested getting the little boy a place to hide. They ended up traveling with a small umbrella-type tent that could be set up wherever they were staying. This gave the boy a consistent place to sleep every night. His behavior improved greatly, and he was happy again.

• I can only speak from personal experience. For most of our deputation, it was easier that I stayed home with our children about two-thirds of the time. Then we traveled with my husband one third of the time, going to places that wanted to see the family or that were near our relatives to take advantage of time with them before going to the field. Our children had the experience of traveling and seeing many places without being worn out from constant travel.

• Kids are very versatile and flexible, but they get tired too. They have real emotional needs that should be met very gently. Being a missionary kid myself, I appreciate the fact that my folks understood each of our personalities and did not force us to participate in any activities that would have been embarrassing. For example, my two older sisters were good at singing specials in churches, whereas my brother and I tend to be shyer, so we were not forced to "perform" in any way unless we volunteered ourselves. Let each kid pack a backpack with his own favorite toys or crafts. This really helps give them some security as they travel from one new place to the next. Also give each kid an area of responsibility. For example, one can be responsible for getting baby sister and the diaper bag from the nursery after church. Another child can be responsible to get out the extension cord for the slide projector and putting it away. Kids love to have a job, and responsibility gives them some security and a sense of accomplishment.

Chapter Three

Taking a Survey Trip and Making Other Preparations

Our friends, Dr. and Mrs. Doug Kalapp, have been involved with missions for many years. Recently, after returning from China, Mrs. Kalapp wrote down some ideas for Mrs. Sandy Domelle's mission class that she was teaching for ladies at Hyles-Anderson College. With her permission, I have reproduced those ideas in this chapter.

Preparations by the Missionary Wife

Preparation Before Going to the Field

A. Go on a survey trip with your husband. This trip is not to decide whether or not you want to go to the mission field. Most missionary wives probably aren't excited about leaving their country, home church, and family. Go with the purpose of learning about the country and to ask God to give you a love and burden for the people. Be honest with your husband about your fears, but never tell him you won't go. You have no right to hold your husband back from doing God's will. Be careful to not discourage him by being negative and telling him all the things you hate. Ask God to help you see things for which to be thankful.

B. While there, try to find out the following: (1) a place to live, the cost and availability of appliances and furniture, (2) language school, (3) a translator to help you when you first arrive in the country to go with you to market, etc., (4) banking; learn the money exchange; find out what you must do to get funds from your Stateside banking account, (5) electrical current; the need for adapters, transformers, and converters, and (6) the foods available in the marketplace and their cost.

C. Make lists of what is available on the field and what is not. Decide what you will need to take with you because it is not available or it is cheaper in the States. Determine how much you will need to take with you until you return to the States or until someone can get more to you. Evaluate the cost of shipping items from the States to your new country. Be sure to include the following: (1) medicine and prescriptions (Most insurances will not allow a year's supply. Therefore, you have to make arrangements to have it sent to you three months at a time, generally.) (2) bath soaps, deodorant, etc. (3) makeup (4) hair care and needs (5) laundry needs (6) paper products (7) school/office supplies (8) school books/curriculum (9) appliances (check voltage; most U.S. appliances will not work on the foreign field) (10) computer, printing equipment, supplies, and paper and (11) church equipment, such as the Lord's Supper dishes, things needed for nursery, song books, Bibles, tracts, Sunday school lessons, music.

D. Be upbeat with your children. Show them pictures of what the country looks like and tell them what it's like. If you are excited, they will be. If you are negative, they will be negative or even fearful. Go to the library and check out books about the country. Learn all you can. If you are leaving behind adult children or parents, be sure to have e-mail or some way to communicate with them.

E. Be sure to get needed passports, visas, etc. Be sure you have all your legal paperwork in order.

F. Be sure to have your Last Will and Testament drawn up before you leave.

G. Be sure that you have health and life insurance that will provide coverage for you on the foreign field.

H. Find out size needed and cost of container in which to pack things you will need to ship to the foreign field. Pack away clothes that will not be needed when you first arrive on the field. Be sure to keep out and take with you on the plane or car enough medicine, makeup, toiletries, etc. to meet your needs between the time you leave and the time the container will arrive. Be sure to insure the container.

I. Visit your family before you leave. Spend time with them and do your best to alleviate their fears and concerns.

J. Though you will be busy packing and visiting family, never be too busy to walk with the Lord each day. This is vital to keep your heart right so your heart will be right when you arrive on the field.

K. The United States uses feet/inches, while most of the world uses the metric system; the United States uses Fahrenheit, while most of the world uses Celsius. Be sure to get a table or some way of converting these equations.

Preparations When Arriving on the Field

A. Get your home established as quickly as possible.

B. Get your banking account established.

C. Have a translator go with you to the market place until you learn enough of the language to be conversational and until you learn your way around your city.

D. Watch for dangers to yourself and your family.

E. Learn the language as soon as possible.

F. Help your husband get his schedule established. Then set up your children, yourself, and your home on a schedule.

G. Keep a digital camera with you at all times. Often send pictures home to family.

H. Give yourself and your children time to adjust to the culture and time to grow to love the people.

I. Be patient and flexible. Realize that shopping and other such things will take much longer on the mission field until you learn the area and the language.

J. Be sure to walk with the Lord every day. Read your Bible twice a day—morning and evening. I use the One-Year-Bible, and I read the next day's Bible reading the night before. I also go through my prayer list at night. I allow about one hour, from 8:00-9:00 p.m. Then each morning I follow Brother Jack Schaap's plan for being filled with the Holy Spirit by reading five Psalms each morning, enabling me to read through the Psalms each month. I then read a couple of hymns and ask God to fill me with His Holy Spirit for the day.

K. Establish a budget for decorating your home. Don't be extravagant, but allow yourself to have a nice, comfortable home. Be sure to have water, including hot showers, indoor toilets, and electricity. Have a first-class home without living way above the average level of the people.

L. Get a map of the area and learn your way around the neighborhood and the surrounding areas.

Some Additional Thoughts

A. Help with the ministry, but not to the neglect of your children or home responsibilities. Be part of the work; go to church.

B. Keep your children's school studies on schedule.

C. Plan occasional sightseeing trips, but not more than you work. Make serving the Lord fun.

D. Don't spoil your children because you feel guilty for taking them to the mission field. Teach them to be humble, yet proud that God chose their daddy to be a missionary and chose them to be missionaries.

E.   Make sure your children walk with the Lord. Have a time they read the Bible and pray each day. Give them a notebook in which they write each day the verse they read that day that spoke most to their heart and what they believe God is teaching them personally from that verse. Have them share with the family during family devotion time what they learned that day or the day before during their personal devotions.

F.   You and your husband should take time to have family time each week with your children, and you and your husband should have a date each week.

I would also like to share the experiences of a young lady regarding her survey trip and deputation. This e-mail was sent to Mrs. Sandy Domelle, who has graciously agreed to let me share it:

Dear Mrs. Domelle,

Please forgive me for having taken so long to respond to your letter. I have been writing down many thoughts and such from our survey trip for your father as he had asked me to do. I have to admit that it has not been easy for me to gather my thoughts and present them the way I want to in order to be a help to someone else in the future. I am so glad that there are classes in which a lady can learn from the experience of other ladies such as you who have been on the mission field and understand more clearly what a lady needs to learn that would benefit her later on the mission field.

I will try to answer your questions so that you understand my thoughts, and hopefully, it will be a help to you. Please give me grace and understanding as you read my answers and realize that I am not trying to be spiritual; I am only opening my heart so that someone else might be encouraged and helped.

As we got ready for our trip, I tried to learn as much as I could about health conditions in the area where we would be. The idea of being in a place that had so much sickness and uncleanness terrified me, so I wanted to be sure that we could adequately care for ourselves. While over there, I realized how much more materialistic I was than I thought I was. I found that it meant a lot to me to be able to see other missionaries and how they lived. I realized how spoiled we are in America and how selfish it is so easy to be without even realizing it. I also realized how much I have relied on my family, church, friends to be my happiness as well as my spiritual, mental, and physical inspiration. I found myself really struggling to keep my head up when faced with the reality of "leaving everything." I had previously thought of myself as a strong person, but I was suddenly being slapped in the face with how weak I really was.

The survey trip opened my eyes to what I have been taught, but what I have never truly understood the meaning of, and that is to have your own personal walk with the Lord. I have heard this all my life. I have grown up in church, reading my Bible daily, praying daily, etc., but now as I look back I realize that I was always "riding the coattails" of my parents, school, teachers, pastor, etc. for the spiritual needs that I had instead of learning to go to the Lord. I have been so blessed by having the opportunity to be a "second-generation" Christian and all that goes along with that blessing, but at the same time I realize how that has made me spiritually like a spoiled child in the world materialistically.

I have had to come to grips with myself and the feelings of bitterness that have crept in with the thought of all my "securities" being taken away from me. I have found myself throwing a mental temper tantrum just the way a spoiled child would when a parent takes away the things he wants. Don't get me wrong, I have not grown up with all the material things; it is more the sentimental things that I have had that are being left behind that I struggle with, but that also includes, on a smaller scale, material things as well.

Of course I have been taught so very well, and I know where my problems lie; but that fact does not eliminate the feelings and thoughts of the flesh. Over the last several months, the spiritual and non-spiritual sides of me have been at war with each other, and nothing is worse than having to fight off selfishness. I have found how quickly I can lose sight of God and the big picture and get caught up with myself and the here and now.

I also realized how much more I need to work at building the friendship as well as the romance between my husband and me. He needs me to be all that I am supposed to be so that he can be all that he needs to be.

Another thing that I learned from the survey trip was how emotional living in another country could be when I saw and heard how the people had to live, the dying children, the chaos, the dirt and trash, the kindness of the people, the harshness of the environment, the frustrations of the language barrier, the desires of the people, the differences in culture, the fear from being so far from protection, and yet being put on such a high pedestal—it was all very overwhelming.

I felt that I was experiencing every possible emotion all at the same time, and to be honest with you, I wanted to run from this "awful place" and never have anything to do with it again. I wanted to go back home where I was safe, happy, and comfortable—where no dying children were lying on the ground or where flies were crawling over old people, where the constant stench of garbage and noise seemed never to cease, where I could talk to someone without an interpreter, or take a walk or go to the store by myself without fear, or put my child down on the ground to let them play without worrying about "wort warbles" or "mango maggots" burrowing under their skin or their getting bit by a poisonous spider. All these things and more were running (and have many times since) through my mind and made me feel like throwing in the towel.

All that keeps me in line is asking myself the question, "Would you rather have all that you want and allow them to go to Hell?" Yes, I realize I am a horrible, selfish person, but I won't give the Devil the satisfaction of seeing me be that selfish. It helped me to read the diary of Ann Judson.

I think what shocked me the most was the constant chaos in all aspects of daily living and the trash in which the people had to live. You almost got the feeling of having no reprieve—no place to go to escape. Even when we came to our house at night, there was the loud, almost obnoxious music till late in the night, and I wished for somewhere to go to have peace and quiet. Everywhere you went, you were thronged by people and their insistent begging and arguing, and this plus the heat would exhaust you quickly. I guess for me, I never really realized how differently some parts of the world were run. We have it so good in America; I wish more people could see what I saw just so that they would appreciate what we have here in America more.

I wish I had spent time talking with someone like your father or mother who could have helped prepare me for the emotional feelings I would face. Of course, it is important to be prepared for the health issues. That is common knowledge, but I was not prepared for how I would feel when faced with those things about which we read or hear stories. I am so thankful your father went with us because I needed that "father figure" to give me the mental reassurance that everything was going to be fine. Of course, my comfort came from my husband, but there is an extra sort of security that comes from knowing that someone with experience is in the room, and he was so kind to me [and the others].

[Things to take on the survey trip] Not all countries will require this but in a third-world country such as ours, take toiletry items, toilet paper, personal items, hand sanitizer (which we used constantly), chapstick, repellent, nonscented hair spray, soap to wash clothes with in case of hand-washing clothes, a converter for electrical appliances, snacks that will help keep up your energy level but will not spoil, and mosquito nets for nighttime. The main thing is to take items that if lost or stolen you would not be devastated. For instance, we did not take our wedding bands. You cannot assume that you will be able to buy something (such as personal items). As far as being prepared emotionally and mentally for a survey trip, I think a lady would greatly benefit from seeking advice from experienced ladies and learn as much as possible about the country beforehand. For me, I found that ignorance and unfamiliarity bred fear and repulsion toward something I did not understand.

Deputation: I am still learning things every day as we travel. We have had many pastors tell us that we are not the typical missionary family. Please don't think I am bragging or being haughty when I say this, but when we ask them why, they say because we are classy, yet real. Whether or not that is true, we can only hope that it is true, but the reason I tell you this is because we have found that the word "missionary" truly does not have a good connotation with all pastors. We, as missionaries, should want to make it a goal to do our part to give the word a good definition by how we dress and act and serve. I hope that something I have shared can be used to help someone else.

I really appreciate this young lady's honesty, and I believe God will use her.

Chapter Four

Furloughs

Many years ago I heard a missionary say there was a surefire test to know when it's time to take a furlough. I would like to share that test.

The first year you are on the mission field, if a fly falls in your coffee, you throw it out and make a new cup.

The second year you are on the mission field, if a fly falls in your coffee, you don't throw out the whole cup. You just get a spoon and flick the little fellow out of the liquid and go ahead and drink your coffee.

The third year you are on the mission field, if a fly falls in your coffee, you don't even bother to flick out the stupid thing. You just go ahead and drink around him.

The fourth year you're on the mission field, if a fly falls in your coffee, you throw away the coffee and eat the fly. That's when you know it's time to take a furlough!

I shared this anecdote with our good friends, Jim and Judy Joines, who had started a church about an hour's ride from us. Brother Jim, who recently went home to be with the Lord, loved that story. Many times, when he saw us, he would laughingly ask if we were eating flies yet!

Here are some more questions and answers from our surveys.

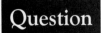 **Question** What can you share about furlough?

Answers:

• Preparing your children ahead of time can make the furlough much more enjoyable for everyone. Your youngest children may not remember anything from back home. They may speak another language better than they speak their mother tongue. They have been absorbing a different culture and a different way of thinking. These are all admirable traits when serving overseas but may make them seem odd and cause them to be shunned when with their peers in their home country.

• These days it is unnecessary for the missionary to go on furlough for an entire year. Travel is much quicker and technology more advanced. Some churches would be content to receive a video update rather than house the missionary and his family. They would still see and hear from the missionary's own mouth what is happening in the ministry without the added expense of hotel, food, etc.

• When planning the itinerary, be sure to plan a few times for sightseeing, fun, and recreation for the whole family. MKs often have the advantage of seeing parts of their home country that their peers never get to see. Take the opportunity to let them experience the richness of their home culture. It really isn't wasted time or expense.

• Help children practice greetings and table manners, especially so if these will differ from what they are familiar with on the field. Help them look forward to staying in different places as an adventure, maybe even a game. In one home the hostess serves cookies and milk to the kids while they watch television. In the next home, children can't drink anything unless they are in the kitchen. In one home toys are scattered all over the house; and in the next, children can only play with one toy at a time. These constant fluctuations are hard on our children.

• Some missionaries expect their children to participate in presentations from their field and to wear national costumes. Carefully consider your child's desire to sit with his peers and not to be part of your "show and tell." The financial support you seek is not worth your child's failure to adjust to life in his home culture.

• For teenagers, furlough can be exciting or devastating. This furlough is laying the groundwork for their re-entry to life in their home country. Be sure to prepare them ahead of time. This would be a good time for them to go to youth camp and visit prospective Bible colleges.

I would like to quote portions of an article regarding furlough that Missionary Tom Vineyard, missionary to the Ivory Coast, wrote for the magazine published by his father, Dr. Jim Vineyard, Windsor Hills Baptist Church, Oklahoma City, Oklahoma.

Then there are the missionary children—from one culture, living in another, and being in a third. Most missionary children grow up never really getting to know their grandparents or other members of their mom or dad's families. Many of them never have the privilege or opportunity to do things like going to a baseball game, going to grandma's house, or getting to watch fireworks on the Fourth of July. These are things that we so often take for granted, and they are an integral part of why missionaries need to take a furlough. One very high priority for my wife and me was that our children get to know their grandparents. We are fortunate enough that both my and my wife's parents love the Lord, live in the same town, and go to the same church. It has made furlough that much better. They have also been able to visit [other relatives]. I am sure that they have no comprehension of it now, but someday they will really appreciate the videos that we were able to take of them with [their relatives].

One of the biggest debates for missionaries is whether or not to settle in somewhere while on furlough or for the whole family to travel together. For me, it was very important that my children get to know the people of our sending church. If anything ever happens to my wife and me, I want them to know the people where they will be living and going to church. I want them to have an attachment to them. I want them to understand that they are a part of that church and that they are to participate in that church's services and activities.

Another thing that was important to us was Katherine's [their daughter] being able to go to the Christian school during the year that we were home. We wanted her to have a good foundation for school and to have identification with that school for later furloughs.

One of the fringe benefits of furlough has been for my children to be able to do some of the things that I was able to do while I was growing up. For instance, the youth group from Windsor Hills went to a rodeo. I took Katherine, and we rode the bus with the teenagers. [She] thoroughly enjoyed it. Furlough made that outing possible.[1]

It is probably a good idea to put children in a Christian school while they are in the United States. Children can get a "taste" of their home—their roots and their culture. Some have experienced problems with this, however, such as their children not wanting to go back to the mission field when the year was over. A year (or at least a few months) of school in the States may be good for them for other reasons too. Boys perhaps need to get in a sports program. Also, teenagers may need to experience dating with Christian young people of their own culture. Hopefully, this will help them to make an adjustment later on when they come back to America for college. Most importantly, this year should be something great in their lives spiritually. A word of caution: monitor your child's friends carefully. Just because kids are in a good church or a Christian school doesn't necessarily mean they will be a good influence for your child. Sometimes we are prone to let down our guard while on furlough. We still need to be very careful.

As with most decisions we must make, there are pros and cons. We have never taken a furlough. My husband opted rather to make short trips home to visit churches now and then. Even when we had to spend two years in America during Rachel's heart surgery, my husband flew back and forth every other month between the United States and the Philippines. When he was in the States, Ricky, Rachel, and I traveled with him to churches. During the time he was in the Philippines, Ricky, Rachel, and I stayed with my folks in Indiana or with his mom in Oklahoma. I could not enroll them in a school as this was the only time we had with my husband, so we did school work on the road.

My husband has never asked for money. He is always very positive and never whines or complains in our prayer letter about how hard up we are to pastors of churches. Perhaps because we had been on the field for so long and God had blessed our work, some people thought we were doing fine financially and did not need any more support. Perhaps because we had not been back for a furlough to raise more support, our support had dropped quite a bit. Regardless, we really needed to travel and raise support. In many ways, those two years were very difficult; yet in many ways, they were wonderful.

In Numbers 11, the children of Israel were complaining to Moses because they were sick and tired of manna. They missed the food from Egypt, and they wanted some meat. This murmuring angered God. He had brought them out of Egypt, where they were slaves, to bring them into a Promised Land. Were they grateful? No. When He fed them with manna and water from the rock, were they grateful? No!

Moses heard everyone weeping, and the Bible said he was displeased. Moses told God he was unable to bear all the people's burdens. God told Moses He could choose some men to help him bear the burdens, and then God told Moses to tell the people that He would give them flesh to eat. In fact, God said He wouldn't just give them meat for a few days, but He would give them meat for a whole month!

This answer blew Moses away! What? How was God going to give millions of people meat for a whole month? What was Moses' reply? Basically he said, "Well God, should we butcher all the herds, or shall we all go fishing? How are we going to catch enough fish to feed everyone, Lord?"

The Lord answered in Numbers 11:23, "...Is the LORD's hand waxed short? thou shalt see now whether my word shall come to pass unto thee or not." I am amazed at Moses' lack of faith! He saw God feed the people with manna from Heaven, and here He is in Numbers 11, doubting that God can somehow come up with enough meat to feed the people! But before I get too critical of Moses, I need to look inward at my own heart. How many times have I seen God answer prayer to provide our needs (and even a lot of our wants), yet every time we have a low statement, I doubt God again. I often agonize, "Why can't I just trust Him?"

When we are on deputation or furlough trying to raise support, we need to trust God. My husband always says, "Work as though it all depends upon you, and pray as though it all depends upon God." We need to trust God with our finances.

Again, with permission, I would like to reproduce an excellent piece written by Mrs. Doug Kalapp. Brother and Mrs. Kalapp had to leave China due to visa problems; therefore, they were more or less on furlough at the time of this writing. The following article was really a blessing to me.

Decide to Be Happy
by Karen Kalapp

So many things in life don't turn out right. A ministry may not turn out like you had envisioned; a marriage, the birth of a child doesn't turn out like you hoped; perhaps you're not even able to have children at all, or children disappoint you and don't turn out like you had dreamed of; friendships can turn sour, and family can abandon you or turn on you; or you may lose finances or a loved one. Many times in life, things don't turn out right. So what do you do? The following are things I learned in China and wrote down, things that I knew I must do if I were to encourage myself in the Lord:

1. **Keep my eyes on the Lord.** James 5:11, *"Behold, we count them happy which endure. Ye have heard of the patience of Job, and have seen the end of the Lord; that the Lord is very pitiful, and of tender mercy."* The word "Lord" means "controller, supreme authority." I had to remember that even when it seems that things are out of control or chaotic, God is in control.

2. **I need to make sure I am counted worthy of His calling.** Sometimes wives of men in full-time Christian service can't take the cost. Sometimes there are rejections, criticisms, loneliness, disappointments, misunderstandings, and frustrations; if you're not careful, you can get bitter and become ugly and ruin your influence or quit before the harvest comes. II Thessalonians 1:11 says, *"Wherefore also we pray always for you, that our God would count you worthy of this calling, and fulfil all the good pleasure of his goodness, and the work of faith with power; That the name of our Lord Jesus Christ may be glorified in you, and ye in him, according to the grace of our God and the Lord Jesus Christ."*

3. **Make good use of the time God gives you to serve Him.** Psalm 90:12 *"So teach us to number our days, that we may apply our hearts unto wisdom."* To "number" means *to weigh* or *to evaluate, to consider as important, to count our days.* If I live to be 70, I have less than 16 years, or around 5,700 days left to serve God. Life goes so quickly. We somehow think we have all of eternity to decide what we want to do or to decide to do something for God. We don't

even have the promise of tomorrow. You never know what a day may bring forth.

4. Be thankful for what you can be thankful for in the past. Remember the good times in the past before things went bad. Though it has not been easy and we seemingly have a setback now, I would not have missed China for anything. Concerning China I think of:

- Souls saved. A light comes on in their eyes. Many said their salvation was the result of family members' prayers, even of those already gone to Heaven. Over 100 came for a Dove bar!
- Russia sending a Christian radio station into China; people praying for someone to come to northern China.
- "Lit a fire from here to Beijing;" lit a fire among Christians throughout northern China; gave hope to underground Christians and how they started having public assemblies.
- Friends of a lifetime, including CMP (China Mission Project) team members and Chinese friends
- So much laughter and good memories. "God gave us memories so we'll have roses in December." When it's the December time in your life, dwell on good memories so you can keep your eyes on your problems and the hard circumstances of life, or you can remember the good of the past and not get bitter.

5. Be thankful for what you can be thankful for. Look for good in the present. Look for what you can be thankful for despite the situation; look for things to be thankful for in the situation. We are still alive; can still serve God; God is not through with us. We have friends, family—we're not alone. We can still go to church. We still have a home in Heaven. So, you can keep your eyes on your problems and the hard circumstances of life, or you can keep your eyes on the good in the present and remain thankful.

6. Watch your spirit and heart. Proverbs 4:23, "*Keep thy heart with all diligence; for out of it are the issues of life.*" Don't be angry and bitter or cynical and distrusting. See the common people; don't look at the officials. Don't be critical and despising. Remember they are lost and full of fear about losing position. Keep things in the right perspective, and remember that people hurt us because they are hurting.

7. Take steps to fight discouragement. Stay in church; you must have preaching. Don't run from God. Stay in your ministry. Don't abandon your husband and your work for the Lord. Keep reading your Bible—day and night. Joshua 1:8 says to meditate day and night. Praise! Satan wants us to keep our eyes on the bad. Read the Psalms. Brother Schaap said he reads five chapters a day. Listen to good music—it will uplift your spirit.

8.   Beware of self-condemnation. Sometimes fear of what man thinks causes us to condemn ourselves. I Samuel 30:6, *"And David was greatly distressed; for the people spake of stoning him, because the soul of all the people was grieved, every man for his sons and for his daughters: but David encouraged himself in the LORD his God."* Encourage yourself. Satan fights good, then makes you feel like a failure, and we fall into his trap. Proverbs 29:25: *"The fear of man bringeth a snare: but whoso putteth his trust in the LORD shall be safe."* When I found out we were going to have to come home to work on our visas, I started feeling like we were failures, so I made a list of our successes. After I made my list, I called Satan a liar! Don't fall into Satan's trap.

9.   Learn to live one day at a time and enjoy each day to its fullest. Philippines 4:6 says, *"Be careful for nothing."* If you're full of care, thinking too much on tomorrow or too much on yesterday; live today to its fullest.

10.   Keep a good sense of humor. I never felt so much oppression from Satan and fear and discouragement, but I never laughed so much in all my life. My husband was investigated for being part of a cult and accused of being a spy sent to overthrow the Chinese government singlehandedly. We gave each other "spy" names—being silly, not to laugh at the Chinese, but to laugh at the situation and to keep us laughing. Be the sunshine of your home.

11.   Don't lose hope. Don't dwell on fears and worries of the future. Make plans for the future. When problems come, I always think: "What's the worst that could happen?" If things don't work out in China (and I believe they will), many other countries would want us and allow us, or we could always continue the work we were doing here before we left. Never stop dreaming!

12.   Decide to be happy. James 5:11, *"Behold, we count them happy which endure. Ye have heard of the patience of Job, and have seen the end of the Lord; that the Lord is very pitiful, and of tender mercy."* Count them happy means "pronounce or esteem them fortunate." *Endure* means "stay under, remain, persevere." Stay in church, stay in the Lord's work; keep serving the Lord. *Patience* means "endurance or constancy." So many people change when the hard times come. *End* means "goal." Keep your eyes on His goals, not yours. *Lord* means "Controller; Supreme Authority." He's in control; it may not look like it, but He knows what's going on. So that's all I need to know. *Pitiful* means "extremely compassionate." *Mercy* means compassionate. He cares!

Don't let Satan tell you that God doesn't care. Don't let the circumstances of life or people or Satan take away your hope, happiness, or joy. Decide to be happy!

I can see that God can use Mrs. Kalapp anywhere with her attitude! I want to be like that!

Conclusion

I would like to close this unit by writing about a missionary who worked with the China Inland Mission started by Hudson Taylor. Taylor was able to instill his financial principles in many of the missionaries who worked under the C.I.M., including Jonathan Goforth.

Rosalind Goforth, the wife of Jonathan Goforth, wrote the following in her book, which is a perfect example of what a missionary's attitude should be toward finances and furlough:

In the summer of 1908, I was obliged to return to Canada with five of our children, leaving my husband in China for the revival work.

Reaching Toronto, I learned that my eldest son was at death's door from repeated attacks of rheumatic fever. He was then almost a day's journey away. On my way there, as I recalled the times in which he had been given back to us from the very gates of death, my faith was strengthened to believe for his recovery again. But, as I prayed, it became very clear that the answer to my petition depended on myself; in other words, that I must yield myself and my will to God.

I had been planning to take no meetings during that furlough, but to devote myself wholly to my children. I confessed the sin of planning my own life and definitely covenanted with the Lord that if He would raise my son for His service, I would take meetings, or do anything, as He opened the way for the care of the children.

There were six difficult doors, however, that would have to be opened—not one, but all—before I could possibly go out and speak for Christ and China, as God seemed to be asking. First, the Lord would need to restore my son to complete health, as I could never feel justified in leaving a sick child. Second, He would need to restore my own health, for I had been ordered to the hospital for an operation. Third, He would need to keep all the other children well. Fourth, a servant must be sent to take care of the house—though my income was so small that a servant seemed out of the question, and only the strictest economy was making both ends meet. Fifth, a Christian lady would need to be willing to take care of the children and act as my housekeeper in my absence from home. Sixth, sufficient money would need to be sent to meet the extra expenses incurred by my leaving home.

Yet, as I laid these difficulties before the Lord, I received the definite assurance that He would open the way.

My son was brought back to Toronto on a stretcher, the doctor not allowing him to raise his head; but on arrival he would not obey orders, declaring that he was so well he could not and would not remain still. Fearing the consequences of his disobeying orders, I telephoned for the doctor to come at once. On his arrival he gave the lad a thorough examination and then said, "Well, I cannot make him out; all I can say is, let him do as he pleases."

As for myself, I did not go to the hospital; for all the symptoms that had seemed to require it left me, and I became perfectly well. A servant was sent to me who did her work sympathetically, as helping me to do the Lord's work. A married niece, living near, offered to stay in the home whenever I needed to be absent.

And so there remained but one condition unfulfilled—the money. But I believed this would come as I went forward; and it did. Each month that followed, as I made up my accounts, I found that my receipts exceeded my expenditure sufficiently to enable me to spend money for work in China, and to purchase things which I needed in China, including an organ. All these accounts were laid before our beloved mission board secretary, who approved them.

Under these circumstances I dared not refuse invitations to speak. Yet so weak was my faith.[1]

Another time Mrs. Goforth recorded the following:

Finally, the husband had the last word, which was, "Oh, let us trust Him. Who knows but that a cheque is awaiting us at Changte?" On reaching home a pile of mail was heaped up on the dining table. Opening the first letter to hand, I read: "Dear Mrs. Goforth, I am a stranger to you. I've never seen you or your husband. I have an old mother, not very well, who has got the idea into her head that you need money. So to quiet her I am sending you the enclosed cheque for fifty dollars. I hope you will find some use for it."

Oh, how humbled I felt! For several moments I could not summon up the courage to hand the letter to my husband, for I expected to hear him say, "I told you so." The good man, on reading it, just smiled, but there was a triumphant look in his eyes which needed no words. Some months later a second letter came from this same lady in answer to my acknowledgment, which read, "My mother was dying when your letter came, but she was able to take in all you wrote. The joy of knowing she had been God's channel to help you in China carried her joyfully through those last three days before she passed away." Mr. Goforth's faith never seemed to waver, even when, as a family, times of severe testing came. He would never borrow, nor ever go in debt, and God always honored His servant's trust in Him.

On reaching Toronto, the Goforths found a welcome haven in the Missionary Rest Home at Mimico, some distance out of the city. Then, by the end of August, they were face to face with a serious financial crisis, the sudden return to Canada and Mr. Goforth's illness having entailed many extra expenses. The hard fact had to be faced that their salary was not sufficient. Mr. Goforth felt he could not lay our needs before the Board and ask for help. The only other alternative was to step out in faith, secure a suitable home in Toronto, and trust the Lord to undertake for the extra expense. This we did, and the Lord never failed us.

While the financial question was being discussed, Ruth, then about seventeen years of age, became very indignant that we should be brought, as she put it, "to a place of beggars." But we assured her that to trust God for what was lacking was not begging. But she seemed only partly convinced. The day came for our taking possession of the new home in Toronto, and on entering, we found a large mail awaiting us. One letter was from [a lady] in Australia whose cooperation with us in the past we have already mentioned. Her letter enclosed fifty pounds with the express wish that thirty pounds be used for work in China, but twenty pounds was to be used for personal needs. I handed the letter to Ruth with the words, "It seems to me as if our Father were beside us saying, 'Take this one hundred dollars as an earnest of what I am going to do for you.'" Tears stood in Ruth's eyes as she handed the letter back. "Oh, mother," she said, "we don't trust God half enough." That little incident was the beginning of a new vision in the life of our dear daughter and ultimately led to her yielding herself as a missionary to Indo-China, where she has been with her husband for some years.[2]

Let's just simply trust God with every area of our life, including deputation, furlough, and finances. He is faithful!

Above: Rachel teaches Sunday school.
Below left: Ricky and me
Below right: Rachel plays violin at church. She has played the violin since she was four years old.

UNIT NINE

Medical Concerns

"...I am the LORD that healeth thee."
(Exodus 15:26)

Introduction

Mary Rachel Martin was born in the Philippines on April 14, 1986. My mom and dad flew to the Philippines for the event, just as they had when Ricky was born. Ricky not only surveyed, but supervised everything—being all of seven years old! Every night he carried a little stool to the nursery window at the hospital to check on his baby sister. The nurses would come out and say, "Ricky, go back to your mama's room and sleep now. We'll take good care of Rachel." He then gave them detailed instructions in Ilonggo—much to their amusement.

That first night when Ricky said, "Mom, Rachel is very colorful," I didn't think much of his remark. At the time I did not know he was referring to what looked like black-and-blue bruises around her mouth. The following morning I begged to see my baby. Because I had had a Caesarean, the nurse put me in a wheelchair and wheeled me to the nursery to see Rachel. The first time I held my precious daughter, I did what all mothers do—counted her fingers and toes and breathed a prayer of thanks that we had a strong, healthy baby. We had no way of knowing the trials our faith would endure in the next few weeks.

Rachel was three days old when her pediatrician told me he thought she had a heart problem and wanted to call in a pediatric cardiologist. The doctor performed an x-ray and EKG. Rachel was immediately put on oxygen and started on the drug dioxin which helps the heart pump stronger. Her doctor explained that Rachel had gone into heart failure. When I was told how serious her condition was, I went to the nurses station to call Rick and to ask him to come. I started crying as I told him Rachel had a heart problem.

Rachel's doctor suggested we fly her to the Heart Center in Manila. My dad somehow persuaded (with money, no doubt!) a professional photographer to come to the hospital to get Rachel's two-by-two photos. We were thinking while we were in Manila that we should get her passport and certificate of birth abroad. My husband still carries that picture of our poor baby in his Bible—her face bloated and an oxygen tube running from her nose.

Rick's niece, Becky Maytubby, had a one-year-old baby named Carrie who also had a heart problem. Carrie had open-heart surgery three weeks before Rachel was born, so Becky was the first person we called. Becky told us she would have taken Carrie anywhere, but she felt the very best hospital was Children's in Oklahoma City. Becky then said, "You know, ever since I found out Carrie had a heart problem I've been asking God, 'Why?' Now I know why. God allowed Carrie to have a heart problem so we could help you with Rachel." Becky was happy that God was already using her precious one-year-old little girl. Becky gave us the names and telephone numbers for Carrie's surgeon, Dr. Ronald Elkins, as well as her pediatric cardiologist, Dr. Jerry Razook. These extremely busy doctors patiently listened, answered questions, and started giving us advice over the phone.

Mom and Dad stayed in Iloilo with Ricky, while Rick, Rachel, her doctor, and I flew to Manila. I remember our dear church members, Mr. and Mrs. Jun Andigan, driving us everywhere we needed to go because we did not have a car. Dad had already gone to the airport to make arrangements for our flight. We soon learned that the Philippine Airlines would not allow any baby under the age of 21 days to fly, and Rachel was only a week old. Dad tried and tried to convince the officials of how vital it was, but he couldn't reason with anyone. Finally Rachel's doctor went to the airport and told them in no uncertain terms that Rachel would die if she didn't fly immediately to Manila, and her death would be their fault.

In 1986, people were still smoking on flights, so the flight attendants asked everyone to refrain from smoking because of the baby on board who was hooked up to an oxygen tank. After the one-hour flight, we landed in Manila where an ambulance met us at the airport and rushed us to the hospital. We had called Mel and Carol Brown, missionary friends in Manila, who graciously met us at the Heart Center. An eminent surgeon had driven to the hospital at that late hour (almost midnight) to look at our baby. He told us to go get some rest, and he would talk to us in the morning after he had performed some tests. Brother Mel and Carol took us to their house.

The next morning I had broken out with hives, and I was having a difficult time breathing as my throat was beginning to close up. I thought I was allergic to the medicines I was on from having the C-section, but it was probably just nerves. Rachel's doctor, Dr. Reyes, pulled some strings for me so I could be admitted to the Heart Center instead of another hospital across town. We needed to be near Rachel; I needed to be near my daughter.

We were allowed to look at her through a glass window for 30 minutes twice a day. Dr. Reyes told us he thought Rachel had a condition called aortic stenosis, which meant her aortic valve was deformed and not functioning properly. He said, "I have performed the surgery before, but none of the babies lived." We thought about contacting Clark Air Force Base, even though we were not military personnel. We had taken Ricky to the base years ago for some rabies shots, so we knew from that experience that it was nearly impossible for a civilian to get help. The doctors and nurses were extremely kind and seemingly wanted to help all they could; but after all, the military has to operate by rules and regulations. Clark Air Force Base was our only hope as Dr. Reyes stressed, "There is no way your baby can survive the long flight to the States. In fact, I am sure the airline will not even allow her to make the flight in her present condition."

We made the initial contact with the military base, but those who really made the difference were Rick's sister Connie and her husband, Bill Graves, who was in the Oklahoma State legislature. They were friends with Congressman Mickey Edwards, a born-again Christian. He very kindly agreed to call Clark Air Force Base and ask for a favor. I was in my hospital room when the nurse summoned me to the phone at her desk. I picked it up in time to hear Rick talking to a high-ranking official at the base.

He explained that Congressman Edwards had called him and asked them to help us. "What can I do?" he kindly questioned. A decision was soon reached for the base hospital, some 60 miles away, to send an ambulance for Rachel. I rode with her while Rick flew back to Iloilo to get Ricky and to give some last-minute instructions to our staff.

I kept calling Mom and Dad and updating them. "We are going to wait here in Iloilo until the doctors know what should be done about Rachel," they told me. At that time I think we believed Rachel would have heart surgery at the base. After all, it was the top neo-natal hospital in Asia. The doctors and nurses were taking care of babies who had been flown in from U.S. bases all over the Asian region.

When we arrived at the base, Rachel was immediately taken to ICU. After she had been examined and her monitors were in place, I was allowed to hold her for the first time in a week. It was extremely difficult to see her submitted to all the necessary blood tests, shots, and IVs. Any mother who has been through that kind of experience knows what I'm talking about.

One of the nurses took me to an empty barracks and made up a bed for me. The next morning I got up early and walked to the hospital. I saw a very young doctor, in fact the same quiet doctor who had ridden with us in the ambulance, doing an echocardiogram on Rachel. Another doctor walked up to me and commented, "Don't let his age fool you—that's Dr. Bradley Yoder, and he's brilliant."

A friend met Rick and Ricky at the Manila airport and drove them to the base. I cried when I saw them. Rick spent countless hours going back and forth from the U.S. Embassy to the base (over an hour's drive), going through mounds of paperwork and red tape, trying to get a passport and birth certificate (certificate of birth abroad) for Rachel. The State Department was really giving him a hard time. It almost seemed as if they did not care whether or not our baby died. Meanwhile, the doctor had decided that Rachel's problem was too serious for even Clark's neo-natal unit to handle. That's when I knew she didn't have a chance. I started preparing myself to lose her while they started preparing her for the long Medi-Vac flight. They explained that when Rachel went into heart failure, all of her major organs would start shutting down. Her lungs were already filling with fluid, and she was being fed through a tube inserted through her nose. Her kidneys and liver were in the beginning stages of shutting down. It was going to cost thousands of dollars for her to fly on the Medi-Vac, and several thousands more for the three of us, so Rick and I decided we had to fly commercial. We were also looking at a heart surgery that would cost thousands of dollars once we reached the United States. We felt helpless.

I sat in the chair in the hospital and held my tiny daughter for what I was sure was the last time. I was crying when Dr. Harry Laws, wearing his dress uniform, walked into where I was holding Rachel. He introduced himself to me and promised he'd take good care of Rachel. She was to be his only patient on that huge plane.

Rick, Ricky, and I took a bus back to Manila. We checked into a hotel and were walking across the lobby when to our complete surprise, we saw Mom and Dad. They thought we were on the plane with Rachel, but as I mentioned previously, the plans had changed very early that morning because it would have cost over $10,000 for the three of us to fly on the Medi-Vac. When Mom and Dad found out Rachel was having surgery in the USA, they quickly packed and flew to Manila to catch an international flight the next day. We explained that Rachel was already on her way and that we were flying the next day. They were too, only on a different flight. We had supper together; and the next morning, we all went to the airport together. Their flight was just one hour after ours.

Needless to say, that was the longest flight of my life. I cried and prayed and read my Bible the whole way. I read I Peter 5:7 and 10 over and over: *"Casting all your care upon him; for he careth for you. But the God of all grace, who hath called us unto his eternal glory by Christ Jesus, after that ye have suffered a while, make you perfect, stablish, strengthen, settle you."*

I just knew Rachel wasn't going to make it. I could see it in the faces of the doctors and nurses at the base. I saw it in the faces of those at the Manila Heart Center. I silently planned her funeral. We landed in San Francisco and called Travis Air Force Base to see if Rachel had survived the flight. We found out she had, and she had already been transported to Children's Hospital in Oklahoma City. We called there and learned that Rick's mother, father, sisters, and brother were waiting outside of surgery. We had given power of attorney to Dr. Laws and the doctors at Children's because we knew Rachel would be arriving there long before us, and would need surgery before we could arrive to sign papers.

My sister Bobbie had driven two hours from her home, in the middle of the night, to meet the helicopter as it flew Rachel from Tinker Air Force Base to Children's Hospital. Bobbie said she sobbed as the nurse handed Rachel to her to hold before she was wheeled into surgery.

When our plane touched down in Denver, we again made some frantic calls to Children's Hospital. Dr. Razook informed us that another doctor, Dr. Ward, had discovered another problem with Rachel's heart called a co-arctation of the aorta. Before they performed the necessary surgery on the aortic valve, the co-arctation of the aorta had to be corrected first. Later we learned if the work had been done on the aortic valve, without correcting the co-arctation first, she would have died on the operating table.

Dr. Razook told Rick by phone that they had opened her from the back for the co-arctation and now that part of the surgery was done. He further explained that she was now being turning over to open her chest. He added that she was stable.

Rick asked what was next after the valve was repaired. Dr. Razook explained that the riskiest part came when they took her off the heart-lung machine because sometimes the heart fails to start beating again on its own.

My husband asked what could be done if that happened, expecting an answer like, "Put her back on the machine and try again."

We were shocked by Dr. Razook's answer: "Then there is nothing we can do—we've lost her." We realized more than ever how important our prayers were for our little daughter's life.

Rick hung up the phone, and we boarded the last plane and flew into Oklahoma City. We were numb. We took our time getting off the plane because we just knew someone was waiting for us to tell us that Rachel didn't make it. With heavy hearts, we slowly walked down the ramp.

Then I spotted my sister Bobbie standing at the doorway, jumping up and down and shouting: "Becky—she's okay! She made it!" I started weeping uncontrollably. In fact, I don't think I had stopped crying for several days. Rick's brothers-in-law, Tom Moll and Bill Graves, were also at the airport waiting for us.

Little did we know that while we were being driven to the hospital, Rachel's heart went into fibrillation while the doctors were sewing up her chest. They immediately ripped open her chest and started massaging her heart. Dr. Razook went in to tell the family.

Totally unaware of the complications, we jubilantly arrived at the hospital. We were hugging Rick's mom and sisters. Finally after we calmed down, Connie took my hand and said there had been a problem since Bobbie, Bill, and Tom had left to get us at the airport. Our spirits plummeted, but before she had time to explain, Dr. Razook walked in to the waiting room. We all froze. He smiled and said, "She's stable."

A few minutes later Dr. Elkins walked in and told us about the surgery. The heart of a newborn is about the size of a strawberry, and the aorta, the largest artery in the body, is smaller than a thread. It was mind boggling to think of opening a tiny hole in her aortic valve, which was almost completely closed. Too large of an opening would kill her. It had to be just big enough to let the blood flow through for a few years—until she would be old enough to have the valve replaced.

The hospital chaplain, Danny Cavitt, came in and introduced himself to us. He had been a close friend of Tom and Julie's from Bible college. From that moment, he became a dear friend. He prepared us for what Rachel would look like; then he took us into ICU. The room was filled with tiny beds cradling tiny patients, with lots of doctors and nurses.

It was terrifying to see countless tubes and machines connected to Rachel. One nurse and one resident were assigned to her and her alone. She was terribly bloated. Danny looked at us and said, "It's okay to cry."

Rick said, "We can't cry. We cried all the way here. We don't have any tears left."

I said, "We can't cry—she's alive." Rachel was now 17 days old.

Chapter One

Suggestions for Mothers of Small Children

A lmost every year our family attends the Baptist International Missions, Inc. (BIMI) field conference. We find it is a refreshing time to get away, to relax, and to fellowship with other missionaries.

While at the meetings, I noticed that the number-one subject the mothers seem to discuss is the illnesses of their children. I remember when my children were small, that subject was also of utmost importance in my mind. When they got older, they didn't seem to get sick as often.

When my children were small, they were constantly sick. This situation can be terribly discouraging and upsetting to a young missionary mother. You can't totally isolate them from friends or your people at church services. The church people love your children, want to hold them and give them candy and other treats. It is so hard to say "No." On the other hand, you don't want your children to suffer with all the diseases they can get. You have to pray for wisdom and use some common sense. I heard about one missionary wife whose house was crawling with huge cockroaches. She did not want to spray her house because she was afraid the chemicals would cause cancer. However, the filthy insects running all over their food and everything else were just as dangerous.

One thing I can say to these young mothers is: "This too shall pass!" Please don't think I am being unsympathetic. Believe me when I say I spent many nights on my knees, many nights crying, and many nights in hospitals. Just remember that Jesus is the Great Physician, and He has the power to heal our children.

Jonathan Goforth, missionary to China, felt God wanted him and his family to travel throughout China, preaching and starting churches. One story that illustrates this chapter so well is the time when Rosalind, the wife of Jonathan Goforth, surrendered her children to God:

Yes, it was a very wonderfully thought-out plan and should be carried out *if there were no children in the question!* As I listened, my heart went like lead! The vision of those women with their smallpox children at Hopei, crowding about me and the baby, the constant danger to the children from all kinds of infectious diseases that this life would mean (for the Chinese cared nothing of bringing infection to others), and the thought of our four little graves—all combined to make me set my face as adamant against the plan. My one and only reason, however, in opposing and refusing to go with my children, as my husband suggested, was because it seemed a risking of the children's lives.

Oh, how my husband pleaded! Day by day in the quiet stillness of that long river journey, he assured me that the Lord would keep my children from harm. He was *sure* the Lord would keep them. He was *sure* God was calling me to take this step of faith. Then as we drew near the journey's end, he went further. He said: "Rose, I am so sure this plan is of God, that I fear for the children if you refuse to obey His call. *The safest place for you and the children is the path of duty.* You think you can keep your children safe in your comfortable home at Changte, but God may have to show you you cannot. But He can and will keep the children if you trust Him and step out in faith!"

Time proved he was right, but, as yet, I had not the faith nor the vision nor the courage to regard it in that light.

We reached our Changte home on a Saturday evening. Sunday morning I left the children with the faithful nurse, Mrs. Cheng. They all seemed perfectly well. Two hours later I returned to be met by Mrs. Cheng saying, "Wallace is ill." The doctor was called who pronounced it "one of the worst cases of Asiatic dysentery he had come across."

For two weeks we literally fought for the child's life during which time my husband whispered to me gently, "O Rose, give in, before it is too late!" But I only thought him hard and cruel, and refused. Then, when Wallace began to recover, my husband packed up and left on a tour alone.

The day after he left, my precious baby Constance, almost one year old, was taken ill suddenly, as Wallace had been, only much worse. From the first, the doctors gave practically no hope. The father was sent for. Constance was dying when he arrived. We had laid her on a cot in the middle of my husband's study. Our faithful friend, Miss Pyke, knelt on one side. My husband knelt next to Constance and I beside him. The little one was quietly passing, all was still, when suddenly I seemed to apprehend in a strange and utterly new way the *love* of God—as a *Father.* I seemed to see all at once, as in a flash, that *my Heavenly Father could be trusted to keep my children!* This all came so overwhelmingly upon me, I could only bow my head and say, "O God, it is too late for Constance, but I will trust You. I will go where you want me to go. But keep my children!"

Oh, the joy that came and peace—so when my husband turned to me saying, "Constance is gone"—I was ready and comforted, knowing that her life had not been in vain. Our little Constance's remains were laid beside her two sister's graves on her birthday, October 13, 1902.[1]

In the book *How I Know God Answers Prayer*, Mrs. Goforth continues:

Was God faithful to the vision He had given me? Or did He allow the children to suffer in the years that followed, when months each year were spent with them right out among the people? As I write this, eighteen years have passed since we started on that first trip, and none of our children has died. Never had we as little sickness as during that life. Never had we so much evidence of God's favor and blessing in a hundred ways.[2]

Ultimately, we must depend on God to keep us safe. However, we can do all that we can do, within reason, to guard the health of our family members. You may find that on the mission field you have to boil your drinking water, soak your vegetables in potassium permanganate, and wash your meat with Clorox to keep your family from getting typhoid, some type of an amoeba, or even a disease like cholera. Study and prepare yourself. Seek advice from older, wiser missionaries. We are fortunate to have a medical doctor in our church, and I am constantly bombarding her with questions. Read and study. To get information for the students and staff at Iloilo, I constantly refer to *The American Medical Association Home Medical Encyclopedia, Prevention's Healing with Vitamins, Dr. Wright's Guide to Healing with Nutrition*, and *The Reader's Digest Good Health Fact Book*.

In the book *The Missionary Wife and Her Work*, author Joy Turner Tuggy comments:

It is the mother's responsibility to safeguard her children in every possible way. She will teach them to keep their hands out of their mouths. She will feed them as wholesome a diet as possible and watch over their eating, drinking, and sleeping habits. She will see to it that their shots and immunizations are kept up to date. She will patiently instruct them and the people in matters of hygiene. And then will simply trust the Lord.[3]

No doubt God is pleased when we step out by faith to do His will. Although He may allow trials and tests to come into our lives, I believe He will reward us for being obedient to His call. Ask Him to protect your family.

Chapter Two

Medical Advice From Other Missionaries

W e asked many other missionaries who were on the field three questions dealing with medical issues. I would like to share their responses.

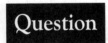 What basic first aid should one know? What basic medication
is needed where you are? How have you dealt with the medical
differences?

Answers:

• The Red Cross offers a basic first-aid class which every missionary
should take. The knowledge of what drugs to take for what problem would also
be helpful.

• All moms should know first aid, how to give massages (back and
neck), and how to wrap ankles and wrists with an ACE wrap. We major on
prevention. We take vitamins and eat our meals mostly at home. As a family,
we also exercise five days a week.

• Thankfully, we are in a modern city and have medical help readily
accessible, although I get frustrated with the government's social-medical system for the people who cannot afford other medical aid. Those who need medical help wait forever to see a doctor who often does not take their problems
seriously.

• Medical needs such as treating burns and cuts and performing CPR
are my most difficult struggle. We can get almost anything in medication. I do
not trust this country's medical system as I have seen many people die need-
lessly. The language barrier also makes me nervous. When you start getting
into technical language, it becomes harder to communicate. God has provided, and we have not needed emergency care on the field. I pray about this fear
daily.

• Pray for health! In a third-world country, the last thing you want to do is have a health problem. We stock butterfly bandages, Johnson & Johnson First Aid Cream, and a basic first-aid and health book. Most missionaries in third-world countries probably have shortened their life due to precarious conditions in the country where the Lord has sent them. It is something we just accept.

• I believe every missionary should take a first-aid class and know how to do CPR. Pain medication, vitamins, cough syrup, antibiotics, eye drops, first aid for minor cuts, Nyquil etc. are available. I bring a lot of things from the States.

• We have basic first-aid books and books on natural first-aid remedies that we study from regularly. I am now re-reading *Standard First-Aid and Personal Safety* by the American Red Cross. Resource materials often mean the difference between life and death when you are isolated like we are. We believe both in the power of prayer and good resource materials.

• I think that a basic course in first aid and CPR is essential. We have taken a short medical course, and it has been so valuable. One of the most used and most referred to books on our shelf is *Where There Is No Doctor* by David Werner, The Hesperian Foundation, Box 162, Palo Alto, CA.

• Medical help and facilities here are very poor in the country where we serve. I have come to the conclusion that if anything serious happens to us here, that is probably the end! We have a few good medical books; *Where There Is No Doctor* is excellent. Another missionary wife told me about colloidal silver liquid which can be purchased at a health food store. It helps with upset stomach a lot. We do not drink the water unless it is purified. We try to wash our hands constantly to help from spreading germs.

• First, find out what kind of facilities your area has and learn things accordingly. We do have a small hospital and some good doctors, but we also realize they have a limited amount of knowledge. One must also make sure you know where to go or what to do when the facility you have is not adequate. Stay in contact with your doctors in the United States. Some of ours have e-mail and have even been of great help in that way. We have tried to learn from others and their needs, also.

• Trust God and go to the doctor! I've submitted to the National Health Service here and so far haven't died—one-day surgery and three successful babies later! We've maintained our U.S. insurance but haven't had to claim in the last five years—praise God! It does help the other ladies [nationals] to accept you if you "trust" the doctors as well. Surely that's completely with discretion according to the country—but at least give them the benefit of the doubt if you're in a developed nation. Take advantage of the free services that may be available. We've no "baby debt;" dental and prescriptions are free during and up to one year post-natal. Also, there are free services/medicines available for children.

The Good Heath Fact Book lists the following suggestions for first-aid equipment and medicines to have on hand:

- Assorted small adhesive bandages
- Individually wrapped sterile gauze pads
- Roll of sterile gauze bandage
- Roll of adhesive tape
- Triangular bandage and large safety pins (for sling)
- Cotton swabs and balls
- Measuring spoons
- Heating pad or hot-water bottle
- Ice pack
- First-aid manual
- Small blunt-tipped scissors
- Tweezers and a packet of sewing needles (to remove splinters)
- Antacid
- Antibiotic ointment or antiseptic for cuts
- Thermometers (oral for adults, rectal for infants)
- Anti-diarrhea medication
- Antihistamine
- Anti-itching lotion or spray (or baking soda)
- Aspirin or acetaminophen
- Burn ointments
- Children's acetaminophen (if needed)
- Cough syrup with expectorant
- Decongestant
- Foot powder
- Mild laxative
- Syrup of ipecac (to induce vomiting)
- Powdered activated charcoal (to absorb poison)
- Rubbing alcohol (70% solution)[1]

Be sure to ask advice from other missionaries—especially veteran missionaries. They will have a lot of knowledge and experience. Let's ask God for wisdom and prepare ourselves.

Chapter Three

When Your People
Need Medical Attention

When you live in a third-world country, it is extremely difficult to see the people around you suffer. You simply do not have the finances to help everyone with their illnesses. My husband has helped countless numbers of people with medical problems in the years we have been here—even people who do not go to our church. The government here has "free" hospitals, but the patient has to pay for everything, meaning he has to pay for all the medicines and any procedure such as blood tests, x-rays, and other diagnostic tests. It is heartbreaking to see someone be diagnosed with cancer, and since the individual cannot pay for even the first chemotherapy, he simply goes home and dies. If a person needs kidney dialysis, his family might sell everything they have and borrow all they can to simply have the first treatment done. What happens when the second treatment is needed? With all of their resources gone, the family has to watch their loved one die. Some in America gripe and complain about healthcare, but they have no idea what it's like in other countries, especially in third-world countries.

About six months ago, we learned that two of our church members had cancer. One had surgery and seems to be doing fine for the time being. The other person just passed away. About the same time, we discovered that two pastors' wives had been diagnosed with cancer here on our island. One is already gone; the other has stage 4. The mother of one of our staff members is presently dying with cancer. A lay person in a neighboring Baptist church, who is a friend of many years, died two months after learning she had cancer.

These deaths from cancer puzzled me, and I asked a doctor in our church: "I always thought most Filipinos had healthy diets—they eat lots of fish, fruits, and vegetables. Why are so many getting cancer?" She explained that Filipinos have gotten away from the traditional healthy diets they once had and are eating lots of junk foods. McDonald's and other fast-food places have opened up. Also, many chemicals are sprayed on the fruits, vegetables, and even the rice fields. When we first came to the mission field, we never saw a Filipino who was overweight. Now we see them all the time. This doctor also mentioned the consumption of processed meats and how the Filipinos are so fond of dried, salted fish.

Another dear friend of ours just passed away with cancer at the age of 43, the same age as Rick's sister Julie when she died of cancer. When Rick and I came to the Philippines in the fall of 1977, we started a Bible study soon after. Two teenagers, who were faithful in those early days, were Werner Catequista and his sister Lorna. Werner and Lorna became very good soul winners. One by one, other members of the family got saved. Two years later, the family moved to the northern island of Luzon; and we did not see them for many years. Family members would occasionally visit our church in Iloilo. Werner and Lorna and their brother and sisters were in different professions. Sometimes they would come back for business, and also they would come back to visit family and friends. Their youngest brother Franklin went to Bible college and became a pastor.

Lorna and her older sister Lira became successful at an insurance company. They were often flying back and forth between Iloilo and Manila because of their jobs. When Lira opened a branch office here in our city, one of the first things she did was ask some of our staff to conduct Bible studies in her office for her employees. Many were saved as a result.

Last year, at the age of 43, Lira was married. She insisted that my husband conduct part of the ceremony, that I play for part of the service, and that Rachel play her violin. She wanted her "beloved missionaries," as she called us, to have a part on her special day.

In May 2003, right before her first wedding anniversary, Lira discovered she had breast cancer. My husband and I helped them financially and prayed for her every day. She died four months later.

Recently Lorna flew back to Iloilo for a visit. After church Lorna came to our house, sat in our living room, and told us about Lira's Homegoing at the hospital in Manila. Lorna shared:

We gathered around Lira's bed, sang hymns, and prayed. Lira looked at all of us and said, "Whatever I have done for God, I want my family to triple it!" She was in a great deal of pain. We all hated to see her suffer.

I said to my dear sister, "It is time for you to go Home." She nodded her head.

I said, "When the Lord comes for you, go. Don't look back." She nodded her head again. I said, "Lira, you know when you always flew back and forth from Manila to Iloilo? You would text me on your cell phone that you made it safely? And I would always text back to you, "Praise the Lord"? She nodded her head. I said, "I want you to do that for me Lira. When you see Jesus, would you let me know? Can you smile or squeeze my hand so I will know you have safely arrived?" She nodded her head again.

Several hours later there was finally no pulse. We all stood around her bed and cried and prayed. Finally, one hour after the nurse told us Lira was dead, my sister suddenly smiled and squeezed my hand! I knew she was with God, and I leaned over and whispered in her ear, "Praise the Lord!"

Ask God to give you wisdom and compassion so you can help your people in their times of illness.

First and foremost, you can pray. Jesus is the Great Physician, and He can heal. The Bible says in James 5:14-16, *"Is any sick among you? let him call for the elders of the church; and let them pray over him, anointing him with oil in the name of the Lord: And the prayer of faith shall save the sick, and the Lord shall raise him up; and if he have committed sins, they shall be forgiven him. Confess your faults one to another, and pray one for another, that ye may be healed. The effectual fervent prayer of a righteous man availeth much."*

Secondly, help them financially. I know you cannot help everyone every time a need arises. Let the Holy Spirit guide you. I John 3:17: *"But whoso hath this world's good, and seeth his brother have need, and shutteth up his bowels of compassion from him, how dwelleth the love of God in him?"*

Thirdly, you can mobilize others to help. When a staff or student knocks on our door and tells us another staff member or a student is sick, my husband will tell that person to go around the dorms and to the staff to help raise money for the patient. Then he will also give. Our people should not depend on the missionary to take care of all their needs. Also, they need to learn to have compassion and a giving spirit, even though they are not as financially well off.

Chapter Four

𝒟epression

My dear friend, Mrs. Linda Vaprezsan, recently sent me a copy of Mrs. Cindy Schaap's new book, *Living on the Bright Side*. It is so good! The truth is, we all go through times of depression. Those times of depression may be related to hormones, emotions, or circumstances in our lives over which we have no control. For instance, December 2003 was Rachel's last Christmas home with us, as next year, Lord willing, she'll be away at Bible college. I tried my best to make it a very nice Christmas, but several outside influences (no doubt the Devil's doing!) tried to spoil everything. To me, it was a very depressing Christmas because of several problems which had to be dealt with, and also because I kept thinking, "This is Rachel's last Christmas." Unfulfilled dreams can cause depression.

We cannot control life's circumstances, but we can try to control our thinking with the help of the Holy Spirit. If you have negative thoughts, you are going to have negative feelings. Maybe we're feeling guilty about resisting God's will in our lives. Maybe there are times when we are even angry with God.

We can do as our pastor's wife, Mrs. Schaap, says in her book—sit around all the time having a pity party and saying, "Poor me!" Or we can choose to live on the bright side. Go to Him in prayer. He is the Healer of broken hearts!

One missionary wife wrote some excellent material on depression, and I would like to share her thoughts because people do face times of depression.

It has been my understanding, with the few experiences that I have had with missionaries who have left the field or have had depression on the field, that it was not one big thing that caused it, but a combination of small failures and simple frustrations that were built up to be a seemingly unconquerable obstacle. Of course, we know Satan will "blow up" any situation or frustration way out of proportion in order to discourage the Christian and cause failure in his life. If the missionary can guard some of the following areas, in my opinion, his chances for depression on the field will be diminished considerably.

1. **One cause of depression is financial struggles.** For instance, you may

encounter major vehicle problems and parts are much more expensive. Maybe the exchange rate will change, making your money worth less. Your house rent could go up. Sometimes churches in the States will have to drop your support or cut back for one reason or another. Whatever the case, you may find your finances are suddenly tighter. Maybe you don't even have the finances to return to the U.S. to raise more support!

One solution is to set aside money each month for your "furlough fund" so that you will have some money saved should you need to return to the United states unexpectedly. Another solution is to set aside money each month for "emergency" situations. Lastly, it is important to make sure that you communicate with missionaries already in your field of service and be sure you have enough support raised before you come. Of course, we know that we must trust the Lord to supply our needs, but we must use common sense in preparing and caring for our family. Let's not heedlessly give the Devil an opportunity to use finances as an avenue of depression and possible failure in our lives.

2. **Another cause of depression is health problems.** Because the modernization of the medical world is often lacking on the mission field, health problems can be a great burden. This area of our lives is something we must trust to the Lord; but once again, if we can live healthy lives, exercise, and watch our diet, we may be able to prevent many unnecessary problems. Also, if you are already aware of existing health problems in your family, make sure you bring plenty of the needed medicines with you to the field.

3. **Loneliness is often a cause of depression.** This cause may more often be the case for women than men because women generally need companionship, communication, and fellowship with other women. Sometimes, depending on your location and the proximity of other missionaries, you may find yourself totally isolated. Having a close and real relationship with God is so valuable in a case like this. Also, it is important to have a good "friend" relationship with your spouse. If you and your spouse share common interests and are willing to listen to each other and take time for each other, the loneliness can be greatly eased. Keeping busy, writing letters and e-mails to friends, and doing for others always helps to take your mind off loneliness. Many times, good books can be wonderful companions. Keep this thought in mind when you are packing for the field.

4. **Depression can be caused by extreme fatigue.** Many times we get so wrapped up in our ministries and other duties that we get plain worn out! It is important to take breaks and mini-vacations to get away occasionally. Choose one day a week that is set aside to rest and relax. You will find it difficult and maybe even impossible to take time for yourself; therefore, you *must* take time

for it. You will have a better outlook and attitude if you take a break or have a change of scenery for a while.

5. A lack of faith, or in other words, worry, can be a factor in depression. This problem was not as prevalent several years ago as I believe it is now. The long deputation process usually weeded out these people. Unfortunately, some missionaries have supported faith right out of missions. Trials and hardships build the Christian's faith. Let's face it—missionaries *will* have hardships; they will have frustrations, and they will have problems. It is better for a missionary to experience these before they get to the field so they can see how God worked through them, supplied their needs, and built their faith. Therefore, when hardships arise on the field, the missionary has a well-developed faith in God; and he can survive hardship. I am not saying I think everyone must have a hard time getting to the field, but God will get the missionary to the field in His time and when He deems the missionary ready. When the missionary does not have a strong faith in God, he will worry; worry can lead to depression.

6. Frustration over a seeming lack of success can cause depression. Some erroneously believe that success is measured in numbers. However, the missionary (as well as any full-time Christian worker) must see success as it is in God's eyes. The missionary should avoid the pressures to "measure up" to others back home or on other fields.

7. Language barriers can also lead to depression. If a missionary is older than most or has a difficult time learning the language and constantly struggles with what to say and trying to understand what is being said to him, it can get depressing. Throughout the world, English is becoming the worldwide language, giving missionaries the temptation not to be diligent in their language studies in their particular field. Just because a national can speak a little in English does not mean he will understand when you try to teach him a spiritual truth. If you work in a small village instead of a big city, you will soon learn the importance of linguistic skills. Lack of these skills can cause frustration and discouragement. I know one missionary who shared with me that he "faked" his ability to understand the locals and ended up agreeing to do certain things that he had no idea he was agreeing to do. Later it caused a great problem in that village when the missionary was unable to do what the nationals thought he had agreed to do. As a result, a good work could not be started in that village simply because of a lack of language skill. Imagine the discouragement of that missionary! Take the necessary time to learn the language, even if you need refresher courses each term or have to pay for a tutor to come to your home for a while.

8. Small, day-to-day frustrations can build up and can eventually

cause depression. Most of these frustrations are daily life in a third-world country. Sometimes, these situations may not seem to bother you. Other times, it can build up until you reach the "boiling point."

    A. The biggest problem in this area is situations when the missionary home is not a "haven" to come home to. Cultural frustrations meet you often as soon as you exit the gate of your house. Throughout any given day, a missionary couple might battle with corrupt government officials, struggle to be understood in the language as they witness, be bombarded with the extreme poverty of the people, and be constantly asked for a hand-out of food or money. After several hours of this, one needs to "get away." If your house is not a home—a haven—with a peaceful atmosphere, you can be sure frustration will invade your lives.

    B. In many third-world countries, it is necessary to have at least one worker on the premises, helping either as a gardener or as a maid in the house. If there are not proper instructions between the missionary and the national worker, the "haven" of the home can easily be disrupted.

    C. Working in a third-world country often with people who have no formal education, can lead to frustration. Many of these people, simply because of their "backwardness," do not have any of the common basic courtesies that we observe as a part of daily life. Without meaning to be, some can come across as rude, unthankful, even hateful. Since they have no sense of time, they don't respect your time. Without keeping in mind that you are there to reach these people with the Gospel and to train them, one can easily get frustrated enough to eventually fail. You must keep your eyes on the Lord and remember that your service is to Him.

    D. Things constantly break on the mission field. Unfortunately, since Wal-mart is not around the corner to replace what just broke, you go without. For instance, the refrigerator breaks. Who will you get to repair it? When you find a repairman from a neighboring town, who often arrives without tools, where will you get a spare part to fix it? More often than not, a spare part is non-existent or extremely expensive. One time a mouse got into the shed where we kept our washing machine and chewed through all the wires. Imagine all the time it took to rewire the entire machine. Then the electricity goes out, and you have an electric range, electric refrigerator, or electric water heater. As you might imagine, your home is paralyzed. The generator that you have is not working right, and even if it was, it would not be big enough to run everything. You go to call the electric company, and you find out your phone is out. When the electric company tried to fix the line, their truck ran over a water main that was not properly covered and broke the pipe, which shorted out the underground cable. Now you are without electricity, water, and a phone; nobody can tell you how long it will take before it all gets fixed. Welcome to the third world! "Fine," you think, "Let's go to the capital city and get a hotel for a few days." You get into your vehicle and head out of town. You make it five miles, and your car starts acting up. The engine stalls and cannot be restarted. Talk about frustration and discouragement! There have been times where we have been without all utilities, vehicle, and it seems, sanity!

One can easily see that without the call of God on one's life, these small frustrations can lead to failure and eventual disaster in the life of the missionary.

I saw myself many times in the excellent material this dear missionary sent. We must not let Satan have the victory in our life, be it through depression or in any other area. I John 5:4 says, *"For whatsoever is born of God overcometh the world: and this is the victory that overcometh the world, even our faith."*

Chapter Five

Taking Care of You and Your Husband

My husband wrote some suggestions about health in his book *Missionary Relationships at Home*. We often joke with each other about this because he is a "Coke-a-holic." However, I can't get after him too much because I am a "coffee-holic." The truth is, however, if we get sick, we cannot serve the Lord as effectively. Some illnesses have even caused missionaries to leave the field. We need to be good stewards of the body God gave us and remember it is the temple of the Holy Spirit, so it should be treated with respect. *"Know ye not that ye are the temple of God, and that the Spirit of God dwelleth in you?"* (I Corinthians 3:16)

In my husband's book, he mentions some areas about which we need to be careful concerning our body; namely, eating, sleeping, and exercising.

We need to start weaning ourselves off junk food and learn to enjoy raw fruits and vegetables, especially as we get older. The only vegetable Rick will eat is French fries and potato chips! (I am preaching to myself as well here!) I will not go into detail about this subject, as good reading materials on the market are plentiful regarding this subject. Take vitamins and get regular checkups. Most of us know what we are supposed to do or not do. However, I have found there is a difference between knowing and doing!

We also need to get the proper sleep. When Rick and I first came to the Philippines, we decided not to buy an air conditioner. An older and wiser missionary advised us that we needed to do so because the tropical heat saps your strength. We soon learned he was right. We bought one for our bedroom, and it has helped tremendously. If I can get out of the heat in the middle of the day and take a nap, or read, or even sit in the air-conditioned room to get my paperwork done, I can get more done throughout the rest of the day. If I do not take time out, the rest of my day is usually useless because I am so tired and drained.

Exercise is very important to keep us from being overweight. If you are overweight, discipline yourself to lose the weight and then keep it off through proper diet and exercise. Plenty of help is available for you to read if you have a problem with weight. Basically, the material boils down to two facts—eat less and exercise more! The motivating force behind weight loss is attitude, which should be controlled by the Holy Spirit. The Bible says, *"I can do all things through Christ which strengtheneth me."* (Philippians 4:13)

Adoniram and Ann Judson, missionaries to Burma in the 1800s, often rode horses for their exercise. Both believed this form of exercise tremendously boosted their health. My husband plays basketball a couple of times a week, and the doctor said his heart is in great shape. I walk. If you can't do anything else, you can at least get out and walk. You can even try doing exercises in the privacy of your home.

In my own life I have found that, in the past, I have been so extremely busy with the Lord's work that I have not been careful with our eating habits. I was perfectly satisfied whenever my husband or I needed to make a trip downtown, just to bring back a burger so I wouldn't have to worry with lunch or supper. We could then continue on with our work uninterrupted.

In recent years, however, I am finding that as we are getting older, it is harder for us to live that fast-paced life without proper meal preparation. If I need to give up some things in order to take better care of my health, and especially my husband's health, I need to do that. No one else can be Rick Martin's wife except me, and it is my responsibility to take care of him. No one else can take the place of my husband and his important work that God has given him. It is better that I relinquish some of my church responsibilities to someone else while I make time to take better care of him. Let's take care of the temple of the Holy Spirit. (I Corinthians 6:19) *"What? know ye not that your body is the temple of the Holy Ghost which is in you, which ye have of God, and ye are not your own?"*

Chapter Six

Returning to America for Medical Problems

When it seems the only solution for medical problems is to return to the States, you and your husband need to pray and ask God for wisdom. Perhaps you need to seek advice from your mission board, from your home pastor, a trusted friend, or your doctor. Your choice will largely depend on the country you are in and what kind of medical care is available.

I will never forget when my dear friend, Suzie Heidenreich, went for an ultrasound here in Iloilo City. Brother Steve and Suzie lived one hour from us where they had started a church and Bible college.

Suzie had recently had a hysterectomy, and she explained to the technician that the hysterectomy had been done in America. Because that particular surgery is now so commonplace in the States, the surgery left only a small scar. The technicians and nurses simply could not believe that Suzie had had this operation because she did not have a large scar!

Brother Steve patiently waited outside for Suzie's procedure to be finished. When she came out, he asked, "Well, what did they say?"

"Steve, you better sit down," Suzie said. "I have stunning news."

Brother Steve, no doubt scared to death, asked: "What?!"

Suzie said, "They said I'm pregnant."

Of course, this diagnosis was totally ridiculous because Suzie had had a hysterectomy! We all had a good laugh over that particular diagnosis, but situations comparable to this can make a person very frustrated. You may feel like you don't even want to have a splinter removed after a story like that. However, for the most part, we have had very good health care in the Philippines.

I have had an ovarian cyst removed, and I delivered two babies through Caesarean section here in the Philippines. I also had a ruptured tubal pregnancy and probably would have died if it had not been for the excellent care of my doctor. When I was about two months pregnant and Ricky was about two years old, I passed out one morning as I was getting ready for class. Since I knew I was pregnant, I just chalked it up to morning sickness and went back to bed. Little did I know that as I rested in bed all morning, I was bleeding internally. My husband insisted that I go to the doctor, but I simply could not get out of bed.

Finally, since we did not have a telephone, he went to my doctor's clinic and told her what happened. She immediately left all of her patients, jumped in her car, and drove to my house. She later told me that when she walked into our bedroom and saw me, she thought I was not going to survive. My husband carried me to her car, and she drove me to the hospital as fast as she could. She asked my husband, "Why did you wait so long?" To make a long story short, it is obvious that I didn't die! I know that God was very good to give us such a great doctor.

My husband had knee surgery performed in America when the doctor here honestly told him that it needed to be scoped. That kind of surgery is not performed in the Philippines.

One advantage of having some procedures done in the Philippines is that the doctors here and in other third-world countries can be much more knowledgeable about tropical diseases. They deal with diseases like dengue fever, typhoid and typhus fever, malaria, certain kinds of amoebas and parasites, dysentery, hepatitis, yellow fever, tuberculosis, and many others. A doctor in America may never come in contact with any of the diseases that plague a foreign country.

Two men who graduated from our Bible college, Leny Funtecha and Juanito Genada, along with their families, are missionaries in Haiti. Two other graduates, Mario Genada and Josue Satunero, and their families are missionaries in Africa. Brother Mario is in Zambia, and Brother Josue is in Uganda.

I often receive e-mails from these precious friends, asking us to pray for their children who are often sick. Probably their biggest problem is malaria, and my heart goes out to them. They have had to learn to trust God in a great way. Brother Mario's wife Dianah recently gave birth to twin girls in Zambia. These babies, along with her two older children, often suffer from malaria. She told me that God graciously gave them an excellent doctor who is from India. This man is a Christian and will not accept any payment for his services. I rejoiced that God heard the prayer of a little Filipina mother in the heart of Africa. How pleased the Lord must have been when Mario and Dianah answered His call to go to the regions beyond. Yes, there are trials and testings and illness, but He sent a Christian doctor, who happens to be an expert in malaria, to see them through those times.

Another advantage of having some procedures done in the Philippines (or your field of service) is the cost. We have to spend a lot of money for our tickets to go home, and the cost of medical care in the States has skyrocketed. Our insurance covers most of the medical expenses we have done on the field because the procedures are much cheaper. By far, the biggest medical incident in our family's history was Rachel's heart problem. Of course, there are emergencies, such as a ruptured appendix, where a person simply cannot just jump on a plane and fly home.

Chapter Seven

Controlling Your Attitude Toward Your Medical Problems

I am devoting a whole chapter to "attitude," and I do want to make a few additional comments. What is your attitude regarding sickness? No doubt, some missionaries are looking for the tiniest excuse to quit the mission field and go home. I'm sure that type of missionary is rare. Most are devoted people who have simply tried to do God's will, and illness is a price they have had to pay.

Definitely, some people have no choice but to go home because of medical conditions. However, some situations rest totally on our attitude. If God wants you to stay on the field, He will make a way. Don't turn aside from His will.

After Rachel had her heart surgery and was recovering, this question hit us: Now what do we do?

First of all, we were facing huge bills. The bill for the Air Force Medi-Vac alone was over $5,000. Rachel's heart surgery at Children's was over $20,000. We also had to consider the airfare charges for Rick, Ricky, and me.

Secondly, and more importantly, could we possibly take such a sick child back to the mission field? It would have been easy to say, "No!" Honestly, I was scared to death. Then God gently reminded me, "Haven't I taken care of Rachel so far? Can't you trust Me to finish the job?"

Have you heard the saying, "God is good, and He's good all the time?" He is not just good when things are going our way; He's good even when things are not going our way.

I argued with the Lord. Did He actually want us to take such a sick baby to a third-world country full of disease, where the hospitals were inadequate? Then the Lord reminded me, "Didn't you give Rachel to Me?"

We waited for His leading. A few days after all the days of contemplating His perfect will, Rachel was doing beautifully. We asked Dr. Razook, "When do you think we can take Rachel home?" We were expecting a shocked look and this answer: "Are you nuts? You're surely not taking this baby to the Philippines are you?" Instead, he asked about our city and the kind of medical care available. We explained that we had a fairly good hospital and that Rachel's pediatric cardiologist was trained in Japan. He was surprised that there was even a pediatric cardiologist in our city. He asked if we would be able to fly Rachel back to the United States for regular checkups. We told him we would do that. We didn't know how we were going to pay for it, so we were going by faith in making that promise.

He said, "Let her stay in America for one month so I can make sure she's doing all right. Then you can take her back to the Philippines as long as her cardiologist in Iloilo keeps a close watch on her. Bring her back here in six months." We were amazed! With that hurdle conquered, we faced the huge financial battle.

I sent the Air Force a check for $1,000, explaining our entire situation. I told them we could not pay the whole amount now but promised we would make payments until it was paid in full. Guess what? The Air Force sent back our $1,000 and said it was gratis! As for Rachel's medical bills, much was taken care of with generous love offerings from God's people all over America. Dr. Jim Vineyard, of Windsor Hills Baptist Church in Oklahoma City, paid the round trip fares for Rick, Ricky, and me. Our pastor, Dr. Jack Hyles, and the First Baptist Church of Hammond, Indiana, gave us an extremely generous love offering to help with the other bills. Countless others also helped. God was obviously opening the doors for us to be able to return to the mission field.

I am amazed when I look back and remember all the miracles involved. The procedure performed on Rachel was fairly new. If she had been born a couple of years before, she probably would have died. Clark Air Force Base closed shortly after Rachel's birth, partly due to the eruption of the Mt. Pinatubo volcano. If she had been born a couple of years later, more than likely, she could not have been put on the Medi-Vac. She would have died in that Manila Hospital. Mickey Edwards retired from Congress shortly after Rachel's surgery. Who else would Connie and Bill know to contact who was in a position to call Clark Air Force Base and ask for this favor? When Rachel arrived at Children's Hospital and had all the preliminary tests done, the doctors and surgeons found three critical heart defects—not just one. If they had gone ahead and performed emergency surgery at Clark Air Force Base, without first correcting the other defects, she would have died at the base hospital. A year after she was born, Dr. Bradley Yoder was transferred to another base. Perhaps another doctor would have gone ahead and tried to perform the surgery on her. All these thoughts kept going around and around in my mind as I kept asking God why He allowed this to happen to Rachel. God could have let Rachel be born without a heart defect, but if our lives are trouble free all the time, how can God teach us anything? If we have no problems, how can we learn to trust Him? If everything is good all the time—you know how it is—we don't need Him! It is when trials come that we learn to lean on Him. When we are going through the fires, that is when the Lord reveals Himself to us and shows us His miracles. He held our hand the whole way and continues to do so.

When the newborn baby arrived at Tinker Air Force Base in Oklahoma City all by her tiny self, a television camera crew was there to meet her. One article said, "Tinker officials said a three-foot incubator was a strange sight in the plane's cavernous cargo hold. The baby was accompanied from the Philippines by Dr. Harry Law, a lieutenant colonel and pediatrician from Clark Air Base in the Philippines." Rachel was on the nightly news three days in a row, as well as on the front page of the local newspaper. Radio stations were calling for interviews. The following clippings are some articles published about her.

Flight to U.S., City Surgeons Rescue Infant

By Jim Killackey

A surgical team at Oklahoma Children's Memorial Hospital operated for five hours Thursday to correct life-threatening heart defects in an 18-day-old daughter of missionaries in the Philippines.

"The operation has been a success," Dr. Webb Thompson, a pediatric cardiologist at Children's, said.

The critically ill baby was brought from the Philippines to Oklahoma City on an Air Force C-141 Starlifter Medivac transport.

The baby, Rachel Martin, had suffered from two heart defects that would have killed her. She was reported in critical condition late Thursday.

Thompson said surgeons corrected a condition known as aortic stenosis, in which there was a narrowing of the aortic valve. The valve separates the heart's left ventricle from the aorta, which carries blood from the heart to branch arteries.

The baby also suffered from a narrowing of the aorta.

"Both problems were repaired," Thompson said. Surgeons at the hospital perform eight to 10 such operations a year.

The child's survival chances are good, although another operation may be necessary later, the physician said.

Rachel is the daughter of Becky and Richard Martin, Baptist missionaries who have lived on the Philippine island of Panay for the past eight years. Martin is a native of Miami, OK.

The infant began to turn blue four days after her birth 400 miles outside Manila. She originally was treated in the Philippines, but a decision was made to seek specialized care at Oklahoma Children's Memorial Hospital, one of two hospitals in the United States reported-

See BABY, Page 2

Baby ——

From Page 1

ly equiped to deal with the baby's ailment.

The medivac flight was arranged by Connie Graves, wife of state Rep. Bill Graves, R-Oklahoma City, and Larry Lesser, an aide to U.S. Rep. Mickey Edwards, R-Oklahoma City.

Connie Graves is the baby's aunt.

The plane carrying the baby arrived at Tinker Air Force Base from San Francisco at 4 a.m. Thursday. The jet had made previous stops in Guam and Hawaii to drop off other patients.

Tinker officials said a three-foot incubator was a strange sight in the plane's cavernous cargo hold. The baby was accompanied from the Philippines by Dr. Harry Law, a lieutenant colonel and pediatrician from Clark Air Base in the Philippines.

Meanwhile, the Martins were expected to arrive in Oklahoma City from the Philippines late Thursday.

Critically Sick Infant Being Flown to City

By Anthony Thornton

An emergency medical plane is expected to land at Tinker Air Force Base early this morning to transport a critically ill American baby from the Philippines to Oklahoma City.

Seventeen-day-old Rachel Martin, who developed heart problems soon after she was born, was given a slim chance of survival by Philippine doctors unless she was given specialized care at an American hospital. She will be taken to Oklahoma Children's Memorial Hospital, one of two hospitals in the country said to be able to handle her special needs.

"This has been the result of much prayer," the baby's aunt, Connie Graves of Oklahoma City, said Wednesday.

The baby girl is the daughter of Richard Martin, a Miami, OK, native and Baptist missionary who has lived on the Philippine island of Panai for the last eight years.

Rachel was born in perfect health, but she began to turn blue after four days, Graves said. She was diagnosed as having aortic stignosis, a rare heart problem among infants.

"They took her to the Asian Heart Center, which is supposed to be the best place for her in the Philippines," Graves said. "But they don't specialize in pediatrics ...

"The doctors said she's a very sick baby," Graves said. "I know they're bringing her here because it's very critical."

Graves, the wife of state Rep. Bill Graves, said she arranged the U.S. Air Force Medivac flight last week through U.S. Rep. Mickey Edwards, D-Oklahoma City.

An Edwards' aide, Larry Lesser, who deals regularly with the armed forces, reserved spots on a Medivac C-141 plane for both Rachel and her pediatrician.

The plane made stops in Guam and Hawaii to drop off other patients before flying to Travis Air Force Base in California Wednesday night. Rachel spent seven hours in the intensive care unit of the base hospital there while doctors stabilized her condition.

The plane was scheduled to leave there at 11 p.m. PST (1 a.m. Oklahoma time) and land at Tinker between 4 and 5 a.m.

Missionary Parents Join Recovering Infant

By Jim Killackey

From Iloilo Baptist Church in the Philippines to the intensive care waiting room at Oklahoma Children's Memorial Hospital in Oklahoma City is a distance of more than 8,500 miles.

Baptist missionaries Richard and Becky Martin said Friday the long trip was worth it — to them and the life of their newborn daughter.

The baby, Rachel Martin, was doing well Friday after life-saving heart surgery Thursday at Children's.

The 19-day-old child was flown from the Philippines to Oklahoma City in an Air Force C-141 Starlifter Medivac transport on Wednesday. Her parents arrived in Oklahoma City late Thursday, and spent most of Friday with their child in the intensive care unit at Children's.

"We want to thank everyone for their prayers," Becky Martin said.

Rachel had suffered from two heart defects that would have killed her.

Martin said Friday that doctors in the Philippines didn't give the baby any chance unless surgery could be performed in the United States.

Martin, a 1970 graduate of Miami, OK, High School, contacted relatives in Oklahoma City and arrangements were made for the medivac and subsequent surgery.

Martin and his wife met while they attended Ozark Bible College in Joplin, Mo.

After graduate work in Hyles Anderson College in Indiana, the couple became missionaries in the Philippines.

For the past 8½ years, the couple has lived on the island of Panay, about 400 miles from Manila.

Martin is pastor of the Iloilo Baptist Church, and the couple works extensively with the deaf, blind and mentally retarded.

During their first six years in the Philippines, the Martins did not return to the United States. They have another child, Richard Jr., 7.

Friday, Rachel Martin was taken off a ventilator and was "progressing well," said Dr. Ronald Elkins, chief of cardiovascular surgery at Children's.

Surgeons repaired a malfunctioning valve in the infant's heart and a narrowing of the aorta.

The Martins will be in Oklahoma City for an indefinite period during their child's recovery.

Further surgery may be required later.

Martin said the family will return to the Philippines to continue missionary work there.

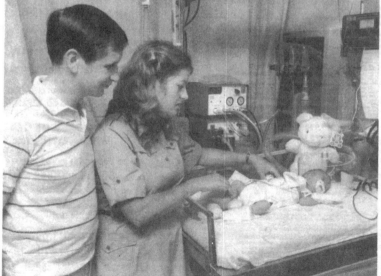

— Staff Photo by George R. Wilson

Richard and Becky Martin check on their daughter, Rachel, in the intensive care unit at Oklahoma Children's Memorial Hospital.

The People Speak

Little Rachel Held in Loving Arms

TO THE EDITOR:

So many people here in Oklahoma City have helped out little baby Rachel Martin from the very moment she was flown here for open heart surgery from the Philippines, and we want to express our thanks to them.

First, we want to thank Dr. Ronald Elkins, the chief surgeon, and his medical team at Oklahoma Children's Memorial Hospital, and Dr. Jerry Razook, the cardiologist. These doctors typify the kind of physicians needed in such a difficult task as this one.

Drs. Elkins and Razook, from the time we first contacted them from the Philippines, interrupted their busy schedules to prepare for the possible arrival of Rachel. In an age when doctors are so often sued unjustifiably for malpractice and are extremely cautious in getting involved, Drs. Elkins and Razook courageously made the decision to give a dying baby a chance for life. It was not only their skill, but also their courage that saved Rachel's life. She is recovering from double open heart surgery and doing well.

Oklahoma Children's Memorial Hospital is very special because it is equipped as only a few hospitals are to help children with unusual heart diseases. It is also special because of the loving concern the hospital staff has for children. We were pleasantly overwhelmed by the care the staff gives to the sick children here.

None of the above would have been possible for Rachel, but for Congressman Mickey Edwards who immediately responded to the call of my sister, Connie Graves, to have Rachel flown here. When I called to thank Congressman Edwards for his help in arranging the Air Force flight that brought Rachel to Oklahoma City, he said, "There are a few times when I've felt I had the opportunity to do something that really counted, and this was one of those times. I am so glad I could help."

Our thanks also to Gen. William P. Bowden and his staff at Tinker Air Force Base, who coordinated the arrival of the Medi-Vac flight that brought Rachel here.

The Oklahoma City news media, both electronic and print, deserve great credit for making the churches and people of Oklahoma aware of Rachel's story. Their prayers made the difference, because in the end it was God who healed little Rachel.

Rick and Becky Martin, City

Author's Note: This is my favorite article which my husband wrote to the paper and which was subsequently published.

Conclusion

A s of this writing, our beautiful daughter will be graduating from high school in a few months. She is planning, Lord willing, to go to Bible college in the fall of 2004. She loves God and wants to serve Him with her life. I know He has something very special planned for her.

My message to her is:

"Trust in the LORD with all thine heart; and lean not unto thine own understanding. In all thy ways acknowledge him, and he shall direct thy paths."

(Proverbs 3:5, 6)

I love you, Sweetheart!

Above: Dr. Jerry Razook, the best pediatric cardiologist in the world (in my unbiased opinion!) with Rachel

Below: Rick with Dr. Jack Hyles, the pastor of First Baptist Church of Hammond, Indiana, from 1959-2001

Endnotes

UNIT ONE — YOUR ATTITUDE

Chapter 4
[1] Rosalind Goforth, *Goforth of China* (Pasig City, Phil.: Lifeline Philippines, 2003), 278.

Chapter 5
[1] Isabel Kuhn, *In the Arena* (Chicago: Moody Press, 1958), 110.
[2] Mrs. Howard Taylor, *The Triumph of John and Betty Stam* (Philadelphia: China Inland Mission, 1960), 45.
[3] Taylor, *Triumph*, 96.
[4] Taylor, *Triumph*, 103-104.
[5] Taylor, *Triumph*, 118.
[6] Taylor, *Triumph*, 119.
[7] Taylor, *Triumph*, 120-121.

Chapter 11
[1] Joy Guinness, *Mrs. Howard Taylor—Her Web of Time* (London: China Inland Mission, 1952) 139.
[2] Guinness, *Mrs. Howard Taylor*, 246-247.

UNIT TWO — YOUR WALK WITH GOD

Chapter 1
[1] Jose Mandoriano, *The Hour Before Sunset* (Butler, Ind.: Higley Press, 1957), 89-90.

Chapter 2
[1] Joy Turner Tuggy, *The Missionary Wife and Her Work* (Chicago: Moody Press, 1970), 19.
[2] Courtney Anderson, *To the Golden Shore* (Boston: Little, Brown and Company, 1956) 385.
[3] Anderson, *To the Golden Shore*, 400-401.
[4] Anderson, *To the Golden Shore*, 412.
[5] Anderson, *To the Golden Shore*, 413.
[6] Anderson, *To the Golden Shore*, 415.
[7] Anderson, *To the Golden Shore*, 416.
[8] Anderson, *To the Golden Shore*, 436.

[9] Anderson, *To the Golden Shore*, 437.

[10] Anderson, *To the Golden Shore*, 439-440.

[11] B. H. Pearson, *The Vision Lives* (Westchester, Ill.: Good News Publishers, 1967), 6.

[12] Pearson, *The Vision Lives*, 15-16.

[13] Pearson, *The Vision Lives*, 17-18.

[14] Pearson, *The Vision Lives*, 21.

[15] Pearson, *The Vision Lives*, 32.

[16] Pearson, *The Vision Lives*, 32.

[17] Pearson, *The Vision Lives*, 36.

[18] Pearson, *The Vision Lives*, 39.

[19] Pearson, *The Vision Lives*, 42.

[20] Pearson, *The Vision Lives*, 60.

Chapter 3

[1] Jack T. Chick, *The Next Step for Growing Christians* (Chino, Cal.: Chick Publications, 1973), 18-19.

[2] James Ray, *Incredible Journey in the Steps of Greatness* (Chattanooga, Tenn.: BIMI Publications, International, 2000), 179.

[3] Ray, *Incredible Journey*, 180.

Chapter 5

[1] Kuhn, *In the Arena*, 44-48.

Chapter 6

[1] Rosalind Goforth, *Climbing* (Manila: Lifeline Philippines, n.d.), 99-102.

[2] Mrs. Howard Taylor, *Her Web of Time by Joy Guinness*, 102-103.

Conclusion

[1] Goforth, *Climbing*, 194-198.

UNIT THREE — YOUR HUSBAND

Introduction

[1] Dr. and Mrs. Howard Taylor, *Hudson Taylor—God's Man in China* (Chicago: Moody Press, 1987) 127.

[2] Taylor, *Hudson Taylor*, 129.

[3] Taylor, *Hudson Taylor*, 129.

[4] Taylor, *Hudson Taylor*, 129.

[5] Taylor, *Hudson Taylor*, 129.

[6] Taylor, *Hudson Taylor*, 129-132.

[7] Ruth Tucker, *From Jerusalem to Irian Jaya* (Grand Rapids, Mich.: Zondervan Publishing House, 1983), 178.

[8] Tucker, *From Jerusalem to Irian Jaya*, 179.

[9] Tucker, *From Jerusalem to Irian Jaya*, 179.

Chapter 1

[1] Frank Norris, *Inside History of First Baptist Church, Fort Worth, and Temple Baptist Church, Detroit* (Fort Worth: n.p., 1938), 38.

[2] Norris, *Inside History*, 38.

[3] Norris, *Inside History*, 40.

[4] Louis Entzminger, *The J. Frank Norris I Have Known for 34 Years* (St. John, Ind.: Christian Book Gallery, n.d.), 48-49.

[5] Entzminger, *J. F. Norris*, 48.

[6] Entzminger, *J. F. Norris*, 49.

[7] Entzminger, *J. F. Norris*, 50.

Chapter 4

[1] Gurdon Langley Hall, *Golden Boats from Burma* (Philadelphia: Macrae Smith Company, 1961), 235.

Chapter 5

[1] Tucker, *From Jerusalem to Irian Jaya*, 116.

[2] Tucker, *From Jerusalem to Irian Jaya*, 117-119.

[3] Ray, *Incredible Journey*.

[4] Tucker, *From Jerusalem to Irian Jaya*, 119.

[5] John B. Myers, *William Carey* (London: S. S. Partridge & Co., n.d.) 99-100.

Chapter 8

[1] Rosalind Goforth, *Goforth of China* (Minneapolis: Bethany House Publications, 1987), 47.

[2] Goforth, *Goforth of China*, 49.

[3] Goforth, *Goforth of China*, 49.

[4] Goforth, *Goforth of China*, 49.

Chapter 9

[1] Rick Martin, *Missionary Relationships at Home* (Iloilo City, Philippines: Iloilo Baptist Church, 2003), 47.

Chapter 10

[1] Joy Turner Tuggy, *The Missionary and Her Work*, 40-47.

Chapter 11

[1] Jack Hyles, *Meet the Holy Spirit* (Manila: Lifeline Press, n.d.), 212.

Chapter 12

[1] Jim Vineyard, *Fundamental Baptist World Missions* (Oklahoma City: Windsor Hills Baptist Church, October, 1997), 31.

[2] Vineyard, *Fundamental Baptist World Missions*, 27.

[3] Vineyard, *Fundamental Baptist World Missions*, 26.

[4] Vineyard, *Fundamental Baptist World Missions*, 26.

[6] Vineyard, *Fundamental Baptist World Missions*, 17.

Conclusion

[1] Tucker, *From Jerusalem to Irian Jaya*, 173.

[2] Taylor, *Hudson Taylor*, 220-221

UNIT FOUR — CHILDREN

Introduction

[1] Winifred Mathews, *Dauntless Women* (New York: Friendship Press, 1974), 33.

[2] Tucker, *From Jerusalem to Irian Jaya*, 144.
[3] Tucker, *From Jerusalem to Irian Jaya*, 145.
[4] Ethel Daniels Hubbard, *The Moffats* (Shoals, Ind.: Old Paths Tract Society, n.d.), 133.
[5] Tucker, *From Jerusalem to Irian Jaya*, 148.
[6] R. J. Campbell, *Livingstone* (New York: Dodd, Mead, and Company, 1930), 71.
[7] Mathews, *Dauntless Women*, 52.
[8] Campbell, *Livingstone*, 71.
[9] Tucker, *From Jerusalem to Irian Jaya*, 149-150.
[10] Mathews, *Dauntless Women*, 56.
[11] Mathews, *Dauntless Women*, 59.
[12] Mathews, *Dauntless Women*, 61-62.
[13] Mathews, *Dauntless Women*, 65.
[14] Campbell, *Livingstone*, 71.
[15] Mathews, *Dauntless Women*, 67.
[16] Campbell, *Livingstone*, 75.
[17] Hubbard, *The Moffatts*, 150.
[18] Mathews, *Dauntless Women*, 71.
[19] Campbell, *Livingstone*, 71.
[20] Mathews, *Dauntless Women*, 71-72.
[21] Tucker, *From Jerusalem to Irian Jaya*, 146.
[22] Mathews, *Dauntless Women*, 49.
[23] Tucker, *From Jerusalem to Irian Jaya*, 151.
[24] Tucker, *From Jerusalem to Irian Jaya*, 152.
[25] Tucker, *From Jerusalem to Irian Jaya*, 153.

Chapter 1
[1] Tuggy, *The Missionary Wife*, 96.
[2] Rick Martin, *Missionary Relationships at Home*, 1.

Chapter 2
[1] Tuggy, *The Missionary Wife*, 81.
[2] Kuhn, *In the Arena*, 67.

Chapter 4
[1] Tuggy, *The Missionary Wife*, 81.

Chapter 8
[1] Tuggy, *The Missionary Wife*, 10-11.
[2] Tucker, *From Jerusalem to Irian Jaya*, 332.
[3] Kathleen White, *John and Betty Stam* (Minneapolis: Bethany House Publishing, 1989), 41.
[4] Martin, *Missionary Relationships at Home*, 5-6.
[5] Martin, *Missionary Relationships at Home*, 6-7.
[6] Martin, *Missionary Relationships at Home*, 3-4.

Conclusion
[1] Ray, *Incredible Journey*, 83.
[2] Ray, *Incredible Journey*, 83.

[3] Ray, *Incredible Journey*, 83.
[4] Ray, *Incredible Journey*, 84.
[5] Ray, *Incredible Journey*, 84.
[6] Ray, *Incredible Journey*, 85.

UNIT FIVE — MINISTRY
Introduction
[1] Evelyn Stenbock, *Miss Terri* (Lincoln: Good News Broadcasting Association, n.d.) 29.
[2] Stenbock, *Miss Terri*, 15-16.
[3] Stenbock, *Miss Terri*, 45.

Chapter 1
[1] Goforth, *Climbing*, 76-78.

Chapter 3
[1] Tucker, *From Jerusalem to Irian Jaya*, 205.
[2] E. Myers Harrison, *Blazing the Missionary Trail* (Wheaton, Ill.: Van Kampen Press, n.d.) 101-102.
[3] Harrison, *Blazing the Missionary Trail*, 105.

Chapter 4
[1] Mathews, *Dauntless Women*, 108.
[2] Mathews, *Dauntless Women*, 110.
[3] Mathews, *Dauntless Women*, 127-140.
[4] Mathews, *Dauntless Women*, 168-169.

Chapter 5
[1] Frank L. Houghton, *Amy Carmichael of Dohnavur* (Ft. Washington, Penna.: Christian Literature Crusade, 1979), flyleaf.
[2] Tucker, *From Jerusalem to Irian Jaya*, 254.

Chapter 6
[1] Rosalind Goforth, *Goforth of China*, 222.

Conclusion
[1] Stenbock, *Miss Terri*, 53.
[2] Stenbock, *Miss Terri*, 54.
[3] Stenbock, *Miss Terri*, 74-77.
[4] Stenbock, *Miss Terri*, 79-82.
[5] Stenbock, *Miss Terri*, 86.
[6] Stenbock, *Miss Terri*, 91.
[7] Patrick Johnstone, *Operation World* (1993 ed.; Grand Rapids: Zondervan Publishing House, 1993), 392.
[8] Johnstone, *Operation World*, 393.

UNIT SIX — RELATIONSHIPS
Introduction

[1] Tucker, *From Jerusalem to Irian Jaya*, 101.
[2] T. D. Allen, *Doctor in Buckskin* (New York: Harper and Brothers, 1951), 212-215.
[3] Tucker, *From Jerusalem to Irian Jaya*, 103.

Chapter Four
[1] Imogene Carlson, *American Family Interned, WWII* (Cebu City, Philippines: Cebu Christian Mission, 1979), 161.
[2] Guinness, *Mrs. Howard Taylor*, 156-157.

Chapter Five
[1] Joe Finn, *In Our Time—An Interview with a Missionary*, Dec. 1998, 33.
[2] Joe Finn, *In Our Time—An Interview with a Missionary*, Dec. 1998, 34.
[3] Edith Buxton, *Reluctant Missionary* (London: Hodder and Stoughton, 1968), 114-118.
[4] Buxton, *Reluctant Missionary*, 118-120.

Chapter 6
[1] Tucker, *From Jerusalem to Irian Jaya*, 295.
[2] Tucker, *From Jerusalem to Irian Jaya*, 296.
[3] Tucker, *From Jerusalem to Irian Jaya*, 297.
[4] Rosalind Goforth, *Climbing* (Grand Rapids: Zondervan Publishing House, 1940), 22-23.
[5] Isobel Kuhn, *In the Arena* (Chicago: Moody Press, 1958), 13-15.
[6] Ray, *Incredible Journey*, 90.

UNIT SEVEN — LANGUAGE AND CULTURE
Introduction
[1] Maria Nilsen, *Malla Moe* (Chicago: Moody Press, 1966), 27.
[2] Nilsen, *Malla Moe*, 29.
[3] Nilsen, *Malla Moe*, 32.
[4] Nilsen, *Malla Moe*, 32-33.
[5] Nilsen, *Malla Moe*, 34.
[6] Nilsen, *Malla Moe*, 37.
[7] Nilsen, *Malla Moe*, 39.
[8] Nilsen, *Malla Moe*, 41.

Chapter 1
[1] Russell Hitt, *Sensi—The Life Story of Irene Webster-Smith* (Lincoln: ICM Press, 2003), 34-36.
[2] Thomas Hale, *On Being a Missionary* (Pasadena, Cal.: William Carey Library, 1995), 94-95.

Chapter 2
[1] Joy Guinness, *Mrs. Howard Taylor — Her Web of Time* (London: China Inland Mission, 1952), 88.
[2] Guinness, *Her Web of Time*, 88.
[3] Guinness, *Her Web of Time*, 121.

Chapter 4

[1] Hale, *On Being a Missionary*, 62-87.
[2] Hale, *On Being a Missionary*, 89-93.

Chapter 5

[1] Verda Peet, *Sometimes I Prefer to Fuss* (Singapore: Overseas Missionary Fellowship, 1985), 33-36.
[2] Peet, *Sometimes I Prefer to Fuss*, 33-34.
[3] Peet, *Sometimes I Prefer to Fuss*, 34.
[4] Peet, *Sometimes I Prefer to Fuss*, 36.

Conclusion

[1] Nilsen, *Malla Moe*, 71-72.
[2] Nilsen, *Malla Moe*, 72.
[3] Nilsen, *Malla Moe*, 73.
[4] Nilsen, *Malla Moe*, 87-88.
[5] Nilsen, *Malla Moe*, 89.
[6] Nilsen, *Malla Moe*, 97-98.
[7] Nilsen, *Malla Moe*, 132.
[8] Nilsen, *Malla Moe*, 171.
[9] Nilsen, *Malla Moe*, 172.
[10] Nilsen, *Malla Moe*, 148.
[11] Nilsen, *Malla Moe*, 149-150.
[12] Nilsen, *Malla Moe*, 150.
[13] Nilsen, *Malla Moe*, 150.
[14] Nilsen, *Malla Moe*, 151.
[15] Nilsen, *Malla Moe*, 167-169.
[16] Nilsen, *Malla Moe*, 172-173.

UNIT 8 — FINANCES, DEPUTATION, FURLOUGH

Introduction

[1] Vance Christie, *Hudson Taylor: Founder, China Inland Mission* (Uhrichsville, Oh.: Barbour Publishing, Inc., n.d.), 32.
[2] Christie, *Hudson Taylor*, 38.
[3] Christie, *Hudson Taylor*, 69.
[4] Christie, *Hudson Taylor*, 127.
[5] Christie, *Hudson Taylor*, 133.
[6] Christie, *Hudson Taylor*, 135.
[7] Christie, *Hudson Taylor*, 137.
[8] Christie, *Hudson Taylor*, 143.
[9] Christie, *Hudson Taylor*, 185.

Chapter 1

[1] Mrs. Charles E. Cowman, *Charles E. Cowman: Missionary Warrior* (Los Angeles, The Oriental Missionary Society, n.d.), 252-253.

[2] Norman Grubb, *After C.T. Studd* (Grand Rapids: Zondervan Publishing House, 1946), 18.

Chapter 4
[1] Tom Vineyard, *Fundamental Baptist Mission*, May 1998, 29.

Conclusion
[1] Rosalind Goforth, *How I Know God Answers Prayer* (Pasig City, Philippines: Lifeline Philippines, n.d.), 81-83.
[2] Goforth, *Goforth of China*, 220-230.

UNIT NINE — MEDICAL CONCERNS
Chapter 1
[1] Goforth, *Goforth of China*, 156-157.
[2] Goforth, *How I Know God Answers Prayer*, 67.
[3] Tuggy, *The Missionary Wife and Her Work*, 87.

Chapter 2
[1] Joseph Gonzalez, *The Good Health Fact Book* (Project ed.; Pleasantville, NY: The Reader's Digest Association, Inc., 1992), 229.

Sources Consulted

Allen, T. D. *Doctor in Buckskin*. New York: Harper and Brothers, 1951.

Anderson, Courtney. *To the Golden Shore*. Boston: Little, Brown and Company, 1956.

Buxton, Edith. *Reluctant Missionary*. London: Hodder and Stoughton, 1968.

Campbell, R. J. *Livingstone*. New York: Dodd, Mead, and Company, 1930.

Carlson, Imogene. *American Family Interned, WWII*. Cebu City, Philippines: Cebu Christian Mission, 1979.

Chick, Jack T. *The Next Step for Growing Christians*. Chino, Cal.: Chick Publications, 1973.

Christie, Vance. *Hudson Taylor: Founder, China Inland Mission*. Uhrichsville, Oh.: Barbour Publishing, Inc., n.d.

Cowman, Mrs. Charles E. *Charles E. Cowman: Missionary Warrior*. Los Angeles, The Oriental Missionary Society, n.d.

Entzminger, Louis. *The J. Frank Norris I Have Known for 34 Years*. St. John, Ind.: Christian Book Gallery, n.d.

Finn, Joe. *In Our Time—An Interview with a Missionary*. Dec. 1998.

Gonzalez, Joseph. *The Good Health Fact Book*. Project ed.; Pleasantville, NY: The Reader's Digest Association, Inc., 1992.

Goforth, Rosalind. *Climbing*. Grand Rapids: Zondervan Publishing House, 1940.

_____. *Goforth of China*. Minneapolis: Bethany House Publications, 1987.

_____. *How I Know God Answers Prayer*. Pasig City, Philippines: Lifeline Philippines, n.d.

Grubb, Norman. *After C.T. Studd*. Grand Rapids: Zondervan Publishing House, 1946.

Guinness, Joy. *Mrs. Howard Taylor—Her Web of Time*. London: China Inland Mission, 1952.

Hale, Thomas. *On Being a Missionary*. Pasadena, Cal.: William Carey Library, 1995.

Hall, Gurdon Langley. *Golden Boats from Burma*. Philadelphia: Macrae Smith Company, 1961

Harrison, E. Myers. *Blazing the Missionary Trail*. Wheaton, Ill.: Van Kampen Press, n.d.

Hitt, Russell. *Sensi—The Life Story of Irene Webster-Smith*. Lincoln: ICM Press, 2003.

Houghton, Frank L. *Amy Carmichael of Dohnavur*. Ft. Washington, Penna.: Christian Literature Crusade, 1979.

Hubbard, Ethel Daniels. *The Moffats*. Shoals, Ind.: Old Paths Tract Society, n.d.

Hyles, Jack. *Meet the Holy Spirit*. Manila: Lifeline Press, n.d.

Johnstone, Patrick. *Operation World*. 1993 ed.; Grand Rapids: Zondervan Publishing House, 1993.

Kuhn, Isobel. *In the Arena*. Chicago: Moody Press, 1958.

Mandoriano, Jose. *The Hour Before Sunset*. Butler, Ind.: Higley Press, 1957.

Martin, Rick. *Missionary Relationships at Home*. Iloilo City, Iloilo Baptist Church, 2003.

Mathews, Winifred. *Dauntless Women*. New York: Friendship Press, 1974.

Myers, John B. *William Carey*. London: S. S. Partridge & Co., n.d.

Nilsen, Maria. *Malla Moe*. Chicago: Moody Press, 1966.

Norris, Frank. *Inside History of First Baptist Church, Fort Worth, and Temple Baptist Church, Detroit*. Fort Worth, n.p., 1938.

Pearson, B. H. *The Vision Lives*. Westchester, Ill.: Good News Publishers, 1967.

Peet, Verda. *Sometimes I Prefer to Fuss*. Singapore: Overseas Missionary Fellowship, 1985.

Ray, James. *Incredible Journey in the Steps of Greatness*. Chattanooga, Tenn.: BIMI Publications, International, 2000.

Stenbock, Evelyn. *Miss Terri*. Lincoln: Good News Broadcasting Association, n.d.

Taylor, Dr. and Mrs. Howard. *Hudson Taylor—God's Man in China*. Chicago: Moody Press, 1987.

Taylor, Mrs. Howard. *The Triumph of John and Betty Stam*. Philadelphia: China Inland Mission, 1960.

Tucker, Ruth. *From Jerusalem to Irian Jaya*. Grand Rapids, Mich.: Zondervan Publishing House, 1983.

Tuggy, Joy Turner. *The Missionary Wife and Her Work*. Chicago: Moody Press, 1970.

Vineyard, Jim. *Fundamental Baptist World Missions*. Oklahoma City: Windsor Hills Baptist Church, October, 1997.

White, Kathleen. *John and Betty Stam*. Minneapolis: Bethany House Publishing, 1989.

Medical References

Clayman, M.D., Charles B. *The American Medical Association Home Medical Encyclopedia*. Random House, New York, 1989.

Feinstein, Alice, Selene Craig, Jennifer Haigh, Brian Paul Kaufman, Gale Maleskey, & Ellen Michaud. *Prevention's Healing with Vitamins*. Emmaus, Penna.: Rodale Press, Inc., 1996.

Gonzalez, Joseph. *The Good Health Fact Book*. Project ed.; Pleasantville, NY: The Reader's Digest Association, Inc., 1992.

Shuker, Nancy, Gordon Bloch, Jean Callahan, Charlene Canpe, Nancy Carothers, Nancy De Korp, Linda Hetzer, Guy Lester, Wendy Murphy, Serena Stockwell. *Reader's Digest The Good Health Fact Book*. Pleasantville, NY: Reader's Digest Assoc, Inc., 1992.

Werner, David, Carol Thurman, and Jane Maxwell. *Where There Is No Doctor: A Village Health Care Handbook*. Palo Alto: Cal.: The Hesperian Foundation, 1992.

Wright, M.D., Jonathan V. *Dr. Wright's Guide to Healing with Nutrition*. 9th printing. New Canaan, Conn.: Keats Publishers, Inc, 1984.

Handwritten inscription on photo:

Rachel,
It was so proud
to have your name
on page. You did
a great job.
Love
Bill
4-11-01

Above: Rachel paging for her Uncle Bill at the state capital. Bill was in the Oklahoma state legislature. He and his wife Connie (Rick's sister) were instrumental in helping to save Rachel's life when she was born.

Inset: Rachel at camp!

Above: Rick, Rachel, and I visiting a Moslem city where one of our graduates and his wife (far left and far right) started a church (shown in the background).

Below: Visitors Ricky brought to his dad's men's Sunday school class on a big day.

Three snapshots of Rick, Rachel, and me and some kids at camp.

Above: The ladies are working to prepare lunch at Mt. View Christian Camp. We go every April and May during our summer in the Philippines.

Below: The ladies are cooking over an open fire. Notice my tent in the background in both of these snapshots. It was too hot to sleep in it!

Above: Rick and Ricky visit a village where a graduate from Iloilo Baptist College started a church.

Below: Some kids on my route pose with me on Saturday visitation. Tata (right) passed away in June 2005.

Above: An overloaded jeepney headed for a Sunday morning service at the church of one of our graduates, Brother Billy Caleem.

Below: This snapshot of some of the street kids who lived on our campus was taken in our living room with Ricky and Rachel. They come and go. (You can take the kid off the street, but you can't always take the "street" out of the kid.) Kano, sitting beside Ricky, still comes to church regularly with his wife and daughter.

Above: A typical wedding

Center: Iloilo Baptist Church orchestra

Left: Buddies since childhood—Rachel, Stephanie (daughter of a staff pastor), and JD (son of a staff pastor) accompanied our Iloilo Baptist Church choir on their CD.

Below: Pastor and Mrs. Mike Johnson are sitting with Rachel and me and some teens from our route. Pastor Johnson has preached for our annual Youth Conference.

Above (and inset): Our son Ricky and his wife Brandie, who are now working with us, going soul winning

Top left: Russ Martin, my husband's father
Top right: Alta Martin, my husband's mother
Below: Vernon and Mary Umbright, my parents